Traces of the Sage

Traces of the Sage

Monument, Materiality, and the First Temple of Confucius

JAMES A. FLATH

UNIVERSITY OF HAWAI'I PRESS

HONOLULU

spatial habitus

© 2016 University of Hawai'i Press
All rights reserved
Printed in Singapore by Markono Print Media Pte Ltd

21 20 19 18 17 16   6 5 4 3 2 1

Library of Congress Cataloging-in-Publication Data

Flath, James A., author.
Traces of the sage : monument, materiality, and the first temple of Confucius / James A. Flath.
pages cm—(Spatial habitus)
Includes bibliographical references and index.
ISBN 978-0-8248-5370-9 (cloth : alk. paper)
1. Kong miao (Qufu Shi, China)
2. Temples, Confucian—China—Design and construction.
3. Qufu Shi (China)—Buildings, structures, etc. I. Title.
II. Series: Spatial habitus (Series)
NA6047.Q345F53 2016
726'.1095114—dc23
2015035283

University of Hawai'i Press books are printed on acid-free
paper and meet the guidelines for permanence and
durability of the Council on Library Resources.

All uncredited photographs are by the author

In memoriam, Rudy Flath, 1930–2013

Contents

Color plates follow page 108

Illustrations

Figures

Plates

Tables

Preface

SUPPOSE THIS PROJECT really began during a brief visit to the One Sky Pavilion (Tianyige), a private library established in 1561 and preserved today as a key part of the cultural and material history of the city of Ningbo, Zhejiang. I recall the moment, while wandering through the corridors, that I realized I was not concerned with the books so much as absorbed in the buildings that contained them and curious about the artfully crafted shelves, the filigree decorations, and the courtyards that tied them all together. Like Phineas J. Nanson, a fictional doctoral student who I would later discover in the pages of A. S. Byatt's *The Biographer's Tale,* it occurred to me that "I must have things."

This is, essentially, a book about a complex thing—Kong Temple, also known as the Temple of Confucius, in the small city of Qufu, Shandong. I would prefer not to follow a statement on what the book is with a statement of what it is not, but having invoked the name of China's greatest sage, I think it only fair to state that this is not a book about Confucius. Readers might also want to know in advance that this is neither a social history of the people who used or sponsored the sage's temple nor a genealogy of his descendants. It does not concern the many other Confucius temples once found throughout East Asia or the international Confucius Institutes designed to extend China's "soft power" to the world. And it studies neither Confucian intellectual history nor the Confucian state nor whether Confucianism should be regarded as a religion or a philosophy.

I do not consider these people, places, and problems as unimportant to the history and development of one of China's proudest heritage sites. I just concluded early on that the only way to write about Kong Temple without digressing into an incomplete history of everything was to treat the temple as a microcosm and to concentrate as much as possible on the material and documentary texts that emerged from or center on its specific locality. Even as a microcosm, Kong Temple presents a formidable challenge to the historian simply because the place is so old and venerable. Following my earlier studies of heritage formation and creation in Shandong's museum culture and at historical sites, including Lugou Bridge near Beijing and the Opium War relics at Humen, I initially intended to focus on a much less ambitious exploration of late-imperial and twentieth-century cultural memory and heritage values. That work now appears in the latter chapters of this book, although in addressing the modern history of the temple it occurred to me that we have much to learn from the premodern *longue dureé*. Having opened that door, I could find no justification for closing it again, and so began the work of unravelling some 2,500 years of Kong Temple history.

I also did not begin this study intending to emphasize building and construction. I initially assumed that Kong Temple would be articulated in more conventional terms as the site of multiple and overlapping communities, negotiated identity, cultural memory, and the social construction of place, much as Brian Dott explores Mt. Tai, as Susan Naquin studies the temples of Beijing, or as Tobie Meyer-Fong writes of the city of Yangzhou.[1] In considering dynastic histories, local annals, and stele inscriptions, however, I was impressed by how many of these documents were concerned with the material conditions of the temple, the negotiation of supporting properties and endowments, and the contingencies of management. I knew, of course, that Kong Temple stood for a good deal more than what could be seen, touched, and managed but could not dismiss the fact that the temple has been under construction, with the occasional pre-Tang intermission, since the Han dynasty. It is somewhat of a tourist cliché that when workers employed at the Forbidden City in Beijing, for example, complete one renovation of the complex they must immediately start over again just to keep decay in check. Cliché or not, that work is essential to the ongoing production of any large-scale architectural group, and it is a phenomenon that has not received the attention that it deserves. And so, while this book remains open to the many abstractions of Confucian material culture and the social construction of place, it is substantially concerned with actual construction and structure and the ways in which societies manage space and material. It is unfortunate that available historical records provide few details on who actually shaped the timbers and fired the tiles for Kong Temple. In looking at the temple's history, however, one cannot escape the conclusion that behind the intellectual and state discourse over Confucianism a great deal of shaping and firing was going on and that beyond giving form to place, material culture has had a formative influence on perceptions and uses of time, space, and history.

Although I take responsibility for the translations not otherwise credited, most were collaborative productions, and I especially wish to acknowledge the linguistic talents of Grace Wei Xu. Selina Gao, Meili Ma, and Hua Huang were each invaluable as research assistants during the gestation of the manuscript. Frank Schumacher reviewed and translated a number of German-language resources. Andy Patton, Alan MacEachern, Sam Clark, and Dave Stasiuk offered their insights regarding the theoretical considerations presented in the introduction. Randy Fox and Jun Fang generously read the entire manuscript at various stages of development. As editors of the Spatial Habitus series on Chinese architecture, Ron Knapp and Xing Ruan encouraged me to pursue the topic, waited patiently for it to materialize, and offered unfailing advice and moral support as the manuscript matured. In Qufu, Luo Chenglie and Lu Houxuan of Qufu Normal University offered their contacts and resources, as did Gao Jianjun in Jining. A grant from the Social Sciences and Humanities Research Council of Canada supported most of the research. Much of the writing was done during a sabbatical year at the University of Queensland, where Chi-Kong Lai provided constant support. When the manuscript reached the University of Hawai'i Press, it was Pat Crosby who steered the work through the review process before handing it over to Stephanie Chun. A generous grant from the J. B. Smallman Publication Fund at the University of Western Ontario made the inclusion of illustrations possible.

Note on Terms and Dates

A WORD NEEDS TO BE SAID about the decision to refer to China's greatest sage as Kongzi (Master Kong) rather than Confucius. My choice in this regard is pragmatic. It is not because I think this name is more authentic than the Western adaptation of "Confucius" but because all Chinese terms and names have been rendered in modern pinyin. I see no compelling reason why Confucius should be the exception, and the same rule applies to Mengzi (Mencius), Sun Zhongshan (Sun Yat-sen), Jiang Jieshi (Chiang Kai-shek), Beijing (Peking), etc. The term "Confucian" is problematic because, as Lionel Jensen argues, the term needs to be understood as a Western construct rather than a native Chinese reality.[1] There is, however, no simple solution in this regard because, as Thomas Wilson notes, in substituting terms like *rujiao* (scholarly teachings) or Kongjiao (teachings of Kongzi) we only create new ambiguities.[2] Therefore, I have chosen to retain Confucian and Confucianism when referring to the diverse system of values and principles stemming from the teachings of Kongzi.

The location of Kongzi's ancient home is known in history as both Queli and Qufu. Queli was a precinct within the county of Qufu (Xianyuan during the Northern Song) until the Yuan dynasty, when the administrative center of Qufu was established in a separate location. This left the older settlement under the name of Queli. In the Ming dynasty, the two were reconsolidated on the site of Queli as Qufu city, which became the administrative seat of Qufu county. Queli continues as the name of a street that runs adjacent to the temple and as a nostalgic address for the old walled city.

The temple in Queli/Qufu has known many formal names depending on the various honorific titles Kongzi has held. These include XuanNimiao

(Temple of the Exalted Ni) between the Han and the Tang dynasties, Wenxuanwangmiao (Temple of the King of Exalted Culture) from the mid-Tang to the Ming dynasty, and Zhishengmiao (Temple of the Ultimate Sage) since the late Ming. Fortunately, most Chinese sources also agree to the generic title of Kongmiao, which I translate directly as Kong Temple. This term has the advantage of uniting Kongzi with his home temple and with his acclaimed descendants who treated the temple, in part, as their lineage property. Although millions of people now share the Kong surname, in referring to the "Kong family" I specifically mean the descent line that resided in Qufu and claimed key titles and properties granted by the imperial state. Temples outside of Queli/Qufu are referred to as Confucian temples, simply as a means of distinguishing them from Kong Temple. It is important to note, however, that while I treat the performance of ritual and rank as being particular to the Queli/Qufu temple, most such performances were universally implemented.

In naming the various architectural components of Kong Temple, I have chosen to provide translations of formal titles. The transliteration of a Chinese term appears only upon its first significant occurrence within the text. The entrance to Kong Temple, therefore, appears as Timeliness of the Sage Gate rather than Shengshimen, and the main temple hall appears as the Hall of the Great Ensemble rather than Dachengdian, etc. The same applies to formal personal titles, so that the late-imperial title of the lineal descendant of Kongzi is given as Duke of Fulfilling the Sage rather than Yanshenggong. Titles belonging to scholar-officials are generally translated according to Charles Hucker, *A Dictionary of Official Titles in Imperial China*. Emperors, according to long-established conventions, are referred to by posthumous names in the Han through the Sui dynasties; by temple names for the Tang, the Jin, the Song, and the Yuan; and by reign name for the Ming and the Qing dynasties.

When romanizing titles of written works, I separate appended words such as *shi* (history), *zhi* (annals), and *bei* (stele). With regard to buildings or temples, all syllables that refer to a single object, be it a building or a temple, are joined except in extreme cases of multiple honorifics when honorary prefixes are separated. When quoting secondary sources that use forms of romanization other than pinyin, these terms have been converted to pinyin.

This text provides dates for dynasties and imperial reigns. Personal dates are provided only where the period of their involvement with Kong Temple is not apparent from the context or where they are necessary for establishing context.

1 | Introduction

A Temple under Construction

DURING THE HEIGHT of the Ming dynasty, at the beginning of the Hongzhi reign (1486–1505), Kong Temple (Temple of Confucius) was already one of the oldest continuously maintained architectural sites in China. After a decade of restoration and reconstruction, it was also one of the largest, second only to the Ming imperial palace in terms of scale and architectural grandeur. At the heart of the refurbished complex, an ornate altar marked the site of an ancient apricot grove where Kongzi (Confucius, 551–479 BCE) was said to have lectured his students. To the north an expansive timber hall sheltered the effigies of the sage and his most accomplished followers. Smaller structures to the east, west, and further to the north served the ritual needs and memory of the sage's family, his ancestors, and his descendants. Although the temple was not an active site for education, cloisters running the length of the central court enshrined dozens of scholars and exegetes of the Confucian classics. Toward the south the grounds extended from one courtyard to another, beyond a towering library hall, through clusters of memorial steles, and past stands of ancient cypress toward the temple's formal entrance, where a vaulted entrance recognized Kongzi as the "timely sage." Technically, the increased dimensions and sumptuous materials were mandated to match the temple architecture to the sage's lofty rank as an uncrowned king and support the perennial rites offered to him on behalf of the Ming state. Implicitly, the completed work recalled that Kongzi had lived and died in this place some two millennia before, that his lineal descendants still resided in a mansion just beyond the temple wall, and that some form of state-sponsored monument had stood in this place for at least fourteen of the past seventeen centuries.

Then, in the summer of 1499, lightning struck the temple and burned it mostly to the ground. The loss was greatly lamented by the imperial court that had invested so heavily in the recent reconstruction, the family who cultivated their ancestor's memory, and the scholar-officials who regarded the edifice as a sacred relic. However, this was not the first time that fire or the slower processes of decay had brought the complex down, and it would not be the last. In its long recorded history, the temple had experienced roughly a dozen near-total reconstructions, twice as many full restorations, and innumerable refurbishments. Now, from its smoking ashes, the temple would be recovered again, to continue in the cycle of repair, erosion, and rebuilding that continues until the present day (fig. 1).

This book is about the work of creating architecture, the art of constructing memorials, and the problem of managing a sacred place. It accepts that Kong Temple is subject to the rhythms of building and decay and interprets conservation as essential to the temple's history and material culture. Noting the potential for decay and destruction, I ask how human interests are constrained and frustrated by the limits of space and material. Conversely, seeing that Kong Temple is perpetuated through maintenance and construction, I interpret the place in terms of random materials arranged in orderly structures; systematic hierarchies that define and differentiate structure and space; and ritual systems that validate and are in turn validated by space, architecture, and building.

By attending to the temple's physical attributes, management, and maintenance, I do not propose that materials overtly determined the ritual or politics of Confucianism. Nor do I claim that the temple or any other architectural structure has anything like "agency." No matter how old, how large, or how spiritually possessed the temple may have become, it can never be said that the relic plotted its own demise or development. However, in tracing the temple's multimillennial transitions and transformations and observing how its rhythms are recorded in space, text, and architecture, one begins to understand that the temple is not merely subject to the agency of its human actors. The temple was and is a "thing," and as a thing, it possesses what Arjun Appadurai describes as a "social life." Through the study of that social life, we may assess both the temple and the society with which it is involved. We are obliged, writes Appadurai,

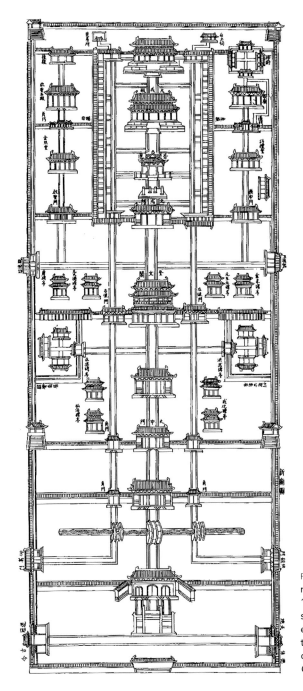

FIGURE 1. Kong Temple after reconstruction between 1499 and 1505 and before the addition of several gates at the southern extreme, an exhibition hall on the north, and stele pavilions constructed during the Qing. *Queli zhi*, 1505.

to follow the things themselves, for their meanings are inscribed in their forms, their uses, their trajectories. It is only through the analysis of these trajectories that we can interpret the human transactions and calculations that enliven things. Thus, even though from a *theoretical* point of view human actors encode things with significance, from a *methodological* point of view it is the things-in-motion that illuminate their human and social context.[1]

Things, in Appadurai's view, are essentially commodities. Through exchange they may follow the pathways laid out by the people who manage them or be diverted by factors that cannot be controlled. Certainly, Kong Temple was never a commodity to be exchanged in the ordinary sense of being bought and sold, but the temple nonetheless owes its existence to an active culture of transaction and calculation that valued and contested—but did not always control—the relic.

Jun Jing's notable study of a branch of the Kong family and their local temple in Dachuan, Gansu Province, has raised the idea that a temple under construction can powerfully influence its patrons. That work draws on Emile Durkheim's theory that rituals and ceremonies were basic to social cohesion and control, Maurice Halbwachs' idea that collective memory maintained that cohesion, and Frances Yates' theory on the role of space in organizing memory.[2] In synthesizing these arguments, Jing shows that the collective memory of the local temple proved critical to sustaining the family through the hardships of the Cultural Revolution and into the present.[3] The emphasis of that study is on memory, although the author also addresses the management and building of the temple as a real and meaningful process. In a later work, Jing observes that "temple reconstruction is a domain of social organization in which existing interpersonal networks can be transformed into powerful institutions and effective providers of the needed knowledge rewarded in terms of honor, prestige, and deference."[4] Accepting that building was in itself an act of social cohesion/negotiation is important to understanding that monumental architecture constantly engages its community, not simply by reflecting or representing individual or group interests or recalling the name of an ancient sage, but by consuming, producing, and obliterating different types of material and symbolic resources.

Kong Temple has been processing these resources and facilitating their movement almost continuously since the Han dynasty, perhaps longer. The historical record, however, is far from complete, so if we are to understand that lengthy past as something other than a long string of random events, it is necessary to foreground the discussion in a principle that accounts for how things change over time regardless of the state of the archive. In this study I conceptualize the temple in terms of open, closed, and isolated systems. My approach can be illustrated in a preliminary way by comparing the tombs of Kongzi and his descendants that lie a short distance to the north of Kong Temple to the pavilions and gates that adorn and protect the cemetery known as Kong Forest (Konglin). The tombs themselves are closed systems. Beyond occasional grooming or sweeping, these earthen tumuli receive little investment of time or energy and thus move toward a state of equilibrium—their "tensions" are reduced, and they ultimately settle into a form that cannot be easily disturbed. The imperial stele pavilions, gates, and ritual halls that surround the tombs are also subject to energy dissipation. Left alone they might stand with some integrity for several generations, but gradually their heavy tiled roofs will force the structures downward, reducing them to heaps of weathered timbers and broken tiles, to be finally dispersed by recycling and scavenging. Without the investment of time and energy, the architecture will erode by degrees and follow the tombs toward oblivion.

In Qufu, however, memorial architecture is not a closed system, and tension-reduction is not its aesthetic principle. Builders and custodians have been intensively involved in creating and re-creating these elaborate structures and extending them from one generation to the next. They do not accept their work as terminal, and they perpetuate the architecture by persistently refining material, adjusting space, and reforming management. Builders resist physical decay while maintaining enough continuity to prevent the decay of symbols and memories embedded in the architecture. Yet memorial architecture is not entirely open to outside influences because of constraints set by building codes, available materials, budgets, and precedent. The traditional architecture of Qufu is neither open nor closed; it is an isolated system that resists change but will change under pressure.

The problem with maintaining an isolated system is that entropy always has the upper hand. Yves Alain Bois explains, "Entropy is a negative movement: it presupposes an initial order and a deterioration of that order. Expenditure, on the contrary, is the regulation, through excess, of an initial disorder and such regulation is never successful because it is always insufficient."[5] Architecture is subject to forces that cannot be anticipated or modelled—politics, economics, vandalism, fire, and dry rot being only the most pervasive sources of discord. A literary description of "weeds in the courtyard" may have alluded to the corruption of Confucian values, but Kong Temple actually had weeds in its courtyard, choking out the greenery, growing out of the cracks between the roof tiles, and slowly breaking down the integrity of the architecture. Managers and custodians strived to maintain architectural relics in their received form, but it was impossible to perfectly preserve them according to what was remembered and idealized as the "model of the ancients." Actions often worked contrary to intentions, adding to an unaccountable chain of events that drove the architecture away from its structural precedents and challenged any sense that architecture embodied permanence and pattern.

Yet one must concede that these managers and custodians were stunningly successful regulators, and it is through the study of this "regulation through excess" that I intend to circumvent the more fatalistic conclusions that classical thermodynamics suggest. Rather than taking decay or entropy as merely a destructive force with only one possible outcome, I see it as a measure of order within the environment and an instrument in the creative effort to reconcile (if not overcome) the problems of time, space, and memory. Complex things cannot be put back together as they once were, but the builder, the conservationist, or the ritualist may compensate by recovering fragments and restructuring them in new forms or formal orders that both reify and efface the past. That, as far as this study is concerned, is the definition of Chinese monumental architecture and the act of conservation.

In advancing these points, I begin chapter 2 by working through two millennia of repairs, restoration, and rebuilding, much in the way that it appears in key historical sources such as *Queli zhi* (Annals of Queli, 1505, 1575), *Queli guangzhi* (Expanded annals of Queli, 1673), *Queli wenxian kao* (Study of Queli documents, 1762), or *Qufu xianzhi* (Qufu county annals, 1774). I recognize, as most historians do, that linear histories and stratigraphic analyses should be read and especially written with care due to their tendency to privilege certain outcomes as inevitable. The aforementioned texts are excellent examples of the propensity to legitimate the claims of the ruling elite that sponsored their production. As Christopher Agnew points out in his social history of the Kong family, in its first edition *Queli zhi* was sponsored by the head of the Kong lineage and his father-in-law, Grand Secretary Li Dongyang, and implicitly served the interests of the Kong family and the Ming court. The early Qing dynasty *Queli guangzhi* was sponsored by a minister of the Board of Ritual and marginalized the Kongs while placing more emphasis on the imperial court. Kong Jifen's *Queli wenxian kao* sought to reclaim the family's pivotal place in history at a time in which their influence was diminishing, and a district magistrate edited *Qufu xianzhi* at a time in which county administrative authority was growing relative to that of the Kong family.[6] In each of these examples, linear history supports the imperial state's often factional claims and interests, or the Kong family that claimed descent from the sage, or the scholar-officials who claimed to understand his teachings. At the same time, these texts do not account for the nonlinear, day-to-day activities of temple management or the routine work of fixing roofs and pulling weeds, without which the temple would have collapsed long before the next donor came along to sponsor a full-scale restoration. And yet, whatever their bias, these sources divulge a need for the continual investment of resources, articulate a desire to control the random events that lie beyond the surface of the text, and effectively perpetuate the appropriate action. In that form the classical texts and engraved steles are not just records of events but a constituent part of the flow of work and materials that give structure and direction to the temple and its history.

Property management and resource allocation were significant issues for the extended temple community, although the temple's continuing development and renewal is not separate from the performance of ritual and the negotiation of status. As Angela Zito argues in respect to the imperial architecture of Beijing, ritual and ritual venues are not distinguishable as "setting" and "action" but are "products of the same ritual process, sensuous embodiments of sagely productive power."[7] Like architecture, ritual and status are fundamentally spatial and have to be constructed, maintained, repeated, and hierarchical in order to be effective. Indeed, it is apparent that building was itself a ritual, although because available records do not substantiate how building ceremonies were performed at Kong Temple, chapter 3 turns to other forms of ritual performed in the context of architecture. These include the ongoing provision of ritual status and property to the Confucian "family" and the nearly perpetual conducting of sacrifices within Kong Temple. The first part of the chapter isolates three distinct periods of ritual entitlement that encompass several centuries each: the Han dynasty, the late Tang through Yuan, and the Ming to mid-Qing. Although these three periods are arranged chronologically and do in fact cover most of the time span of imperial China, I do not intend them as a complete and continuous record of ritual or as a ritual-centered history of China. As with the overview of building, in discussing more than two thousand years of patronage, sacrifice, and title adjustment this survey passes over the finer gradations and complexities in favor of a long-range perspective that addresses the question of why the temple was more than just property. History, society, and the cosmos were embodied in the temple, but the temple also generated dynamics that cannot be explained by simply looking at the motivation of the worshippers. For many, the temple seemed literally enveloped in an aura of cosmic harmony. It had attained that reputation not by reflecting personal goals or supporting private or state motives but by remaining beyond individual or institutional control and never passively representing either the symbolic or the material capital of its patrons. Kong Temple synthesized architecture; imperial activism; music; rites; and the myriad social, political, and cultural concerns that circulated through and about the complex. But it did so in ways that could not be predicted or easily controlled. Poetic accounts and eulogies translated in the latter part of the chapter show how the enormity of the temple's architecture and history and the unimaginable commitment to maintaining the ancient civilization (siwen) erased day-to-day existence, intrigues, and politics and left an indescribable feeling that overawed the faithful.

Chapter 4 studies another form of organization by following Kong Temple as it spatially unfolds along a central axis that extends from the formal entrance in the south to the memorial halls in the north before branching out to the more complicated eastern and western courts. Although these architectural systems and networks appear to be linear, the longue durée shows them to be less an expression of preconceived order and more the product of a centuries-long reaction of space, material, and ideals.

The second part of this book finds the temple on the dramatically altered terrain of modernity. It would have been difficult for anyone to perceive Kong Temple's traditional aura after the end of the nineteenth century, when the collapse of the Qing dynasty and the ritual structure over which it had presided undid the spatial-moral-temporal equation that supported the institution. Change was not new to the temple, but the nature of change in the twentieth century produced a profound identity crisis. Walter Benjamin's analysis of art in the age of mechanical production calls our attention to the less than subtle transformations in the nature of authenticity brought on by modernity:

> It is significant that the existence of the work of art with reference to its aura is never entirely separated from its religious function. In other words, the unique value of the "authentic" work of art has its basis in ritual, the location of its original use value. . . . But the instant the criterion of authenticity ceases to be applicable to artistic production, the total function of art is reversed. Instead of being based on ritual, it begins to be based on another practice—politics.[8]

Kong Temple was deeply associated with the old order, but owing to its relative durability, the edifice preserved dynastic remnants long after the termination of the last imperial regime. At the same time, the temple had to cope with an emerging sense of modernity that cast doubt on the value and the authenticity of ritual while becoming a problem for those who were not willing to tolerate a purge of antiquity. The capacity for the temple to inspire its pilgrims and patrons was diminished, and for some it became an unambiguous object to be managed according to the uncertain needs of the new society.

In accounting for modern political uses of Kong Temple in chapter 5 and for modern cultural and economic uses in chapter 6, this study assumes a divide or disjuncture between late-imperial and modern experience. That assumption reflects the predominant Chinese practice of identifying the mid-nineteenth century as the turning point for Chinese architecture,[9] although of more interest to this study is Pierre Nora's widely cited concept of *lieux de memoire* (sites of memory). Nora's point is that a *milieu de memoire* (environment of memory) was "perpetually actual"—evolving, unconscious, open to manipulation and appropriation, and forgettable as well as memorable. *Lieux de memoire,* on the other hand, are described as the reconstructed remains of the past—produced through analysis and criticism and devoid of any sense of the sacred, heroic, or mythical.[10]

That French-inspired idea cannot be transferred directly to China because even in the modern era, China has not undergone a comparable process of demarcating the boundaries of history and memory and making them mutually exclusive.[11] As Madeleine Yue Dong points out in her study of Republican Beijing, because the people of Beijing actively "recycled" their past, both in terms of material and culture, there was no clear-cut distinction between "tradition" and "modernity."[12] Nonetheless, with respect to Kong Temple at the very least, the premodern relationship between Chinese culture and politics is qualitatively different from the patterns that began to emerge in the late-nineteenth and twentieth centuries. Early devotees of Kong Temple had always lamented the destruction of the *siwen* by politics, and yet these feelings were typically subsumed by the hope that, like ancient junipers that miraculously revived after decades and even centuries of dormancy, Confucianism would eventually recover. Rather than being mutually destructive, culture and politics worked together to maintain the temple as perpetually actual. I would venture to say that culture and politics continue to work together even now, although I am less certain that they are mutually supportive. Formerly discarded rituals and materials may be used again, but recycling has taken on the character of down-cycling, and while the remnants of the past may be infused with new values they do not reclaim their historical stature.

As recently as the first decades of the twentieth century, the temple had been pivotal in Confucian culture. However, by the late-nineteenth century a longer tradition of scholarly skepticism had begun to coalesce into a political cynicism that undermined the temple's claim to privilege. State-sponsored ritual fell into a terminal decline. In losing the support of canonical texts, sacred practices, and revered associations, Kong Temple became subject to a different set of values dominated, as Benjamin claims for modern aesthetics, by politics increasingly unalloyed by faith. Revisionist scholars had already begun to debate the value of Confucian worship in the last decades of imperial China. With the passage of the 1911 Revolution, support for the sage's relics narrowed to disconnected scholarly associations and political factions seeking to bolster conservative legitimacy through appeals to sacred traditions and the dwindling influence of the Kong family and their illustrious ancestor. Republican rule also presided over the debasement of cults and cultures that had no formal relationship with Kongzi but had helped to sustain the general milieu nonetheless.[13] What remained of the aura suffered continual erosion as the state-sponsored ritual structure was hollowed out and bent to the needs of self-serving warlords and the fragile Republican state. Modern scholars recognized the past to be unrepeatable, conceding only that certain relics might be maintained for posterity. By the 1930s Kong Temple had been enlisted as national patrimony—subject to the politics and economics of heritage designation, protection, and exploitation.

Nora's nation-centered formula helps to explain the fate of Kong Temple because the Chinese nation-state has played a central role in heritage-related activities. Even today local civic leaders are bound to the conviction that the temple and its implied culture qualify their region to take a leading role in guiding the "national consciousness." In the absence of state-sponsored ideological support during the mid-twentieth century, these claims did not carry a great deal of weight, but increasingly, these local conceits are taken seriously as Kongzi emerges as a renewed, if contentious, symbol for modern China. The renewed attention in turn drives the rising stock in Kongzi's temple and leads at times to a eulogistic praise that echoes tributes of a bygone era. Patrimonies, however, tend to be contested by their heirs. By its enduring physical presence and material existence, the temple is capable of undermining or destabilizing nationalist histories and even complicating its own heritage status. Like building dams or planning cities, heritage is often a process of managing conflict.

There is a growing literature on the role of conflict in Chinese heritage management. In addition to Jun Jing's aforementioned book, which includes the threat of actual dam-building to the local Temple of Memory, Dong Wang considers how government agencies in charge of the Longmen Grottoes had to manage not only various preservation issues but diverse domestic and international tensions that arose in the discursive space of the relic.[14] In a similar approach, Xiaobo Su and Peggy Teo demonstrate how often conflicting local, national, and global power relations have shaped tourism in the Naxi homeland of Lijiang.[15] Robert Shepherd's study of the Buddhist site of Wutai Shan concerns conservation and the creation of heritage through negotiating the diverse interests of forestry, tourism and security officials, preservationists, economic planners, and religious affairs bureaucrats, as well as the needs and interests of religious pilgrims and secular tourists.[16] Anna Sun's ethnographic research likewise finds that "confusion and controversy" underlies the new discourse on Confucianism, even as more people are drawn into the remaining Confucian temples.[17]

These diverse studies all recognize that heritage is not under the control of any one person or managerial entity. My finding in relation to Qufu is that it is not just the space or use of the temple but also the material and structure of the relic that either facilitates or frustrates its would-be agents. Ritual can be liquidated or appropriated, but the temple cannot be disassociated from its foundations and so continually creates both opportunities and problems for those who use it to promote their own initiatives. Witness the abortive reinvention of Kong Temple as a site of Republican political rituals, the intense ideological struggle that erupted there in the opening days of the Cultural Revolution, or more recent controversies over the commercial exploitation of the property. Each of these initiatives claimed the mantle of the nation, but failure to manage the space and material of the temple warped and derailed efforts to involve it in any notion of progress as those respective regimes defined it. Paradoxically, it is contradiction and tension that keeps Kong Temple relevant. It may variously be the subject of appropriation, criticism, preservation, and transformation, but in never confirming those positions the monument claims a continuing role in the development of modern China.

2 | Kong Temple as Structure

I**N ONE SENSE** Kong Temple is China's oldest continuously maintained architectural complex, dated by classical sources to the fifth century BCE, when the sage himself is thought to have occupied the grounds. Yet no physical remains exist from the time of Kongzi nor can any structures be dated to or even seen to resemble the architecture of the Han, the Tang, or even the Song dynasty. Several stele pavilions survive in part from the Jin and the Yuan, but all of the larger buildings were repeatedly destroyed, either by the fires that periodically swept through the temple or by more pervasive forces of decay. Only from the post-1499 reconstruction period do a few significant buildings survive as legitimate examples of Ming architecture. The balance of the temple dates to the period of reconstruction that followed a catastrophic fire in 1724.

This contradiction between built reality and what is assumed to be the temple's past raises a basic problem when studying Chinese architecture. Is value defined by the material substance of the building or by its textual record and intellectual abstractions—the monumental or the memorial? It has been suggested that the Chinese traditionally placed greater emphasis on the textual associations and underlying cosmic patterns of architecture than on the architecture itself. Following the early twentieth-century writings of Victor Segalen, Simon Leys used the example of a Ming scholar who once proposed liberating oneself from real gardens and imagining a space purely of the mind; the implication being that the idea or the name was what mattered and not the object it signified.[1] Frederick Mote made a comparable argument that "Chinese civilization did not lodge its history in buildings. Even its most grandiose palace and city complexes stressed grand layout, the employment of space, and not buildings, which were added as a relatively impermanent superstructure. Chinese civilization seems not to have regarded its history as violated or abused when the historic monuments collapsed or burned, as long as those could be replaced or restored, and their functions regained."

Mote, of course, was correct—names and associations are vital to the identity of the monument, and built reality is indeed temporal. What is problematic, I think, is the assertion that since Chinese building materials were ephemeral, the past therefore "was a past of words, not of stones."[2] From this perspective, materials seem to be constantly fading away, and it is not the presence of architecture that denotes value but its absence. While it is true that few literati wrote about building and structure in terms that the modern observer might prefer, in accepting cultural abstractions as the substance of the monument, cultural and social historians tend to overlook the role of building and temporality in overcoming absence and giving presence to Chinese architecture.[3]

One exceptional, although highly evocative, articulation of the relationship between ritual, memory, and building appears in Wu Jingzi's classic eighteenth-century novel *The Scholars*. Set in the Ming dynasty, one of the novel's key incidents happens to be a grand sacrifice at the Temple of Tai Po (Tai Bo)—a proto-Confucian luminary and founder of the ancient state of Wu. In preparing for that sacrifice the sponsor, Mr. Chi, raises contributions for the temple's construction and the provision of fine sacrificial wares.[4] The gathering unites scholar and commoner, high class and low, and is recorded as the most memorable event to have occurred in the community in generations.[5] At the novel's conclusion, the focus shifts to the declining years of the Ming and to a later generation of scholars who return to the temple only to find it in ruins. The ritual wares—and even the cabinets built to store them—had disappeared:

> Having climbed the left side of Rain Flower Mount, they saw the main hall of Tai Po's Temple with the front half of the roof caving in. Five or six children were playing football beside the double gate, one half of which had fallen to the ground. Going in, they came upon three or four old women who were picking shepherd's purse in the temple courtyard. All the lattice-work in the hall had disappeared, and the five buildings at the back were completely stripped—not even a floor plank was left. After walking around, Kai sighed.[6]

The semifictional Tai Bo Temple shares something with the actual Kong Temple because it has the potential to evoke a magnificent past as well as a ruined present. The temple is remembered as a complete and uncorrupted structure that anchored a ritual system, formed a pattern, and helped to define political and social order. However, as its decay advances, Tai Bo Temple loses the capacity to represent that narrative or uphold that memory. Although it is a constant point of reference, the temple is neither physically nor symbolically stable. The effects of decay are not restricted to the physical relic and extend to the temple's mental and social space. The temple registers certain traces—Tai Bo's spirit, the history of the ancient Wu, and the renowned sacrifices of the high Ming, as well as the remnant traces of a once-great temple. The traces, however, are fragments, fading impressions, and material ruins, and the protagonists take no comfort in the perpetuity of any texts that might survive, either as inscriptions or in their memory.[7]

Mote observed that so long as a relic could be rebuilt, the literati would not feel their culture had been abused by the loss of the architecture. But *The Scholars* illustrates a problem; under certain circumstances the relic could not be rebuilt because these precious associations were at the same time dematerializing.[8] Wu Jingzi tells us, through his characters, that without the cabinets the ritual wares could not be stored, without the ritual wares the sacrifices could not be performed, and without the performance the memories or associations could not be made. From this example we may better understand that losing a historic building to fire or decay was more than a temporary inconvenience and that reconstruction was more than the addition of superstructure. The physical destruction/construction of the place was inseparable from the devastation or recovery of its social and cultural milieu.

In texts relating to Kong Temple, the concern for decay—at least from the Song dynasty onward—was expressed most passionately as an assault on the vaunted *siwen*—a concept that Peter Bol explains as going well beyond the literal translation of "This Culture of Ours" and referring to "a civilization based on both the models of the ancients and the manifest patterns of the natural order."[9] Construction was conceived of as part of this pattern, and although certain forms of reasoning may have held that its subsequent decay was natural and inevitable, in practice, few patrons could accept erosion as healthy or desirable. In contrast to the Ise Shrine of Japan, where elaborate decoration, glazed tile, and stonework were eschewed in the expectation that the structure would be dismantled twenty years after its construction, Kong Temple was never willingly surrendered and rarely subjected to any intentional force of destruction.[10] Nor did builders use inferior materials with the intent of having them decay. They certainly did not, as Segalen imaginatively overstated, build on sand with the intent of expediting the collapse of the tiled roof.[11] To permit or promote decay was to deny a received order or invalidate the embedded values; conversely, to restore and rebuild was to enact a higher principle, to correct deviation from the Way, and to create the powerful illusion of mastering time and space. In colloquial terms, as Tracy Miller finds with the Jin Shrine in Shanxi, architecture had a spiritual power and had to be maintained lest that spirit abandon the site.[12] That was something Kong Temple patrons and custodians understood even when they were not able to act upon their concerns.

Considering the age and the morphology of Kong Temple, it is neither possible nor preferable to reconstruct the changing socioeconomic circumstances and interests of each of the past seventy or so generations of temple managers, custodians, and sponsors. Instead, in examining the records I look for the management ethic that governed the construction of the monument at various stages of its development. In defining those stages, it is worth considering Michael Nylan and Thomas Wilson's well-founded position that the imperial cult of Kongzi developed through three distinct historical eras. Before the mid-third century, the cult was localized in nature, with little imperial involvement. The second stage, from the mid-third to the mid-eighth century, saw a greater frequency of state sacrifice, but the era was marked by a continuing uncertainty as to whether the principal sage of the cult should be Kongzi or the Duke of Zhou. Finally, between the mid-eighth and the late nineteenth century, the cult was fully integrated with the state and followed a standard liturgy based on classical precedent.[13] The building and maintenance of that cult's foremost temple can also be organized into three stages, although with substantial differences in their nature and time. Before the mid-second century CE the temple was under local management, after which it received only occasional assistance from the early imperial state. This regime changed in the late tenth century when the Song dynasty began to undertake greater responsibility for the material condition and the architectural standardization of the temple. Only with the geopolitical shifts at the beginning of the fourteenth century does the temple become fully integrated with the Ming state, and only in the Qing era does it fall under the direct control of state ministries (reversion to a looser form of management at the end of the last dynasty will be discussed in a later chapter). There is, in other words, no direct correlation between the development of Confucianism as an ideology and the development of the bureaucratic and management systems that governed Kong Temple. Confucian interests were expressed in and through the temple, but the interests of the literati must be considered together with those of the imperial state and Kongzi's resident lineal descendants, who I will refer to simply as the Kong family. These institutions never claimed independent control over the temple, and the key to understanding long-term change in the temple's production is in weighing the relative balance of authority between these stakeholding institutions and in considering the changing nature of the institutions themselves.

This chapter is more concerned with the evolution of Kong Temple than with its anatomy.[14] However, in surveying more than two millennia of its notable past, this account will do little to illuminate the details of temple building or management. The records that survive seldom relate technical data and appear instead as a poetics of building and conservation expressed as a longing for the historical or the imagined Kongzi, tales of myth and portent, the pursuit of individual and collective virtue, and the perpetuation and cultivation of the sagely spirit through material means. It is also a story about the growth, expansion, and negotiation of sacrifice and ritual authority; the contending schools of thought; the networking of elite scholars; and, most grandly, the rise and fall of practically every major Chinese dynasty. Less grandly, these texts and narratives served the interests of the temple's managers and patrons.[15] "Confucians" might claim to be pious in donating their salary to the memory of the sage, but they could also be driven to invest in the temple as a means to affirm their position and status or to manipulate the relic in pursuit of political or material gain. Even the "grand ancients" were not above signing their name to every memorial stele, and while many desired to restore the great temple halls, few claimed to improve the drainage, pull the weeds from the temple's courtyard, or sweep the cobwebs from its rafters.

Kong Temple patrons nonetheless developed a remarkably direct sense of the relationship between revering the sage (or protecting his aura/ demonstrating his virtue) and maintaining his relics. Actions were taken not just out of respect for Kongzi but also for the many past generations that had repaired the temple and were thus responsible for delivering the relic up to the present. In recognizing that they had subsequently allowed the temple to deteriorate, these supporters implied that their own generation had a responsibility to restore and to rebuild and thus to deliver the same legacy to the future. Of course, this was a constructed past and an imagined future, but these builders and patrons sought to consolidate ideals and follow the example of Kongzi in their own present. This same principle drove every major dynasty except the Qin to maintain, restore, and rebuild.

In the history of building, even the greatest monuments are transitory. Among them, Kong Temple has always been in a state of flux and subject to the situational demands of its patrons. But rather than producing a sense of fatalism, that rhythm of building and decay gave substance to the ideological and increasingly political imperative to uphold integrity, contain corruption, and search for order. In contextualizing that imperative within a single architectural complex, one begins to understand that even for erudite literati and agents of the imperial state, building was not an abstraction—it was something that had to be acted out through the assembly of brick, mortar, timber, and tile.

Building Walls to Protect the Sage: From Ancient Origins to the End of the Tang

The emergence of Qufu and the Lu region as a "sacred precinct" under imperial China seems almost preordained by a remarkably deep preimperial history.[16] Qufu's fertile plain has been under cultivation for over seven thousand years, and it is one of the key archaeological sites of both the Dawenkou and the Longshan prehistoric cultures. Some archaeologists argue that these early cultures gave birth to the Xia and the Shang dynasties, which would involve Qufu in China's earliest political and cultural developments leading to an organized polity.[17] According to legend, Qufu is linked with three of the five ancient sage kings. It is said that Emperor Huang (Huangdi) was born in nearby Shouqiu and that at one time or another Emperor Yan (Yandi), Emperor Huang, and King Shao Hao each maintained their capital at Qufu. The last is believed to be buried near Shouqiu in an unusual stone-clad pyramid that once rivaled the tomb of Kongzi for patronage, especially under the rule of more Daoist-minded emperors such as Song Zhenzong (r. 997–1022).[18]

During the rule of the Western Zhou, in the latter part of the eleventh century BCE, the lands of Shao Hao's clan were enfeoffed to the Duke of Zhou, who sent his son Bo Qin to rule the land. Thereafter, Qufu became the capital of the state of Lu and remained so until it was conquered by the southern state of Chu.[19] According to tradition, Kongzi was born into humble, even illicit, circumstances in Changping, near Qufu, in 551 BCE. Although his father, Shuliang He, claimed descent from a king of the ancient state of Song, he was no more than a local official with a marginally honorable military record. Kongzi's mother, Yan Zhengzai, prayed for conception at Mt. Ni (Niqiu) and was rewarded with the child whom she called Kong Qiu (courtesy name Zhongni). Legends add to the origin of Kongzi. Some suggest that Shuliang He joined in the mother's adoration while others say that Kongzi was so ugly at birth that his father abandoned him at Mt. Ni. Several days later, Yan Zhengzai found baby Kongzi alive in a cave being suckled by a tigress and fanned by an eagle's wing.[20]

As a young man, Kongzi sought official employment first at home and then abroad, but failing to find a suitable employer, he returned to the state of Lu. At the age of nineteen, he married the Lady Qiguan and fathered a son named Li, who would go on to perpetuate China's most famous lineage. After a period of study and teaching, Kongzi took up official duties in Lu and was appointed chief minister at the age of fifty-six. Dissatisfied with his post, he resigned and took to the road, traveling the land for fourteen years before making a final return to his home state. Taking up residence in Qufu, the master occasionally dispensed advice to the ruling Duke Ai of Lu (Lu Aigong, r. 498–468) but spent most of his remaining days teaching, resurrecting the ancient rites and music perfected by the Duke of Zhou, and editing the works that would become the classics of Confucianism. In 479 BCE Kongzi died at the age of seventy-three.

The accepted wisdom is that Duke Ai of Lu established Kong Temple two years after Kongzi died. Although he had never provided Kongzi with gainful employment, the ruler evidently saw the value of preserving his memory and built a hall near Kongzi's house, using it to display some of the deceased's personal articles. Sima Qian's biography of Kongzi, inspired by the historian's journey to Qufu in 127 BCE, is the usual source for this event.[21] During his visit Sima observed Kongzi's personal effects and inquired into the history of the memorial. Based on what scholars from the area told him and on scant references in earlier works, the *Records of the Grand Historian* (*Shiji*, ca. 109 BCE) notes that after Kongzi was buried, his students stayed on to observe three years of mourning. Even then, they could not tear themselves away from their master, going again to weep at his grave before returning to their homes. Zigong, the most loyal, built a hut near the tomb and remained there for another three years. In time, says the *Shiji*, a village grew up near the grave:

> The building which had formerly been used by the disciples during their mourning was made into a memorial temple (*miaotang*) by following generations, in which were kept the clothes, ceremonial hat, and the lute of Kongzi, besides his chariot and his writings. This was continued during more than 200 years until the beginning of the Han.[22]

This passage is often cited as proof that a memorial had existed in Qufu since shortly after Kongzi's death, although several unresolved issues with the statement exist. First, Sima Qian's account was written more than 350 years after the death of the sage, and there are no earlier references to this commemoration. The earlier *Chunqiu Zuozhuan* records Duke Ai's eulogy for Kongzi, and Mengzi (Mencius) notes the mourning of the disciples, but neither have anything to say about a memorial or a shrine.[23] Sima Qian also does not explain how such a prominent memorial could have survived the anti-Confucian campaign of Qin Shihuang (r. 221–210 BCE). Nonetheless, the evident desire to have an unbroken brick-and-mortar lineage reaching back to Kongzi's time has given this account an authority that effectively

dismisses such contradictions. The more gaping inconsistencies were resolved through tales of miraculous intervention that claim, for example,
that Qin Shihuang was startled into retreat after discovering either a white
rabbit in Kongzi's tomb or a tablet that prophesied its own unearthing and
the emperor's impending death.[24] As to the existence of the temple in the
early Han, Sima Qian wrote that Emperor Gaozu (r. 206–195 BCE) visited
Qufu in 195 BCE and offered the supreme Sacrifice of the Large Beast
(*tailao,* involving a bull, a boar, and a ram) before the tomb of Kongzi.[25]
The text does not explicitly mention a temple, although it is reasonable to
assume that if one did not already exist, a facility would have been constructed for the imperial sacrifice. Still, the historian's personal observation
made some seventy years later stands as the first reference to an actual
structure that was distinct from the sage's tomb.

Although the Han dynasty was probably never as "Confucian" as it was
made out to be, it was during this time that certain factions of scholars—
and eventually the dynasty itself—began to recognize Kongzi as an
uncrowned king (*suwang*). The image of nobility, however, lacked two key
markers of status—namely material wealth and a dignified family. In addressing that deficiency, the Confucian scholars began to develop the only
property and the only lineage that could be associated with the sage: his putative home and descendants in Qufu. Patronage of these relics and heirs
was inconsistent before the end of the dynasty, but a loose record does
begin to appear, as inscriptions on stone tablets and steles, showing that
visiting dignitaries made donations to the temple and worked to preserve it.
Most of these inscriptions merely cite the dates and names of these dignitaries or record eulogies to "the Sage." Some, however, include details on the
construction and maintenance of the temple and begin to illustrate how its
preservation was connected with imperial rule, state ritual, and the rising
fortunes of the Kong family.

In 152, long after the authority of the Han had fallen into decline, the ex-
cellency of works publicly urged the dynasty to repair the temple. The next
year Yi Ying, the chancellor (*xiang*) of Lu placed the site under state management.[26] According to the Yi Ying Stele inscribed at that time, Kongzi
had created the basis of the Han ruling system and therefore deserved the
respect of the dynasty. The temple had thus been established as a place to

offer sacrifices to Kongzi, but once the ceremonies were completed, the facilities were neglected. Thus, it was proposed that an inspector be appointed at the rank of a hundredweight of grain (*baishi zushi*) to manage the temple and to collect donations to fund the sacrifices in the spring and the autumn. The position was awarded to one Kong He, who had obtained an appropriate age (over forty), certain skills, knowledge of sacrifice, and the approval of Kongzi's descendants.[27] Erected three years later, the Liqi Stele (156 BCE) sponsored by Han Chi, chancellor of Lu, includes the first record of a temple restoration. The stele explains that the chancellor prepared the sacrifice wares, composed music, washed dishes, roasted venison, cut beans, prepared bamboo wares (*bian*), and decorated the temple. Arriving early and departing late, he worked to preserve the integrity of the old buildings or, as the memorial phrases it, "used lacquer without dilution, hired labor without counting salary" and "channeled clear water into the temple."[28]

These documents indicate that the temple had come under a form of state management in the Eastern Han and that a scheme to maintain regular sacrifice had been implemented. No formal system yet existed for funding repairs or restoration, however. Han Chi had been obliged to use his own resources to complete the project. These funds had apparently been sufficient in the short term, although for at least two reasons, private donations could not have continued as the sole source of support. First, the growing size and complexity of the temple likely made its maintenance prohibitively expensive. Second, and perhaps more importantly, to fund a temple devoted to Kongzi through private donors would miss the point of having such a temple in the first place. For Han Confucians to reach their objective of reforming society, they required the state to become financially as well as symbolically and "cosmically" invested in the temple. In the late stages of that dynasty, however, the state did not commit itself to the Confucian movement, and consequently, no further records exist regarding the condition of the temple before the end of the dynasty. The temple may have been neglected for as long as a century, and it was said that a fire swept through and destroyed the chariot of Kongzi during the reign of Han Xiandi (r. 189–220). There is no indication that the site was subsequently restored.[29]

After the Wei dynasty took control of northern China, the new emperor Wen (Cao Pi, r. 220–226) followed the earlier Han example of recognizing

Kongzi as a sage. Where Han rulers were content to leave temple affairs to the regional authorities and the Kong family, the Wei ruler set a new precedent by ordering the governor (*jun*) of Lu to restore and expand the temple. The stated purpose of this work was to honor Kongzi and facilitate sacrifice. Yet the associated stele inscription makes it clear that beyond symbolic restoration, the Wei saw the proper form of restoration and construction as a means to assert authority. While few details survive regarding the standardization of early architectural forms, it is known that the Wei had developed a complex building code by the time this restoration was commissioned.[30] A postscript to the emperor's text suggests these regulations and their link to the centralized authority of the state while implying that building and architecture are expressions of discipline, order, and power: "Repairing the old hall and aggrandizing the palaces and buildings, this is how diligent students show respect for their study and this is how we make the rules and laws. When the work is done the sage and the gods will protect the realm . . . and honor will be known to the wastelands."[31] The text marks a noteworthy development in understanding the relationship between architecture, ideology, and authority—first, in suggesting that custodial work provides a distinct political advantage; second, in suggesting that it is indistinct from scholarship; and finally, in suggesting that it is in accord with cosmic pattern.

Despite the gravity of such pronouncements, the Wei and its promise of ongoing funding collapsed within five decades. Responsibility for Kong Temple must have reverted to the Kong family at this time, although two hundred years pass before the relics surface in the records of the Liu-Song dynasty as an object of Emperor Xiaowu's (r. 424–453) patronage.[32] The temple's maintenance concerns next appear during the successor Northern Wei, when Li Daoyuan's *Shui jing zhu* (ca. 515–527) tells how Zhong Liyi aspired to become prime minister of Lu during the Yongping era (508–512), in part by commissioning a facsimile of Kongzi's long-destroyed chariot and commanding his subordinate Zhang Bo to refurbish Kong Temple. When clearing the weeds from the hall, the text continues, Zhang found seven jades in the earth. Concealing one for himself, he placed the others on the temple's altar. The discovery of a vermillion text inside a container that had once belonged to Kongzi revealed this deceit. "Later generations," the text read, "will study my works, and Dong Zhongshu [179?–104? BCE] will compile my books, preserve my chariot, clean my shoes and open my bamboo vessel. Seven pieces of jade will be found." Seeing that one was amiss, Zhong Liyi inquired about the jade, whereupon Zhang Bo confessed his crime and returned the missing item.[33]

The perception that supernatural forces resided in the temple and acted through the expression of portents was muted in later dynasties when scholars began to seek their models in ancient culture rather than mystical phenomena. Yet the sense of a lingering spiritual presence continued to motivate generations of renovators to come. The Li Zhongxuan Stele of 541 describes the feelings of the Yanzhou commander upon beginning a renovation of the temple under the authority of the Eastern Wei. The objective was technically to restore the effigies of Kongzi and his followers, but the description of the project shows that in addition to restoring the temple's function, builders also sought to restore its spirit:

> The palace was destroyed and the pools and stairways were overgrown with weeds, but in the temple courtyard the pines and cypress trees endured the severe winter . . . and the palace is surrounded by huge phoenix trees. The wild geese depart with the coming autumn, the moonlight touches the frost on the branches, the swallows return in the spring, the green leaves unfold to catch the wind. . . . This lends comfort to the sagely spirit, and that is why every generation restored [the temple].[34]

Li makes no mention of portents in this text, but in associating the temple with the four seasons he does act within a metaphysical framework informed by the *Book of Changes* (*Yijing*), wherein natural, material, spiritual, and moral phenomena were seen as part of the same process of growth and regeneration. It is well established that Confucian scholars saw the correct performance of ritual as essential to harmonizing the individual with the cosmos. If that concept is extended to building and restoration, then we may better understand why the Yanzhou commander, perhaps like Han Chi centuries earlier, felt the need to pursue this project even without the express approval of his emperor.

There is, nonetheless, a persistent concern within the available texts that respect for Kongzi, as expressed through the preservation of his temple, would not be complete without the support of the state. In the late sixth century, the Sui emperors were nominally more respectful of Kongzi and aware of how ritual could enshrine the value of deference to imperial authority. Yet Kong Temple continued to rely upon regional officials and family patrons for its maintenance, and it was in that environment that the magistrate (*xianling*) Chen Shuyi inscribed an initiative that absolved the emperor and assumed his own responsibility for restoring the temple: "Many matters are left to the local officials," he wrote, "so it is time to change the means of honoring the Duke of Zhou, and the heritage (*yifeng*) of Kongzi should be regarded as the principle followed by the hundred rulers. The old traditions and rites are not enough, so the capable Magistrate Chen of Qufu must follow the heavenly command, respect the First Teacher (*xianshi*) [Kongzi], and persuade the Kong family to repair the temple."[35] In recording his initiative, Chen was careful to show proper respect for imperial authority, yet his message betrays frustration with the court and even the Kongs, who seem reluctant to take a leading role in preserving the memory of their own ancestor.

Kong Temple began to capture greater imperial attention under Tang emperor Gaozong (r. 649–683). When Gaozong visited the temple during an imperial tour of 666, he ordered the conscription of laborers to clear the weeds, dredge the canals, expand the exterior walls, acquire timbers, and collect rocks to decorate the gardens. The record states that interior walls were painted, roofs and windows were repaired, archways were constructed, pavilions were renovated, the temple was furnished and supplied with books and stationery, and the effigies of Kongzi and his followers were restored and repainted to give them a dignified appearance. The emperor gave the project his seal of approval but did not assign the work to the Board of Works or Board of Rites (Libu). Instead, the project was delegated to the governor of Yanzhou, who in turn raised funds from the local elite.[36]

Although the dynasty was following precedent in this regard, scholars in the state's employ had begun to see the status quo as inadequate. The relationship between temple and state was addressed most forcefully in 719 when noted calligrapher Li Yong petitioned Emperor Xuanzong (r. 712–756) to pay greater respect to the descendants of Kongzi and Confucian scholars, to adopt Confucian texts as the state orthodoxy, and to support state sacrifice at Kong Temple. As to the temple itself, Li recorded a demure suggestion that the relic owed its survival not to the state but to those who pursued virtue of their own accord. Where Chen Shuyi may have implied that the Kong family were reticent custodians, they now appeared as models of virtue, demonstrating ancestral devotion by actively preserving the trees around the sage's tomb, building walls for the sage's protection, and erecting steles to record their achievements.[37]

It should not be presumed that Xuanzong responded to this specific example, although he did supplement the local initiatives by commissioning an expansion of the main hall appropriate to the sage's promotion to the rank of king. The end of the reign, however, was marred by the An Lushan Rebellion, and in its weakened state, the Tang effectively lost control of Qufu.[38] During that time private initiatives reappear as a critical means of funding major renovations. The "Record of the New Gate of the Temple of King of Exalted Culture" testifies that when Meng Xiujian and Lu Tong visited in 773, they were dismayed to find the temple run down, the "red gate" about to collapse, half the roof tiles missing, and commoners freely wandering about the grounds—blasphemy, in their view. Only after Meng and Lu had taken up the initiative to repair the temple did officials begin to collect money to purchase materials and conscript labor to rebuild walls and gates. The alarming security problem was thus corrected, and the sacrifices could continue with due ceremony.[39]

A century later, the next restoration on record was paid for entirely by Kong Wenyu, a regional authority titled Duke of Lu (Luguogong). Although belonging to a collateral branch of the Kong family, the duke felt a personal responsibility for the temple and lamented that the buildings were decrepit and the walls reduced to broken relics. The main sacrifices were held in spring and autumn, but the rites were said to be disorderly, the music vulgar, and the sacrificial objects "discarded amongst the weeds." This state of affairs weighed heavily on Wenyu and so, even though the temple was not in his jurisdiction, the duke used his own resources for a full-scale restoration. On receiving court approval in 869, Wenyu sent one of his trusted officials to supervise the work. Gates and high walls were constructed to "show the continuity of virtue" and to guard the sage's aura (*lingguang*), the statues of Kongzi and his acolytes were restored, and couplets were hung on columns. Without the nobles, it was written, "Orchids were planted, and without the governor the weeds were expelled," meaning that the restoration was completed without resorting to state funds. When the work was finished, it was recorded, the "gentle breeze [i.e., the teachings of Kongzi] rises again and Queli will remain fragrant for 10,000 years, serving as a model for the people of our times."[40]

It would be ambitious to claim the handful of texts that refer to the temple's early condition as a "history" and problematic to claim the temple achieved a substantial monumental form before the end of the Tang, when available sources portray it as a ruin more often than not. These may be fragmentary pages from an imperfect history, yet the documents, many of which have occupied the site as steles since ancient times, do show that the temple retained a physical presence throughout early imperial China. By accounting for the material of the temple and relating it to the sentiments expressed in text, it is possible to conclude that Kong Temple contained two basic potentialities: in good repair the temple embodied the ideal of Kongzi and the Duke of Zhou, and in decay it exposed the deterioration of the rites and the loss of the Way. Through the interaction of its potentialities, the relic was subject to constant change—never far from ruin and yet never beyond recovery. There is, however, a sense that by the beginning of the Tang dynasty, custodians and sponsors were motivated to do more than simply keep the temple in stasis. Nothing in early Confucian theory or cosmology suggests that the promotion of ancient virtue or the protection of the sagely aura demanded better monuments, but the urge to expand and improve the temple—to regulate it through excess—implies that ritual building had developed a political and economic dimension in early imperial China. Individuals like Chen Shuyi and Li Zhongxuan acted on their aesthetic sensibilities and partnered with the Kong family to establish the temple as a legitimate concern for the highest levels of state. Art and politics were in tension but not necessarily in contradiction as long as it was understood that the expansion or elaboration of the system was a means to achieve its harmonization.

A Temple for a King: Song, Jin, and Yuan Transitions

The Song dynasty represents a major turning point for Kong Temple. Having endured untold centuries of ruin interrupted only by haphazard construction and conservation efforts, the relic expanded beyond its continuing role as an ancestral temple and memorial shrine and gradually emerged as a symbol of imperial legitimacy. At the same time, responsibility for restoring the temple began to shift from private citizens and the "feudal" authority of regional governors toward a more direct involvement with the state. The centralization of authority coincides with the rise of the scholar-official as a force in politics and with the rising entitlement of senior members of the Kong family, who appear increasingly eager to transcend their role as filial descendants and keepers of the temple. In their respective roles and often in partnership, the family and the scholars begin to act more as the temple's agents, using the poetics of decay to hold the state responsible for what was increasingly seen and accepted as an imperial obligation.

In 983 the Song emperor Taizong (r. 976–997) initiated a major restoration and expansion of Kong Temple. Details on the site's improvements are few, although it was noted that before the project began, the effigy of the sage was not sufficiently venerable, the grounds were overgrown, and the temple buildings were unappealing. Thereafter, Taizong implemented new architectural standards and sent his envoy to conscript labor and supervise the new construction, which now included multiple stories and mezzanine levels for the temple's more prominent buildings. When the repairs were complete, the archetypical scholar-official Lü Mengzheng did not impoverish his prose by reciting the technical details of the new style, but he did comment that a new prospect had revealed itself through the work: "Rooftops reach to the clouds, the eaves curve like spreading wings, gates open in succession, and many storied buildings tower about one another."[41] Lü was no architect, but he understood aesthetics and the meaning of scale and sequence as well as his obligation to publicly acclaim the imperially mandated upgrades.

In the next generation, Emperor Zhenzong advanced the temple's prestige by paying a visit to the county that he would rename Xianyuan (Source of the Immortals). On his arrival in 1008, the Daoist-inclined sovereign was arguably more interested in the nearby tomb of Shao Hao, sponsoring the construction of not one but two magnificent Daoist temples near the site.[42] Zhenzong nonetheless did his duty to Confucian heritage by sponsoring the reconstruction of the ancient ruins of the Temple of the Duke of Zhou (Zhou-gongmiao) a short distance to the east of Queli, performing a sacrifice at Kong Temple, and inscribing the Stele for the Profound/Dark Sage and King of Exalted Culture.[43] This stele was sheltered by a new pavilion in the temple's main courtyard, although further construction had to wait until 1018–1022, when it was undertaken by the local notable Kong Daofu. On receiving Dao-fu's report that the temple was "unfittingly shabby," the emperor charged his transport commissioner (zhuanyunshi) with raising the necessary funds and provided materials left from the construction of a temporary hall that had been erected for the emperor's personal use.[44] Using these resources, Daofu went well beyond simply restoring the old premises, adding new structures, and expanding its dimensions to about two-thirds its modern size. As depicted in the following Jin dynasty, the new temple included multiple gates, a library hall to honor literature, pavilions to shelter imperial steles, and sacrifice halls dedicated to Kongzi as well as his son, grandson, wife, and father (fig. 2).[45] The forms and designations of the new temple reflect the developing tripartite nature of the temple—state, family, and scholar enshrined together within its expanding walls.

This work was principally an act of piety, although like his close colleague Fan Zhongyan, Kong Daofu was also part of an increasingly mobile generation of scholar elites who sought to strengthen their lineages by compiling genealogies, founding charitable estates, and maintaining ancestral homes and cemeteries. Since Kong Temple was in effect his family's ancestral shrine, Daofu's project can be seen as an effort to boost the profile of his kin. The political implications of these actions will be discussed in the following chapter, although it is presently worth noting the impact that these political and ritual changes had on temple management. Raising the social status of those directly responsible for the temple changed the way in which the monument was "produced." In the Song dynasty, Kong elders went from simply observing restoration projects sponsored by other Confucian officials to being partners in a campaign to advance the mutual interests of the scholars and the family by involving the state in temple maintenance. Although only gradually drawn into the equation, it was a responsibility that the state found increasingly difficult to avoid.

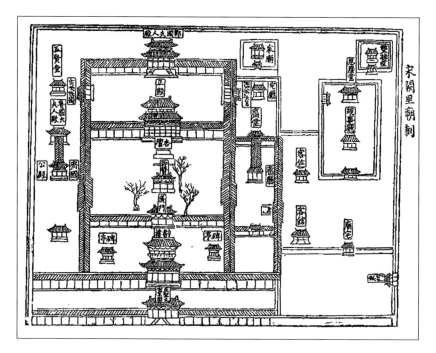

FIGURE 2. Song dynasty Queli Temple configuration. By the eleventh century, the core of the temple had been established, including the Pavilion of the Literary Constellation, two stele pavilions, Yimen (Gate of the Great Ensemble), the Main Hall (Hall of the Great Ensemble), the Hall of the Matron of Zou (Lady Qisheng), side halls for the son and grandson of Kongzi, and the Apricot Altar as an uncovered terrace. The memorial architecture for Kongzi's parents and the five worthies lies to the west, and the Abstinence Hall and the Family Temple lie to the east. The Kong Family Mansion and the guest quarters are on the extreme east. Many of the lesser structures are not extant. Kong Yuancuo, *Kongshi zuting guangji*, 1227.

The Jin conquest was initially problematic for Kong Temple. In 1129 the relic was damaged by fire and it was some years before Jin emperor Xizong (r. 1135–1150) sponsored a restoration of the cloisters and main hall.[46] Prospects improved when Emperor Shizong (r. 1161–1189) threw his support behind Confucian ritual, according to the eminent Hanlin scholar Dang Huaiying, as a means to "civilize the barbarians, inherit the past rites and restore that which had been wasted (*feizhui*) in the past."[47] According to Dang's record, the contemporary head of the Kong family, entitled as Duke of Fulfilling the Sage (Yanshenggong), rejoiced in asking: "Is now not the time to restore the courtyard of my ancestor (*zuting zhifu*)?" After submitting the proposal, however, Kong Zong learned that his budget had been slashed and the project scaled back. The duke had few reservations about recording his displeasure or using the reputation of his illustrious ancestor to dun the court for funds that he felt were his due:

> [Kong Zong] remarked in consternation "how can such a Front Hall suit one with the title of king (*wang*)?" He continued "I am in charge of the sacrifice affairs and responsible for guarding the temple and tombs, my ability is limited, but as the leader of the family I held an ax and went deep into the Dongmeng area with the temple men, experienced the harsh conditions, felt the wind and the rain, and worked with the laborers in searching out good timbers. Finally we found several thousand in a valley. My brother and I spent a lot of money on the sacrifice wares to ensure their suitability. Many big pagoda trees in the cemetery suddenly withered and these were deemed suitable for columns and rafters, which was fortunate because the two million [i.e., two thousand strings of one thousand coins, provided by the court] was only enough to pay the craftsmen."[48]

The material in this account is no longer an abstraction of the temple's metaphysical condition. It is real. The means of engaging those materials, moreover, is not an exercise of ritual in the usual sense of the word but an exercise of labor. It should not be presumed that this or any of the increasingly detailed building budgets to come reflect the actual costs of building so much as indicate the relative value of a building project and its place within the building hierarchy. In his appeal, however, the duke asserted that the temple had financial worth and cited that specific monetary sum to argue that the temple had been undervalued by the state.

Kong Zong's complaints failed to capture the attention of Shizong, although the supporters of Kong Temple found a more sympathetic ear in the person of Emperor Zhangzong (r. 1189–1208), who approved a major expansion of the site in the first year of his reign. The associated commemorative stele remarks that just as construction was about to begin, nine supernatural *lingzhi* fungi were found in the cemetery of Kongzi, at his birthplace on Mt. Ni, and in the dwelling of the Kong family. Under this auspicious sign, a

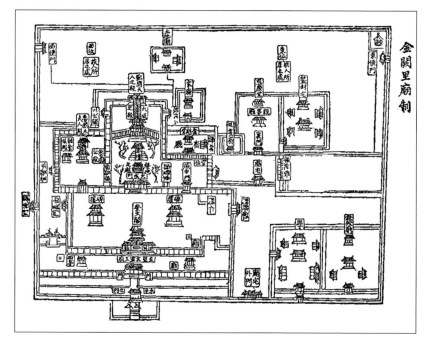

FIGURE 3. Jin dynasty Queli Temple configuration, showing the main components of the Song dynasty still in place. The perimeter has been expanded, the Apricot Altar is equipped with a pavilion, and an additional gate has been added to the south. A school has been added to the southeast on the opposite side of what will later become Queli Street. Kong Yuancuo, *Kongshi zuting guangji*, 1227.

capable official supervised the work, the army supplied labor, and craftsmen were hired from the community. At that time the temple was in such degraded condition that only one-third of the existing buildings could be salvaged; the remainder were torn down and rebuilt according to "proper sequence and order" (i.e., as prescribed by building codes). Pavilions were repainted and surrounded by high walls, and small items such as balustrades, window frames, screens, and protective mesh were positioned according to strict regulations (fig. 3). The construction work was finished within a year, and another was spent painting and decorating and replacing statues and "dressing them with dignity." The stated cost of the project was 76,400 strings of cash (*min*), and the official record notes that the emperor vowed to pay it without recourse to a special levy on the people.[49] A postscript to that record, however, mentions that much of the pledge did not materialize. The

cash-strapped court had to renege on its commitment amid a series of financial challenges resulting from major floods along the Yellow River and
the rise of the Mongol Empire.[50] The miraculous discovery of a hoard of
coins in a well and a quantity of building materials submerged in a pool recovered some of the costs, but in the end the Kong family and their scholar-
official allies supplied the funds to restore the Apricot Altar (Xingtan).[51]

When the Jin did fall to the Mongols, the transition proved disastrous.
For the second time in less than a century, the temple came to ruin when
"barbarians from the north" burned most of the major structures and three
junipers thought to have been alive since the age of Kongzi. In the aftermath
of the assault, it was said that a five-colored cloud appeared containing a flock
of cranes that continuously circled the sky above the temple. Seeing this as
an omen, members of the Kong family collected the remains of the junipers
and had them carved into statues of Kongzi and other sages.[52] That omen
portended the revival of the temple's fortunes under Mongol rule, although
in the early decades of that regime the responsibility for temple maintenance
reverted to the family and their supporters. Between 1237 and 1267 the Kong
family and local officials were able to rebuild the basic ritual infrastructure,
but not the main sacrifice hall.[53] Jining route commander (*zongguan fushi*)
Liu Houyong turned his attention to the temple in 1282, noting that while
the government often spoke of restoration, the necessary funds were in short
supply, and repairs were outpaced by deterioration. Liu attempted to address
the problem by raising money from his provincial colleagues and schedul-
ing work during the agricultural off-season in order to use surplus labor from
the estates of the gentry. These gentry willingly cooperated, the evidence suggests, "because it brings glory to our native place," but without the imperial
court their resources were only sufficient to rebuild the crumbling temple
wall, clear out the weeds, and plant trees in and around the temple.[54]

Two decades later, the political climate had changed for the better. Where
Commander Liu had failed to attract more than the court's tacit acceptance,
in 1301 the Mongol governor of the Jining district claimed to "follow the
example of the Grand Ancients" in contributing ten thousand *min* toward
renovations. By the time the project was completed after three and a half
years, it had grown into a full scale state-sponsored restoration and expansion
costing an additional one hundred thousand *min*.[55] Physical deterioration

and status promotions were cited as justification for another round of renovations that began during the reign of Emperor Wenzong (r. 1328–1332). The Jining route was provided with 314,400 *min* for maintaining the temple and restoring the Pavilion of the Literary Constellation (Kuiwenge). Because Kongzi's father had been promoted to the rank of King Who Fathered the Sage (Qishengwang), the temple was altered to follow the "model of a royal palace" (*wang gong zhizhi*), meaning that new walls were erected around the temple and distinguished by corner towers.[56] When the work was completed in 1336, it was said that the pavilions looked grand, walls surrounded the cloisters, and gates soared upward.[57]

To reprise an earlier point, the Song, the Jin, and the Yuan texts show that the Kong family and their scholar-official allies involved those dynasties in the maintenance of Kong Temple. And though these successive courts did not necessarily commit to this responsibility, the growing scale of the temple meant that it was no longer possible for the Kong family and even the wealthiest private donors to properly maintain the place without assistance from the state or its regional subdivisions. Under these circumstances, it is notable that the available texts do not dwell upon "restoring the ways of the ancients" so much as describe a more grandiose vision of the temple that points to the necessarily greater responsibilities of the imperial court and the serious consequences of the occasional failure to honor those duties.

The insistent tone of these texts indicates the Kong family's growing power and sense of entitlement, although Kong Temple was not simply a reflection of that influence. As an institution the temple was increasingly available to the official class as a means to build networks, control resources, and enact authority. As the temple and its networks grew more complex and prestigious, the state could no longer afford to remain on the sidelines or to delegate the responsibility and benefits of temple maintenance to its agents. Nor could the state simply trust its officials to conduct large-scale restorations according to abstract "cosmic patterns." In adopting actual patterns and budgets, the Song, the Jin, and the Yuan began to define and circumscribe the "social life" of the temple and its patrons. In reaffirming the temple's kingly status, the late Yuan court in particular imposed a system on ritual architecture, appropriated its hierarchies, and subordinated it to the state rather than leaving it to serve only as a model. In subsequent dynasties that system would be subject to negotiation, and at times it was weakly executed or openly challenged. Yet together with the manipulation of imperial titles, the emulation of imperial architecture would continue as the defining principle for forthcoming restorations and reconstructions. Under that principle the temple would advance to new heights of material development, although it cannot be said that it came to represent the state any more than a knot represents the net that it ties or the tree in which it grows. Kong Temple had always been open to diverse strands of interest, and that diversity would persist even as centralized bureaucratic management in the Ming and Qing dynasties wove those strands more tightly together.

Emulating the Imperial Court in Ming and Qing

If the Song-Jin-Yuan era suggests a growing, if still problematical, relationship between the temple and the imperial court through the intermediary role of the Kong family, then that relationship, with all of its responsibilities, comes to maturity under the Ming. It has been shown that the Kong family may well have manufactured their affiliation with the court, perhaps even fabricating records of imperial patronage in order to legitimize their base.[58] Nonetheless, it is clear that the Ming and later the Qing dynasty invested heavily in Kong Temple, becoming its principal shareholders and the driving force behind its architectural and spatial development. More than ever, from the Ming onward, the fate of the temple was tied to the fate of the dynasty because it was inextricably tied into the system of rule. It could strengthen when the system flourished, but the extraordinary expense associated with restoration or rebuilding meant that the temple was exposed to the elements whenever the system began to break down.

The late Yuan had been a chaotic time for the Lu region, and by the time the Ming dynasty was founded the temple was overdue for restoration. The founding Hongwu emperor (r. 1368–1398) decreed repairs in 1374 and again in 1387, when the Board of Works sent one thousand artisans to restore the temple.[59] More significant investment came after the Yongle emperor (r. 1402–1424) moved the capital from Nanjing to Beijing and restored the Grand Canal as the lifeline between the North and the South. Because of its close proximity to the canal, Kong Temple became an asset in the effort to control the perennially restive lands of western Shandong by upholding the state-sponsored orthodoxy against the allegedly heterodox tendencies of the local people. More importantly, the temple gave the family and the officials charged with maintaining order in the region ample opportunity to enact their authority by sponsoring temple-based building projects.

Kong Temple's last major expansion began in 1411, two years after Yongle initiated the construction of his own tomb, the same year in which construction work began on the renewed canal, and the same year in which the Confucian temple in Beijing began to undergo a major renovation.[60] The Board of Works initially committed 230 convict laborers to the Queli project. The emperor subsequently barred this despised class from the temple and ordered the Shandong administration commissioner to assemble a civilian force of three thousand workers to undertake the bulk of the project, leaving the convicts to work on the temple's peripherals.[61] In 1434 the attendant (*shilang*) to the Board of Works (Gongbu), Zhou Chen, "donated his salary" to have large timbers shipped from the South (presumably along the Grand Canal), although he entrusted the completion of the project to the head of the Kong family—the Duke of Fulfilling the Sage.[62] Providing for the reconstruction and expansion of the architecture for Kongzi's father three decades later, a subsequent duke made it clear that the work was done "without official funds or corvée."[63] Although the nature of this project might imply a resurgence in family and patron sponsorship, on coming to power in the next generation the culturally adept Chenghua emperor (Xianzong, r. 1464–1487) reasserted the imperial prerogative by ordering the Shandong grand coordinator (*xunfu*) to renovate the temple in preparation for a major sacrifice.[64] Chenghua wrote the eulogy for that sacrifice and had it inscribed in his own calligraphy on a giant stele that loomed over the temple grounds. When the Duke of Fulfilling the Sage requested permission to address the condition of the temple in 1477, the resulting overhaul would be total in scale. In addition to the main ceremonial buildings and decorative elements, the work was extended to include construction or renovation of service and storage buildings and external offices for ritual and property managers. When the work was completed in 1487, the cost of the project was reported as one hundred thousand *liang* of government silver.[65]

The accomplishment was utterly eliminated just twelve years later when storm clouds gathered over Queli, setting the temple's eastern court ablaze with a flash of lightning. The fire quickly spread to the central courtyard, incinerating most of the ritual architecture as well as gates, stele pavilions, auxiliary buildings, and trees throughout the temple.[66] Looking over the charred ruins in the aftermath, Prefect Zhao Huang was philosophical, writing that like its greenery, the temple itself was subject to the cycle of life.[67] Such musings aside, however, little time was lost in lamenting the tragedy, and almost as soon as the smoke cleared, Investigating Censor (*jiancha yushi*) Yu Lian applied for and received court permission to rebuild.[68] The records do not explain why Yu in particular (or indeed anyone else in similar levels of authority) undertook this responsibility, although it may be speculated that he was following a bureaucratic procedure by which major building projects had to be requested by high officials not associated with the court or the Board of Works.[69] Once the project was approved, Grand Secretary Li Dongyang, who happened to be father-in-law to the Duke of Fulfilling the Sage, undertook its general management. Under the authority of the Board of Works, grand coordinators He Jian and Xu Yuan raised funds, coordinated regional officials, recruited artisans, and hired laborers. With no suitable timber reserves in the vicinity, the managers spared no expense in procuring wood from as far as Hunan/Hubei and Sichuan. Stone was easier to acquire from local quarries that were said to have been "divinely created to serve the needs of the temple." The task of carving that stone into elaborate dragon columns was entrusted to skilled artisans from Huizhou in Anhui.[70]

Equipped with quality materials and skills and an army of laborers, the project managers enlarged the front gates to suit the expanded temple, rebuilt all the bridges and stairways, and refurbished all the tablets and plaques. The Hall of the Great Ensemble (Dachengdian), associated with Kongzi, and the Hall of Repose (Qindian), associated with Kongzi's wife, were upgraded with "royal" two-tier gable-hip roofs and reconstructed using the highest quality *nanmu* wood for the columns, beams, rafters, lintels, and door sills. The ceilings were decorated with hundreds of panels accented with golden dragons, the door panels were decorated with water-chestnut flower and tortoise-shell lattice (*linghua guibei*) designs, and the timber columns were painted in a rich silver vermillion. The eave-support brackets (*dougong*), beams, lintels, and purlins were decorated with the highest grade of blue and green paint with gold accents, the roof was sheathed in green-glazed tiles, and the floors and walls were paved with bricks. The double-tier stone terraces that lifted the main halls above the courtyard were carved and fitted with stone balustrades.[71] Memorial halls and chambers in the eastern and western courts were expanded from three bays to five; the eastern and western cloisters were extended to one hundred bays in length; the Pavilion of the Literary Constellation was overhauled; and many secondary structures and stele pavilions were renewed, along with nearby *pai-fang* arches adjacent the streets. The total cost of the project was given as 152,600 *liang*.[72]

Eulogists throughout the ages had expressed the sentiment that to repair Kong Temple was to restore peace, order, and prosperity, not just in the cosmic sense but also in real terms of maintaining social stability. That logic, however, failed a decade after the temple's most recent sumptuous restoration when insurgents attacked the defenseless county, killing hundreds of its citizens and forcing the Kong family to evacuate. Breaking into the temple, the rebels vandalized the premises and sacrilegiously "fed their horses in the courtyard and soiled the books in the sewer."[73] When the rebels were finally driven off, Zhao Huang, now serving as Shandong grand coordinator, ordered the officials who had failed to provide adequate security to pay for the repairs. Recognizing that moral authority alone was insufficient to guarantee the temple, Zhao further recommended bolstering the contingent of indentured servants committed for its maintenance and protection.[74]

The actual response would involve moving an entire city. Since the Yuan dynasty, the temple and the ducal mansion at Queli had been separate from the administrative center of Qufu, which a rival branch of the Kong lineage occupied and controlled. Because both Queli and Qufu had suffered from inadequate defenses during the insurrection and Grand Secretary Li had recently helped the duke regain control of the county administration from his cousins in Qufu, it was decided to move the county offices to Queli.[75] Surveillance Commissioner (*anchashi*) Pan Zhen and a legion of corvée laborers started work on the requisite city wall, completing the massive construction in nine years at the expense of 35,800 *liang*.[76] The temple had

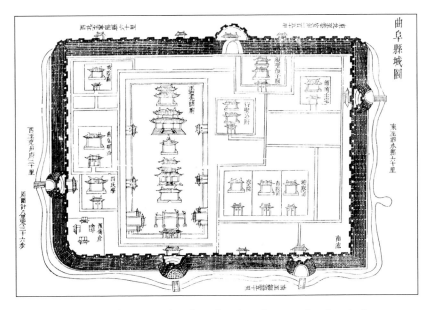

FIGURE 4. Diagram of the city of Qufu in the Ming dynasty, showing the key structures of Kong Temple, *center-left;* the magistrate's office and schools to the west; the schools and the Kong family compound to the east; and the Yanzi Temple and the Yan family compound to the northeast. The Qufu city wall and moat surround all. The city assumed this scale and configuration in the early sixteenth century. *Queli guangzhi,* 1673.

already begun to affect imperial pretensions in the Yuan dynasty when builders were permitted to add corner towers to its walls. Now Qufu would follow the pattern established by Beijing, with temple and mansion dominating the center in the way that the Forbidden City occupied imperial Beijing (fig. 4).[77] Not only did the temple occupy the center of the city, but the city now occupied the center of a conceptual "state of Lu" that included other relics of the ancient past such as the ancient state wall, the temples of Yanzi and the Duke of Zhou, the cemetery of Kongzi's father, and the tomb of Mengzi. According to a map printed in the *Expanded Annals of Queli,* the state of Lu even includes imperial China's most sacred site, the Eastern Marchmount—Mt. Tai (fig. 5). By enhancing the sage's ritual architecture, developing his hometown, and investing his lineal descendants with extraordinary ritual and political authority, the Ming state had begun to treat Kongzi as a king in both name and in practice.

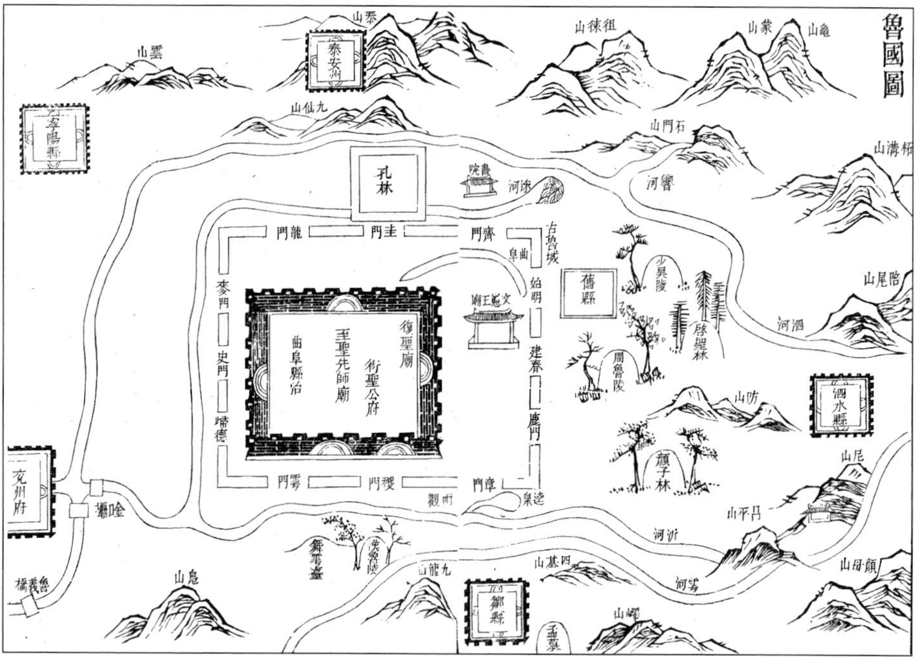

FIGURE 5. Map of the state of Lu. Qufu County is imagined in relation to its ancient Lu State relics, including Kongzi's birthplace of Mt. Ni, his burial site in Kong Forest, and his temple (Zhishengxianshi Miao). Other notable sites include the burial ground of Kongzi's parents, the tomb of Mengzi, the tomb of Shao Hao, the outer wall of the ancient Lu State, and the dispossessed old county seat. Mt. Tai, although actually much farther to the north, is included as an apparent affirmation of the sacred qualities of the home of Kongzi. *Queli guangzhi*, 1673.

Kong Temple suffered a dramatic reversal in its fortunes under the reign of the controversial Jiajing emperor (Shizong, r. 1521–1567). For reasons to be discussed in the next chapter, the emperor withdrew the kingly title granted to Kongzi in the Tang dynasty and declined to provide material support to the sage's temple for the next four decades of his reign. When it came due for restoration in the 1550s, the prefect (*shou*) who initiated the work prudently did not cite the veneration of Kongzi as his rationale, claiming instead that without Kong Temple the Lu region would be destabilized by "heterodox religions." Even so, the imperial censor who sponsored the project did not forward the request to the Board of Works or the Imperial Household Department but returned it to the regional administrators of Jinan and Yanzhou with the instruction that they supervise and contribute toward the renovation of thirty-seven dilapidated buildings within the temple.[78]

The death of Jiajing in 1567 coincides with the resumption of a more active repair cycle, but the emperor's position had fundamentally changed the way in which Kong Temple was managed. The officials who undertook these projects in the late sixteenth century had to do so without aid from the Ming court or the Board of Works and appear increasingly reliant on personal networks, contingency funds, and private donations. In 1577, for example, Chief Censor Zhao Xian found the temple "run down" and initiated repairs with the help of two colleagues.[79] Fourteen years later, the Hall of the Sage's Traces (Shengjidian) was constructed through the cooperation of an imperial censor, the Shandong surveillance vice-commissioner (*ancha fushi*), and the magistrate of Qufu.[80] In 1594 Censor Lian Biao raised three thousand *liang* of gold (equivalent to twelve thousand to fifteen thousand *liang* of silver) from the Censorate's "atonement fund" (*liangtai zhi shuhuan*), "incense tax from mountain sacrifices" (*yuesi xiangshui*, i.e., funds donated by pilgrims to Mt. Tai), surplus from the Palace Buildings Office (*Jiangzuo*, a subsidiary of the Board of Works), and tax surplus (*guanku xianjin*).[81] On completion the temple and surroundings were said to resemble a "palace of the heavenly realm" (*juntian zhi gong*) and to "emulate the imperial courtyard" (*yixiang chaoque*), but in 1601 the governor of Shandong noted that the temple was once again in desperate need of repair. After pressing his subordinates for two thousand *liang* of gold, the governor was able to initiate the work. Repairs to the Western Cloister, however, were delayed until 1608 when the work was undertaken by the Jining vice-military commissioner (*bingxun fushi*).[82]

More serious shortfalls were noted in 1614, when 105,270 *liang* the state had earmarked for regular maintenance failed to materialize, leaving the temple exposed to worms that infested the timbers and to storms that battered Qufu in 1619. Responding to the emergency, Assistant Censor in Chief Bi Maokang dismissed a suggestion that funds be redirected from taxes collected at the Grand Canal customs station of Linqing and from the pilgrims to Mt. Tai, arguing that those who paid the fees were themselves facing financial difficulties and that in any case Shandong Province alone should not assume the responsibility for Kong Temple and other sacred relics. The censor called for an immediate infusion of cash from imperial coffers and proposed a fundraising mechanism by which each province would donate five thousand to ten thousand *liang* every ten years. Although Bi was able to raise money for makeshift repairs, such a scheme had little chance of working once the dynasty began to struggle with bankruptcy and chronic rebellion during the last decades of its mandate.[83]

The rebellion that ultimately ended the Ming dynasty helped bring the Manchu to power in 1644, but for once Kong Temple passed through a dynastic transition without a serious threat to its integrity. During its first decades, the Qing court continued the Ming practice of deferring temple maintenance to local supporters.[84] In 1683, however, a short inscription indicates the provision of official supervisors and funds from the state treasury (*neitang*) for temple restoration.[85] As the temple's acting manager, the budding dramatist Kong Shangren claimed ignorance of the dynasty's motive until it was revealed that these funds were intended to prepare the temple for an audience with the Kangxi emperor (r. 1661–1722). When Kangxi arrived the following year, Kong Shangren was assigned to act as both erudite scholar and expert tour guide, and in that capacity succeeded in arousing the emperor's enthusiasm for the Confucian relics. Kangxi subsequently granted permission to increase the size of the family cemetery and pledged an additional 86,500 *liang* to fund a full temple restoration. In contrast to the late Ming practice of entrusting building and restoration to regional officials, provincial governors, and imperial censors, the Qing emperor assigned the two-year project to the director of the storage office (*guangchusi langzhong*) of the Imperial Household Department (Neiwufu).[86]

Klaas Ruitenbeek hypothesizes that similar administrative methods, when used in rebuilding imperial palaces in the Ming and the Qing, indicate a shift away from the personal initiatives of the scholar-official in the former dynasty and toward a more highly bureaucratized procedure in the latter.[87] That appears to have been the case with Kong Temple as maintenance became a state prerogative during the Kangxi reign. Under that system the temple could benefit from imperial largesse, although the drawback to the system was that, having once received the emperor's financial contribution, Kong Temple had to endure the remaining decades of the long Kangxi reign without significant follow-up funds either from the emperor or his regional officials.

The temple was thus due—perhaps overdue—for attention when the Yongzheng emperor (r. 1722–1735) came to the throne, although the decision to rebuild was ultimately forced by a bolt of lightning that set the Hall of the Great Ensemble ablaze in the summer of 1724. The Duke of Fulfilling the Sage was immediately alerted, but with the fire starting high up in the rafters there was little the attendants could do but evacuate the spirit tablets and watch the fire burn through the night.[88] Upon surveying the damage, the duke submitted a report reflecting his expectation that the temple would be rebuilt using state funds and included the precise monetary calculations associated with Qing building codes.[89] The resulting budget proposed a generous, though not exorbitant, increase in spending relative to the costs submitted for the same work in the Ming dynasty:

> Five rooms on the east and all the rooms on the west [of the Pavilion of the Literary Constellation] were destroyed leaving only the foundation. These places should be rebuilt at the cost of 938.986 *liang*. Other places in poor condition include Apricot Altar, Pavilion of the Literary Constellation, Spirit Kitchen and Abattoir (Shenchu, Shenpao), Houtu Shrine (Houtuci), the four corner towers, stele pavilions, Gate of Unified Texts (Tongwenmen), Gate of the Great Mean (Dazhongmen) . . . All should be repaired or replaced at a cost of 14,548.207 *liang*. Then there are those buildings that were partially destroyed and scorched, such as the Hall of the Sage's Traces, Shrine of Esteemed Sages (Chongshengci), Chamber of Odes and Rites (Shilitang), Ritual Instruments Repository (Liqiku), Fathering the Sage Hall of Repose (Qishengqindian), Gate of Fathering the Sage (Qishengmen) . . . All should be repaired at the cost of 2,432.952 *liang*. Additional expenses needed to complete these restorations and repairs will be 17,920.145 *liang*. In total, the cost of repairs will be 167,507.918 *liang*. These expenses were carefully considered, and all the items have been inventoried and sent to the government.[90]

The building costs detailed in this document were generated by a specific formula prepared by the Board of Works and reflected the value the state placed on the project and not the final expense that, as the following will show, would have to include a wide margin for graft.[91] What the figures do indicate is an extraordinarily high level of regulation that reached to the person of the emperor himself.

On receiving this report, Yongzheng pledged to restore the temple to its former greatness, and in the months and years to come a parade of high officials, led by the controversial but well-connected Shandong governor Chen Shiguan, arrived to conduct rites and to manage the reconstruction.[92] In addition to untold numbers of workers and craftsmen, these influential statesmen oversaw a coterie of lower officials, the record of which illustrates the reach of the temple and the range of bureaucrats who could be called upon to contribute to the project.[93] These included eleven general managers (*chengxiuguan*), six managers (*banshiguan*), thirteen coordinators (*xiexiuguan*), eight foremen (*xiaoliguan*), one inspector (*xunshiguan*), and one quality controller (*xunchayuan*). The ranks of general managers and managers consisted mainly of magistrates and prefects from surrounding districts; coordinators tended to be lower officials, ritual officers, and scholars. Foremen were magistrates or vice-magistrates (all sharing the Kong surname); the inspector was a district junior officer (*youguan*).[94]

In spite of this extensive management, the work did not proceed smoothly. Documents from early 1725 note significant delays caused by racketeering in the local tile-making industry and the need to import large framing timbers from south-central China.[95] Having resigned his provincial office, Chen Shiguan now stepped in to manage the project, but continuing difficulties led to his replacement with Governor Saileng'e. Once Saileng'e proved his even greater incompetence, the redoubtable Chen was returned to the job under the nominal supervision of Governor Yue Jun and Hanlin academician Liu Bao.[96]

It would take another four years to assemble the necessary materials, but late in 1729 the builders finally observed auspicious clouds in the shape of *lingzhi* fungi and in the color of the phoenix settling over Qufu and gave the order to raise the main beam of the Hall of the Great Ensemble.[97] The completion of Kong Temple in its grand form the next year did not prevent the

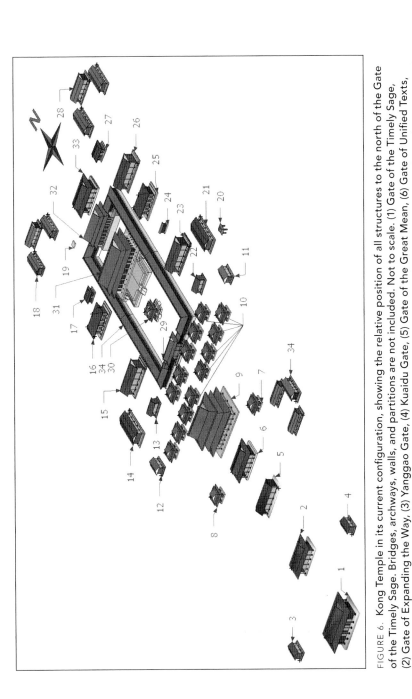

FIGURE 6. Kong Temple in its current configuration, showing the relative position of all structures to the north of the Gate of the Timely Sage. Bridges, archways, walls, and partitions are not included. Not to scale. (1) Gate of the Timely Sage, (2) Gate of Expanding the Way, (3) Yanggao Gate, (4) Kuaidu Gate, (5) Gate of the Great Mean, (6) Gate of Unified Texts, (7) Ming Stele Pavilion, (8) Ming Stele Pavilion, (9) Pavilion of the Literary Constellation, (10) Thirteen Stele Pavilions, (11) Yucui Gate, (12) Guande Gate, (13) Gate of Fathering the Sage, (14) Hall of Musical Instruments, (15) Chamber of Gold and Silk, (16) Hall of the King Who Fathered the Sage, (17) Fathering the Sage Hall of Repose, (18) Spirit Abattoir, (19) Incinerator, (20) Ancient Home of Kongzi Stele Pavilion, (22) Gate of Inherited Sagacity, (23) Chamber of Odes and Rites, (24) Lu Wall, (25) Shrine of the Esteemed Sages, (26) Family Temple, (27) Houtu Shrine, (28) Spirit Kitchen, (29) Gate of the Great Ensemble, (30) Apricot Altar, (31) Hall the Great Ensemble, (32) Hall of Repose, (33) Hall of the Sage's Traces, (34) Cloisters.

supervising governor general from subsequently demoting many of the managers, but the reconstruction was grudgingly deemed satisfactory. Two years later, a long-dormant juniper in the main courtyard obligingly sprang to life, suggesting a great resurgence in Confucian ritualism.[98]

Surviving documents provide little further detail on the new construction, although we need only consider the architecture that stands today as a guide to how it appeared in the eighteenth century (fig. 6). Most buildings in Kong Temple display the Ming-Qing standard of relatively high and straight roofs graded by structure, color, and decoration according to their status and function. Late-imperial building regulations in general prescribed the most common constructions with simple gable-end roofs and flush or overhanging eaves and higher status buildings with hip roofs or combination gable-hip roofs (fig. 7). At Kong Temple many of the rooftops are of the combination gable-hip variety—the upper section ending in a gable with the lower forming a continuous eave. The technique is used in most central axis

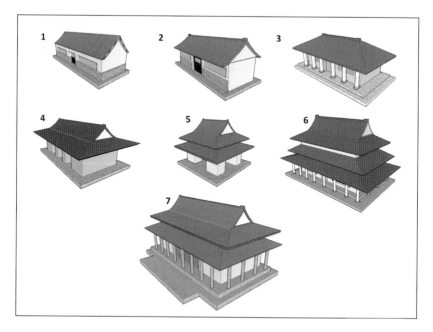

FIGURE 7. Standard roof designs found in Kong Temple: (1) flush gable, (2) overhanging gable, (3) single hip, (4) single gable-hip, (5) double gable-hip pavilion, (6) triple gable-hip, and (7) double gable-hip.

buildings except for the simple overhanging gable of the Gate of the Great Mean (Dazhongmen) and the regular-hip roofs found on the shrines in the eastern and western courts. Interior structures, including the pavilions housing imperial steles and sites associated directly with Kongzi and his wife, are given higher status through the addition of a second tier of eaves. In total, therefore, Kong Temple possesses a nearly complete building hierarchy, lacking only the double-hip roof of the type found on the main hall of the Confucian temple in Beijing and a handful of other constructions that were directly associated with the Ming-Qing court.

Rooftops throughout the temple are clad in one of three distinct grades of roof tile; lowest-status gray tiles can be found on service buildings at the rear and sides of the temple, and middle status green-glazed tiles adorn ceremonial buildings and gates around the peripheries. Green-glazed tiles had also been standard for the core buildings through most of the late-imperial era, but over the course of the Qing dynasty these were upgraded to an elite shade of yellow, with the last such promotion granted to the Gate of Unified Texts by the republican state in the early twentieth century.[99] The grade of the building is defined again by the number of glazed figurines that adorn the ridges. Conventionally, between one and nine figurines depicting various auspicious beasts are arranged in odd numbers depending on the importance of the building. At Kong Temple these arrangements faithfully indicate status, although their numbers fluctuate between odd and even with little discernable pattern except perhaps to associate even-numbered buildings with the passive *yin* and odd-numbered buildings with the ascendant *yang*. Buildings at the periphery of the temple have as few as one or two of the beasts, and secondary gates and pavilions may have three or four. Toward the heart of the temple, the totals rise to six for the Gate of Great Ensemble and the Pavilion of the Literary Constellation, eight for the Hall of Repose, and the maximum of nine for the Hall of the Great Ensemble.[100]

Like the roofing hierarchy, the range and style of *dougong* within Kong Temple define the site as second in status only to imperial palaces and mortuaries. Side gates and buildings associated with Kong family descendants in the eastern section of the temple have the simplest sets; the Gate of Inherited Sagacity (Chengshengmen) uses *santiao* (three jump) brackets, and the Chamber of Odes and Rites uses *yidou ersheng* (double rise) brackets. Most of the pavilions, gates, and altars along the southern reaches of the central axis and in the western section of the Shrine of Fathering the Sage have five *puzuo* (major part) brackets, except for the Gate of the Great Mean (Dazhongmen), which is limited to *yidou sansheng* (triple rise) brackets. The primary buildings are supported by more elaborate *dougong*.

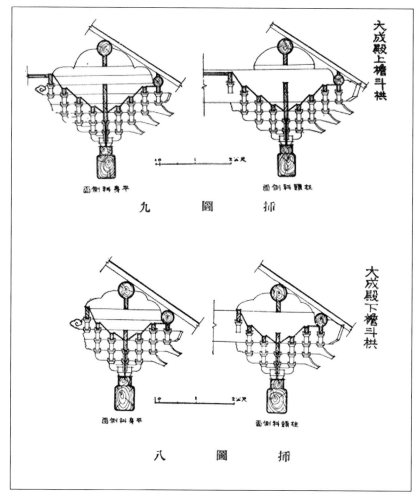

FIGURE 8. Hall of the Great Ensemble, upper and lower brackets. Upper brackets display three descending cantilevers; lower brackets have two descending cantilevers. Drawing by Liang Sicheng, 1935.

FIGURE 9. Close-up of bracket set, observed during disassembly of the Temple of Yanzi. Similar in style to the lower bracket set of Kong Temple's Hall of the Great Ensemble.

The Pavilion of the Literary Constellation uses a combination of three, five, and seven part brackets; the Hall of Repose uses a combination of seven and five part brackets in its upper and lower eaves; and the Hall of the Great Ensemble employs seven part brackets to support its lower eaves, reserving the upper level for its extreme nine part bracket sets (figs. 8 and 9).

Generally, these *dougong* adhere to Ming and Qing standards and demonstrate that builders understood formal building methods and employed them according to imperial building codes. Slight variations, however, demonstrate a certain amount of slippage in the adoption of building codes and show that the system left room for innovation. In Qufu, builders often extended certain bracket arms inward, so they emphasized the central bay of the more prominent buildings. In the Hall of the Great Ensemble, builders used unorthodox triple *ang* (downward-slanting cantilevers) in addition to the double *ang* prescribed by the Qing-era *Technical Instructions and Regulations for Handicrafts*.[101] More unusual was the practice of replacing standard timber posts with inscribed or carved stone exterior columns, some of

FIGURE 10. Hall of the Great Ensemble columns, showing the carved dragon iconography unique to Kong Temple. Photograph by Ernst Boerschmann, 1911.

which were so audacious that temple custodians felt compelled to cover them with red silk sleeves on the occasion of an imperial visit lest they imply an inadequacy in the emperor's palace in Beijing (fig. 10).

The framework of most Kong Temple buildings is characterized by the Ming-Qing dynasty standard of straight columns of equal height, each topped with lateral extensions and tied together by elaborately decorated beams. In contrast to Tang, Song, Jin, and Yuan period architecture, the roofs of these buildings do not rest on a few large bracket sets supported by the columns but float above the structure on the strength of intermediate brackets placed shoulder to shoulder along the length of the tie beams. Instead of only linking the columns, as they must have done in earlier times, the tie beams support the eaves and the intermediate brackets.

The expansion, weight, ornamentation, and elaboration of the structure lend the architecture considerable power, although as the architectural historian Liang Sicheng complained, the straighter lines, extra brackets, column extensions, and heavier beams also suggest overregulation.[102] The temple's use value had never been exclusively based in ritual and respect for ancient ideals, and there had always been a political subtext to ritualized maintenance and rebuilding. In late-imperial China, however, temple restorations and reconstructions arguably did less to embody the "order of Kongzi and the Duke of Zhou" or to demonstrate the Way than they did to illustrate the political order of the dynasty. The increasingly pragmatic use value of architecture challenged any sense that the temple embodied culture and pattern and retained the traces of the sage. Subsequent chapters, however, will show that Kong Temple was never simply a tool of the state and never completely devoid of its aura, even under periods of intense politicization in the twentieth century.

3 | Ritual as Material Culture

THIS CHAPTER INTERPRETS RITUAL in the way that the former interpreted structure and the next interprets space—that is, as an active culture of transaction and negotiation. There is no question that ritual was more than a system of exchange. As Joseph Lam writes, ritual, especially imperial sacrifice, was at the heart of Chinese intellectual practice: "Performed with a wealth of ritual paraphernalia that displayed government control of human and material resources, state sacrifices were copiously described in classical documents and enthusiastically discussed by scholar-officials. Projecting a representation of the natural and supernatural worlds of the emperors and scholar-officials, state sacrifices revealed the ways in which they understood, in abstract and specific terms, their existence and the roles they played."[1] If on one level, Chinese elite ritual was impenetrably complex and cerebral, Kai-wing Chow explains how on another it was refreshingly simple and tactile: "Ritual does not appeal to the intellect in achieving its goal of inculcating values. It manipulates material symbols and the ritual setting to create awe and to arouse the emotions of the participants. The participants may not know or understand the meaning of the specific ritual, but by taking part in it, they submit to the authority and values encoded in the ritual structure."[2] At Kong Temple the configuration of rituals, including the specific configuration of sacrifice, the conferral of titles and honors, the appointment and salary of officers, and the provision of endowments, was determined in relation to a wider discourse on ritual. Yet the value of those rites and privileges still relied upon the performance, negotiation, and manipulation of the ritual setting, including its space and material.

That is not to imply that materialism produced an ideal ritual structure. The following analysis confirms that the practice of negotiating and increasing the assets of the cult drove ritual from its presumptive roots, so it is doubtful that any part of an "ancient" rite actually survives in later articulation. To the contrary, manipulation created unaccountable chains of events that compelled managers to develop ritual through acts of compulsion and accumulation as well as harmonization and finesse. The futility of recovering or re-creating a pure and unadulterated rite, however, did not invalidate the reproduction so long as the observer or participant believed the performance was not a decaying echo of the past but an ancient tone renewed every time it was struck.

After attending a sacrifice in the mid-sixteenth century, for example, Zheng Guangwan wrote that "the hall of Lu was honored with a new configuration (*chong xin zhi*) and the shrine (*ci*) stood in the glow of auspicious light. This is where the primal essences (*yuanqi*) of the cosmos (*qian* and *kun*) converge, and that is why [Kongzi] became the mentor of emperors past and present."[3] Zheng did not explain how Kong Temple fit into the complex ritual system nor did he analyze the moral qualities associated with certain ritual vessels or dance steps. He implicitly understood the place as a point of connection or a nexus that channeled music, rites, architecture, nature, and the myriad social, cultural, and spiritual concerns that circulated through and about the complex. What Zheng did not state is the reality that no educated person of his generation could ignore: for reasons that will be made clear, in Zheng's time ritual was highly politicized. Far from blunting the sanctity of the temple, however, the constant negotiation and adjustment of titles, performances, and endowments and even conflictive politics helped to create a sense of depth and renewal that kept rituals from ringing hollow. Between the brick-and-mortar relic, ritual negotiation, and the active sacrifices, the temple was experienced in material, body, and spirit. In seamlessly merging the intangible with the tangible and joining the permanence of space with the fabrications of its inhabitants, the temple inspired the heartfelt belief in its most sincere patrons that the ancient relic of Kongzi simply transcended history.

Building the State Cult in the Han Dynasty

According to Sima Qian, the state of Lu began to conduct sacrifices to Kongzi shortly after his death: "Transmit[ing] from generation to generation the custom of sacrificing to Kongzi at fixed times during the year. Scholars performed the rites of the District Banquet and the Archery Bout [*xiangyin dashe*] at the tomb of Kongzi."[4] Sima was told that this custom had been perpetuated until the beginning of Han, and so it may have been current when Emperor Gaozu interrupted a tour of the provinces to visit the home of Kongzi in 195 BCE. Arriving in Queli, the emperor honored the sage by performing the highest-level Sacrifice of the Large Beast and entitling a member of the Kong family as Lord Heir (*fengsijun*).[5] Although Gaozu's example set an important precedent, the Han dynasty would not commit to Confucian ritual until the reign of Emperor Wu (r. 141–87 BCE), who followed the advice of the scholar and statesman Dong Zhongshu in designating five texts as the basis of the Confucian canon and appointing five erudites, including two members of the Kong family, to specialize in those texts. The policy may have been calculated to undermine the authority of regional rulers by bringing nonaristocratic scholars to court, yet it also strengthened scholarly interest in Kong Temple. It was during the reign of Emperor Wu that Sima Qian visited the home of the sage—by his own account not the first scholar to do so, and as with so much of what he wrote, the historian set the tone for generations of scholar-pilgrims to follow. For all his knowledge of Kongzi, it was only upon visiting the sage's relics that the historian could really come to terms with his subject: "When I read the writings of Master Kong, I longed to see what kind of person he really was. So I went to Lu and took a close look at his temple, hall, chariot, robes, and ritual vessels, as well as the many students practicing the rites at the appropriate times at his grave. I tarried there awhile, awestruck."[6]

Sima Qian's record suggests two different modes of ritual performance: one fixed to the tomb and another based in the temple. As Wu Hung asserts, movement between tomb and temple demonstrates contrasting forms of monumentality: "A temple was a 'living monument' of a lineage—its religious content (the ancestors being worshipped) and physical components (ritual vessels) were subject to constant renewal; a tomb was a static symbol of an individual."[7] This observation actually pertains to an earlier age, although the contrast between temple and tomb is no less relevant to Han dynasty Qufu because, as Sima Qian observed, sacrifices and rituals had always taken place not at the temple but at the tomb of the sage. In sacrificing at the tomb, these scholars and descendants focused their efforts on something beyond recovery and exclusive of the living. At the same time, these devotees had begun to develop the temple/memorial hall as a more inclusive place by ennobling descendants who could serve the memory of the sage, and by developing a place to more effectively regulate and manage ritual. In sacrificing at the tomb, the descendants and the followers could keep the memory of Kongzi, but in performing sacrifice in a distinct temple they were drawing the past, ritual, and memory into a controlled environment where these "traces of the sage" could be recovered, developed, and exploited.

In the early Han, those traces began to be exploited most notably in favor of the Kong family. In addition to earning more than fifty government appointments, the family was honored with a succession of titles and enfeoffments.[8] Kongzi's thirteenth-generation ancestor, who had already been named tutor to Emperor Yuan (r. 49–33 BCE), was ennobled as Guannei Marquis (Guanneihou), endowed with a fief of eight hundred households, and conferred the title Lord of Baocheng (Baochengjun).[9] The role of those original eight hundred households was not specified, although the courtier Mei Fu later clarified their duties in calling on the Han to follow the Zhou precedent of granting fiefs to the descendants of Xia and Shang (Yin) for the purpose of continuing ancestral sacrifices. Since Kongzi was supposed to be a descendant of Shang kings, it was argued that the same privilege should be granted to his heirs so that they could sacrifice to the Shang founder, King Tang.[10] Emperor Cheng (r. 33–7 BCE) obliged with a hereditary endowment of 1,670 households and the title of Marquis Who Continues and Honors the Yin (Yin Shaojiahou).[11] Emperor Ping (r. 1 BCE–5 CE), presumably at the behest of the idealistic regent Wang Mang, raised Kongzi to the rank of Duke XuanNi of Baocheng (Baocheng xuanNigong). The sage's sixteenth-generation descendant was at the same time entitled as Baocheng Marquis (Baochenghou), endowed with land (*shiyi*), and charged with the responsibility of sacrificing to Kongzi.[12] Emperor Guangwu (r. 25–57), having pledged to follow Zhou ritual, sent an official to sacrifice to Kongzi in Lu and entitled a Kong descendant as Duke Who Continues and Honors the Yin (Yin Shaojiagong) with responsibility for conducting sacrifices to Tang.[13] That title was later changed to Duke of Song (Songgong), and another descendant was given the lower title Baocheng Marquis, with the responsibility of sacrificing to Kongzi.[14] The sacrifices to Tang ended with the Guangwu reign, but the sacrifices to Kongzi continued in a form that implied that the sage was descended from ancient Shang kings and was an uncrowned king in his own right.[15]

In the following century, Qufu received three more imperial audiences with emperors Ming (72 CE), Zhang (85 CE), and An (124 CE), although in 153 a local magistrate reported that the performance of Kong Temple rituals had fallen into abeyance. The chancellor of Lu responded by appointing an official to manage the temple and to collect money to conduct sacrifices.[16] In one respect this action brought the temple into the dynasty's orbit, although in another, the intention to control the rites reflects a more pressing need to bring order to the increasingly factionalized court and to the restive region of southwestern Shandong. When peasants in the Mt. Tai area to the north of Qufu broke into rebellion in 154, Emperor Huan (r. 146–168) adopted severe measures to crush the insurrection, but he also met resistance from certain regional officials who opted to use peaceful means to "[lead] those fierce rebels back to virtue and loyalty."[17] The rebellion, according to the *Book of the Later Han,* was resolved by military force and mass execution, although the chancellor assigned to the Lu region in 156 noted the benefits of culture and civility. Once he had displayed the ceremonial and ritual wares in Kong Temple, Han Chi's stele inscription claims, "Heaven sent rain, the common people were blessed with harmony, and the whole land celebrated."[18]

From his inscription, Han Chi seems to have believed in Confucian ritual as a means to resolve the dynasty's problems. However, the fact that an influential faction in the capital was at the same time preoccupied with raising its own memorial stele to a deceased eunuch suggests the court's differing opinion.[19] There is no evidence that this monument was intended as a response to Han Chi, although considering the ongoing and highly public conflict between court eunuchs and Confucians, the subtext must have been apparent to anyone with knowledge of the dynasty's politics. In 159 Emperor Huan gained greater infamy by colluding with eunuchs to purge family members of the imperial consort, who had begun to dominate the court.[20] As Confucian scholars pressed their criticism, the emperor escalated his persecution of them, bluntly directing his patronage toward the temples of Laozi and performing a grand sacrifice for the sage of Daoism in 166.[21] The political situation improved for the scholars with the promotion of the Confucian Dou Wu to a position of authority in the capital and the emperor's subsequent decision to spare Confucian officials charged with treason in the Disaster of Partisan Prohibition. When the emperor died without an heir in 167, however, the court was left deeply divided between the eunuchs and the faction loyal to Dou.[22] It was in this troubled political climate that a third chancellor of Lu inscribed the first extant document to clearly articulate the sanctity of Kong Temple, the vital nature of sacrifice, and the ongoing respect that ritual earned for the dynasty. Given his position, it was not possible to directly censure the court for its policies, although Shi Chen did use the temple to infer that the court had failed to fully live up to its responsibilities:

> I was assigned as Keeper of the Seal (Fushou) to "reside in the Kuilou Building" [i.e., hold official appointment], and so I am in command of the original abode of Kongzi and the domain of the Duke of Zhou. Night and day I worry about how best to represent the emperor's virtuous policy and restore the splendor of the past. With great anticipation I fulfill my duty and bow with great obeisance. I arrived at my post in the first year of Jianning [168], performed the autumn ceremony and sacrificed wine in front of the academy (pangong), and then paid a ritual visit to the home of Kongzi and worshiped his spirit tablet (shenzuo). Looking about, I can feel the spirit of Kongzi, yet there is no public sacrifice, so I purchase meat and wine at my own expense to show my respect.[23]

The "virtuous policy" that Shi Chen mentions undoubtedly alludes to the period following the coronation of Emperor Ling, when Dou Wu and Chen Fan gained control of the government and took the opportunity to invite a lineal descendant of Kongzi to advise the court and serve as prefect of Luoyang.[24] The politics surrounding this chain of events were intense and finally resulted in the destruction of Dou and Chen at the hands of the eunuchs, but Shi Chen's message scrupulously focuses attention on the "true virtue" of the past. In contrasting the model of Kongzi and the Duke of Zhou with his own present, the chancellor exploited the temple's archived potential, not just in the sense of physical ruin noted in the previous chapter, but in terms of ritual erosion. Performed in the proper time and place, sacrifice might recall a past order and exhibit cohesion and growth. The problem for Han Confucians was that, in spite of their best efforts, the performance of ritual could not re-create this order. Shi Chen could "feel" a sagely spirit, and he made a personal effort to connect with it, yet his greatest concern was with the lack of "public" sacrifice. In the socially complex environment of the temple, he understood that ritual could be individually performed, but it could not be fulfilled without the collective performance of court, lineage, and scholar. The saving grace for Confucian ritualism was that this was not a failure of the past—rather it was a failure to recover antiquity and to develop harmonious social relations in the present. The durability of that logic would allow future generations of Confucians to return to Qufu in search of their ideal, although anyone approaching Kong Temple at the end of the Han might well have wondered what was left to salvage. As the dynasty crumbled under its last eunuch-dominated reigns, it was said that the old home of Kongzi had collapsed, ceremonies were forgotten, Confucian works were not discussed, and the descendants of the sage were nearly extinct.[25] The Way, it seemed, had been lost.

Recovering the Way in the Tang, Song, Jin, and Yuan

By the end of the Han dynasty and for centuries to follow, anyone with Confucian sympathies would see that it was not only Kong Temple that needed to be rebuilt from nearly complete ruin but also the Kong family and the ritual system that tied their interests to the court and the scholars. A review of the formative issues in post-Tang ritual will demonstrate the difficulty in reaching a consensus on how that ritual system should be organized. Confucian scholars were themselves divided over how to interpret ritual. The various political regimes under which the scholar-officials operated had different and sometimes conflicting priorities, as did the various branches of the Kong family that competed for control of the progressively valuable local assets. The interested parties may have agreed that Kong Temple should serve as a model of harmony, but that model was conflicted by dissonant tones of politics and wealth that were inevitably tied to philosophical interpretation. The temple would experience multiple crises after the Han, including centuries of ruin, domination by a murderous grave sweeper, factional disputes, and a bitterly contested family feud, to name only the more blatant conflicts. Dissonant as the politics may have been, however, the temple never came to represent that fractured reality because it was not allowed to degrade as a consequence. Conflict was always, in time, addressed through the expansion and rectification of ritual so that by the mid-fourteenth century the ritual system had become, if not "fulfilled," then at least stable. The ongoing expansion and rectification, however, would also create a system that was more complicated than elegant and more materialistic than idealistic.

Little is said about the state of ritual in the centuries following the Han dynasty except that sacrifices became increasingly standardized, and Kongzi and his descendants continued to receive titles and property from a succession of imperial patrons.[26] By the Tang dynasty, Kongzi was grandly entitled as First Sage (Xiansheng), his acclaimed lineal descendant was entitled as the Marquis of Baosheng, and temple sacrifices were supported by a large landed estate and a corps of bonded servants. These so-called "sweeping households" (sasaohu) had originally been assigned to maintain the family cemetery but over time had begun to perform maintenance work for the greater Queli ritual complex. The temple cult had likewise expanded to include sacrifices for Confucian disciples, including the Ten Savants (Shi Zhe, much later increased to a total of twelve) who were regarded as the sage's most capable students and the first of many exegetes on the Confucian canon who were honored in the temple as "first teachers." Critically, the temple once again attracted imperial visits: Emperor Gaozong (r. 649–683) in 666 and then Emperor Xuanzong (r. 712–756), who performed a Sacrifice of the Large Beast and increased the number of bells and chimes to be used in the rite. Xuanzong also promoted Kongzi to the title of King of Exalted Culture (Wenxuanwang) and conferred the head of the Kong lineage the title of Duke of Exalted Culture (Wenxuangong).[27]

Having reached this apex of entitlement, the support for ritual began to decline, perhaps as a consequence of the devastating An Lushan Rebellion (755–763), perhaps, as Han Yu famously charged, due to a surging interest in Buddhism and Daoism. Han would rally the educated elite in defense of Confucianism, although there were few immediate benefits for Qufu, where the weakened court now had little authority. The Kong family continued to receive certain privileges until the end of the dynasty, but the local ritual infrastructure had so declined that its managers could only lament that the rites had been replaced by vulgar music and that the ritual instruments were "left to waste away."[28] After the fall of the Tang, the Kong family barely escaped extinction when a hereditary grave sweeper by the name of Kong Mo murdered the lineage head, installed himself as magistrate, and nearly (or perhaps actually) succeeded in exterminating the rest of the senior clan members.[29]

At that point the Kong family and the ritual system they managed had been reduced to the point of annihilation. But if the enigmatic Kong Mo represents the nadir of the local establishment, then the Later Tang/Song dynasty would provide for its redemption by eliminating the usurper, installing a rightful heir to Kongzi, and patronizing the sage at his home and in the capital of Kaifeng.[30] In 1008 the Song emperor Zhenzong announced that his performance of rites at Mt. Tai would be followed by a sacrifice at Kong Temple. The *Song History* is worth quoting at length for the insight it provides into the implied connections between imperial reverence, ancestral devotion, poetic composition, title adjustment, property awards, and temple construction and maintenance:

> The temple was decorated with yellow banners and hangings, and the clan of Kongzi assisted at the sacrifice. The emperor wore the robes and boots of state, and offered the *Zhou xian li* [Rites of Zhou]. He also visited the hall of the father of Kongzi and asked members of his suite to pour a libation to the seventy-two disciples and to the *xianru* [first scholars]. In former times the officials prepared the sacrifice, and the emperor merely bowed [before the altar], raising his folded hands, but on this occasion the emperor performed the kowtow as an expression of his reverence for Kongzi and the canonical learning. He wrote an ode, which was engraved on a stone monument placed in the temple. After this he visited the grave, riding on a horse, not in his palanquin,

where he offered a libation of wine, and kowtowed twice. He issued an edict conferring on Kongzi the title of *Xuansheng wenxuanwang* [Profound/Dark Sage and King of Exalted Culture]. At the sacrifice a prayer was read, and the victims were those of the Tailao [large beast]. The temple was repaired, and ten local families of the Kong clan were appointed to look after the grave and the temple.[31]

The statement, based here on Edouard Chavannes' translation, defines the imperial state, the Confucian scholars (*ru*), and the Kong family as the temple's ruling trinity and suggests how, in advancing the level of sacrifice, the supplicants reached a consensus over Kong Temple's ritual status and management. If that consensus actually existed, however, it was only for the moment. In the century to follow, the state, the scholars, and the family would become increasingly complicated entities prone to factional discord and subject to disruptive geopolitics. As in the late Han dynasty, the temple continued to register an ideal past, but in the eleventh century the temple's shareholders would reach an impasse over how to interpret that model.

The figure of Kong Daofu (986–1039) is essential to understanding how and why Kong Temple's ritual system continued to develop during this century. As noted previously, Kong Daofu had used temple construction as a means to raise the stature of his family. It must also be considered that Daofu was using the temple to express his affiliation with Ancient-style Learning. That faction of scholar-officials stressed responsible government over the central authority of the emperor and believed that the Way of Kongzi had survived beyond the death of the sage. In 1034 Daofu put his beliefs into action by taking a high-profile stand against Emperor Renzong (r. 1022–1063) in a sensitive case concerning the ejection of the empress.[32] The scholar was subsequently demoted to service in the provinces, and it was during this time of exile that he sponsored the construction of the Chamber of the Five Worthies (Wuxiantang) in Kong Temple's western court. In Daofu's interpretation these worthies included the ancient sages Mengzi and Xunzi, as well as the more recent Han, Sui, and Tang dynasty scholars Yang Xiong, Wang Tong, and Han Yu.[33] While serving as prefect of Yanzhou in the late 1030s, Daofu also sought out the tomb of Mengzi in Zou County and erected a memorial temple (reconstructed in its present location in 1121), identified the legitimate heirs of the sage, and supported the establishment of a Meng family estate in Zoucheng—all within twenty kilometers of Queli.[34]

These initiatives demonstrate several important trends in Song dynasty Confucianism. First, Kong Daofu used his authority as a disgraced but still influential regional official to help the members of a local lineage develop an ancestral temple, cemetery, and estate. Second, Daofu acted on the Mencian principle that morality is inseparable from economic welfare such as a landed estate might provide. Finally, in celebrating Mengzi among other later sages, he was asserting that Mengzi had recovered the Way of Kongzi and passed it on to later scholars such as Han Yu. Like Fan Zhongyan, who was at virtually the same time developing his own lineage and sponsoring the construction of a Confucian temple in Suzhou, Daofu appears to have been working under the expectation that a stronger lineage would contribute toward the stability of the region and ultimately, the state.[35] His actions suggest that he understood Mengzi to be the key to building an ideal society in which proactive state, local government, and lineage organizations worked to achieve stability and economic prosperity within a framework governed by ritual.[36]

Kong Daofu's experiment with Mengzi was cut short by his untimely death in 1039, and it is not clear what influence his work may have had in state or scholarly circles. It is interesting, though, that Fan Zhongyan was brought back to court as chancellor in 1040 and given the opportunity to implement a Mencian-inspired reform program on a much larger scale. These reforms ended when a conservative faction deposed Fan in 1045, although the principle was reintroduced through the New Policies of Chancellor Wang Anshi after 1058. Wang made liberal use of Mengzi and his teachings to support a program of government activism, leading to the philosopher's promotion to the rank of Duke of Zou in 1083 and his introduction to Kong Temple's main hall as a correlate to Kongzi in 1084.[37] Wang's death in 1086 allowed Sima Guang and a revitalized conservative faction to dismantle the reforms, although the change in political fortunes had no effect on the ritual status of Mengzi. Nor did the Kong family interpret the politics of the new regime as detrimental to their own interests, even taking the reversal as an opportunity to complain to the new court of "deficient ceremonies of the scholars' temple" and to request that even more households be assigned for maintenance of the temple and its ceremonies.[38]

When yet another faction claiming to represent reform came to power in 1093, the Song court declared that one hundred *qing* (1,640 acres) of land granted to the Kong family earlier in the dynasty be distributed among the lineage members, with another one hundred *qing* declared as an endowment for Kong Temple.[39] A decade later, Emperor Huizong granted the temple's main hall its *Mencius*-derived title of Great Ensemble (Dacheng), thereby advancing the reformist claim that Kongzi was best understood through the interpretation of the later sage. If there was any doubt as to the politics behind this action, it could not have survived the simultaneous initiative to bring Wang Anshi into the temple as a third correlate to Kongzi. In going to that extreme, the reform faction decisively crossed the line of what the opposition was willing to tolerate. When conservatives returned to power in 1126, Wang was demoted and eventually ejected from the temple altogether.[40] Mengzi and all the titles and properties that had accompanied his rise in Kong Temple remained in place, however, even as the faction that promoted him was held responsible for the rapid disintegration of the Northern Song under the threat of the Jurchen invasion.

The point to be observed here is that in the eleventh and early twelfth centuries, Confucianism was diverse, and that diversification produced factions. Wang Anshi, like Kong Daofu and Fan Zhongyan, drew on the teachings of Mengzi to support a view of the ritual system as open, organic, and capable of change. Sima Guang, the most vocal member of the conservative faction, contrastingly saw ritual as a balanced structure comparable to the "finished model" of a building.[41] In Peter Bol's explication of Sima's analogy, "When the pieces are in good repair and kept in place, the structure will not collapse. The union survives, not because when joined correctly the parts are transformed into a single body taking directions from a single mind, but through diligent and deliberate maintenance."[42] Unable to find common ground, the reform and conservative factions struggled to define the temple system according to fundamentally opposing philosophical positions. Although Kong Temple had spent much of the last century of the Northern Song under the influence of reform factions, it cannot be said that the institution had emerged as a reform icon—nor for that matter was it conservative. The efforts to reform the temple, as well as the efforts to preserve its status quo, had failed to generate an ideal system by either definition, even though the tensions between them had permanently altered the temple's material and ritual composition. Politics had become an inextricable part of the temple's culture. In never declaring allegiance to one faction or another, however, the temple was able to negotiate those tensions and not only survive the turmoil but realize a net gain in terms of enshrinement and material resources.

The establishment of the Jurchen Jin dynasty in North China in 1127 created a new problem for the Queli ritual system. During the Jurchen conquest Duke Kong Duanyou fled to the Southern Song, leaving the younger Kong Duancao in Queli to accept the patronage of the Jin client state of Qi. The resident Duancao acquired an endowment of one hundred households and the title of Duke of Fulfilling the Sage even as Duanyou continued to hold the same commission in the southern city of Quzhou, Zhejiang.[43] The rift presented a compelling problem for the Jin because in adopting Song rituals the dynasty also accepted the descent line system, meaning that only a lineage head could sacrifice to the family's ancestors.[44] The Jin had indirect control over the temple, but the duke with whom it was now allied was technically illegitimate. Lacking the authority to rule on the Southern Song exiles, the Jin wavered—initially revoking the northern entitlements after it took control from Qi and then renewing the ducal title of Kong Duancao in 1140.[45] In 1190 the Jin Ministry of Revenue (Hubu) revived the practice of endowment, granting the Duancao lineage control over six villages totaling more than 123 qing of land as compensation for assets lost during the conquest, sixty-five qing of "sacrifice land" (jitian) and four hundred jian of houses for unspecified purposes.[46] The provision of title and property to support Kong Temple and the Duancao lineage had not resolved the descent-line problem, although it set an important precedent in recognizing temple possession as an adequate substitute for lineage legitimacy when determining the right to perform sacrifices for Kongzi.

When the Jurchen were in turn eliminated by the Mongols, the politically astute northern duke Kong Yuancuo sought to extend his family privileges by paying tribute at the new court. The initial attitude of the new rulers proved to be ambiguous. In 1237, the Mongol regime resumed sacrifices in Qufu and endowed one hundred households to serve as the temple guard.[47] Two decades later, the regime broke with tradition to withdraw some of the family's key ritual assets. Duke Kong Zhen was disentitled for "not serving with learning and refinement," and the provision of sweeping households ended on the grounds that the system was being used to hide taxable property.[48] Disdain for the family, however, did not necessarily extend to the sage. An inscription of 1269 tells how a Mongol officer first presented a sacrifice before proceeding to the tomb of Kongzi with a company of armed warriors. Before entering the cemetery, the commander cautioned his followers against displaying signs of ignorance and ordered them to dismount and walk. "His respectful behavior shows," the inscription concludes (wishfully, perhaps), "that he followed the rites."[49]

The decisive factor in reviving the temple's ritual system was not, however, a Mongol conversion to Confucian values but rather the final conquest of the Southern Song in 1271. As a consequence, the northern Confucian relics were integrated with the innovative southern Dao School of Confucianism (Daoxue), which emphasized connection with the "true sages of antiquity" through a principle of genealogy that transmitted their virtue into the present.[50] Although Kong Temple was not immediately affected, the decision to restore the ducal title to the northern line in 1294 begins one of the most active periods of ritual practice on record.[51] In performing his duties, the rehabilitated Duke of Fulfilling the Sage began preparations for the autumn sacrifice, and seeing that the temple's ritual wares were inadequate, he enlisted the support of local and higher officials in assembling a 1,391-piece set of Han dynasty sacrificial vessels. The success of the venture was remembered for being as essential to the recovery of ritual as it was to demonstrating the civility of the dynasty. The presiding envoy commented at the dedication: "The relics seemed to have been waiting for the Sage . . . more than mere vessels, they represent the ancient civilization of our homeland (*guojia siwen*)."[52]

In the following decades, the Yuan affirmed Kongzi's kingly title and implemented the Southern Song precedent of offering correlate sacrifices to Zengzi, the reputed author of the *Great Learning* (*Daxue*) and Zisi, the reputed author of *Doctrine of the Mean* (*Zhongyong*). This action completed the set of "four correlates" (*sipei*) in accordance with Cheng Yi's (1033–1107) interpretation of the canon: "When Kongzi died, only Zengzi transmitted his Dao. Zengzi transmitted it to Zisi and Zisi transmitted it to Mengzi. When Mengzi died no one received the transmission."[53] The inclusion of Cheng Yi and other founders of the Dao School in the temple as "former scholars," also following the Southern Song precedent, further recognized Zhu Xi's claim that the school had in fact recovered the essence of the Way from Mengzi and transmitted the ideal into the present.[54] Completing the apotheosis, in 1330 the four correlates and the father of Mengzi were enfeoffed posthumously as dukes of long extinct Warring States territories, and Shuliang He was advanced to the rank of King Who Fathered the Sage.[55] When those titles were given space and supported by architecture, it could finally be said that the "spirits were settled" (*ning shen qi*); that the precious teachings were shown respect; and that Kongzi was respected as having sageliness within, and kingliness without (*neisheng waiwang*).[56]

The realization and recognition of these titles and honors in the Yuan dynasty was the culmination of a lengthy process of debate and negotiation that finally established *daotong*, the "transmission of the Way," as orthodoxy, although there is no mistaking the noncanonical elements in this ritual structure. For centuries the imperial court and Confucian literati had debated, as Thomas Wilson phrases the question, whether Kongzi should be honored with "titles, caps, and liturgies appropriate to someone of his station in his own day" or recognized "within the context of his august status as teacher of the ten thousand generations."[57] Was Kongzi, in other words, better represented as an honorable official according to the canon or according to the Han dynasty interpretation of the sage as an uncrowned king deserving commensurate rites and music and noble peers? The debate had never been entirely settled, and even with the adoption of *daotong* the noncanonical tradition continued to influence the material culture and aesthetics of the temple. The relics of Kongzi had been restored and legitimized, the scholars and kinfolk responsible for delivering the sagely spirit into the present had been enshrined in effigy and granted feudal titles, and endowments and salaries ensured that sacrifices could take place with due splendor and ceremony. This structure was not the result of one interpretation of Confucianism overcoming another but the product of centuries of conflict, compromise, transaction, and negotiation. The temple preserved the traces of that history and merged them into a monumental whole, although in doing so it also brought the inherent contradictions into greater relief. When carried forward to the Ming dynasty, those contradictions would have severe implications for the integrity of the cult of Kongzi.

Consolidating the Imperial Prerogative in the Ming and Qing

Where ritual may have helped to legitimize Mongol rule after the conquest of the Southern Song, there was no disguising the factionalism and mass rebellion that undermined the regime later in the fourteenth century. When the Red Turban Rebellion reached Shandong in the 1350s, the Lu region suffered immensely in the ensuing warfare, and the Duke of Fulfilling the Sage was forced to abandon his properties for refuge in the capital. The counterattack brought him back, but not before its Mongol commander had claimed some eighty thousand severed heads, left the landscape "strewn with corpses for 4,000 *li*," and reduced Queli to what locals perceived as a "demon-infested ruin." In light of that record, the commander's statement that the remaining population might be pacified through the resumption of Kong Temple sacrifice seems nothing short of cynical.[58] Yet the simple fact that sacrifice remained an option in the aftermath of such epic violence indicates just how resilient the temple's ritual structure had become by this point in history. It also explains why the site would continue to prove of vital interest to subsequent dynasties—the temple had outgrown its classical role as a locus for the negotiation of diverse interests and was becoming an asset to be controlled in the interests of gaining imperial legitimacy.

This sense of legitimacy still demanded that the dynasty exhibit ritual propriety, yet the Ming and the Qing recognized that any shortcomings in that regard could be recompensed through sheer monumentality. Investment on this scale would transform ritual into a system in which political connections and managerial practices were as critical to the temple's perpetuity as respect for its impersonal and intrinsic values. In claiming vast resources and having their interests linked to the state through court appointments, the managers and custodians of Kong Temple became part of a ritual infrastructure that could hardly be dismantled without destabilizing the dynasty, the scholar-official establishment, and the "sacred precinct" of the Kong Family.

The Hongwu emperor (r. 1368–1398) demonstrated a firm appreciation of the political benefits of monumental ritual performance at the outset of the Ming dynasty. Although initially distrustful of the scholar-official establishment, the emperor understood that the preferred means to keep that establishment under control was to act as its patron. One of Hongwu's first acts as emperor was to send an envoy to conduct sacrifice at the sage's home temple in Shandong.[59] Lineage head Kong Kejian had remained loyal to the Yuan through the transition to the Ming and was reluctant to attend the new court as his ancestors had done at the beginning of the two previous dynasties. On receiving a summons to attend the court in Nanjing, he excused himself on account of illness and sent his son (who in fact held the ducal title) in his place. Hongwu did not take the elder Kong at his word, pointing out that the Kong family had "served each and every ruling house," including "barbarian rulers," throughout history and hinting ominously: "I doubt that you are ill, it would be better if you came to see me—think about it."[60] Although Kong Kejian would pay a high price for his incertitude, he obeyed the command and thereby earned the emperor's support for Kong Temple and particularly for the Kong family.[61] In 1369 Hongwu cancelled the regional spring and autumn sacrifices but ordered annual disbursements of livestock and funds to support those same sacrifices in Queli.[62] The sacrifice wares were at the same time increased to ten in number and improved in quality; the preparation of the sacrificial animals was upgraded from raw to cooked; and there was an increase in the number of appointed sacrifice dancers, musicians, apprentices, and conductors.[63] In 1374 twenty local musicians and dancers were sent to undergo training at the Office of Imperial Sacrifice in Nanjing.[64]

There is some discrepancy concerning the value of the property that was "imperially granted" to the Kong family at this time, although there is no question that the family profited under the new administration.[65] Local records indicate that the emperor humbled all his predecessors by granting the lineage a vast estate of two thousand large *qing* (nearly one hundred thousand acres) of land. The income from this land was to be used to support sacrifice and pay salaries, with the duke retaining the surplus. In addition, 115 households were assigned to temple maintenance, one hundred to the cemetery, and seven to the local academies.[66] The imperial bounty continued in subsequent reigns. The family was provided with seventy-three *qing* of land in 1407, and in 1439 the Ministry of Revenue approved the family's right to retain five hundred households (two thousand *ding*, i.e., able-bodied workers) for the purpose of "cultivating grains for sacrifice."[67] The relationship between family and court was further strengthened by the marriage of Duke Kong Hongxu to the daughter of Grand Secretary Li Xian. Although Hongxu had to be removed from office under charges of serial rape and murder, his replacement was nonetheless able to extend the elite family status by arranging the marriage of the ducal heir to the daughter of Grand Secretary Li Dongyang.[68]

The sacrifice structure likewise continued to grow. Having earlier approved a major reconstruction and expansion of Kong Temple, in 1477 the Chenghua emperor resumed the century-old precedent of advancing the level of sacrifice by increasing the number of sacrifice vessels to a total of twelve and advancing the number of dancers to eight rows of eight.[69] The configuration was appropriate to a subject with the rank of king, and in 1496 the Hongzhi emperor (r. 1487–1505) went to the greater extreme of increasing the number of dancers to the maximum nine rows of eight, appropriate to the rank of emperor.[70]

The destruction of the temple by fire in 1499 provided further opportunities for the Ming court to enhance ritual, and almost as soon as the ashes had cooled chief minister of the Court of Imperial Sacrifice (Taichangsi) Li Jie arrived to perform sacrifice and initiate the temple's reconstruction.[71] In undertaking general management of the project, Li Dongyang provided more than building materials, recommending his in-laws for a series of extraordinary honors, including the recognition of the second and third sons of the duke as Hanlin Erudite of the Five Classics (Hanlinyuan Wujingboshi) and Erudite of the Court of Imperial Sacrifice (Taichangsi Boshi), respectively.[72] These inheritable titles were, in addition to more than eighty official temple positions, provided mainly to members of the Kong lineage. The duke received the right to attend court audiences and to take up a position just behind the grand secretaries, which implied that his status was equal to that of the highest officials in the court.[73]

In sponsoring upgrades to both the temple and its keepers, the emperor was, according to an inscription of 1504, acting on a perceived obligation to improve upon the ritual of the alien Jin and Yuan.[74] After 1521, however, the logic of promotion would take a radical turn as the temple's inflated ritual infrastructure entered a period of highly controversial deflation. The Zhengde emperor had died without leaving an heir, resulting in the placement of his cousin on the throne as the Jiajing emperor. The transfer of power within the same generation was already a breach of protocol, although more serious conflict ensued when Jiajing refused to accept his status as an effective adoptee and insisted upon worshipping his own father as an imperial ancestor. This action formally interrupted the imperial succession, leading to the start of the Great Rites Controversy in 1530 and an ongoing struggle between the emperor and the scholar-officials over who defined the "rites and music." It was a fight the scholars could not win. Jiajing used his authority to overturn earlier ritual upgrades on the understanding that although he had the "way of the king" (wangdao), Kongzi had never been a ruler in his own lifetime. The decision to grant him the rites of a king was judged to be an error dating back to the time of Tang emperor Xuanzong, and Kongzi's title was accordingly altered to Ultimate Sage, First Teacher, Master Kong (Zhisheng Xianshi Kongzi). The ritual vessels and dancers were reduced in number to ten and thirty-six, respectively, and since Kongzi had lost his nobility the same principle necessarily extended to all titles of duke, marquis, and earl granted to various correlates, savants, and ancestors throughout the temple.[75]

Deborah Sommer observes that the practice of inflating titles and representing Kongzi and other sages with figural images had been a matter of contention since the early Ming, when scholars like Qiu Jun complained that far from showing respect for Kongzi these recent inventions were "obstacles to a direct personal understanding of the subtleties of the Way."[76] This attitude was reflected in the policies of the dynasty as well. Although Hongwu had advanced the level of sacrifice and the property of the Kong family, he and his immediate successors had abstained from advancing the actual honorifics of Kongzi. Jiajing was more aggressive than the dynasty's founders in actually retracting the noble titles, although the reasons for doing so had less to do with grasping the subtleties of the Way than they did with controlling the ritual system. As Huang Chin-shing argues, in challenging long-held conventions the emperor was acting to weaken the resolve of the scholar-officials and reinforce his dominance over the court.[77]

Kong Temple, however, also demonstrates the limits of Jiajing's ambition. The perpetuity of the Confucian monument is reflected in the concessions offered to the Queli temple, where historical statuary and architectural attributes continued to refer to the former kingly status in substance if not in name.[78] The practice of linking the Kong family to the imperial court also continued through the marriage of Duke Kong Zhen'gan (1519–1556) to the daughter of the powerful imperial in-law Zhang Yanling and the marriage of Duke Kong Shangxian (1544–1621) to the daughter of Grand Secretary Yan Song.[79] These alliances did not produce status appointments for the Kong family as they had under Li Dongyang, but given that the court subsequently punished both Zhang and Yan for treason the Kongs might be considered fortunate to have avoided guilt by association. As it was, the local institution emerged from the troubled Jiajing reign facing no more than unrelated charges of corruption, which led to the stricter separation of duties between the office of the duke and the office of the county magistrate.[80] The substance of imperial patronage had thus changed relative to the early Ming, yet the pattern was the same. Like the dynasty's founder, Jiajing had identified a need to impose authority, to claim the right to define ritual, and to reserve important exemptions and privileges for the sage's family. Yet he could not make the temple and the ritual system respond to his wishes. Kong Temple absorbed the emperor's demands but never affirmed his position.

The Qing dynasty approached Kong Temple in much the same way as the Ming in that it used the institution as a tool for governance and legitimacy. However, the Manchu were more aware that because it did not discriminate against their ethnicity the temple was ideal for connecting with a past not their own. In patronizing the institution, the Manchu were not simply acting as authoritarians. They were more broadly concerned with what Alexander Woodside describes as an "imaginative refeudalization and mystification of a dead philosopher in order to compensate for the continuing defeudalization and demystification of specific living political ties."[81] The problem was to revive or reinvent the ideals of the sage-king, legitimate governance (*zhitong*), and the transmission of the Way, through which the dynasty might attract the loyalty of the scholar-official and the obedience of the public.

In doing so the Manchu relied upon a long-established strategy—appeal to the sage's family, manipulate his titles, and advance the level of his sacrifice. Soon after taking power, the dynasty declared that the descendants of Kongzi would retain all the rights granted them under the Ming, including the balance of their estate and the right to recommend their own magistrate.[82] The next year, the Qing court confirmed the sage's late Ming title with one addition. Kongzi was now recognized as Great Completer, Ultimate Sage, First Master of Exalted Culture (Dacheng Zhisheng Wenxuan Xianshi), although the cumbersome title was soon simplified to the form still in use today—Ultimate Sage and First Master (Zhisheng Xianshi).[83] That in itself does not suggest an improvement in status for the sage, and it certainly fell short of restoring the contentious kingly title affirmed in the Tang and the Yuan, although the Manchu appeared increasingly willing to compensate for that deficiency through patronage. When the Kangxi emperor (r. 1661–1722) came to the throne, he tacitly allowed the renewal of the temple's regal Yuan-era corner towers and the Gate of the Timely Sage, sent envoys to sacrifice on at least three occasions, and decreed that these sacrifices return to the large beast form. It was determined that because Kongzi had never been a ruler per se, the number of sacrificial vessels and dancers would remain at ten and thirty-six. Yet Kangxi made an extraordinary concession in reviving the custom of the imperial tour and introducing a full "three kneelings and nine prostrations" (*sangui jiukou*) as the standard salutation for a visiting emperor.[84]

The emperor's tour of 1684 did not generate any major upgrades to the ritual status of the temple, although it did yield many lesser honors and symbolically important gifts. Gifts of embroidered robes were made to thirty-five senior lineage members and degree holders, and three hundred local licentiate degree holders and students of the local academies received the sum of five *liang* of silver each. As a licentiate, Kong Shangren was among this latter group, although he and cousin Kong Shangli would soon receive the much greater honor of being named Erudites of the Imperial Academy (Guozijian Boshi). The imperial favor also extended to the common people of Qufu in the form of a year's exemption from corvée and land taxes.[85] The temple received a scroll in the emperor's handwriting that evaluated Kongzi as "Paragon and Master of Ten Thousand Generations" (wanshi shibiao) and a yellow imperial parasol detached from the emperor's personal retinue. Both tributes suggest that while the emperor could not advance the sage's title, he nonetheless wished to revere Kongzi as an uncrowned king.

In the subsequent reign, the Yongzheng emperor (r. 1722–1735) encountered a compelling problem with ritual saturation. The Tang, the Song, and the Yuan had elevated Kongzi to near the top of the ritual hierarchy, and Kangxi had essentially matched the Ming example of endowing Kongzi's descendants with property and privilege. So one of the few avenues of promotion left open to Yongzheng was to ennoble more of the sage's kin. This he did, promoting Kongzi's "Five Generations of Ancestors" to the rank of king, which was in itself an honor normally reserved for those holding the rank of king.[86] The emperor also made the master's name taboo, another privilege normally reserved for royalty, and ordered his subjects to abstain from eating meat on the sage's birthday, recognized as the twenty-eighth day of the eighth lunar month.[87] When the temple was reconstructed after the fire of 1724, Yongzheng increased the sacrifice budget and asked the Duke of Fulfilling the Sage to select forty "men of good character" from his family to serve as manager-officials for the temple. Each was to be compensated with an annual salary of twenty liang—a modest sum for the day but in keeping with the station.[88]

Since Yongzheng had completed the ritual system, at least according to his own terms, it now fell to his successor, the Qianlong emperor (r. 1735–1796), to honor Kongzi as his grandfather had done. That is, by paying personal tribute at the home of the sage, accessorizing the temple through gifts and inscriptions, and conferring titles on members of the Kong family. Qianlong would outdo his predecessors by visiting Qufu a total of eight times over the course of his long reign.[89] On his first trip in 1748, the ruler rewarded keynote lecturer Kong Jifen with a promotion to secretary in the Grand Secretariat (neige zhongshu) and created a special civil service examination category for family candidates.[90] The relationship between family and emperor soured somewhat after the lineage heads were accused of sponsoring massive corruption and consequently deprived of the right to submit their own candidates to serve as Qufu's magistrate.[91] In a related scandal, Kong Jifen was convicted of sedition, stripped of rank, and exiled to China's far West for having discussed ritual in terms that disagreed with the canon as defined by Zhu Xi. The scholar's statements were alleged to show extreme disrespect for the dynasty although his family kept the balance of its privileges in spite of these charges. And although the Qing code demanded capital punishment for sedition, Kong Jifen kept his head.[92]

Qianlong had dictatorial authority over Qufu, but in spite of the notable shortcomings of China's proudest lineage the emperor was not inclined to dismantle the "Sacred Precinct." The reason is plain. However fractious its institutions had become, Kong Temple remained a monument to the Chinese state, scholar, and family. Ritual performances, titles, properties, and architecture continued to embody the cosmos and re-create essential moments in history—the ancient Zhou, for example, when ritual was thought to have been perfected or the Tang when Kongzi was formally granted the title of king. The temple also embodied the politics and discord of ritual negotiation, such as the Ming when that title was taken away and the Qing when it was symbolically returned. By the Qianlong era, the relic had served as ancestral temple to over sixty generations of Kongzi's descendants; had received the support of every major dynasty since the Han; and had attracted countless Confucian scholars, hundreds of imperial envoys, and a dozen emperors. Huang Chin-shing argues that "both emperors and Confucian scholars continually manipulated the ritual practices of the temple to serve their own interests."[93] Yet it must be recognized that the system was not fully under the control of any actor or set of actors, did not passively represent the performer, and could even create profound difficulties for its subscribers. In remaining perpetually open to investment, contradiction, and "regulation by excess," Kong Temple had become a system too big to control and too big to fail.

Sacrifice

Angela Zito, in a study of the Qianlong emperor's grand sacrifices, asks the question, "What did it mean to be the Son of Heaven?" The answer, essentially, is that in the context of sacrifice the "self" was constantly shifting and contested and emerged through the construction and negotiation of boundaries. "Arrangement of space and movement within it, recitation of hymns, and the deployment of objects all produced certain positions for the actors, especially showing how manipulation of high/low and inner/outer produced the emperor as the embodiment of yang power," Zito writes.[94] Since Kong Temple sacrifices were directly related to these imperial performances, one might ask whether the same also held true of the seasonal sacrifices performed by the Duke of Fulfilling the Sage. Did sacrifice "center" the cosmos—perhaps at a lower level—in the person of the duke? Did the manipulation of texts, clothing, food, music, dance, and architecture allow him to order his domain, manage his bureaucracy, and affirm his relationship with the populace and his emperor? Or, as Peter Carroll notes with respect to local performances in Suzhou, did it simply invite the sage to bless society with peace, tranquility, and bountiful harvests?[95]

The problem in this section is not to explain the entire social psychology of ritual, to decode the many symbols and cultural references embedded in performance, or to understand the many subtle ways in which ritual participants defined their place in the universe. My object here is to account for the space, skills, and resources created and deployed in the production of Kong Temple sacrifice. In treating sacrifice as material culture, it is possible to show that beyond performing social relations and centering the cosmos in the self, sacrifice formed the apex of a hierarchy that controlled, with varying degrees of success, the distribution and movement of objects and people through space and time. As Joseph Lam suggests, ritual was the object of scholarly obsession and vital to the scholar's self-identification; furthermore, as Kai-wing Chow argues, the material culture of ritual produced an affective relationship, which allowed the ritual participant to view the temple as much more than a site of status negotiation.[96]

A thorough analysis of this problem would necessarily follow the movement of sacrifice objects/people beyond the confines of the temple, where one might study the productive capacities and social hierarchy of the surrounding community that provided many of the raw resources of sacrifice.[97] The study might also consider more distant regions—Nanjing or Beijing, for example, which were known to provide instructors for music and dance, or Hunan, which produced timbers suitable for architecture. The hierarchy might also extend upward to the Ministry of Rites and the imperial court, which regularly endowed the temple with sacred texts and highly refined ritual items, such as the Qianlong emperor's ancient Shang and Zhou bronze vessels (fig. 11). My focus, however, remains on the temple proper and on the manipulation of these resources within the temple and in the context of sacrifice and other rituals. In tracing the movement of skills and resources through that limited space, it is possible to conceive of ritual as an active and constructive spatial hierarchy and to appreciate how the manipulation of "complex things" could support the perception of cosmic alignment and the sense of spiritual presence.

Kong Temple was perpetually engaged in ritual. Among the lesser rituals performed on its grounds, salutary incense (*xingxiang*) offered incense at the Hall of the Great Ensemble, the Hall of Fathering the Sage, and the Shrine of the Esteemed Sage on the full moon of every month. Sacrifice and report (*jigao*) were held to commemorate important events such as the revision of a genealogy. Timely offerings (*shixiang*) were held in the Family Temple on the fifth day of the first month of each season. Simplified vegetarian oblations (*shicai*) were held for Confucian disciples and elders on the first day of each month in the Hall of the Great Ensemble, the Shrine of Fathering the Sage, and the Shrine of Esteemed Sages. Repeated renewal (*jianxin*) was an ancestor sacrifice using fresh grain and fruit on key calendar dates. Family sacrifice (*jiaji*) evolved from imperial funeral ceremonies and was performed as an ancestral ceremony in the Family Temple on the first day of the last month. Although in decline since the Yuan dynasty, imperial envoy sacrifices (*qianguan zhiji*) were occasionally held during the Ming and the Qing dynasties to mark important events—namely the reconstruction of the temple after the fires of 1499 and 1724. More common were sending envoys to sacrifice and report (*qianguan jigao*), held when communicating important promotions for Kongzi or his family members, providing news of important affairs such as the suppression of a rebellion, marking an important imperial birthday, or celebrating the appearance of an auspicious omen.[98]

Amid that active schedule, the definitive Kong Temple ritual was the seasonal sacrifice (*ding ji*), held on the first *ding* day of the second, fourth, eighth, and twelfth lunar months (spring, summer, autumn, and winter).[99] Preparations for these sacrifices always began with a formal notification

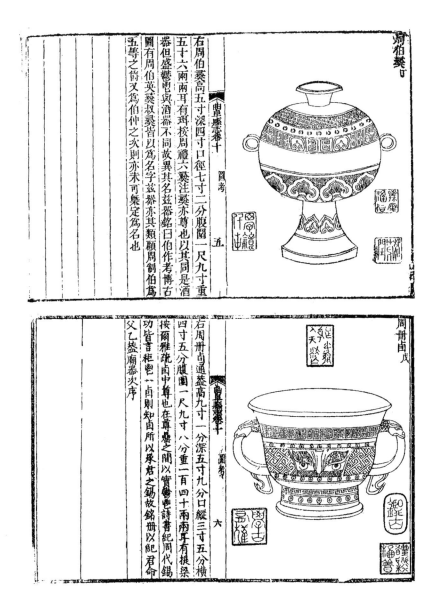

《曲阜縣卷十 圖考 五

右周伯彝高五寸深四寸口徑七寸二分腹圍一尺九寸重
五十六兩兩耳有珥按周禮六彝注彝亦尊也以其同是酒
器但盛鬱鬯與酒器不同故異其名茲器銘曰伯作考博右
圖有周伯彝英彝叔彝皆以爲名字茲器亦其類顧周制伯爲
五尊之首又爲伯仲之次則亦未可繫定爲名也

《曲阜縣卷十 圖考 六

右周冊卣通蓋高九寸一分深五寸九分口縱三寸五分橫
四寸五分腹圍一尺九寸八分重一百四十兩年有橫梁
按爾雅疏卣中尊也在尊罍之間以實鬯詩書紀周代錫
功皆曰秬鬯一卣則知卣所以尊君之錫故銘冊以紀君命
父乙茲廟彝次庫

FIGURE 11. Illustrations of two of the Ten Shang and Zhou gifts granted to Kong Temple by the Qianlong emperor. From Pan Xiang, *Qufu xianzhi*, 1774.

TABLE 1.
Items Procured for Seasonal Sacrifice, 1755

Item	Quantity	Item	Quantity
Oxen	2	Wine	122 bottles
Deer (as substitute for usual sheep?)	3	Leeks	71 *jin*
Hogs	29	Greens	125 *jin*
Hares	10	Water chestnuts	30 *jin*
Onions	5.2 *jin*	Gorgon fruit	35 *jin*
Bamboo shoots	10	Fish, various kinds	40 total
Dates	144.8 *jin*	White sugar	1 *jin*
Chestnuts	186 *jin*	Prickly ash fruit	8 *liang*
Hazelnuts	17.8 *jin*	Fennel	8 *liang*
Broomcorn millet	1.6 *dou*	Dill	4 *liang*
Panicled millet	3.8 *dou*	Sesame oil	3 *jin*
Rice	3.8 *dou*	Firewood	4330 *jin*
Foxtail millet	1.1 *dou*	Silk	20 *duan*
Buckwheat	2 *jin*	Incense, various	Various quantities
White flour	2 *jin*	Candles, various	371
Salt cakes	22	Miscellaneous	Miscellaneous
White salt	4 *jin*		

Source: Kong Deping et al., *JiKong liyue* (Rites and music for the sacrifice to Kongzi) (Beijing: Zhongguo shehui chubanshe, 2010), 293–294.

Note: 1 dou = approximately ten liters, 1 jin = approximately six hundred grams

made twenty days in advance of the event. Over the next fifteen days, the relevant officials would procure the necessary viands and sacrifice goods, including several dozen head of livestock, dozens of fish, many bushels of grain, gallons of wine and refined oil, crates of vegetables, sacks of sugar and salt, rolls of silk, and more than a ton of firewood. The sacrifice of 1755 detailed in table 1 may be an extreme example because it appears the Qianlong emperor conducted it himself during one of his many visits to Qufu. As a state sacrifice, however, the procurements were standardized, and regardless of the identity of the chief officer it was necessary to obtain massive quantities of material, for the most part from the "sacrifice lands," looms, and distilleries of the Kong family estates—four times a year, every year.

A second logistical undertaking in the context of sacrifice was the management of personnel. In the weeks and days leading up to the sacrifice, the temple's music and dance director would select the finest performers from a class of as many as 240 music and dance students to begin rehearsals in the courtyard of the Chamber of Gold and Silk. Other officers prepared the eulogy, submitted sacrificial silk, posted the final program of events on the Gate of Unified Texts, and prepared the list of participants (table 2). Three days before the sacrifice, the duke approved the roster, and the participants would proceed to the Gate of Unified Texts to recite vows and begin ablutions. A day later, the duke took charge of preparations in the Chamber of Odes and Rites and the Chamber of Gold and Silk, and on the last day before the ceremony the duke and his officers received the raw animal and vegetable sacrifices in the outer courtyard and delivered them for processing to the Spirit Abattoir (Shenpao) and the Spirit Kitchen (Shenchu) (fig. 12). Finally, the duke retired to the special Abstinence Quarters (Zhaisu) to the east of the Gate of Unified Texts.[100]

When the drums sounded in the predawn hours on the day of the ceremony, the appropriate gates were opened, and the duke and his officers took up their positions in front of the Apricot Altar. Kong family members, local officials, visiting dignitaries, degree holders, teachers, and students who could keep up the pretension of scholarship would stand in formation and join in the prostrations but otherwise served a passive role. The ceremony as experienced in the court of the Hall of the Great Ensemble began with the rite of *yimaoxue,* designed to stimulate the spirits by burying some of the blood and fur of the principal sacrificial animals outside the front gate. Once all the attending officials had taken up their positions in the temple, the sacrifice vessels were opened as the eulogist ordered the commencement of welcoming spirits (*yingshen*) by bringing the spirit tablets out of storage and setting them in their correct position on the altars. All stages of the sacrifice were performed to the accompaniment of carefully prescribed ritual music.

TABLE 2.
Officers Serving at Kong Temple Seasonal Sacrifices during the Mid-Qing Dynasty

Title	Rank	Number (in eighteenth century)	Position/duties
Zheng xianguan	Zheng 1	1	Chief sacrifice officer (usually Duke of Fulfilling the Sage).
Fen xianguan	various	?	Conduct sacrifice for twelve savants (zhe).
Dai xianguan	various	?	Conduct sacrifice at Hall of Repose.
She xianguan	various	?	Conduct sacrifice at Shrine of the Esteemed Sages, Family Temple.
Baishi zushi	4	1	Manager of sacrificial vessels.
Zhangshu	7	1	Manager of letters, archives, certificates, etc.
Dianji	7	1	Manager of imperial texts, lisheng (acolyte) tutor.
Siyue	7	1	Direction and choreography of music and dance, maintenance of music and dance instruments and props, training performers.
Shanzhang	?	2	Headmaster of Nishan Academy and Zhusi Academy.
Sanshi xue jiaoshou	?	1	Headmaster of "Three Surnames" family school.
Xuelu	5	1	Assistant to Duke of Fulfilling the Sage.
Zhiyin	7	1	Manager of official letters.
Shuxue	?	1	Assistant to Duke of Sagely Posterity.
Guan'gou	7	1	Estate manager.
Tunguan	?	8	Assistant estate managers.
Baihu	4	1	Chief of temple and cemetery security and maintenance divisions.
Banguan	7	6	(Court) Retainers to Duke of Fulfilling the Sage.
Jizou	7	1	Assistant to Duke of Fulfilling the Sage.
Shuxie	7	1	Assistant to Duke of Fulfilling the Sage.
Zhishi	3, 4, 5, 7, 8, 9	Total of 40	
Hanlinyuan Wujingboshi	8	15	Appointed to Hanlin Academy.

Source: Kong Deping et al., *Ji Kong yuewu* (The music and dance of the sacrifice to Kongzi) (Beijing: Zhongguo shehui chubanshe, 2010), 24–32; Kong Jifen, *Queli wenxian kao* (Investigation of documents in Queli) (1762).

FIGURE 12. Spirit Kitchen (Shenchu), ca. 1730, following earlier precedent. Three five-bay buildings with flush-gable roofs, traditionally used to prepare sacrificial foods, currently house Han dynasty tomb engravings.

After the assembled officers had performed the *sangui jiukou*, the sacrifice could proceed with the first of three offerings (*chuxian, yaxian,* and *zhongxian*) that involved the "Music and Dance for Sacrificing to Kongzi" (fig. 13).[101] During the offering the officials repeatedly cleansed both their hands and the vessels and proffered incense, silk, and wine in the Hall of the Great Ensemble. The recitation of the sacrifice eulogy and a second performance of *sangui jiukou* followed this offering.[102] The second and third offerings followed a procedure similar to the first except for the position of the dancers and the absence of the silk, incense, and the eulogy. As the duke paid similar respects to the four correlates, subordinate officers went to make offerings at the Family Temple and before the images and tablets of the savants; the former worthies; the former Confucians; Lady Qiguan; the five-generations of Confucian ancestors, Shuliang He and Yan Zhengzai; and the tutelary spirit Houtu, who retained a shrine at the rear of the temple (fig. 14). With the completion of the offerings, the sacrifice entered the stage of *chezhuan,* when the sacrificial foods were withdrawn, and *yinfu shouzuo,* during which the officials drank the sacrificial wine and accepted a portion of sacrificial beef. Having disposed of the offerings, the spirit tablets were

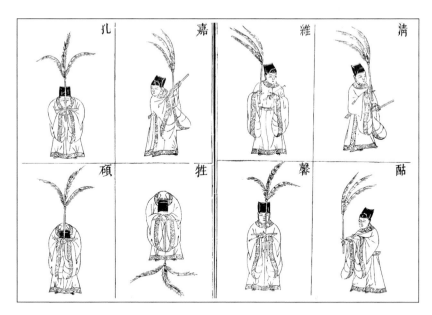

FIGURE 13. Music and Dance for Sacrificing to Confucius (*Ji Kong yuewu*), illustrating sacrifice dancers in Ming costume and holding reed pipes and peacock feathers. *Queli guangzhi*, 1673.

FIGURE 14. Tutelary God Shrine (Houtuci), ca. Qing dynasty, following earlier precedent. Self-contained compound containing three-bay hall with overhanging gable roof.

returned to storage (*songshen*), and the written eulogy and silk offerings were incinerated (*yizhuan*) in a facility to the rear of the temple (Liaosuo). With the closing of the doors to the Hall of the Great Ensemble and the return of the Kangxi emperor's imperial parasol to storage, the ceremony was declared complete, and officials, dancers, and musicians were allowed to withdraw to the beat of the Apricot Altar drums.[103]

These details are reconstructed from the same ritual texts that individuals like Kong Shangren consulted when directing and choreographing music and dance and effectively describe the various movements and articulations of hierarchy within the performance. They do not, however, indicate how the ritual might have been perceived as something more than a complex act of resource and personnel management. Some sense that sacrifice was spiritually possessed or aesthetically sublime can be recovered from memoirs and prose collected in local annals, although in turning to those records one faces a problem that should be familiar to the readers of this book. Much of the available evidence suggests that the Chinese literati were less concerned with material culture than with the various ethereal qualities of ritual. Poems and eulogies contained in texts such as the *Annals of Queli* seldom dwell upon the substance of the edifice or its sacrificial wares, choosing instead to focus, as Mote argued, on the "imperishable associations . . . realized in words."[104] The point, however, is that attention to words and associations does not imply that material was regarded as mere infrastructure. This was no temple of the mind unencumbered by architecture, and it should be clear from all the preceding that intangible forms of culture were not held in isolation from the built environment.

It should be noted, first of all, that while the temple north of the Gate of Expanding the Way was formally closed to casual visitors, this exclusivity could be breached and at times relaxed altogether so that ordinary people could pass through the center of the temple and linger in its park-like setting. The practice suggests a flaw in the temple's security system, although the appearance of commoners within the temple also demonstrates movement between the temple and the surrounding community. In the formal sense of sacrifice, the passage between inner and outer and the boundaries between higher and lower were carefully circumscribed and ritualized. However, in the nineteenth century, the office of the Duke of Fulfilling the Sage issued the following statement demonstrating that these movements and boundaries were continuous throughout the community and not always constrained by propriety:

> The environment of the temple should be serious and quiet out of respect to the Sage. Therefore the two gates of Yucui and Guande were always controlled by appointed guardians and security was maintained by opening and closing them on schedule to avoid incidents. But recently anyone can enter and exit freely and people have taken to sitting and lounging about the stele pavilions. This kind of behavior is remarkably vulgar and in violation of the regulations—how rude! The guards are to be punished and free entry and exit through these gates should be expressly forbidden. Let the guards be warned to take their duties seriously in the future. Only those working for local authorities preparing to offer sacrifice in the temple may pass through these gates. Those who are not dressed formally and look strange and suspicious are forbidden from entering. Anyone who violates this prohibition may be reported to the local authorities and summoned to trial. Guards, however, must not abuse their power. All heed these prohibitions.[105]

The interior court of the temple beyond the Gate of the Great Ensemble was more tightly controlled, but even here it seems that given the right connections or sufficient funds most anyone could gain access outside of sacrifice. Craftsmen and custodians, of course, were regularly admitted to perform maintenance and construction, although their presence was otherwise invisible. Travel accounts from other visitors are typically unexceptional, providing unembellished descriptions of the temple's architecture and the appearance of various relics.[106] In the Ming dynasty, Wang Gen wrote a more telling account of how he, the barely literate son of a salt worker, came face-to-face with the Kongzi effigy and was enlightened by his realization that "Kongzi is a man, just as I am."[107] Zhang Dai was somewhat less inspired by his encounter, noting that he had paid for the privilege of entering the temple. Inside he found a strange plaque proclaiming, "This is the place where Liang Shanbo and Zhu Yingtai studied"—in reference to the classic tale of the "butterfly lovers," who could only by the longest stretch of the imagination be associated with Qufu.[108] Zhang also noted wryly that the sacred vessels on the altars in front of the sages were nailed down, presumably to deter souvenir hunters, who seem to have been admitted to the temple in larger numbers than official records care to mention.[109]

With these texts as a reminder of the permeability of the temple's supposedly exclusive walls and the fact that the temple could be experienced in ways other than as "pure" ritual, we turn to the literati accounts that commemorate the temple in the context of sacrifice. Much of this prose is united by the sense that rather than attaining a singular monumental stature, the temple stood at the intersection of manmade works and nature/cosmos, heaven and earth, life and death, and present and past. In so doing it allowed the visitor to commune with the sage. Others surveying the temple in a state of ruin sometimes saw it as evidence that the Way of Kongzi was lost. Many more saw the temple, especially its iconic trees, as the ultimate symbol of the rebirth and regeneration of the Way.[110] Most importantly, commemorative prose suggests that the spirit of Kongzi was, or at least should be, present at the sacrifice.

In the late Yuan dynasty, Zhou Boqi was an established court poet and principal of the Hanlin Academy. In writing of his visit to Kong Temple, the scholar did not entirely ignore its architectural qualities, recording his impressions of the surrounding walls, the imposing stature of the Pavilion of the Literary Constellation, the expansive cloisters, the elaborately carved dragon columns of the Hall of the Great Ensemble, and other buildings that "reached to the sky." However, the scholar focused his attention on the sacrifice that he had been sent to conduct:

> As an envoy I prayed wholeheartedly on the emperor's behalf. Torches brightened the towering temple, and incense arose from the burners as we observed the ritual of Zhou and building site of Han. Today's ceremony not only continues this tradition but expands upon earlier practices. Buildings surrounded by one wall after another, stelae erected on tortoise backs, ten thousand volumes of books arranged in proper order, two pavilions stand amid green bamboo, rooftops

meet the natural vistas, spring water pours from the well and wets the ground.[111]

Zhou went through the temple as he went through the sacrifices, awed by the implied complexity of the architecture and the depth of history. The temple, as he put it, was "a mass of ritual and music"—architecture, ritual, literary culture, and nature being indivisible. The scholar believed, or at least professed, that he was experiencing rituals and a ritual environment that were truly ancient.

When Hu Zuanzong arrived in the sixteenth century, the provincial governor was likewise overawed by the depth of the ceremony. In contrast to the evident faith of Zhou Boqi, however, Hu was gripped by existential doubt. In the first of three poems commemorating his sacrifice, the governor remembered:

Climbing on the temple wall in the early morning,
Solemnly we approached the altar,
Suppressing the sound of our jade ornaments,
The fragrance of grass, like osmanthus, spread through the temple,
The officials assembled for the sacrifice,
Their high caps met the branches of pines and junipers,
Even a hundred prostrations cannot fully express our respect for
    the Sage,
Anxiously seeking his traces,
Open a door, an apparition,
Close the door and the trace is gone,
Even a thousand sacrifices cannot recompense the death of
    the Sage.[112]

On entering the temple, Hu surrendered to his senses—the merest sound of a dangling ornament reverberated across the courtyards, and faint scents were magnified into powerful aromas. Having cleansed his body and mind before the sacrifice, the governor had disposed himself toward this type of awareness, cultivating the level of reverence that would, as the *Record of Rites* prescribed, allow him to catch "faint glimpses of the spirit upon entering the shrine and the gentle sense of their murmuring at every point during the rite until he turns to leave."[113] Yet the spirit of Kongzi was elusive, and the governor could not escape the feeling that the sage was gone forever and that all the later works of building and sacrifice compensated poorly for his absence.

Hu's contemporary, the Hanlin academician Yang Weicong (1500–?), shared the governor's misgivings. Referring to the story of Kongzi leaving his footwear behind as a symbol of the wish to return (a custom followed by departing magistrates), Yang wrote that although the temple was in good condition after its recent restoration, "the shoe [of Kongzi] has been gone a long time, and there is no sound of ritual music. Standing there overlooking the several *ren* high wall I feel apprehension."[114] Hu and Yang may have been inspired in their pessimism by the Great Rites Controversy that had shaken the Confucian establishment a few years earlier, but the attitude of loss was not unique to the sixteenth century. In the Sui dynasty, Liu Bin lamented that "in the dusk one feels melancholy on the desolate steps covered by falling leaves of ancient trees blown by the autumn wind. The so-called sacrifices are only a means of seeking consolation in the past."[115] Visiting the temple in the Tang dynasty, Emperor Xuanzong set the standard for woeful remembrance of Kongzi:

How is it with you, Master Kong,
Who strove for your belief a whole age long?
This place is still the Zou family's ground,
Your home became a palace for the Duke of Lu.
You sighed for a phoenix and lamented your ill luck.
You grieved for the unicorn and mourned the failure of your teaching.
As I watched the libation poured between two columns.
I thought of your dream—all was just the same![116]

Later in the dynasty, when the prospects of Confucianism were at a low ebb, Liu Cang equated the ruined state of the temple with the depletion of virtue: "When I passed Queli I mourned the relentless passage of time, like a river flowing endlessly toward the east. Weeds and mosses cover the ancient palace walls . . . Standing on the Zhu and Si Rivers I feel the wind blow, and when the moon climbs to the top of the autumn mountain I sense the darkness of night."[117]

These reminiscences are laments, known in Chinese poetry circles as *huaigu*—literally "yearning for antiquity." In Wu Hung's interpretation, *huaigu* goes beyond poetic musing to form "a general aesthetic experience: looking at (or thinking about) a ruined city, an abandoned place, or a silent 'void' left by historical erasure, one feels that one is confronting the past, both intimately linked with it but hopelessly separated from it."[118] Jonathan Hay has productively linked *huaigu* to the literati perception of the former Ming Palace of Nanjing, observing that in having no prospect of being rebuilt the ruins served as a reminder of the mutability of history.[119] Kong Temple similarly traced the path of ruin, and some visitors evidently found it difficult to overcome the feeling that even a well-maintained temple was a pale reflection of the long-lost spirit of Kongzi.

But not all ruins were beyond recovery, and Kong Temple's history of decay was matched at every turn by its history of reconstruction. The temple, never simply a void nor something that merely stood for an absence, was a place that inspired the conviction that the Way of Kongzi would rise again. Working under the Yuan dynasty, Wang Yun (1227–1304) wrote that the teachings, rules and regulations, and much of the temple itself had fallen into decay. When he approached Queli, however, the Shandong surveillance commissioner (*ancha*) witnessed an auspicious mist hanging over the deteriorating halls and hurried to offer his sacrifice to the "Three Sages, (Kongzi, Yanzi and Mengzi) Towering like Mt. Tai":

> The sage's [virtue] is like an ocean—how can it decay like timber columns and rafters? I hastened back to the Chamber of Gold and Silk, it seems like the abode of an emperor because of the sound of heavenly music. My ears were refreshed, and I forgot the taste of meat . . . I stayed long in the temple, until the sun sank below the junipers.[120]

Viewing the depleted conditions, Wang might easily have succumbed to resentment over the neglectful policies of his Mongol overlords, yet on hearing the strains of ritual music he was able to more profoundly appreciate his environment. As Mote suggested with respect to scholars' attitudes toward famous sites in Suzhou, on entering the temple Wang's attention was drawn to the intangible, especially the music and its association with Kongzi, who had originally "forgotten the taste of meat" upon hearing *shao* music in his own day.[121] But the temple was hardly inconsequential to the scholar official; the music was enhanced by its venue, and the rotting beams were in turn cognitively restored and enhanced as they pulsed with the music. Together, ritual and place appeared to Wang not as respectively essential and expendable but as indivisible parts of the same ritual process.

In the late sixteenth century, Zhang Cheng did not have to tax his imagination quite so vigorously as Wang Yun. Seeing the temple in good repair, the Hanlin academician noted that although sacrifices occurred across the land, nothing could compare to that witnessed in Queli. Looking over the temple's magnificent trappings, Zhang cursed the "villainous" Qin dynasty and praised the Han before lapsing into a more poetic evaluation of nature's embrace of eternal Confucianism:

> Rains fall with the sound of reverberating jade,
> Dragon heads drenched in dew.
> A halo appears above the towering pavilions.
> Beautiful sounds heard before dawn in the golden chamber . . .
> Although mountains may crumble,
> Confucian learning carries on . . .
> The [Kongzi] juniper always verdant . . .
> Spring rain falls on Apricot Altar.[122]

In observing the continuity of Confucian learning, Wang was firm in his belief that the Way of Kongzi had been transmitted into the present, finding the ideal in the predawn musical performance associated with sacrifice. Shao Yiren, although skeptical of efforts to represent the sage in pictorial form at the Hall of the Sage's Traces in the 1580s, wrote of his joy at experiencing the relics of Kongzi: "I climbed the Apricot Altar, waded in the Zhu and Si Rivers, and saw the beauty of the Temple of Confucius [Kong Temple]. And my desire to study increased by leaps and bounds over what it had been in the past."[123] The Kangxi emperor echoed the sentiment a century later: "Crossing the high wall . . . I discover the Master's profound learning, perpetuating the tradition of the Way of Yao and Shun, and extending like the Rivers of Zhu and Si."[124] Zhu Gun (*Jinshi,* 1502) required less hyperbole to express the importance of attending a sacrifice, but his statements, harkening back to those that Sima Qian had penned some sixteen centuries earlier, capture most effectively how important it was for men of his generation to keep the temple as a living artifact. Although he had pursued Confucian studies his entire life, Zhu wrote, it was only upon arrival in Qufu that he was able to gain affirmation: "As I wandered through the temple I felt that I was stepping two thousand years into the past. How fortunate I am to experience the grand ceremony and enjoy the beautiful scenes. Without coming here, how could a scholar resolve his questions and doubts?"[125]

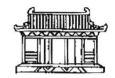

4 | Kong Temple as Space

KONG TEMPLE STANDS as a peerless example of a sacred space formed through the graded separation of a consecrated interior from an external domain. Earlier, the temple was described as concentric quadrangles extending outward from the Apricot Altar, although from a frontal perspective the site is revealed as a progression of gates and courts leading from south to north, through solid walls and open courtyards, toward imposing structures and exclusive sanctuaries. Unfolding as it does, each gate, hall, and pavilion retains an individual identity through its title and architectural qualities, and as an ensemble the relative position and history of the structures form a spatial sequence and temporal rhythm. Finally, these constructive and memorial components work together to define a focal point at the heart of the temple that is not dissimilar from the phenomenon that Mircea Eliade describes as the "absolute reality" at the center of the sacred place.[1]

In Kong Temple that "reality" corresponds to none other than Kongzi— the perceived conductor or originator of an ideal form of governance, a perfect culture, and a noble family. However, the problem with accepting Kong Temple as absolute in any sense of the word is with the imperfect distinction between what Eliade refers to as the inner "sacred" and the external "profane." A sequence of walls or an arrow-straight axis may appear as a flawless expression of spatial hierarchy and cosmic symmetry, although a study of the temple's *longue durée* shows that what passes for order owes a great deal to chance, contingency, and creativity. Managers and builders have always had to deal with precedent, restrictions on space, conflicting building codes, political motives, personal interests, and the forces of nature. These contingencies, often in combination, had the potential to subvert any patterns that may have been envisioned and to complicate any effort to develop the site as an expression of specific ideals and values. Yet those same contingencies prompted the builders to carry on building. They assembled and harmonized space and material, but their work seldom dictated meaning. Kong Temple parallels but does not imitate nature, and although it recalls scholarly and political discourse, it is not a discourse in itself. As Kenneth Frampton argues, "One may assert that building is ontological rather than represen-tational, and that built form is a presence rather than something standing for an absence."[2] Writing from a different perspective but arriving at a similar conclusion, Li Zehou proposes that Chinese aesthetics, architec-ture included, be evaluated in terms of the "line" that does not merely re-strain but "can unfold and express tension, climax and resolution just as musical compositions do."[3] Those tensions and resolutions form the spa-tial dynamics of the temple, and from those dynamics we may better understand how the temple acted on—and was acted upon by—its patrons and participants.

Tones of Bronze and Resonances of Jade: Southern Gates and Arches

This survey begins by defining Kong Temple's formative influences, which include the Chinese state that invested in the temple over many centuries, a loosely organized but enduring community of scholars and ritual specialists who revered Kongzi and saw the temple as a sacred relic, and the acclaimed descendants of the sage who managed the site in part as their ancestral shrine. It is not possible to strictly assign any component of the temple to one set of investors or another because those interests were integrated and mutually supporting. Different institutions, however, did leave differing impressions. The imperial state imposed its authority through precise building codes and by inscribing memorials. The literati appear in the temple's ritual apparatus and the expression of cultural patterns or paradigms (*wen*). Alongside the state and the literati, the acclaimed lineal descendants of the sage maintained a constant presence by residing in the temple precinct, scrupulously main-taining their lineage records, enshrining family members, and asserting their lucrative claims to "sagely posterity" through architecture and ritual. In those respects the temple might be read as a monument to state, literati, and family—arguably the three pillars of late imperial Chinese society, although it just as often inscribes the conflicts between them.

From the perspective of the entrant, the state-literati-family relationship begins to take shape in the temple's forecourt, where symbolically charged gates, archways, and bridges divide, subdivide, and regulate the formal approach to the temple. Yet, as discussed in chapter 2, the most imposing features of that forecourt do not stem from some arcane plan for social engineering or cosmic synchronicity but rather from the combined influences of a bitterly contested family feud and a sixteenth-century peasant uprising. Both the feuding and the banditry were addressed by consolidating the county offices, the ducal Kong Family Mansion, and Kong Temple within a massive wall that defended against outside attack while concentrating regional authority in the person of the Duke of Fulfilling the Sage.

The wall, therefore, was conceived out of exigency, but in resolving a tangible problem the sponsors found the opportunity to pay homage to Kongzi. This tribute was accomplished in several ways: by leaving the temple at the center of the newly enclosed city, by distinguishing the enclosing wall with a high gatehouse of the kind normally reserved for higher administrative cities, and by titling that entrance the Gate of the Esteemed Sage (Yangshengmen) (plate 1). After 1538 the gate was engraved with the calligraphy of Shandong governor Hu Zuanzong and proclaimed as the Ten Thousand Fathom Palace Wall (Wanren Gongqiang). To the classical scholar, that notation referred to an *Analects* passage in which the disciple Zigong dismisses his own learning and lauds the wisdom of the sage. "Let me use the comparison of a house and its encompassing wall," Zigong declares. "My wall only reaches to the shoulders. One may peep over it, and see whatever is valuable in the apartments. The wall of my Master is several fathoms [*ren*] high. If one do[es] not find the door and enter by it, he cannot see the ancestral temple with its beauties, nor all the officers in their rich array."[4] For his part, Hu altered "several" to "ten thousand," and his inscription remained in place until 1748, when the Qianlong emperor had it reinscribed in his own calligraphy. Consequently, the wall became more than a means of centralizing local authority and security and more than a symbol of state and society.[5]

In Qufu the inscribed calligraphy made the wall an extension of a governor's hand, a monument that spoke for an emperor, and a memorial to the sage who had once served his people within the walls of the ancient state of Lu. The wall demonstrates a tension between the written word and the material relic that is basic to understanding all of Kong Temple's major architectural components. The calligraphy alludes to something absent or hidden (Mote's "imperishable association") while the role, status, and "presence" of the architecture is defined by its construction—the laying of brick upon brick; the hauling of earth; and finally, the separation of space. The effort of wall building is categorically different from the effort of calligraphy, but the two forms are contingent upon one another and allow the architecture to emerge as a flow of work, materials, and ideals, not merely a concrete edifice stamped with an eternal impression.

Although the Gate of the Esteemed Sage was typically closed to all but members of the imperial family and their envoys sent to conduct sacrifices to the sage, those that did pass through were faced with another set of archways and gates leading to the temple's main ceremonial entrance. Where the city gate was a practical, if overelaborate, effort to manage a set of concrete problems, the inner archways employed symbolism to manage contingencies of a more abstract nature. Hu Zuanzong commissioned the southernmost memorial arch, known as the Tones of Bronze and Resonances of Jade (Jinsheng Yuzhen), in 1538 (fig. 15). To the north the almost identical Original Qi of Supreme Harmony (Taihe Yuanqi) was sponsored by Imperial Censor Zheng Yun and Shandong governor Zeng Xian in 1544.[6] In choosing the title in the first instance, Governor Hu took a passage from *Mencius* that praises Kongzi as "the timely one among sages" (*sheng zhi shizhi ye*) who achieved the "perfect ensemble" (*ji dacheng*) that "begins with the tone of the bronze bell and ends with the resonance of jade chimes."[7] There is no distinct classical literary source for the second phrase, although *taihe* (Supreme Harmony) and *yuanqi* (Original Qi) refer in a general way to the original and perfectly balanced substance, energy, or material force of the universe that gives rise to myriad things.[8]

Outwardly, these archways uphold a cherished ideal of social and cosmic harmony brought together in the context of music and sacrifice. The timing of their construction, however, suggests the less salubrious political subtext of the Great Rites Controversy, which had erupted eight years earlier and was ongoing at the time that Hu, Zheng, and Zeng commissioned their

FIGURE 15. Tones of Bronze and Resonances of Jade (Jinsheng Yuzhen). Commissioned and inscribed by Hu Zuanzong in 1538. Stone columns topped with *chaotianhou*.

memorials. There is nothing particularly subversive about the appearance of the archways, except perhaps that their columns are finished with mythical "roaring toward the sky" (*chaotianhou*) beasts typically reserved for the palaces of those holding a kingly title or greater.[9] Nor is there any obvious sign that the archways were designed to sanction the emperor or inspire resentment in the literati and scholar-officials who participated in the downgraded sacrifices within the temple. What matters is the way in which the architecture and iconography materialize conflict between the ideal of harmony and the stressful political circumstances under which the scholar-officials worked. The sponsors of these archways could not challenge the imperial court or reverse its decision regarding sacrifice and the rank of Kongzi, and they could not perform the rites as they may have wished, but they could compensate for the erosion of the temple's ritual status by performing an act of construction.

This chapter makes the case for studying architecture as an expression of space and material, although temple nomenclature is a forceful reminder of the role of *wen* in defining temple architecture. Often translated as "literature," "culture," or "text," Cary Liu explains that *wen* must be interpreted both as writing or words and according to its ancient meaning as "heavenly pattern" and "earthly pattern."[10] The Gate of the Lattice Star (Lingxingmen) (plate 2) provides an unusually transparent illustration of these principles. Without delving into the complexities and ambiguities of Chinese astrology and at the risk of giving a fixed interpretation to a system that was highly abstract, it may be noted that the Lattice, or Ling, star belongs to the Beidou constellation (part of Ursa Major) and thereby forms part of a heavenly pattern.[11] The gate, originally raised with timber columns and lintels in the early 1400s, is one of many comparable gates found in similar positions throughout China and so might be interpreted as part of a terrestrial network or earthly pattern.[12] More significance can be attached to the gate if it is observed in conjunction with the Panshui (Semicircular Water) and Panshui Bridge that control access to the gate. First appearing in the Qing dynasty, the waterway and the bridge are relatively recent additions to the temple, but they reference both the Confucian classics and a nearby pond known as Gupanchi (Ancient Semicircular Pond). The name of that pond derives from a passage in the *Book of Odes* (*Shijing*) that praises a seventh-century BCE Marquis of Lu for having created an "academy with its semi-circle of water (*pangong*)."[13] There is no evidence that Gupanchi is the same pool the Marquis of Lu excavated, although from the perspective of the Qing dynasty the pond was nonetheless a relic of ancient China, a tangible connection to the place and time of Kongzi, and a link to a text that the sage is supposed to have edited.[14] In constructing a version of Panshui and the Panshui Bridge in front of the temple, all of those associations—the classics, the sage, and local sacred geography—were imaginatively transferred and contextualized through proximity to the Gate of the Lattice Star.

These relics, individually and in combination, allude to a set of profound ideals, but they could also be used for purposes other than attaining cosmic symmetry. Few transactions involving the Gate of the Lattice Star appear in the historical record. However, it is known that in 1754 the gate was reconstructed with stone columns and lintels under the sponsorship of the contemporary Duke of Fulfilling the Sage.[15] This was a time in which the duke and his family were facing two high-profile challenges: to retain control over the Qufu county magistracy and to prepare for a visit from the Qianlong emperor.[16] The gate makes no definitive statement about these local political or social issues. But where cosmic and imperial associations were only implied in the former timber construction, they were now made explicit in the stone through the addition of carved figures of the atmospheric "kings" of wind, rain, lightning, thunder, and the calligraphy of Qianlong. The available documentation gives little further insight into how the duke understood his actions and the construction that he sponsored. But similar to the archways of 1538 and 1544, the simple fact of the gate's regeneration endows it with multiple potentialities. The gate appeals to an abstract sense of cosmic order or pattern, is a visible monument to imperial power, and, when read in context, appears to address local political and social tensions. The Gate of the Lattice Star had no discernable influence on politics. Nevertheless, it can be read as an effort to defend a particular ideal, to enact it in the present, and to use construction to compensate for the real and potential loss of that same ideal.

The erosion of that ideal and the effort to recover it through the management of ritual architecture is suggested in a more tangible way by an early nineteenth-century incident occurring in the temple forecourt. Through architecture and iconography, the temple forecourt symbolically drew the imperial state, the literati, and the Kong family together under a model of cosmic pattern, although this idealized space could not be made exclusive to those sanctioned parties. Exclusivity may have been less of a problem during the temple's early and middle ages when the precinct of Queli was relatively insular, but when Queli was integrated with the city of Qufu in the Ming dynasty those spaces were abruptly positioned at the center of a socially diverse community. Because of the size of the temple grounds relative to the girth of the city wall, the only convenient way to travel between the southeast and the southwest of the city was to pass through the temple's forecourt. Although the temple managers had reluctantly accepted a certain level of traffic, their concerns were realized on one documented occasion in 1820 when an oxcart belonging to a local scholar "recklessly crashed" into one of the horse-dismounting steles that stood outside the temple.[17] It is not clear whether the driver technically violated the terms of the stele inscription or perhaps an unrelated restriction against livestock in the immediate temple zone, but the temple security chief was determined to make an example of the case. The driver was punished with a severe beating, and all draft and night soil carts were thereafter banned from passing in front of the Gate of the Lattice Star.[18] The circumstances of this case are unusual, although the response demonstrates the ongoing need to protect architecture from physical decay and prevent the erosion of its collateral and embedded values. The point is that while the temple forecourt was highly structured, it was still subject to random occurrences, personal initiatives, and the incursion of "pathways of desire" that find their way through even the most highly controlled spaces.

Inscribing Time on Space: The Outer Temple

In contrast to the mostly symbolic regulation of the forecourt, the formal entrance to Kong Temple is distinguished by the considerable bulk of the Gate of the Timely Sage (Shengshimen). Initially titled the Great Gate (Damen) after its construction in 1415, the portal is similar to the formal entrance of the mortuary of the Yongle emperor at the Ming tombs north of Beijing and the China Gate (Zhonghuamen) that once guarded the approach to Tiananmen Square in the capital. Like these contemporaries, the Gate of the Timely Sage includes an imposing vermillion façade, triple vaulted entrances, and adjoining walls. After burning in the fire of 1499, the entrance was resurrected slightly to the north, and after the fire of 1724 it was finally named the Gate of the Timely Sage according to the passage from *Mencius* cited above.[19] The new entrance was accented with a marble arch engraved with the characters "Temple of the Ultimate Sage" (Zhishengmiao) according to the title imposed on Kongzi during the controversial reforms of the Jiajing emperor and confirmed by the Qing dynasty in 1645 (figs. 16 and 17).

Inside the Gate of the Timely Sage, the first of the temple's courtyards is defined by another waterway and bridge, much as the forecourt is defined by the Gate of the Lattice Star and Panshui Bridge. There are references to "channeling clear water" into Kong Temple and "dredging channels" from as early as the Han and the Tang dynasties, although there is no firm evidence of an interior waterway until the Jin dynasty and no evidence of a name for the system until the Ming, when it appears as Bridge on Jade Disk Moat

FIGURE 16. Temple of the Ultimate Sage Archway (Zhishengmiao), ca. 1730, following precedent of 1415 and ca. 1505.

FIGURE 17. Gate of the Timely Sage (Shengshimen), ca. 1730, following precedent of 1415 and ca. 1505. Single gable-hip roof, five bays wide, two bays deep.

FIGURE 18. Bridge on Jade Disk Moat (Bishuiqiao), ca. 1500, leading to the Gate of Expanding the Way.

(Bishuiqiao) (fig. 18). That name refers to the *Rites of Zhou,* which identifies the jade disc (*bi*) as an appropriate offering to heaven, and to the *Zuo zhuan,* which suggests ways in which *bi* might have been used in the performance of ancient rituals.[20] A more conclusive interpretation offered by Ouyang Xiu in the Song dynasty was that "the ancient imperial academy was called biyong, literally 'moat surrounds like a jade disc,' but meaning that when rites and music are clear then heaven and earth are in harmony."[21]

By definition, the courtyard space was meant to be exclusive to literati and representatives of the state. That exclusivity was more implied than actual and under constant pressure from the mundane realities of the surrounding city. When the temple was enlarged in the Ming dynasty, the extended walls initially isolated this space and diverted the public away from the entrance at the Gate of Expanding the Way (Hongdaomen) just north of Jade Disk Moat (plate 3).[22] The enforced separation proved to be counterproductive because it motivated pedestrians to cross the temple even farther to the north, practically on the threshold of the sage's inner sanctuary. The problem was addressed by installing the east and the west gates that allowed public access to the Jade Disk Moat courtyard, even though this concession defeated the purpose of the enclosure.[23] Having granted the easement, the Duke of Fulfilling the Sage found it necessary to impose rules on its use. Peddlers and actors—and in one documented case a belligerent mule driver—were barred from plying their trades within the courtyard, and the public was implored to respect the tranquility of the surroundings.[24] The need for such regulations, however, suggests the inevitable. For all their efforts, the temple's managers could not overcome the fact that they were part of a community that never fully accepted the temple's exclusive status. Like the forecourt to the south, the intermediate courtyards were subject to multiple layers of order and control, strict regulations and idealized patterns were followed in creating and governing the monuments, yet the monuments were exposed to contingencies that challenged the initial vision of order and facilitated the appropriation of their spaces.

Beyond its median point at the Gate of the Great Mean (fig. 19), the temple begins to exhibit an archival quality that is most apparent in the towering Pavilion of the Literary Constellation (fig. 20). In its original capacity as the temple's library, the pavilion served the local academies and helped to consecrate the past by preserving the histories and historical classics that were fundamental to Confucian education.[25] The first unambiguous reference to a "book repository" appears in an edict dated 997. This is undoubtedly the same building that was repaired circa 1018 by Kong Daofu and renamed after the Literary Constellation at the request of Emperor Zhangzong (r. 1189–1208) in 1191.[26] The pavilion was one of the few structures to survive the fall of the Jin dynasty in 1234, and it may have survived the fire of 1499. However, the record of that disaster states that the books were destroyed, indicating that the upper floors had been damaged.[27] At the time, the surveillance commissioner assigned to manage the reconstruction proposed that the remainder be demolished and the pavilion rebuilt in its entirety. The commissioner was overruled by the provincial grand coordinator, and the remnant was restored in 1504.[28] The library collection was also renewed at this time, then damaged when rebels broke into the temple in 1511, then restored through a donation of Confucian texts from the Ministry of Rites, and finally developed as a comprehensive library with the support of provincial officials and local scholars after 1519.[29] The collection

FIGURE 19. Gate of the Great Mean (Dazhongmen), ca. 1505, after earliest precedent in the Song dynasty. Five bays wide, single gabled roof.

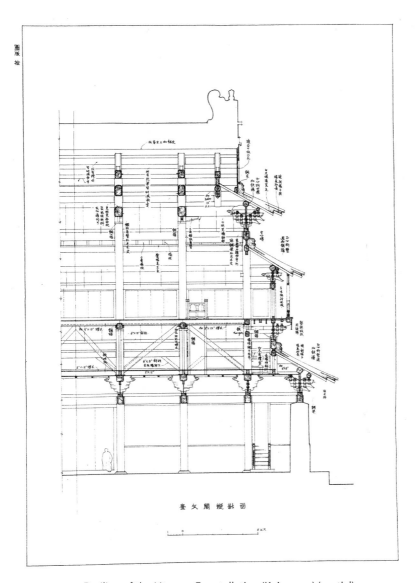

面 剖 縱 閣 文 奎

FIGURE 20. Pavilion of the Literary Constellation (Kuiwenge) (partial), ca. 1505, following precedent of 1018 or earlier. Seven bays wide, five bays deep with a triple gable-hip roof. Drawing by Liang Sicheng, 1935.

seems to have dwindled thereafter and was finally lost, with little fanfare, to the more pervasive forces of neglect in the nineteenth century.[30] The pavilion itself was renovated several more times in the nineteenth and the twentieth centuries. Until the present, however, there has not been a serious effort to restore the library collection or to revive the temple's reputation as an actual site of learning.

Many more of the temple's literary credentials are preserved in a collection of some 1,300 inscribed steles and tablets dating from the twentieth century to as early as the Western Han. In turning to the question of how steles perform in Kong Temple, it is necessary to preface certain considerations: first, steles are monuments that occupy space and architecture; second, because they are moveable, they are subject to manipulation and may be consciously used to control space; third, although relatively durable they are nonetheless subject to erosion; and finally, because they include inscriptions steles are subject to copying by the technique of rubbing.

The temple has been accumulating steles and tablets since the Han dynasty. Early sources do not refer to their position within the temple, and it can only be assumed that they once stood within the central courtyard and were later moved into the adjacent cloisters, probably in the early Tang dynasty.[31] The orientation of the steles comes more clearly into focus after the early eleventh century when Tang and Song stele pavilions were built to the southeast and southwest of the original temple gate and in the shadow of the newly constructed Pavilion of the Literary Constellation.[32] After the Mongol conquest, the Yuan imperial steles, including a notable example engraved in Mongol Phags-pa script, were erected in pavilions directly between the Tang and the Song pavilions, conspicuously nearer to the temple's central axis (fig. 21, plate 4). The logic of stele placement changed in the Ming dynasty when the Duke of Fulfilling the Sage had the aforementioned "conversation" between himself, his father, and the dynastic founder Zhu Yuanzhang (Hongwu emperor) inscribed on a prominent stele to the southeast of the Pavilion of the Literary Constellation.[33] In associating the court with the Ming founder, the duke was effectively setting a precedent. The Stele of the Yongle Emperor was erected on the opposite side of the same courtyard in 1417, and the enlargement of the courtyard at that time made it possible for the Chenghua emperor's eulogy for Kongzi (1468)

FIGURE 21. One of thirteen imperial stele pavilions in the fourth interior courtyard. Portions of some pavilions completed as early as 1179; others date to the Yuan and the Qing dynasties.

and the record of the Hongzhi-era temple restoration (1504) to occupy the free space further to the south.[34]

No imperial steles were raised during the remainder of the Ming, but court commemoration resumed with vigor in the Qing dynasty. In leaving their impressions, Manchu emperors did not follow the Ming example of developing the temple's outer courtyards and began to direct memorials and testimonials back toward its heart. When the Kangxi emperor sent a notoriously heavy commemorative stele direct from its quarry near Beijing, the monolith was erected in a pavilion within the limited space remaining to the north of the Yuan steles, virtually on the doorstep of Kongzi's inner sanctuary.[35] Subsequent emperors and numerous court officials followed, inscribing details of pilgrimages, eulogies, sacrifices, and restorations. By the nineteenth century, the stele pavilions were crowded into such tight quarters that their eaves began to overlap with the gate in a pattern presently known as "intriguing from all angles" (*gouxin doujiao*) (fig. 22). Although often represented as the builders' clever solution to restrictions on

FIGURE 22. *Gouxin doujiao* (intriguing from all angles), intersecting eaves of Qing dynasty stele pavilions, and the Gate of the Great Ensemble.

space, the pattern of stele placement within the outer temple also demonstrates the limits of any obligation to follow precedent and a tendency to manipulate space in order to gain the monumental advantage over a dynastic predecessor. Power, in other words, did not generate balance, and an archive—even one consisting of massive inscribed stones—is subject to continual pressure from disorder advanced by time, neglect, willful destruction, and, paradoxically, even sincere patronage.

Patrons who inscribed texts on stone typically sought to eternalize their eulogies for Kongzi, to make a lasting record of their sacrifice, and/or to state for posterity their initiative to restore the temple. While more durable than printed texts, however, these steles and tablets are still subject to erosion, both from exposure to the elements and from the act of reproducing the text by taking rubbings. As detailed by Wu Hung, since the upsurge of antiquarianism in the Song dynasty, and especially in the Qing dynasty, rubbings from early inscriptions in particular had been highly sought after, implicitly as a means of connecting with classical antiquity and explicitly as calligraphic models. But, they were also collectibles. As Wu explains, the rubbing was often of greater interest to the antiquarian than the actual stele because it could be taken away, collected, and compared, perhaps to earlier rubbings taken from the same stele.[36]

From a conservation point of view, the problem of stele rubbing is that while it takes an impression of the stele at a particular moment in history the physically aggressive act of copying contributes to erosion and leads to significant change in the quality of the text over time.[37] In Kong Temple the growing interest in steleography prompted local authorities and scholars to transfer the most venerable steles into a converted gatehouse formerly known as Cantongmen and since the Yongzheng era of the Qing dynasty as the Gate of Unified Texts (fig. 23). The revised title, while reflecting on the nature of the gate's contents, was chosen from a passage in *The Doctrine of the Mean:* "Now over the kingdom, carriages have all wheels of the same size; all writing is with the same characters; and for conduct there are the same rules."[38] While early records do not indicate which steles were chosen for inclusion in this gate or when they began to migrate to this location, in 1684 the collection primarily included Han dynasty inscriptions such as the Yiying Officer's Stele (Yiying Qingshi Baishi Zushi Bei, CE 153), the Han Stele

FIGURE 23. Gate of Unified Texts (Tongwenmen), ca. 1730, following earliest precedent of Song dynasty. The gate served as the front entrance to the temple during the Song dynasty. When the temple expanded to the south, the gate became a stand-alone structure used to store ancient steles. Five bays in width, single gable-hip roof.

of Ritual Vessels (Han Liqi Bei, CE 156), and the Han Provincial Inspector Kong Qian Tombstone (Han Junzhu Caoshi Kong Xian Mujie, CE 155).[39] In the eighteenth century many of Qufu's remaining Han and some of the more compelling Tang and Song inscriptions were moved into the gate.[40] These included tablets that had traditionally stood within the inner temple cloisters as well as examples brought from the Temple of the Duke of Zhou in the suburbs of Qufu, the nearby Temple of Yanzi, and most notably, from the Kong family cemetery. In 1793 the noted antiquarian Ruan Yuan, acting on a tip from the intrepid stele hunter Huang Yi, unearthed the Xiping Canbei (CE 172) outside the walls of Qufu. Although that inscription makes only vague reference to an early political order and never to Kongzi, the antiquity of the relic nonetheless qualified it for removal to Kong Temple. Following the custom of the time, Ruan Yuan inscribed the stele with his own text detailing the circumstances of its recovery, and it is

PLATE 1. Gate of the Esteemed Sage (Yangshengmen), ca. 1530. As seen from within the outer gate, facing north. Gate house reconstructed in 1989 after destruction in 1930.

PLATE 2. Gate of the Lattice Star (Lingxingmen). Sponsored by the Duke of Fulfilling the Sage in 1754 following earlier timber precedent. Stone archway decorated with dragon and phoenix motifs, cloud patterns, and "four kings," inscribed by the Qianlong emperor.

PLATE 3. Gate of Expanding the Way (Hongdaomen), ca. 1730, following earliest precedent of 1377. Five bays wide with single gable-hip roof.

PLATE 4. Steles on tortoise-back bases in one of the Thirteen Stele Pavilions.

PLATE 5. Apricot Altar (Xingtan), 1569, following earliest precedent of 1018. Double gable-hip roof, containing the stele of Dang Huaiying and the stele of the Qianlong emperor.

PLATE 6. Eastern Cloister (Dongwu) (interior) and altars holding tablets of exegetes of the Confucian classics, ca. 1730, following earliest recorded precedent in the Song dynasty. Identical to the Western Cloister.

PLATE 7. Hall of the Great Ensemble (Dachengdian), ca. 1730, following earliest recorded precedent of 739 and likely precedent of the Han dynasty. Double gable-hip roof with yellow tile, nine bays wide, five bays deep, with a two-tier platform appropriate to rank of king. The hall contains effigies of Kongzi and his twelve most accomplished followers, sacrifice altars, and Qing imperial placards.

PLATE 8. Gate of the Sagely Posterity (Chengshengmen), ca. 1505, following earliest precedent of Northern Song (recently renovated). Three bays wide, single overhanging gable roof. Sign in foreground: "Ancient architecture within the scenic area is undergoing restoration work, visitors please pay attention to safety."

PLATE 9. Fathering the Sage Hall of Repose (Hall of Lady Qisheng) (Qishengqindian), ca. 1730, following earliest precedent of 1048. Three bays wide, single gable-hip roof.

PLATE 10. Modern sacrifice dance with costumes and props in the Ming style. In contrast to traditional regulations, the dance troupe now consists of both men and women and performs daily during the tourist season.

likely that he was the first of many to subject the stele to rubbing. In 1838 the stele was given a place of honor in the Gate of Unified Texts.[41]

These actions illustrate the basic contradiction of monument conservation. In bringing the relic into Kong Temple, an antiquarian such as Ruan might limit natural erosion and may have intended to control the circumstances of reproduction. But in making it available "for the appreciation of the scholars," as he wrote, Ruan exposed the relic to more intensive copying and damage from handling. This was known to be the case in the Forest of Steles at the Confucian temple in Xi'an, where one observer noted that rubbing was being conducted on an almost industrial scale in the nineteenth century.[42] Physical evidence provides ample testimony to rubbing on a comparable scale in Qufu. In an example raised by Wu Hung, a comparison of early rubbings of the Han dynasty Stele of Kong Zhou shows that while the relic had deteriorated prior to its removal to the Gate of Unified Texts in 1739, later impressions show that more intensive rubbing in the nineteenth century had damaged many of the inscribed characters. Others, according to one modern expert, had "become blurred and lost their spirit."[43]

The treatment of the Stele of Kong Zhou demonstrates a fundamental point—to experience the relic is to change it. This "observer principle" is as pertinent to the temple's architecture as it is to the resident steles. Management and reproduction of the relic was a means of cultural survival and the thread, or trace, that connected the present to antiquity. But it also hastened the demise of the relic. The outer temple embodied that paradox. It allowed the patron and participant to act as agents of both construction and erosion, engaging them in ways that both affirmed and negated the past.

The Great Ensemble and the Inner Temple

Where the outer temple alludes more to Kongzi's patrons than to his person, the final court of the central axis encourages the visitor to look for the "traces" of the sage and to listen for the lingering echo of ancient rituals. Like the archival qualities of the outer temple, the material elements of the inner temple lent substance to the sage's spirit and implied power over decay. More idealistic scholars argued that antiquity could not be recovered in the literal sense and condemned the effort to reproduce it in effigy. But the structure, configuration, and contents of the inner temple demonstrate the will of those moved to reconstitute and amplify the past by creating a system that allowed it to resonate with their present. The space preserved or reproduced material referents to Kongzi; configured facilities to support the ancestralism of the Kong family; and linked the architecture to scholarship, statecraft, and cosmology. The inner temple thereby created an idealized and presumably ancient social and political structure that legitimized the dominant actors and affirmed the tensions between them.

The main entrance to the final courtyard of the central axis is through the Gate of the Great Completion (Dachengmen), or as I prefer, the Gate of the Great Ensemble (according to the Ivanhoe and Bloom translation of *Mencius* quoted above).[44] The earliest reference to a main Ceremonial Gate (Yimen) appears in Kong Daofu's account of 1018, although there are no further records of the gate until 1302 when Yan Fu wrote that the "sacrifice place of the scholars" was accompanied by a gate called the Great Ensemble.[45] The structure was destroyed by the fire of 1499, rebuilt and destroyed again by the fire of 1724.[46] When it was rebuilt for the last time in ca. 1730 the new entrance was flanked by two minor gates: Tones of Bronze on one side, Resonances of Jade on the other. Like the single archway in the temple forecourt, these three gates work together to reference *Mencius*. "The great ensemble" begins with the bronze bell and ends with the jade chime.

At five bays in width, the Gate of the Great Ensemble is one of the largest temple gates in China. However, it is less noted for its architectural attributes than for the tree that stands immediately to its north (fig. 24). The juniper is so ancient that it is reputed to have been "touched by the hand" of the sage (*shouzhihui*). The claim is certainly fiction, although the tree's reputation for reviving and regenerating itself after long periods of dormancy and even complete destruction has come to be identified with the perpetuity of virtue passed down from Kongzi. As chronicled by Zhang Dai in the Ming dynasty, the Kongzi juniper lived through the Zhou, Qin, Han, and Jin dynasties before it withered away in 309 CE. The Kong family preserved the relic until it revived in the Sui dynasty before withering again in 688. After 374 years this tree sprang back to life during the reign of Song Renzong, but it was scorched by fire in 1215. The bare trunk stood for eighty-one

FIGURE 24. Gate of the Great Ensemble (Dachengmen), ca. 1730, following earliest recorded precedent of the Song dynasty. Five bays in width, single gable-hip roof. Kongzi juniper, reputed to be ancient but dating to the mid-eighteenth century.

years until reviving in 1294, sprouting new growth in 1389, and flourishing for ten years before it withered.[47] The fire of 1499 scorched the tree again, although its trunk persevered. Encountering this remnant in the early sixteenth century, Li Jie and his companions nursed a feeling of dismay yet remained hopeful that the tree would restore itself:

> The temple was renovated, but sadly only the root of the Kongzi juniper remains. . . . The pines and cypress surround this juniper like sentinels. The fire dares to destroy civilization (*siwen*), the heritage of "the uncrowned king" (*suwang*) was lost in a single night . . . we hope that it will regenerate from the relic, yet it will take time to recover its former greatness.[48]

Others, seeing the tree in the same condition, were more optimistic that even the scorched trunk symbolized the perseverance of civilization. In the aftermath of the fire, an anonymous observer wrote that "although the tree was burned, civilization (*siwen*) was not lost and will be restored when the juniper is reborn."[49] The relic likewise inspired Gu Menggui, who noted "auspicious clouds over the great building" and observed that "although dead, disappearing like the qilin, Kongzi will shine forever like the juniper in front of the [Apricot] altar."[50]

For the next two hundred years, the tree stood limbless and bare yet so solid that it was known as the "iron tree." Seeing the relic in 1629, Zhang Dai wrote that when he touched its trunk the long dormant tree felt "smooth, moist, firm and shiny. The pattern of its bark swirled to the left. When struck, it produced a sound like that of metal or stone. The descendants of Kongzi have always regarded its flourishing and withering as a sign of the times."[51] The trunk burned in the fire of 1724. Before long, however, the roots produced a shoot that eventually grew into the tree that now stands behind the Gate of the Great Ensemble.[52] Owing to the natural longevity of the species, probably some creative grafting or transplanting, and a measure of faith to help knit the centuries together, the temple custodians, historians, and scholars used the tree to establish a connection to the hand of Kongzi.

As Gu Menggui had observed in the Ming, the Kongzi juniper was historically associated with another relic that summoned the memory of the sage and traced the temple's ancient past. Before the Song dynasty, the memorial hall of Kongzi occupied the center of the existing courtyard. When that hall was moved northward during the reconstruction of 1018, the position was filled by a raised altar planted round with apricot trees.[53] In naming the site the Apricot Altar (plate 5) its builder, Kong Daofu, invoked the historical Kongzi and his students by referencing a passage in *Zhuangzi*: "Kongzi, rambling in the forest of Ziwei, stopped and sat down by the Apricot Altar. The disciples began to read their books, while he proceeded to play on his lute, singing as he did so."[54] The name was eternalized by the Jin dynasty scholar-official and calligrapher Dang Huaiying, who wrote the characters for a stele that still occupies the site. Dang mentioned elsewhere that the Apricot Altar was restored or augmented in 1190, and the "Jin dynasty" temple diagram appearing in a thirteenth-century text shows the altar covered by a single-tier roof.[55] The Apricot Altar evidently survived the fire of 1499 and was upgraded with stone balustrades and a "kingly" double-tier roof in 1569, by no coincidence, one year after the end of the oppressive

Jiajing reign.[56] There is no record of damage in the fire of 1724, so it is possible that the altar remains substantially as it was in the late Ming.

These attributes make the Apricot Altar a relatively stable point of reference for the temple, although as a monument it is essentially "empty." Even the Dang Huaiying Stele, the altar's only permanent fixture before the eighteenth century, lists no more than the author's name and the characters for "Xingtan." The emptiness, however, like everything else in the temple, is constructed. Standing at the center of the courtyard, the altar connects the central axis and the implicit genesis of the cult of Kongzi to a lateral axis that points to the former scholars (*xianru*) and former worthies (*xianxian*) enshrined in the Eastern and Western Cloisters (Dongxi Liangwu) (plate 6).[57] In this position, the Apricot Altar is both connected to and removed from the canonized disciples and exegetes, much as Kongzi as seen by Zhuangzi is both at rest and "rambling"; leading his students but not lecturing to them; and passing his time with music, not the contemplation of texts. In naming and configuring the altar, Kong Daofu may have been inspired by the Daoist belief that a space only becomes useful when empty, although it seems just as likely that he desired to please Emperor Zhenzong, who had demonstrated explicit Daoist sympathies by sponsoring the major memorial project at the Tomb of Shao Hao.

The Hall of the Great Ensemble and the effigy of Kongzi form the pinnacle of the central axis (plate 7). Little is known of the main temple building before 739 when it was expanded from three bays to five and titled Hall of the King of Exalted Culture (Wenxuanwangdian) according to Kongzi's title.[58] The hall, reconstructed on its present location in 1018, earned its current title in the twelfth century according to Mengzi's evaluation of Kongzi.[59] The structure was destroyed during the Jurchen invasion, rebuilt in 1149, and destroyed again during the Mongol invasion less than a century later. When it was restored in 1302, the new hall was extended to seven bays and supported in part by the dragon columns that remain its most distinctive feature.[60] In 1487 the hall was extended to its maximum nine bays and then leveled by the fire of 1499. When rebuilt a few years later, the new hall gained a host of architectural attributes and material upgrades that reflected the Ming court's decision to grant Kongzi the rites of a king.[61] However, the use of green-glazed tiles rather than yellow was a compromise to the knowledge that Kongzi had never held any such title during his lifetime. Although Kongzi lost his noble title altogether in 1530, the hall retained its regal status markers through the late Ming and into the Qing. When it was finally rebuilt after the fire of 1724 the new structure recovered all of the former details except for the provision of nine "eave creature" (*yanshou*) figures on each of its ridges and the substitution of elite yellow-glazed tiles. The configuration implied that although Kongzi still held no imperial title, he was nonetheless worthy of the highest honors the dynasty could afford.[62]

Singular as the Hall of the Great Ensemble may be as a specimen of architecture, it cannot be fully appreciated without an account of the resident effigies of Kongzi, his closest followers, and the controversies that have surrounded them (fig. 25). These effigies are not original to the temple—when the regional governor visited Kong Temple in CE 169 he reported only a tablet (*shenzuo*) of Kongzi.[63] Three centuries later Li Daoyuan's *Water Classic* (*Shuijingzhu,* ca. 515–527) mentions that the "temple has an image (*xiang*) of Kongzi accompanied by two students holding books and standing at his side, as if listening to his teaching."[64] The *xiang* in this instance may refer to a portrait rather than an effigy, although a statement recorded a decade later provides stronger evidence that the temple had begun to house statuary by the middle of the sixth century. In visiting the temple in 539–541, the local Yanzhou commander Li Zhongxuan asked his workmen to "repair the effigies (*xiujian rongxiang*)," further requesting that

> ten savant effigies be erected around Kongzi. Dress these sages in black scholar's robes. Although the past is past, and our time is not their time, their appearance and teachings are never obsolete. . . . With the death of the sage, the Way was also lost. Now, the effigy of the sage is restored, and the ten savants stand by their teacher, smiling, keeping silence, as if listening carefully to his lecture. Under the influence of their sincere countenance visitors to the temple will feel eager to study—it is a good way to enlighten the people.[65]

Li harbored no illusions about reviving antiquity and conceded the passing of the Way, although the commander decided to create the effigies because their physical presence provided him a means of influencing his constituents.

FIGURE 25. Effigy of Kongzi, ca. 1730, following earliest precedent of sixth century. Located inside the Hall of the Great Ensemble, facing sacrifice altar and dressed in nine-insignia robes and nine-bead-string cap, appropriate to rank of king. This model was destroyed in 1966 and replaced by a copy in 1984. Photograph by Ernst Boerschmann, 1911.

Statuary was likewise valued by the Tang, and when Kongzi was granted the title of king in that dynasty his effigy earned to right to face south and wear the nine-insignia robes and nine-bead-string cap appropriate to his status.[66] In the Song dynasty, certain scholar-officials questioned the propriety of representing Kongzi in effigy owing to the inevitable failure to capture his likeness. Add to this the anachronistic portrayals of Kongzi sitting in a chair (there were no such contrivances during his time), wearing Han dynasty regalia, or most obviously wearing the robes and cap of a king or an emperor. Critics like Zhu Xi and Song Na also worried that even if the spirit of Kongzi were to reside in such an object, the custom of placing offerings on the ground might require the sage to crawl about in order to receive them. A more fundamental concern was that the effigies altered the nature of sacrifice by drawing attention to a physical entity and away from the higher principles (i.e., the Way) that Kongzi represented.[67] Amid the Great Rites Controversy the Jiajing emperor acted on his own inclination to remove statuary from Confucian temples throughout China. However, the Kong family was able to claim an exemption for Qufu on the grounds that Kong Temple was effectively an extension of their ancestral hall, and thereby eligible to retain the statuary of Kongzi and his closest followers.[68]

The Hall of Repose, occupied by the tablet of Kongzi's wife, is thought to have descended from the women's quarters of Kongzi's ancient household. These quarters were evidently still standing in the sixth century CE,[69] although there are no further records of a space assigned to Lady Qiguan until 998, when Song emperor Zhenzong (r. 997–1022) ordered the construction of a sacrifice hall appropriate to her contemporary title—Matron of Yun.[70] When Kong Daofu restored the temple in 1018, he moved the building to its current position behind the Hall of the Great Ensemble. It was destroyed in that location during the Jurchen invasion, rebuilt in 1179, and burned again in 1214. When it was recovered in 1246, the hall was reserved for the effigies of Kongzi and his disciples, pending the long-delayed restoration of the Hall of the Great Ensemble. The matron's hall was next destroyed in the fire of 1499 and then lavishly reconstructed with the dimensions of seven bays and decorated with appropriately gendered phoenix and flower patterns that complement the dragon iconography of the main hall. Ritually subordinate to her husband, Lady Qiguan never received more than the basic offerings, but in terms of architecture she was matched to Kongzi through the use of the same high-quality materials, the same double eaves, and the same two-tiered foundation.[71] The hall perished in the fire of 1724, but records state that the new building of 1730 adhered closely to Ming standards, retaining the dimensions and style that mark it as the architectural consort to the Hall of the Great Ensemble (fig. 26).[72]

The final element on the central axis, the Hall of the Sage's Traces, was added to the north of the Hall of Repose through a joint initiative of Shandong provincial officials and the Duke of Fulfilling the Sage in 1592. Because it escaped the fire of 1724 it remains one of the temple's few vintage Ming structures.[73] The hall is something of an anomaly because it lacks a ritual function and was designed as a gallery for a set of stone-cut images depicting the life and afterlife of Kongzi. Although based on Sima Qian's biography of

FIGURE 26. Hall of Repose (Qindian), ca. 1730, following earliest recorded precedent of 998, and likely precedent of Han dynasty or earlier. Double gable-hip roof, seven bays wide. Contains the memorial tablet of Kongzi's mother.

the sage and following the example of pictorial narratives originating elsewhere in China, the set carved for Kong Temple in the 1590s emphasizes Qufu as both the home of Kongzi and the geographic center of his cult. Those claims were affirmed not only by physically locating the engraved narrative in close proximity to the main sacrifice hall but also by including depictions of Kongzi passing doctrines and texts to his disciples, burying his parents, and "crossing his courtyard to discuss the *Odes and Rites* with his son." As Julia Murray explains, by affirming that Confucian principles were transmitted to later generations and by depicting scenes of filial piety and parental benevolence, the Pictures of the Sage's Traces demonstrates the fundamentalist beliefs of the late imperial Cheng-Zhu school of Confucianism, which had maintained close ties to the Kong family in Qufu. By further detailing the pilgrimages of Han Gaozu and Song Zhenzong, the temple's custodians and managers were asserting the tradition of imperial patronage that had advanced the status of Kong Temple and the Kong family over previous centuries and which had sharply declined since the beginning of the Jiajing reign some sixty years earlier.[74] It is fair to say that as an artistic expression, the Pictures of the Sage's Traces did not receive universal acclaim from the temple's more idealistic patrons, who may have felt that "traces of the sage" were better found in the study of ancient texts than in the cursive review of graphic reproductions.[75] Those reproductions, nonetheless, acquired a permanent place in the temple and continue to illustrate the value of narrative expression and the material representation of Confucian ideals.

Fathering Sages and Inheriting Sagacity

In accounting for the shrines immediately to the east and the west of the main temple's central axis, the emphasis here turns from the cult of Kongzi to the extended cult of his ancestors and descendants. The specific nature of the concerns embedded in these collateral axes differs from those expressed along the central axis, although the spatial strategies and structural dynamics are similar. Gates control access to the interior, courts provide space, and architecture and inscriptions archive patronage. Like the central axis, the collateral axes use relics to link the temple directly to Kongzi and to the early imperial state, and buildings are ritually configured to establish a spiritual connection between sagely progenitors and their descendants. The main difference is that while the scholar and state dominate the center, the collateral axes primarily embody the Kong family. Here too, however, it is necessary to consider the influence of the imperial court and the scholar-officials in determining who should be worshipped as ancestors, in what location, and with what rites.

Much of the authority of the eastern court hinges on the claim that the house where Kongzi lived with his wife and mother once stood in the immediate vicinity and had been converted into the Kong family ancestral temple at some point in the ancient past.[76] It is believed that the early descendants of Kongzi built their residence to the south of that ancestral hall and lived there until fleeing Queli at the end of the Warring States period. In 159 BCE, for reasons unexplained in the classical texts, the Prince of Lu (Lu Gongwang, d. 127 BCE) was supervising the demolition of "the former residence of Kongzi (Kongzi *guzhai*)" when he heard mysterious strains of jinshi (gold chime) and sizhu (silk string) music. This music heralded the discovery inside a wall of original copies of the *Book of History* (*Shujing*), the *Book of Rites* (*Liji*), the *Classic of Filial Piety* (*Xiaojing*), and *The Analects,* which Kong Fu had hidden before abandoning the property several centuries earlier.[77] Although their authenticity was deeply suspect, those texts would go on to play an important role in developing a school of Confucianism that remained influential practically until the end of imperial China some two millennia later.[78]

The "Lu Wall" was thus eternalized in memory, yet it remains curiously absent from later records. Ban Gu's *Hanshu* does not indicate what the Prince of Lu did with the wall in the aftermath of his discovery, and it is only assumed that he preserved the relic. A millennium later a regional official observed a certain wall within the temple and pronounced it an authentic relic, yet there is scant evidence of its existence in the intervening centuries or the centuries to follow.[79] It seems possible, therefore, that the legend of Lu Wall had been perpetuated without a physical referent for as long as a thousand years.

As the temple became more highly organized in the Song dynasty, the relics gained a physical presence and began to support the temple's provenance and the family's lineage. In the eleventh century, Kong Daofu wrote that the location of the old wall was occupied by the Chamber of Gold and Silk (*Jinsitang*). The origins of that building are unknown, although its name refers to the Prince of Lu's discovery of texts and, by extension, to the pivotal role the Kong family played in preserving the memory of their ancestor.[80] The chamber stood throughout the Song, the Jin, and the Yuan dynasties, functionally serving to warehouse the musical instruments used to perform the sacrifices to Kongzi and symbolically linking temple and family to the Han dynasty and early ancestors, if not Kongzi himself. After the chamber perished in the fire of 1499, it was reconstructed in the temple's western courtyard, where it continues to serve as a storage and practice facility for the temple's musical instruments and musicians (fig. 27).[81] The removal of the hall to an entirely different location might suggest that Kongzi's descendants cared more for the name and function of the building than with maintaining a physical connection to the sage. However, those same descendants compensated by constructing a distinct "Lu Wall" in Kongzi's ancient courtyard (fig. 28). The chamber and the wall had long been

FIGURE 27. Chamber of Gold and Silk (Jinsitang), ca. 1730, following earliest recorded precedent of Song dynasty. Five bays in width, single overhanging gable roof. Used to house sacrifice instruments and ritual wares.

FIGURE 28. Lu Wall (Lubi), ca. Ming dynasty but occupying the former site of the Chamber of Gold and Silk. Reputed to be the place where Confucian texts were recovered in the Han dynasty.

emptied of the relevant texts, and by the Ming dynasty the texts themselves had been declared irrelevant, but that textual absence seems only to have strengthened the role of the physical relics in perpetuating and giving presence to claims of Confucian posterity.

At the southern end of the eastern axis, the Chamber of Odes and Rites, accessed by the Gate of Sagely Posterity (fig. 29, plate 8), performs the narrative of Confucian heritage in a more subtle manner. The original version of this chamber was likely built in 1008 as a ritual "abstinence hall" to serve Emperor Zhenzong. Zhenzong's record states that when the rites were concluded, the building was decommissioned and granted to the Kong family as a banquet and lecture hall.[82] In the Yuan dynasty, the hall was used to receive temple visitors and as a teaching space for the associated academy. In the Ming it stored ceremonial costumes, vehicles, and instruments.[83] After the fire of 1499, the hall was reconstructed in an enlarged and open form using lightweight beams, rafters, columns, and purlins that were conducive to its continuing role as a venue for entertaining guests and hosting

FIGURE 29. Chamber of Odes and Rites (Shilitang), ca. 1505, following earliest precedent of 1008 (recently renovated). Five bays in width, single gable-hip roof and green roof tile. Signage in foreground: "Construction brings inconvenience, please understand."

ritual lectures.[84] In a development that seems intended to support the Kong family prerogative, the new building was named the Chamber of Odes and Rites, in reference to a phrase in *The Analects:* "Kongzi called his son Boyu (Kong Li), who was hurriedly striding through the hall, and bade him study the Odes and Rites."[85] The admonishment has a universal value in stressing the value of mental cultivation, although in referring to the first descendant of Kongzi, the text and the associated architecture also imply the role of the Kong family in safeguarding and developing the sage's legacy.[86]

The remaining structures of the eastern and western courts are effectively ancestral halls, although they cannot be regarded simply as reliquaries of the Kong family. They are, in effect, a materialization of what Thomas Wilson refers to as the "genealogy of the Way"—a centuries-long process of determining the "correct" interpretation of how Kongzi should be remembered and how his teachings were transmitted to later generations.[87] That genealogy stems from the central court and branches out to the eastern and western collateral axes, where it projects forward in time to include the descendants of the sage and back to include the ancestors of Kongzi and his correlates. The effort to implement that principle through architecture, however, was complicated by ongoing changes in the genealogy and by the fact that architecture could not keep pace with that change. The collateral axes, therefore, are not simply the reflection of an externally conceived principle but the product of a long-term reaction of ideals, spaces, and materials.

The catalyst for that reaction was a Song dynasty declaration that whenever a posthumous title was conferred upon a sage, a commensurate title and sacrifice must be given to the sage's father. Accordingly, in 1008 the Song emperor Zhenzong ennobled Kongzi's father as Duke of Qi. A decade later Kong Daofu reconstructed Shuliang He's shrine as the Hall of the Duke of Qi, and in 1048 the Fathering the Sage Hall of Repose was added to the rear of the compound to lodge the tablet of Kongzi's mother.[88] Shuliang He was thus accommodated as father to the temple's principal sage, although the temple could not be considered "rectified" because the father's rank was still not equal to that of his son.

The fact that Kongzi was not the temple's only sage further complicated the matter. Yanzi had been ennobled as a correlate during the Tang dynasty, and in the Song dynasty he was joined by Zengzi, Mengzi, and Zisi (Kong

Ji, son of Kong Li and grandson of Kongzi). According to the precedent set for Shuliang He, each of their fathers required a title and a place in the temple. Most were ennobled during the Song and the Jin dynasties, although like Shuliang He their ranks were still subordinate to their sons. Moreover, while Kong Li retained a shrine in the central courtyard owing to his descent from Kongzi, the fathers of Yanzi, Zengzi, and Mengzi had no distinct memorial space in the temple.

The central incongruity generated by this sequence of entitlements was addressed in 1330 when Shuliang He received the title of King Who Fathered the Sage. That title in turn prompted the renovation and entitlement of his memorial as the Hall of the King Who Fathered the Sage (Qishengwang-dian), and the addition of corner towers to the temple proper, which marked the premises as a virtual "kingly palace" (fig. 30).[89] The other sagely fathers remained in flux until 1530 when the Jiajing emperor revoked their noble titles and assigned them as correlates to Shuliang He under the title of former worthy (*xianxian*).[90] That configuration lasted until the Qing dy-

FIGURE 30. Corner Tower (Jiaolou), ca. 1730, following earliest precedent of 1336. Corner towers symbolically marked Kong Temple as a kingly palace, according to imperial sumptuary regulations.

FIGURE 31. Family Temple (Jiamiao) and ancestral altars, ca. 1730, following earliest recorded precedent of Song dynasty and likely precedent of Han dynasty. Seven bays wide, single overhanging gable roof.

FIGURE 32. Hall of the King Who Fathered the Sage (Qishengwangdian), ca. 1730, following earliest precedent of 1018. Five bays wide with single-hip roof and columns carved in dragon iconography.

nasty, when Yongzheng resurrected Shuliang He's former title and extended royal privileges to four more of Kongzi's ancestors. The tablets of those ancestors, Shuliang He, and all of the correlates were then moved into the former Kong Family Temple on the eastern axis, which had been redesignated as Shrine of the Esteemed Sages. A new and enlarged Kong Family Temple was then erected immediately to the north, where it lodged the tablets of the descendants of Kongzi (fig. 31).

The western court, including the Chamber of Gold and Silk, the Hall of the King Who Fathered the Sage, and the Fathering the Sage Hall of Repose, would undergo one final reconfiguration in 1724. The destruction of the premises by fire in that year provided the opportunity to harmonize the architecture with the eastern axis, which had survived with only cosmetic damage. The Hall of the King Who Fathered the Sage (fig. 32) was fitted with coiling dragon pillars and a high-grade roof to match the Ming-era Shrine of the Esteemed Sages, and the Chamber of Gold and Silk was reconstructed with the same dimensions as the Chamber of Odes and Rites. The only structure not upgraded at this time was the Fathering the Sage Hall of Repose, which remained the only single-bay memorial hall in the temple and the formal terminus of the western axis (plate 9).

Given that there have been no major structural additions or losses to Kong Temple since 1730, it may be said that after centuries of reaction Confucian ideals, imperial politics, space, and architecture have settled into a stable pattern that we now understand to be Kong Temple. The ongoing processes of inscription, erosion, and reproduction and the active creation of separation and rank have produced an environment with profound associations and a clearly defined hierarchy. It is not, however, a pattern that could have been planned or imagined at any point in the temple's development.

5 | Kong Temple and the Modern Politics of Culture

THIS BOOK'S INTRODUCTION made the case for interpreting Kong Temple as a site of memory on the grounds that the politicized "modern" temple was distanced from the "perpetually actual" tradition of cultural production. This interpretation was proposed under the caveat that Chinese civilization has never developed a firm distinction between culture and politics, and no single political or cultural authority has ever been in total control of Kong Temple. Yet the temple was profoundly affected by changes in the understanding of antiquity and the continuity of culture that occurred during the nineteenth and twentieth centuries and by the evolving nature of governance as the last dynasty gave way to the first republic. New scholarship at that time undermined the myth of continuity and gave cause to see decay as irrevocable rather than as an opportunity for improvement or investment in the temple or its ritual infrastructure. Imperialism and war crippled the authority of the government that continued to defend the deflated institution. The crises made it difficult for even sincere Confucians to view the temple as a true reflection of antiquity rather than a symbol of Qing political authority.

With the collapse of the Qing dynasty in 1911, Kong Temple assumed an especially awkward position, having lost both its principal means of support and the last vestiges of imperial legitimacy essential to its perpetuity. With the debasement of ritual under Republican rule and the rise of legalistic interpretations of heritage in the twentieth century, the artifact and its management/restoration aesthetic became subject to political exploitation. Under the new heritage system, the supporters of Kong Temple were continually forced to justify its existence. This would be a problem that various incarnations of heritage management would struggle with throughout the twentieth century, never finding a wholly satisfactory solution. The new politics would ultimately prove capable of maintaining the relics of Kongzi under the condition that they serve the erratic demands of a modernizing society. Where it was once oriented toward the past, the temple was now situated within the political space of the nation. Those politics did not entirely dissolve the temple's aura of sanctity, and there is continuity with the past in that architecture has always been treated as a means to accumulate merit. In the late nineteenth and early twentieth centuries, however, national politics became increasingly divorced from the values of scholarship, filial piety, antiquity, and ritual that had been associated with the temple through most of its history. It is important to consider, nonetheless, that during that departure Kong Temple was not ignored or dismissed so much as it was sacrificed, in the sense discussed by Georges Bataille: "To break up the subject and re-establish it on a different basis is not to neglect the subject; so it is in a sacrifice, which takes liberties with the victim and even kills it, but cannot be said to *neglect* it."[1]

Kong Temple and the End of Imperial China

In having its restoration provisioned and managed through channels controlled by the courts of Kangxi, Yongzheng, and Qianlong, Kong Temple received generous funding through the seventeenth and eighteenth centuries. When the court began to face dire financial straits in the nineteenth century, the institution lost its lifeline to the imperial treasury, making it necessary for concerned officials and managers to access financial resources beyond state coffers in order to fund restoration work.

This problem emerged most notably in 1868 when Ding Baozhen, the regional commander charged with suppressing the Nian Rebellion, invited viceroys Zeng Guofan and Li Hongzhang to Qufu and requested their aid in restoring Kong Temple. At the time Zeng was already engaged in rebuilding the Confucian temple in Nanjing as a means to provide moral and economic relief (*shanhou*) from the lingering effects of the Taiping War. Now in Shandong the viceroys agreed to sponsor a four-year restoration project that included repairs to most of Kong Temple's main buildings and gates, at a cost of forty-five thousand *liang,* with a further fifteen thousand *liang* provided as an endowment for ongoing repair and maintenance.[2] It is not clear from what budget Zeng and the others secured their funds, although it is worth noting that much of the reconstruction in Nanjing was afforded through a disaster relief fund on the understanding that material reconstruction was an essential service.[3] Similarly, in Shandong, Ding Baozhen managed the work of rebuilding Kong Temple in conjunction with a river conservation project, again suggesting a relationship between disaster relief and temple construction.[4] The temple, it appears, was not being repaired merely for its own sake or to sustain scholarly and ritual associations. It had been provided with a "rationale" as the moral education component of a wider agenda of economic reconstruction and the prevention of rebellion.

The need to assemble a maintenance package from contingency funds arose again in 1897 after the Shandong governor had twice failed to raise the necessary capital. His successor Li Jiantang convinced the court of Guangxu (r. 1875–1908) to provide ten thousand *liang* in support. This amount was not secured from the central treasury but from the Office for Disaster Relief (Shanhouju) and Grand Canal transport revenues appropriated from the Linqing Customs Fund (Linqing Guanjie Kuan). Following Li's transfer to Sichuan, the project was handed over to a third governor, who completed the work by requisitioning timber from the Jining Prefecture and covering financial shortfalls out of the provincial budget. Still, the repairs were limited to the temple's peripherals, including Bridge on Jade Disk Moat, various gates and archways, and the surrounding walls.[5]

The dynasty's final gesture toward Kongzi had a grander intent, and late in 1906 it was decreed that the temple and sacrifice be upgraded to match the sage's promotion to the rank of emperor.[6] Yet it was left to the provincial government to finance the project by releasing fifty thousand *liang* from its reserve fund (*kuping wenyin*). Although well in excess of the amount raised ten years earlier, these funds evaporated with little effect. A lower district official made two excursions to acquire timber in Jiangsu, but records do not mention how or where the material was used. When the project was declared complete in the summer of 1908, the only conspicuous upgrade had been to the roofing tiles of certain temple halls, which had been altered from green to the appropriate shade of imperial yellow.[7]

Read against the background of the last decades of the last dynasty, these measures reflect imperial China in its final stage of decline—fighting rebellions, delegating power and prestige to regional authorities, seeking Confucian restorations, pandering to conservative factions, and finally resorting to desperate appeals to a hollow authority. If these strategies suggest desperation on the part of the Qing, the ongoing investment in Kong Temple also reflects a continuing and not entirely groundless belief that architecture and building could potentially sustain the devotion of imperial constituents. The Manchu investment in that enterprise has been widely interpreted as motivated by self-aggrandizement and undermined by graft, yet the nature of the funding sources tapped for architectural restoration demonstrates a policy of combining Confucianism with infrastructure spending, following the example of Zeng Guofan. Temple restoration had become part of a wider endeavor to address the suffering and humiliation the country had experienced over the previous half century. In retrospect it may have been a waste of resources, but compared to the enormous investment required to build infrastructure, improve education, or fight effective wars, temple reconstruction was a cost-effective measure by which the dynasty could attempt, however vainly, to rally its officials, restore pride, and pursue social stability. Kong Temple had begun to accommodate the emerging discourse on the nation and nationalism.

Kong Temple in Republican China

By the turn of the twentieth century, the Qing dynasty had managed to keep the high-Qing Confucian ritual structure intact. The only significant alterations were a 1904 board of education (*xuebu*) decision to redefine Kongzi's birthday as a state school holiday and a 1906 decision to raise the level of sacrifice for Kongzi.[8] At the time Kong Temple was sufficiently impressive to inspire the Japanese sinologist Uno Tetsuto to describe his visit there in rapturous terms: "Unconsciously, I bowed my head as if I were closely approaching the spirit of the Sage. Without looking I saw his spirit; without listening I heard his voice. And my insignificant little body immediately became absorbed in the great spirit of the Sage."[9] Yet for many others the temple was fast losing its relevance. In stark contrast to Suzhou, where Peter Carroll finds the prefectural Confucian temple to have been an "enchanted bastion" at the heart of a vibrant community of restoration scholarship, in Qufu the county magistrate had to admit to a disappointed Uno that the local tradition of Confucian ritualism was nothing more than "chatter."[10]

When the Republic of China was inaugurated in 1912, Confucian ritual became the subject of heated debate, leading the provisional government to formally suspend state sacrifices. Pro-Confucian associations led by the newly established Kongjiaohui (Association for Confucian Religion) fought back with the help of powerful allies such as General Zhang Xun, a reactionary who brought the Confucian relics under his personal protection as commander of the Yanzhou Garrison in the summer of 1912, and especially President Yuan Shikai, a self-appointed dictator who quashed radical dissent and restored the state sacrifices in June 1913.[11] The following September, Yuan's Ministry of Education followed the Qing precedent of declaring Kongzi's birthday as the Festival of the Great Ensemble (Dachengjie).[12] Schools were organized to conduct appropriate ceremonies in recognition of Kongzi's guiding wisdom, and in Qufu the event was organized in conjunction with the first annual gathering of the Kongjiaohui. The week-long observance extended beyond the formal ceremony to include meetings and study sessions in the Pavilion of the Literary Constellation and an extensive sightseeing itinerary that took the delegates to all the regional sites of interest. Special emphasis was placed on those sites that could be identified with the Confucian classics, such as the Spring and Autumn Terrace (Chunqiutai), named for the Confucian *Spring and Autumn Annals,* and the Rain Altar (Wuyutan), which was illuminated by a public reading of the *Analects* passage: "Fan Chi rambling with the Master under the trees about the rain altars, said, 'I venture to ask how to exalt virtue, to correct cherished evil, and to discover delusions.'"[13]

After the formal inauguration of Yuan's leadership, Duke Kong Lingyi arrived in Beijing, where he offered the president gifts and stele rubbings from Qufu and secured the guarantee that the Kongs would retain their imperial privileges under the republic. True to his word, in February 1914 Yuan declared that the sacrifices would occur on the first *ding* day of fall and autumn as observed in the Qing dynasty. To support this edict, Yuan issued a Worshipping the Sage Code to govern the commemoration of Kongzi and maintain his relics. This code included an annual disbursement of ¥12,000 to afford the direct costs of the sacrifice; ¥2,000 in salary for the duke; ¥30 in salary to each of forty ceremonial officers; and a total of ¥4,000 (tax free) to support the salaries of publicly appointed guards, managers, and workers to replace the indentured Hundred Households that had served as custodians to the Confucian relics for much of the previous two millennia. As to temple maintenance, the code ordered Qufu's magistrate to report any needed repairs to the Ministry of the Interior (Neiwubu).[14]

When Yuan Shikai installed himself as emperor on January 1, 1916, he signaled the bias of his regime by conducting a formal, if somewhat modernized, sacrifice at the Confucian temple in Beijing.[15] His political capital and whatever remained of his moral authority, however, soon disintegrated, and within months of taking the throne the dictator was dead. The Confucian question might well have died with him, but when Parliament resumed it was veteran monarchist Kang Youwei who kept the proposal to adopt Confucianism as a state religion on the table through his influence with President Li Yuanhong and Premier Duan Qirui. Kang's position became a lightning rod for the opponents of Confucianism. Chen Duxiu, the founder and editor of *New Youth,* wrote a particularly scathing reply in his "Refutation of Kang's Letters to Li and Duan" that denied the religious nature of Confucianism and attacked Kang's proposal on the grounds that it contradicted the draft constitution article on religious freedom.[16] Later in 1916 the critiques of Kongzi grew more public and personal when *New Youth* published Yi Baisha's "Commentary on Kongzi." Rather than just questioning the institutional form of Confucianism as others had done, Yi took the bold step of attacking the sage and charging him with promoting autocratic government. This accusation was followed by Wu Yu's argument that the Confucian ethical system had done nothing but "turn China into a big factory for the production of obedient subjects."[17] Hu Shi was so impressed with Wu that he commended him as the "old hero from Sichuan Province" who single-handedly "beat the Kong Family Shop" (*da* Kongjiadian). With that, Hu coined the slogan that would, through several variations, unite generations of anti-Confucian radicals.[18]

In fact, the Confucian conservatives were not quite ready to concede. In 1917 Zhang Xun, who now boasted the supplementary title of honorary president of the Kongjiaohui, briefly restored the Qing dynasty and prompted Kong Lingyi to seek a personal audience with Emperor Puyi.[19] Nor did the failure of that restoration silence the supporters of the sage, and later that year President Feng Guozhang followed Yuan's precedent in leading officials of the Ministries of the Interior, Education, and Civil Administration to conduct the autumn sacrifice to Kongzi in Beijing.[20] Early in 1919 President Xu Shichang and his Ministry of the Interior ignored the growing anti-Confucian rhetoric and approved the addition of two new exegetes to the body of Confucian adepts who received sacrifices in Confucian temples.[21] Later that spring the May Fourth Incident and the following May Fourth Movement, which had grown from an initial anti-imperialist stance into a larger critique of political and cultural conservatism, produced even stronger denunciations from students. Among them, a faction from Qufu Normal College took to the streets of their hometown with demands to close down the "old Kong shop." When Kong Lingyi died in January 1920, however, his family successfully petitioned Xu and other members of the national and provincial political elite to confirm the infant Kong Decheng as the new Duke of Fulfilling the Sage.[22]

The Kong family's dilemma was that the renewed title did not come with renewed funding, and since it had become difficult for the family to collect rent and tax from its land endowments, Kong Temple was deprived of its two most important financial resources.[23] The problem was not entirely unanticipated, and from the beginning of the Republican era various national and regional authorities had been experimenting with alternative means to support the relics. Most of the measures were strong on symbolism and weak on substance, beginning with a 1914 Ministry of the Interior order to "investigate the condition of the sacrificial vessels and instruments" in Kong Temple.[24] Yuan Shikai's Worshipping the Sage Code had implied that the Ministry of the Interior might be called upon to support major repairs or restorations, although when it came time to conduct such repairs in 1915 it was the magistrate who undertook and paid for the restoration of the Hall of Repose and the dredging of Jade Disc Moat.[25] Following policies established by the Qing government in 1909, in October 1916 the Ministry of the Interior ordered regional authorities to assess, register, and preserve the tombs of emperors and sages, ancient garrisons, walls and caves, buildings and temples, pavilions, towers, dikes and levees, bridges, ponds, wells, springs, and "anything related to famous people."[26] The Shandong government responded by compiling a provincial registry that included a comprehensive listing of artifacts in and around Qufu, yet the government could not provide for the material conservation of these sites other than to offer a vague suggestion that "local gentlemen and communities" take responsibility for their upkeep.[27]

No further alterations were made to the structure of heritage management under the Beiyang government, and into the late 1920s heritage conservation continued to be at the sole discretion of the so-called local gentlemen and communities. The irony for Qufu in particular is that one of the more reliable patrons was Zhang Zongchang, who contradicted his reputation as a brutal and ignorant warlord governor by hosting the autumn sacrifice at Kong Temple in 1925. The ceremony was marked by a strong military presence and secured by a Russian armored car, but it succeeded in attracting representatives from the Beiyang government's Ministry of Education; the Kongjiaohui; and scores of militarists, civil administrators, and educators—not to mention the newspaper reporters who covered the event. Beyond the formal ceremony, the event prominently featured Governor Zhang, who performed the *sangui jiukou* and attempted to lead selected delegates through a Confucian study session in the Pavilion of the Literary Constellation before admitting to the assembled: "I'm a military guy, how silly for me to talk about Confucian scripture at the gate of Kong Temple."[28] Zhang nonetheless appreciated the symbolism of his action and further distinguished his regime by sponsoring the renovation of the Hall of Repose, cultivating a close relationship with the Kong family, and helping to clear squatters from the Kong estates. In return Zhang received the privilege of being quartered (together with his infamous harem) in the Kong Family Mansion.[29]

In cultivating the likes of Zhang Xun, Xu Shichang, and Zhang Zongchang, the Kong family was able to retain at least the shades of imperial privilege by negotiating the divided political authority of the early Republican state. With the consolidation of the Guomindang (GMD) mandate and the establishment of the capital at Nanjing, however, the family and their allies found themselves subject to political circumstances beyond their control. In 1927 the University Council (*Daxueyuan*) that served as the Nanjing government's ministry of higher education proposed a set of sweeping changes designed to secularize and nationalize the institutional forms of Confucianism that had survived. As Anna Sun notes, the Republican government fatally undermined the movement to establish a Confucian state religion, or "Confucianity," even demanding that the Kongjiaohui alter its title to the Kongxuehui (Association of Confucian Learning).[30] The University Council further proposed cancelling spring and autumn sacrifices, abolishing the ducal title, confiscating lands previously endowed to the Kong family, and converting Kong Temple to a library and exhibition hall complex.[31] The Ministry of the Interior concurred with the proposal to abolish sacrifice on the grounds that it was "superstitious" and promoted "idol worship" but offered to extend material protection to Confucian temples nationwide with the understanding that Kongzi's character was not at fault and his temples would be repurposed as libraries or educational facilities.[32]

Although the revision was tabled out of respect for those who had a "spiritual attachment to Confucianism," it was of little consolation to the supporters of the institution. Modern Confucians issued harshly worded counterattacks in the press, including a stinging denunciation from Chen Huanzhang, chairman of the Kongjiaohui:

> What did Kongzi do to offend the Republic of China, why should he and his descendants be treated this way? If Kongzi is overthrown how can the Republic of China educate its people? When Japan claimed Shandong during the Paris Peace Conference our ambassador's strongest argument in favor of retaining sovereignty was that Qufu was the birthplace of Kongzi. Since then Chinese Confucians have visited Qufu every year to prove to the world how important Qufu and Kongzi is to the Chinese people. Now the whole world sees Qufu as the Jerusalem of Confucianism, and when the Europeans and Americans recognized that fact they asked Japan to return Shandong to Chinese sovereignty. Our government has declared a mandate to end imperialism, but they treat the Confucians worse than they do the imperialists. In these past two years I visited Europe, America and Japan, and when the foreigners heard about China's movement to abolish [Confucianism] they were shocked. Now is the time to promote nationalism, so why would we abandon our greatest teacher?[33]

Chen Huanzhang's diatribe is unlike any mission statement ever articulated for Kong Temple, but it lucidly identifies the situation in which the temple was enmeshed. Any residual belief in the temple's transcendent qualities had been subsumed by the need to locate the temple within the space of the nation and the international community. In order to justify its existence, it was necessary to relate the temple and its properties to political trends having little to do with Kongzi or his teachings.

The Kongjiaohui also found support from a variety of public and private organizations that traditionally might have been discouraged from patronizing the sage owing to a perceived deficit in moral cultivation. These included at least one division of the National Revolutionary Army and the Chinese Chamber of Commerce. The latter argued that the Confucian relics and ancestral lands of Qufu were the legal property of the Kong family and ought to be recognized as such.[34] The most powerful and deciding voice on the matter belonged to Kong Xiangxi (H. H. Kung), who used his status as a Kong family clansman and chairman of the Ministry of Commerce and Industry to block the University Council initiative and preserve the family privileges.[35]

These loosely affiliated conservative interests had managed to preserve the status quo in Qufu, yet the debate had cast the remains of the local establishment in an unflattering light. The sage and his descendants suffered further damage to their reputation when radical students at the Qufu Second Normal College organized anti-Confucian and anti–Kong family protests on the streets of Qufu in the summer of 1929, culminating in a deeply critical performance of the Lin Yutang play *Kongzi Saw Nanzi* (*Zi jian Nanzi*). The plot of this drama follows an incident recorded in the *Analects* 6:28, in which Kongzi meets privately with Nanzi, consort of the Marquis of Wei. Questioned by his student on the propriety of this action, Kongzi responds: "Wherein I have done improperly, may Heaven reject me, may Heaven reject me!" In Lin's interpretation Kongzi is confronted by a liberal and progressive woman who expresses her thoughts on gender segregation and the qualities of love poetry and entertains him with a suggestive ode. Stricken by her beauty and forward behavior, the sage is briefly caught up in the moment before leaving the stage in nervous consternation.[36]

Lin's treatment of Kongzi was relatively benign, although the Qufu performers played up the drama, portraying the sage as a blackened-face degenerate on the threshold of his most sacred temple.[37] It is difficult to imagine that the sedate town travelers encountered at the time might be the scene of a scandal that would abruptly "shock the nation."[38] Nonetheless, ten days later the students were accused of insulting Japanese cabinet minister (and future prime minister) Inukai Tsuyoshi and GMD legislator Zhang Ji as they jointly addressed a college assembly on the topic, "Kongzi as the Root of the Nation." Kong family elders charged the college headmaster with "insulting the descendant of Kongzi" and demanded that the Shandong Education Office dismiss him and two of the student union leaders. In the aftermath the newspaper *Huabei ribao* commented that this action was a case of "feudal forces attacking modern thought and art"; *Dagongbao* commented more charitably that "Kongzi is being used by politicians to advance their agendas, just as he was used by emperors in the past."[39] Lu Xun would refer to this case as a "total victory" for the Kong family, illustrating his point by publishing a full set of documents relating to the case in the journal *Yusi* (Threads of talk).[40] Kong family influence may have carried the day, however, their institution had suffered irreparable damage in being dragged through the national press.

Insult turned literally to injury during the Central Plains War of 1930 when, less than two years after China had been nominally unified under the GMD, generals Feng Yuxiang and Yan Xishan joined forces against the command of Jiang Jieshi (Chiang Kai-shek). During the counteroffensive GMD troops engaged Yan's forces near Qufu before taking cover behind the city's massive walls. Yan's artillery proceeded to shell Qufu, and by the time the siege was lifted ten days later, Kong Temple, Yan Temple, and Zhougong Temple had each sustained heavy damage. Yan Temple was the most severely affected, yet Kong Temple also suffered punctures and general damage to the roof and eaves of the Hall of the Great Ensemble and the Hall of Repose, damage to the roof and the wall of the Western Cloister, and the destruction of one of its scholar's shrines. Several gates had damage to their eaves. The walls and eaves of the Pavilion of the Literary Constellation, the Gate of the Great Mean, and the Gate of Unified Texts were punctured. There was damage to the balusters and the walls adjoining the Gate of the Lattice Star and widespread injury to the temple's greenery, including the destruction of at least six of the ancient trees. The temple, not to mention the life of the

KONG TEMPLE AND THE MODERN POLITICS OF CULTURE | 137

young duke, was saved from a more tragic fate by the poor quality of the ammunition, which often failed to explode.[41] Jiang Jieshi blamed Yan Xishan for the travesty and claimed that his own troops were under orders to protect the tomb and the temple of Kongzi. He never answered Yan's counterclaim that the GMD force had endangered the temple by placing a machine-gun nest on the roof of one of its buildings.[42]

Serious as the physical damage may have been, it was known that in the past the temple had recovered from far worse. But for the custodians and supporters of Kongzi, the more compelling issue was the irreversible violation of the temple's sanctity. It was part of local lore that throughout the temple's history, no matter how great the prevailing chaos, no army had ever been so bold as to inflict damage directly on Kong Temple. A corpus of apocryphal tales had developed illustrating how potential attackers from the Mongols through to Li Zicheng and the Taiping had arrived at the city gates, only to retreat in awe of the sage or his descendants.[43] In the twentieth century, the temple had been able to withstand the actions of radical students and government meddling, but the mystique was decisively shattered when modern militarists brazenly put their self-interests ahead of the need to protect the relics. A delegation of Korean scholars who embarked on a journey from Seoul to Qufu with the express purpose of "bringing comfort" (*xingwei*) to the sage and his descendants poignantly captured the despair in the Confucian community.[44]

The Central Plains War helped to demonstrate that an artifact like Kong Temple could no longer simply depend on the faith of its constituents, and in the 1930s the conservation logic began to shift decisively away from vague appeals for respect and toward legal protection. Since 1928 the GMD Nanjing government had introduced the Regulations Protecting Scenic and Historical Sites and Antiquities,[45] the Regulation Protecting the Property of All Confucian Temples (June 1929),[46] a Committee for the Protection of Scenic and Historical Sites and Antiquities in Shandong,[47] and the Antiquities Protection Law—drafted June 1930 and implemented July 3, 1931.[48] Even the student radicals at Qufu Normal College had previously demanded that, once expropriated by the state, Kong Temple and Kong Forest should be given permanent protection as national historic sites.[49]

These measures may have helped to deflect contemporary proposals to paint all Confucian temples in the GMD colors of blue and white and to secularize the premises by removing their honorific signage.[50] In general, however, none of these committees, laws, regulations, or proposals had actually managed to protect Kong Temple from damage and depredation. On the other hand, even failed measures could contribute toward defining government responsibility. In early 1931 the Shandong provincial government assessed the temple's needs, identifying an immediate need for ¥100,000 to conduct urgent repairs and preparing an estimate for total restoration that called for funds in excess of ¥1.1 million. Governor Han Fuju took a personal interest in the project and conducted his own inspection of Qufu, but as the provincial coffers were allegedly empty the governor telegrammed Jiang Jieshi and other members of the Nanjing government with a budgetary request. That request was submitted together with a reminder of the state's historical obligation: "For 2,000 years [the temple] has been formally protected by the state, and funds have been provided for its upkeep, as a means to honor culture and respect the ancients."[51] Two weeks later Dai Jitao and Liu Jiwen responded on behalf of the Nanjing government, countering that the temple had not been so badly damaged and required just ¥200,000 to address relatively minor problems with its finish. Dai and Liu nonetheless saw an opportunity to appropriate the Confucian heritage, offering to develop Qufu and Zouxian as "model counties for education" by restoring Kong Temple and the memorial halls of each of the Four Correlates, including the seriously decrepit Yan Temple, the Mengzi Temple and Zisi Shrine in Zoucheng, and the Zengzi Temple in Jiaxiang. Dai also offered to support the restoration of the Kong and Meng family mansions under the condition that the respective families surrender their tax-free farmlands, forgo military and government service, reject non-Confucian religious and political party affiliations, abstain from commerce, and accept state management of Confucian ritual duties and properties.[52]

The negotiation of these conditions would be ongoing and generally unresolved by the beginning of the Anti-Japanese War.[53] In the short term, the interested parties focused on the priority of restoring Kong Temple, beginning with the organization of a Planning Committee for the Repair of Kong Temple in Qufu. Chaired by Han Fuju and including the Shandong provincial government secretary and the respective heads of the provincial Departments of Education, Construction, and Civil Administration, the committee's first order of business was to review the repair estimates. In doing so the Department of Construction was unable to find any savings and in fact raised the estimate to ¥1.3 million for repairs to the Hall of the Great Ensemble alone and submitted an additional budget of ¥700,000 to cover the repairs to the temples and the shrines of Mengzi, Yanzi, and Zisi.[54] In April the GMD Executive Yuan approved the plan in principle and urged the Shandong government to "preserve the ancient relics and promote the national inherent culture." Yet Nanjing's pledge amounted to a mere ¥100,000.[55] It was hoped that the remainder could be secured through a national fundraising campaign organized by Dai Jitao, who contacted the national press and sent telegrams to every government department with the message:

> The Confucius [Kong] Temple in Qufu attracts visitors from all over the world. To promote culture, for more than two thousand years, Chinese governments have paid special attention to its preservation . . . In antiquity, Chinese cultural relics were delicate and brilliant. Their fame even spread to Asia and Europe. If we permit their dilapidation, how can we promote education and advocate national glory?[56]

The appeal was ineffective. By the beginning of 1934, the campaign had raised a paltry ¥35,000, which was earmarked for urgent repairs to Yan Temple.[57] Faced with the inadequacy of the government fundraising campaign, in the summer of 1934 the Executive Yuan and the Ministry of Finance agreed to provide an additional ¥100,000 to conduct basic repairs on Kong Temple; to prepare a display of the "cart, clothes, and ritual wares"; to repair the ancient musical instruments; and to recruit musicians. The cost to the Shandong provincial government was the loss of control over the planning committee, which was surrendered to the nominal leadership of Wang Jingwei and Jiang Jieshi.[58]

As the temple moldered away under stopgap repairs, some devotees found other ways to display their material support. Echoing the earlier initiatives of Zhang Xun, the garrison commander from nearby Yanzhou expressed his dedication by building a highway to Qufu and naming it for Kongzi. The road would have been more efficient had the Kong family allowed it to traverse directly across the open plain; instead they obstinately protected both their lands and their feng shui and caused the road to follow an indirect route that included no fewer than twenty-five detours over its fifteen kilometers. Though the highway was a technical failure, the builders compensated by punctuating the route with Confucian commemorative steles at important intersections and adding a series of classical pavilions to represent ancient Chinese postal stations. Certain wealthy devotees and high-ranking GMD officials paid for these pavilions and inscribed them with Confucian titles. In order of appearance, the traveler on the so-called Kong Highway (Kongdao) would encounter the pavilions of Han Fuju, industrialist Song Feiqing, General Song Zheyuan, and Song Ziwen (T. V. Soong) before arriving outside Qufu's Gate of the Esteemed Sage, where the final pavilion bore the inscription of Kong Xiangxi.[59]

The completion of Kong Highway in early 1934 preceded a more ambitious effort to re-create Kong Temple as a Republican icon. In February of that year, Jiang Jieshi announced his intention to set the nation on a path of pseudo-Confucian moral development through the New Life Movement. To mark the renewed commitment to Kongzi, the Executive Yuan, like the declining Qing dynasty and Yuan Shikai before it, designated the sage's birthday as a memorial day. Having been variously celebrated as the Birthday of Kongzi (Kongzi Danchen); the Festival of the Great Ensemble; and, since 1928, as Kongzi Memorial Day (Kongzi Jinian Ri), it was now determined that the national event would include an annual memorial meeting (*jinian hui*) in Qufu and be known as the Kongzi Birth Memorial Day (Kongzi Danchen Jinian Ri). Where the GMD departed from precedent was in using the occasion to promote awareness of the historical Kongzi, to explain Confucianism, and to clarify the relationship between Kongzi and "the revolutionary thought of National Father Sun Zhongshan (Sun Yat-sen)."[60]

The commemoration was observed by various units of government, military, schools, and other public organizations, but the main event was a modernized "state sacrifice" at Kong Temple. Next to the funeral of Sun Zhongshan in 1929, the ceremony held in Qufu in 1934 stands as one of the highest-profile public events ever held under the auspices of the GMD. Certainly, few other events drew as much attention from the Nanjing government, which sent representatives from every central ministry and state organization. The delegation was led by Ye Chucang and included Chu Minyi and Pu Ti of the Executive Yuan as well as representatives of the Legislative Yuan, the Judicial Yuan, the Examination Yuan, the Control Yuan, the Ministry of the Interior, and the Ministry of Education. Han Fuju led the contingent from the Shandong provincial government, and Qufu County was represented by its magistrate. Students attended in a formal capacity, as did a group of unranked women—significant in that their gender had traditionally been barred from entering the temple within three days of any formal sacrifice. Less formally, the ceremony attracted the press, tourists, and some five thousand spectators from the community.[61] Kong Decheng, still clinging to the title of duke, was present, but he did not perform his hereditary duties, reserving them instead for a "family sacrifice" to be conducted later that evening.[62]

Certain elements of the state ceremony were traditional. Following the late imperial example, the main gates of the temple were left closed, with visitors and officials registering and entering through the side entrance at Gate of Nurturing Essence (Yucuimen). Visitors were required to dress formally, although in place of ceremonial robes the attending officials wore the Republican-fashion black mandarin jacket and long gown, and students and military personnel (including a military band) wore their respective uniforms. The Hall of the Great Ensemble was laid out according to custom with the three animal sacrifices, the Shang and Zhou dynasty ritual bronzes bequeathed by the Qianlong emperor in the eighteenth century, and a selection of the temple's ancient (but mostly nonfunctioning) musical instruments.[63]

Many other elements of the ceremony seem to have been designed to keep distance from tradition, beginning with the simple conversion of the lunar calendar date of Kongzi's birthday (then recognized as the twenty-seventh day of the eighth month) to the solar August 27. On that day in 1934, the public ceremony commenced at 7:00 a.m. in front of the Apricot Altar, with chief officiant Ye Chucang shunning the offerings of silk and wine in favor of a floral wreath placed at the Republican altar. Chai Zuyin of the Central Ceremony Bureau was then asked to read the formal eulogy. The audience thereafter bowed in unison to the tune of whichever ancient musical instruments could still be played, but the ritual dance was not performed.

The ceremony was also significantly shorter than the classical version, ending with a final collective bow at 7:20 a.m. Members of the Kong family and the Kongjiaohui, however, spoke for another two and one half hours before the audience was finally released to pay respects at the tomb of Kongzi.[64]

For all the pageantry of the ceremony, Kong Temple was in alarmingly poor condition and still exhibited much of the damage suffered in 1930. Fresh from the grand Republican rite of 1934, Han Fuju renewed the demand for repair funds, revising the budget to ¥1.15 million, including a request for ¥500,000 in start-up funds.[65] In October the Executive Yuan appointed Dai Jitao to draw up plans for repair and maintenance of Kong Temple and Kongzi's tomb, financed by a one-time payout of ¥200,000 from the central government. Under the plan the provinces and municipalities were expected to contribute through a framework already established for the Sun Zhongshan Mausoleum in Nanjing. Dai further planned to solicit private donations and proposed a tax requiring that students of upper-level colleges and schools contribute ¥1 upon graduation, with ¥0.4 coming from high school graduates and ¥0.2 from middle school graduates. Han Fuju personally donated another ¥40,000, and Jiang Jieshi followed up with a donation of ¥50,000. A committee of central, provincial, and Qufu government representatives and members of the Kong family were to manage the endowments.[66]

On the strength of these funds, the Ministries of the Interior and Education called upon Liang Sicheng to provide a thorough diagnosis of Kong Temple. As China's preeminent architectural historian with a declared preference for relics of the Tang and the Song dynasties, Liang was uninspired by the predominantly Qing-era architecture of Kong Temple, referring to it as an example of "clumsy rigidity."[67] He accepted the commission, however, and produced a book-length study of the complex, complete with recommendations for restoration. Liang's wider mission was to construct a new awareness of architectural heritage through education and scientific evaluation. Peter Carroll points out that Liang's interest in scientifically appraising China's architecture formed part of a broader movement to investigate China's past as a means to transition to modernity.[68] The architect's drawings of Kong Temple illustrate this transition by focusing on the detail of the architecture, dissecting individual structures, and documenting the internal structure. The building thus appears as a technical anatomy rather than a monument (fig. 33). In developing this perspective Liang was proposing a new identity for ancient architecture—one that would demand a new form of conservation. The emphasis, he argued, should not be to facilitate the "merit" of the party that sponsored the restoration by giving it a "bright, new look" (*huanran yixin*) but rather to respect the patina of time and the qualities of the ancient.[69] As he wrote in his Kong Temple study, "[In the past] the only goal was to restore collapsed buildings to make them splendid and grand palaces and mansions: those who would demolish the old ones and build new ones would be praised as possessing unrivalled merits and virtues." In contrast, he argued, "Today what we are seeking is to extend the longevity of the extant structure, unlike ancient people, who demolished the old structures and built new ones."[70]

At the heart of Liang's position was a shift in values that emphasized the work of anonymous craftsmen over the supposed merit of the sponsors of his own time, like Zhang Zongchang, Han Fuju, or Jiang Jieshi. In arguing for preservation, Liang implied that the past was unrepeatable, contradicting those who saw restoration as a means to reinvigorate the current regime. If Liang thought Kong Temple was about to receive a bright, new look under the sponsorship of the rich and powerful, however, he need not have worried. Although his proposed repair budget of ¥797,060 was substantially lower than those submitted by provincial authorities, the Nanjing government failed to follow through on the project.[71]

The 1934 celebration had not gone unchallenged—Hu Shi criticized the GMD for its recidivism through the respected journal *Independent Critic* (*Duli pinglun*): "Pitiful and despairing old revolutionary party! You wanted a revolution, but now that the revolution has achieved these twenty years of unprecedented progress, you disown it. What progress there has been in these two decades was not a gift from Confucius, but the result of a common revolutionary struggle, the result of a common acceptance of the new civilization of a new world."[72] In a caustic rebuke Hu continued: "You can't ride a broken-down cart back to a golden world created by morality that never existed in the first place."[73] The Nanjing authorities paid little heed to Hu's remarks, although in years to come the resolve of the GMD, as well as the public enthusiasm for Republican sacrifice, faded nonetheless. In 1935 the

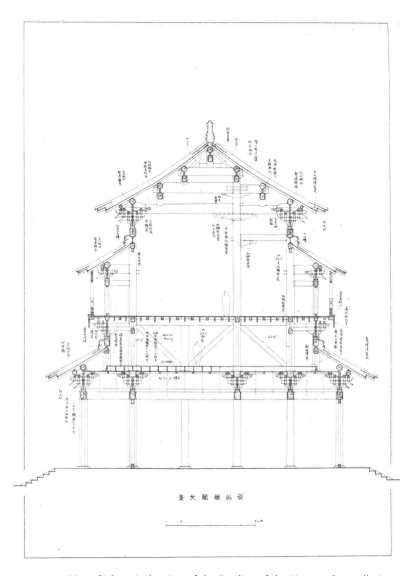

奎文閣橫剖面

FIGURE 33. Liang Sicheng's drawing of the Pavilion of the Literary Constellation (side elevation), prepared for the government of the Republic of China as part of a comprehensive survey of Kong Temple. From Liang Sicheng, *Qufu Kongmiao jianzhu jiqi xiuqi jihua* (Plans for the construction and renovation of Kong Temple in Qufu). Beiping, China: Zhongguo yingzao xueshe, 1935.

sacrifice attracted Governor Han Fuju; the superintendents of the provincial Departments of Civil Administration and Education; the chief of the provincial GMD office; the Kongjiaohui; the respective heads of the Yan, Meng, and Zeng family lineages; and a thousand casual participants. Kong Decheng again represented the Kong family, but by this time he had accepted the anachronism of his status and surrendered the ducal title in exchange for an appointment as chief sacrificial official (*fengsiguan*).[74] President Lin Sen stood to represent the Nanjing government as the master of ceremonies. However, the lack of any additional representation from Nanjing and the lingering effects of a major flood from the Yellow River diminished the ceremony. Qufu had not been inundated, but many of the citizens that might have joined the ceremony were evidently distracted by the wider disaster, as the previous year's attendance of five thousand now fell to only six hundred. Dividing his time between the ceremony and the local refugee camps, Han Fuju used the opportunity to lecture the county magistrate on the need to educate the people, to enforce the ban on footbinding, and to restore social order. In contrast to the traditional argument that temple reconstruction was essential to achieving social stability and enlightenment, Han now declared that any further repairs to Kong Temple would have to wait until after the resolution of the humanitarian crisis.[75]

The repairs were scheduled to resume the following spring, although the new year brought little relief and no additional funding for the project. The state sacrifice of 1936 was essentially a provincial affair, attended by the governor and the usual county and provincial officials but not the ailing President Lin Sen. The former chief officiant Ye Chucang had noted the deficiencies of previous sacrifices, and the Nanjing legislator recorded his intention to sponsor the Great Ensemble Ancient Music Academy to train the 128 musicians and dancers necessary to conduct proper rites. The funding, however, did not materialize, and although the province disbursed ¥2,000 in support, the academy failed to recruit more than a fraction of the acolytes required and was unable to find an instructor who understood the complexities of the ancient music.[76]

As the last trappings of imperial privilege and pageantry unravelled around it, Kong Temple was plunged into limbo when Han Fuju surrendered Shandong to the invading Japanese Imperial Army. Qufu fell without a fight in January 1938, and Kong Decheng joined the fleeing GMD at Hankou, where he could do little but broadcast a message declaring that "Kongzi's thought on war will guide the Chinese people in their fight against the invaders."[77] Now in control of Kong Temple, the Japanese occupiers had their own views about the propaganda value of Kongzi and Kong Temple. This was not a recent revelation by any means, as Japanese agents had promoted Confucian ritual in temples under their control since the early 1930s and had sought favor with the Kong family since the late 1920s. Lacking even Zhang Zongchang's sense of propriety, the Japanese Imperial Army now began to host Confucian studies classes in the sage's home temple, sending Chu Minyi to conduct state sacrifices under the auspices of Wang Jingwei's "puppet" government in 1942 and 1943 and using the puppet China United Provisional Bank to print currency featuring the images of Kongzi and the Hall of the Great Ensemble (fig. 34).[78]

Kong Temple and Qufu's many other Confucian relics survived the war under Japanese management; however, the uncertainty over the status of the temple continued into the postwar era, as the GMD and the Chinese Communist Party (CCP) struggled for control of western Shandong. When the Republican army lost control of Qufu in 1946, the Communists changed the city's name to Chengguanzhen (Wall Pass Town), painted slogans on the

FIGURE 34. Puppet currency issued by China United Provisional Bank, ca. 1930s, illustrated with images of Kongzi and the Hall of the Great Ensemble. Author's collection.

walls surrounding Kong Forest, and abolished some of the Kong family's more objectionable disciplinary measures, but did not expropriate Kong Temple or any of the remaining Kong family properties.[79] When the city was recaptured later that year, the GMD countered by awarding Qufu the more distinguished sobriquet of Yangshengzhen (Town of the Esteemed Saint, after the Ming-era gate of the same name) and erasing the Communist slogans but played no apparent role in the resumed sacrifices of 1947.[80] Kong Decheng made a brief return in 1948, although by the summer of that year the People's Liberation Army (PLA) had overrun the region. With the Communist victory assured, the chief sacrificial officer could do little but prepare for evacuation, leaving his staff to make a desperate last effort to salvage the ancient musical instruments and the priceless Ten Shang Zhou Gifts of Qianlong.[81] The bronzes were placed under the protection of a Catholic church in Yanzhou until they could be evacuated by train. No such train ever arrived. When the artifacts returned to Qufu four years later, Kong Decheng had transferred his mandate to Taiwan, leaving the ancient home of Kongzi firmly under the control of the CCP.[82]

The Homeland of the Four Olds: National Heritage in Communist China

When the PLA entered Qufu for the last time on June 11, 1948, the CCP had not articulated a position on Confucian heritage. Supporters of the sage might have found hope in Mao Zedong's 1938 comments that "we should sum up our history from Kongzi to Sun Zhongshan and take over this valuable legacy."[83] They may also have been heartened by the fact that PLA commanders once observed a sacrifice during their first deployment to Qufu. More dubious assurances may have come from knowing that when the PLA layed siege to Qufu they avoided the use of heavy artillery, allowing GMD defenders to leave the city by the South Gate and meet their executioners on the river bank.[84] Once in control of the city but wary of the potential for counterattack and the ongoing militarization of local society, the PLA posted a bluntly appropriate directive outside the temple that suggested at least a rudimentary appreciation for its heritage value:

(1) Do not fire weapons or shoot birds within the temple,

(2) Do not damage artifacts or trees,

(3) Do not defecate or urinate in the premises,

(4) Note the location of air raid shelters,

(5) Obey the instructions of the security guards.[85]

More formal conservation measures were implemented later that summer when the magistrate established a provisional Cultural Artifact Preservation Office. Under the supervision of a representative from the provincial cultural relics agency, that office was reorganized as the Preparatory Committee for the Preservation of Qufu Antiquities, later the Qufu County Ancient Artifacts Preservation Committee, and given control of the Musical Instruments Warehouse and the Spirit Kitchen as storage facilities for the temple's antiquities.[86] When the Communist mandate stabilized in the early 1950s, the provincial government began to provide Qufu with annual maintenance budgets.[87] These funds initially only covered repairs to the Hall of the Great Ensemble and the cloisters. There was no provision for major renovation until 1957, when the provincial cultural relics office formally implemented protection measures for local heritage sites, including ¥50,000 for major repairs to the roof tiles, beams, and brackets of the main hall.[88] In 1958 Kong Temple received another ¥50,000 for general maintenance and ¥10,000 for repairs to the Pavilion of the Literary Constellation.[89] When British sinologist Joseph Needham visited Qufu in 1958, he found the temple closed to the public but in a state of "excellent preservation and carefully looked after. Much repainting and regilding had been done."[90]

These tentative steps toward conservation demonstrate that Kong Temple was a significant unresolved issue for an administration that had yet to come to terms with history and material culture. When the PRC celebrated its decennial in 1959, the CCP shed its reserve, commissioning a series of building projects that included the restoration of high-profile architectural relics. For its share Qufu received a comparatively large grant of ¥350,000 for general restoration of the so-called Three Kongs (Kong Temple, Kong Forest, and the Kong Family Mansion) and ¥100,000 to prepare the Hall of the Great Ensemble, the Hall of Repose, and the cloisters as a showcase for the soon-to-be reopened temple.[91] To mark the occasion, Guo Moruo, then serving as president of the Chinese Academy of Sciences, made a carefully scripted tour of Qufu. In his dispatch to the provincial newspaper *Masses Daily* (*Dazhong ribao*), Guo declared that the temple was being maintained not out of respect for Kongzi but because Kongzi and his relics were historical entities that could be appreciated independently of modern politics. As a Leftist scholar in the 1930s, Guo had already played an influential role in identifying Kongzi as a progressive reformer working to overthrow an earlier "slave society." He now described Kongzi as a "teacher of great patience, who taught his students according to their needs." As to the temple, the Hall of the Great Ensemble was a unique structure built by "carpenters who never read the Confucian classics," where the bells and drums were "not necessary in teaching the Way." Instead, Guo noted: "The temple hosts an industrial exhibit, it is a good way to shed new light on Kongzi and Mengzi."[92]

In the years to come, there were signs that Guo's position might claim political respectability. Following local protection measures introduced in 1957, the state council extended formal protection to the Three Kongs by adding them to an elite list of national heritage sites in March 1961.[93] By 1962 Kongzi too seemed be on the rise, and the sage's teachings began to garner discussion at academic institutions across the country, including a conference on Confucian thought organized by Liu Shaoqi and Zhou Yang at the Historical Institute of Shandong in Jinan.[94] In light of its modern history, however, and in spite of Guo's inclinations, Kong Temple now represented not just Kongzi but an entire class of conservative political authorities ranging from dynastic emperors to Yuan Shikai, Jiang Jieshi, and now Liu Shaoqi. As the prevailing politics began to shift against Liu and his allies, the temple was about to be dragged into the midst of a major intraparty dispute. Although the impact on Qufu was not immediate, it was inevitable. As during the 1920s, when Qufu attracted both conservative political pilgrims and radical protesters, activists from both extremes would eventually draw a connection between the abstract philosophical debate and the concrete historical relics.

Signs that the "reactionary" Liu faction was preparing to tap the political capital of Kong Temple emerged in September 1964 when both Deng Xiaoping and Peng Zhen traveled to Qufu for a visit to the Three Kongs.[95] This event was not widely reported, but later that year, just days before the sage's publicly recognized birthday, the *Guangming Daily* (*Guangming ribao*) published a barely veiled and inflammatory response calling on readers to "please look at the 'morality' of the 'sage's family.'"[96] That editorial now appears as an opening shot of the Cultural Revolution, which would bring down alleged reactionaries and destroy the remnants of the "old society" that seemed to support them. In being associated with Liu Shaoqi and among the most visible and vulnerable representations of the old society, Kong Temple was in peril once the Cultural Revolution reached its activist stage. On August 25, 1966, three months after Mao had launched the Cultural Revolution with his May Sixteenth Directive, the Qufu Normal College Red Guards realized that although they lived in the very heart of the so-called Four Olds (old customs, old culture, old habits, and old ideas), they had inexplicably failed to lift a finger against the Three Kongs. Intending to make amends, the group descended on Kong Temple and the Kong Family Mansion, only to be turned away by vigorous opposition from local middle school students, political cadres, and workers associated with the temple. When reinforcements arrived from the Tai'an Naval Academy the following day, the new Red Guard coalition encountered an even larger group of defenders who continually frustrated the radicals' efforts in the weeks to come. Without the support of the central government and the PLA, however, local opposition could do little to resist the mounting force of the Cultural Revolution and the Four Olds campaign. On November 7, 1966, the Beijing Normal University Mao Zedong's Thought Red Guard's Mount Jinggang Brigade issued its manifesto, "Declaration of the Crusade against Kongzi":

> The heinous Kong Family Shop ruled and enslaved the Chinese people for 2000 years. It drank the blood of countless working people, swallowed up hundreds and thousands of lives, earning innumerable blood debts for its monstrous crimes. . . . Today we raise the great red banner of Mao Zedong Thought and solemnly declare to the people of the nation, we will rebel against the Kong Family Shop and set it on fire. We will pull Kong "suwang" [the uncrowned king] off his horse and crush him. We will overthrow all the representatives of the old forces, your Dukes of Zhou and Lu, Zongsheng [Zengzi] and Fusheng [Yanzi], your imperial edicts, all your imperial gifts can go to hell. . . . [Chairman

Mao wrote] "we count the mighty as no more than muck."[97] This means we must shit on the head of the "saint," open fire on the Kong Family Shop, open fire on the old world, and defeat it.[98]

When Red Guard leader Tan Houlan led the Beijing Normal University Brigade to Qufu on November 10, the Qufu County Committee realized that its position was no longer tenable and made a final appeal to the state council. In a sequence of two telegrams, the Communist Party Central Cultural Revolution Leadership Committee ordered the preservation of ancient steles and extended protection to the Three Kongs so that they might be converted to a museum like Sichuan's Rent Collection Courtyard. However, it granted the Red Guards permission to dig up the tomb of Kongzi and to destroy all of the Qing dynasty steles.[99] Over the next two weeks, the Red Guards reorganized as the Rebuke Kongzi Contact Station and carried out their work with dedication. On November 13 the mob forced its way into the temple, demolished an agricultural exhibit set up in a hopeless effort to shield the Hall of the Great Ensemble, and plastered the temple statuary with slogans declaring that, among other things, Kongzi was the "#1 Hooligan" (*touhao da hundan*). Two days later the Red Guards reassembled to smash the 1966 state council's "imperialist plaque," pulling it down and ceremoniously crushing it with sledgehammers. Having destroyed this last vestige of state protection, the Red Guards swarmed the temple, smashing Qing steles, destroying the statues of the Twelve Savants and the Four Correlates, and further desecrating the effigy of Kongzi (fig. 35). Two weeks later the Rebuke Kongzi Headquarters organized an Utterly Smash the Kong Family Shop Ceremony, loaded the remains of the Kongzi effigy onto a truck, and paraded it through the town before throwing it and many other relics into a bonfire.[100] The next day the Red Guards sent an exultant telegram to their leader:

Dearest Chairman Mao,

One hundred thousand members of the revolutionary masses would like to report a thrilling development to you: we have rebelled! We have rebelled! We have dragged out the clay statue of Kong the Second Son (*Kong lao'er*); we have torn down the plaque extolling the "teacher of ten-thousand generations"; we have leveled Kongzi's grave; we have

smashed the stelae extolling the virtues of the feudal emperors and
kings, and we have obliterated the statues in the Confucius Temple![101]

The Beijing Red Guards thereafter declared their work finished and returned
home, although local Red Guards and common vandals continued the destruction in the months to come, wrecking the intricate altars that remained
in the Hall of the Great Ensemble and the two cloisters and smashing many
of the stelae that had been ordered preserved.[102] The stele recording the conversation between Kong Kejiah and Zhu Yuanzhang was reprieved, allegedly because Tan Houlan associated the peasant-bandit founder of the Ming
dynasty with Mao Zedong. Few other artifacts could be similarly construed.
Just meters away the towering Chenghua and Hongzhi steles were pulled
down and broken in two, and by the end of the year the temple grounds were
littered with the broken fragments of ancient tablets (fig. 36).[103] For Kong

FIGURE 35. "Kongzi, the #1 Hooligan."
Effigy of Kongzi defaced in 1966 and
later destroyed. Photographer
unknown.

FIGURE 36. Imperial stele, severely damaged during the Cultural Revolution and pieced back together, presumably in the late 1970s.

Temple most of the drama ended by early 1967, although one final threat emerged in 1968 when the Preparatory Team for Renovating the Three Kong Sites Office developed a plan to permanently "oppress the old nest of Kongzi." This plan, which never came to fruition, would have replaced the front portion of the temple with a massive Long Live the Victory of Mao Zedong's

Thought Exhibition Hall and used the remaining structures to commemorate the "modern struggle between Confucians and Anti-Confucians."[104]

In the late 1960s, the situation in Qufu began to stabilize, with the temple receiving limited financial support as early as 1967 and a relatively generous support package of ¥130,000 in 1970.[105] A second wave of anti-Confucianism cut that funding short. In 1971 Kong Temple shared just ¥10,000 in state support with the tomb of Shao Hao, and although funding recovered slightly in 1972 the release of a highly laudatory biography of the arch anti-Confucian Qin Shihuang in that year implied that Kongzi was still persona non grata. That same year Guo Moruo published an article in the political journal *Red Flag* updating his periodization of history and placing Kongzi on the wrong side of the ancient transition from "slave society" to "feudal society." Because Kongzi was on record as having opposed the inscription of legal codes on tripods and ordering the execution of the "Legalist" Shaozheng Mao, he was judged a supporter of slavery and a reactionary opponent of the comparatively progressive Feudalists.[106] The anti-Kongzi movement reached new heights in September 1973, beginning with the organization of the Forum on Criticizing Kongzi and leading to mass rallies in Beijing by the beginning of 1974. At that time the CCP Central Committee had begun to establish a link between Kongzi and Lin Biao, using as key evidence the allegation that before his failed attempt to oust Chairman Mao and seize power Lin and his wife had decorated their quarters with scrolls that extolled the Confucian principle of "Restrain oneself and restore the rites" (*keji fuli*).[107]

The rhetoric of the Anti-Lin Biao Anti-Kongzi (*pi*-Lin, *pi*-Kong) movement was no less vitriolic than the 1966 Red Guard campaign, although the more recent campaign was less destructive. Instead of seeking to destroy the Confucian relics in order to declare the singular supremacy of Mao Zedong, the radicals were now more interested in using the Three Kongs as material evidence of the crimes committed by their "reactionary" enemies. Having narrowly survived a regime that claimed legitimacy through heritage destruction, Kong Temple was again subject to a regime that recognized, however perversely, the political value of conservation.

In setting Kongzi as a reactionary protector of the old order and establishing the traitorous Lin as a Confucian, it was possible to re-create both as supervillains. As seen during the criticism of Liu Shaoqi, one of the most effective means to prosecute the counterattack was to appropriate the relevant historical relics. The local arm of the campaign was launched on February 7, 1974, when the Qufu County Cultural Artifact Management Committee, the Shandong Provincial Museum, the History Department of Qufu Normal College, and the Shandong University History Department invited some seven hundred "worker, peasant, soldier representatives" to assemble in front of the Hall of the Great Ensemble for an inaugural Criticize Lin Biao and Kongzi rally.[108] In March the Shandong Department of Propaganda and Culture used the Kong Family Mansion to host a *Criticize Lin Biao, Criticize Kongzi* exhibit that illustrated the oppressiveness of the former residents. For its part Kong Temple was interpreted as symbolic of the higher authority of the imperial dynasties. One representative pamphlet portrayed the architecture as emblematic of "the reactionary ideals of feudal rulers, its entire design, every pavilion and every gate reflects the feudal controlling class and their respect for Kongzi." The Gate of the Lattice Star, for example, demonstrated how reactionary rulers deified Kongzi. The Hall of the Great Ensemble preserved Kongzi as a political "mummy" (*jiangshi*) in order to "delude the people and perpetuate their reactionary rule." The cloisters were expanded in the Qing dynasty, exposing the "desperate ploy to use the Way of Kongzi and Mengzi to stop the imperial decline," and the Apricot Altar represented Kongzi's "black line of 'the student, having completed his learning, should apply himself to become an official (*Analects* 19.13).'" While excoriating the former ruling class, interpreters were careful to include by name the modern criminals—noting that when he visited the Hall of the Sage's Traces in 1952 the "traitor agent provocateur scab Liu Shaoqi" sang: "Great Kongzi, Great Kongzi, our people's government should also sacrifice to him." The books stored in Lu Wall were said to represent the ancient attempt to "restore the reactionary slave owners"—sentiments, it was asserted, that were identical to Lin Biao's counterrevolutionary principles.[109]

Little qualitative evidence exists from which to draw a more nuanced portrait of the local campaign, although comparing two photos of the time may suggest the tensions that defined the Qufu campaign. The first looks down on the front of the Hall of the Great Ensemble and captures the February 7 rally at the moment an unknown speaker addresses the assembly. From that perspective the hall appears to perform as it always has—framing and amplifying the speaker and diminishing the observer to generate a sense of awe and perhaps even an aura (fig. 37). However, a second photograph, taken from ground level with the Apricot Altar in the background, suggests the difficulty with using architecture as a political tool. In the foreground of the image a middle-aged man leads a small group, presumably in denouncing Kongzi and Lin Biao, but with little of the fury that the leaders of the Anti-Confucius Campaign had sought to inspire. Fists are weakly raised, and the facial expressions of these "workers and peasants" betray a deep uncertainty over what has drawn them into the drama of twentieth-century Confucianism (fig. 38). Amid the most intense politics to have involved Kong Temple since the sixteenth century, the Apricot Altar remains aloof, a present absence that neither confirms nor denies the passions of the day.

Rehabilitation and Political Appropriation

Kongzi of more than 2,000 years ago was a pseudonym with which they attacked by insinuation contemporary people. They wanted to knock down this person today, and this person was "Kongzi", they wanted to knock down that person tomorrow, and that person would be "Kongzi." . . . They invariably took "Kongzi" as a lump of clay to mould at will a double of that person in the contemporary era according to their needs.[110]

When political trends finally turned against the Cultural Revolution and its Gang of Four leaders in 1976, they also began to turn in favor of Kong Temple. As observed in the above quote, published in *People's Daily* at the end of that same year, Kongzi was now recognized as the unfortunate proxy of a disenfranchised political faction. Now that this faction had returned to political viability, Kongzi and the temple that best represented him would continue to serve as a proxy, albeit in a far more subtle and constructive manner. In October 1977, one year after the formal conclusion of the Cultural Revolution, the Qufu Cultural Relics Office received approval for a full-scale restoration of the Pavilion of the Literary Constellation.[111] In May 1978, with Deng Xiaoping vying for control of the state, the embattled vice-premier

把批林批孔的斗争进行到底

FIGURE 37. Anti-Lin Biao, Anti-Confucius Campaign, Peasant, Worker, Soldier assembly in front of the Hall of the Great Ensemble, 1974. Xinhua tongshu she, *Juebu yunxu kai lishi daoche* (1974), 42.

received a strong gesture of support when Li Xiannian became the first senior leader to visit Kong Temple since Deng's own appearance there fourteen years earlier.[112] Having been a focal point of the Cultural Revolution, Kong Temple now stood for rehabilitation, and through rehabilitation the temple inevitably gained an association with the new politics of "reform and openness" (*gaige kaifang*) that Deng would confirm at the Third Plenum of the Eleventh National Congress later that year.

When Kong Temple reopened to domestic and international visitors in 1979, the host province and city carefully avoided the ideological pitfalls that had nearly doomed the temple in the past. That milestone was nonetheless essential to the general rehabilitation of Kongzi and the renewal of

FIGURE 38. Anti-Lin Biao, Anti-Confucius Campaign, Apricot Altar, 1974. Photographer unknown, after *Jielu 'sanKong' zui'e: pipan Lin Biao, Kong Qiu* Beijing, Wenwu chubanshe, 1974.

Confucianism as a subject of academic discussion, which would in turn help to draw the Confucian relics back into the public eye. The rehabilitation of Kongzi had been gathering momentum in academic circles since 1976, when historian Pang Pu issued his "Critique of the Gang of Four's False Criticism of Kongzi."[113] While the critique was more of a repudiation of the gang's historical method than an explicit call to support Kongzi, in 1978 Pang raised the stakes by calling for a "Re-evaluation of Kongzi Thought."[114] In 1979 Zhang Dainian followed with "An Analysis of Kongzi's Philosophy," and in 1980 Li Zehou published his "Re-evaluation of Kongzi."[115] Later that year Qufu Normal College (later Qufu Normal University) joined the trend by sponsoring a Symposium on Kongzi Studies and publishing Yan Beiming's essay "Correctly Evaluate Kongzi" in its journal *Shandong Studies*.[116] As one of the original participants in the 1962 Jinan Conference, Yan had been harshly criticized by more radical intellectuals for arguing that although Kongzi was a reactionary, his ideas were nonetheless progressive. In 1981 Yan revised this position in repeat publications of his article "Rehabilitate Kongzi, Down with the Kong Family Shop," arguing that "Kongzi was not the boss of the antique shop. The shop was kept running by the feudal system that ignored the progressive, reformist aspects of Confucianism and upheld its backward aspects."[117]

By most accounts Qufu's civic leaders had historically served less as the sponsors of enlightened Confucianism than as protectors of the so-called antique shop, but now the city's educational, cultural, and political institutions would seize the opportunity to amend that reputation and stake a claim to this mounting renaissance. Although Qufu Normal College was better known for its history of radically rejecting Confucianism, the institution now began to take a leadership role in reviving interest in the sage. In 1979 the college opened a new Kongzi Research Section, sponsored a second Kongzi Studies Symposium in 1983, and gained the support of the provincial government in creating an expanded Kongzi Research Institute in 1984. Also in 1984, the local Confucian studies enterprise moved to the national stage with the formation of the China Kongzi Foundation. With its head office located in the Kong Family Mansion and many of its founding members drawn from among politically connected Kong descendants, regional and provincial politicians, provincial and local educators, and local heritage conservators, the foundation had a strong local base. This base reflected the organization's original goals, which included building a Kongzi research center and Kongzi museum, researching and publishing material concerning Kongzi, protecting and restoring Kongzi's relics, and recognizing the accomplishments of those who made special contributions to the study of Kongzi.[118] Three of those five goals specifically concerned building and conserving Qufu's heritage infrastructure, yet in naming Vice-Premier Gu Mu of the CCP and President Kuang Yaming of Nanjing University, respectively, as honorary chairman and chairman, the foundation was able to represent those interests on the national and the international stage. In 1987 Gu Mu addressed Qufu's concerns directly to the state council, advising that "in order to meet the needs of domestic and international Kongzi research, it is necessary to create an organization in the hometown of Kongzi that combines antiquity protection, scholarly research, museum displays, to construct relevant architectural facilities, and to gradually build Qufu into a global center for academic research on Kongzi and Confucianism and Chinese cultural tourism."[119]

Throughout the 1980s and the 1990s, Kong Temple's political credentials were burnished by a stream of high-profile public visitors, including party elders like Deng Yingchao, international leaders such as Singapore prime minister Lee Kuan Yew, party ideologues like Hu Qiaomu, and political heavyweights such as Wan Li and Zhao Ziyang. Li Ruihuan appeared in 1990, leaving ¥8,000,000 in funding to renovate the Kong Family Mansion archives.[120] Li Peng visited in 1991, leaving a couplet inscribed "Extract the Essence of Kongzi's Thoughts; Develop the Excellent National Culture." Having already given his explicit support to Confucian ideology through an address to the Kongzi Foundation's Beijing branch in 1989, in 1992 Jiang Zemin ended his tour of Qufu with the advice, "Build the Famed Cultural City; Make Qufu's Economy Prosper."[121]

China's political elite is naturally entitled to heap praise upon Kongzi and to promote Confucian cultural activities, but as with the Qianlong emperor, Zhang Zongchang, the Japanese Imperial Army, or Li Xiannian, this form of engagement must be understood as politically motivated. Kong Temple was being used as historical evidence of the material progress that could be achieved under an authoritarian "Confucian" managerial regime—the point being that similar results might be achieved under the authoritarian leadership of the CCP. These policies were normally implied rather than stated, although when the Three Kongs were nominated for recognition as a United Nations Educational, Scientific and Cultural Organization (UNESCO) World Heritage Site in 1994, this rationale was made explicit. In contrast to the premodern emphasis on Kong Temple as a symbol of cultural continuity, the official nomination stated that the Three Kongs complex should be valued not just for its "outstanding artistic value" but because it represented "China's progress in material civilization in terms of architecture" and the "huge impact" of Confucianism on "modern ideological and management systems." Kong Temple could also validate China's rising international status through reference to its master's influence on Korea, Japan, Vietnam, and even Europe, where Confucianism was said to have exerted "a great impact on the Enlightenment Movement."[122] In claiming that at least some of the roots of the present-day political economy are lodged in Kong Temple, these statements imply an uninterrupted continuity in Chinese material, ideological, and "management" culture from ancient times until the present. Although the Chinese government would not formally adopt the term for another decade, Kong Temple was already becoming enmeshed in a "soft-power" initiative that would see Chinese cultural capital and the renewed interest in Kongzi extended to the global stage.

China's UNESCO agents were not the first to file claims of extraordinary significance on Kong Temple's behalf. Indeed, such plaudits, or more rarely the reactions against them, had been part of the temple's identity for more than two thousand years. Just as the premodern narrative studiously excluded or marginalized evidence that contradicted the preferred narrative, the new narrative did not recognize that China had been deprived of consistent progress, ideology, and management through most of its modern era. Owing to its symbolic ties with political conservatism, Kong Temple's reputation and material condition had shifted repeatedly between honor and integrity and ignominy and depredation—all depending on fluctuations across the political spectrum. Looking back over the twentieth century, Michael Nylan points out that each of the four Confucian movements (May Fourth movement, New Life movement, Cultural Revolution, New Confucianism—"two for, two against") took place in the context of national identity crises and demands for rapid modernization. Each movement called

for a dynamic transformation of traditional culture, although these movements originated not from a careful consideration of Confucianism but
rather on slogans and "messianic" political programs in which the terminol-
ogy of Confucianism coexisted with nation, tradition, and modernity.[123]
The fate of Kong Temple was directly tied to these movements. By the same
token, its material circumstances depended not on any particular concern
for heritage but on the need to demonstrate the sincerity of the political
program by acting it out through building, neglecting, or outright abusing
the architecture.

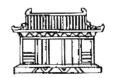

6 | Kong Temple Inc.

I N HIS STUDY of *The Heritage Crusade and the Spoils of History* (1996), David Lowenthal observes that modern heritage "aggravates chauvinistic excess; it mushrooms into mindless incoherence; it sells what should be sacred and beyond price; it is run by exclusive elites; and it distorts the true past."[1] All of these charges could be leveled at modern Qufu, where Kong Temple now anchors a heritage industry that has permanently altered the historical environment, spawned frivolous amusements, and marketed Kongzi quite literally and without irony as a regional brand. Few visitors today would see the temple as vital to the modern development of nation and commerce in the way that Zheng Guangwan long ago perceived it to be the place where the "essences of the cosmos converge." And yet, in spite of its modern history of exploitation, Kong Temple still commands respect. A century after the dissolution of its imperial credentials, the temple also holds enough influence to frustrate the claims of political authorities and subvert the best-laid plans of developers and conservationists alike. In distorting the process by which collective decisions are made about the past, Kong Temple actually conflicts with the heritage enterprise, and conversely, in generating such influences and contradictions Kong Temple assures its own survival.

This chapter will chronicle a few of the ways in which the erosion of a principle of aesthetics informed by the emulation of antiquity left Qufu's historical relics subject to an ambivalent program of development that has often been erratic and contradictory. Rebuilding, revision, and rectification are not new phenomena, and the defenders of neoritualism are right in pointing out that all Chinese traditions have been made anew according to the needs of the time. Except that in place of a principle of aesthetics that once suppressed development, politics, and commerce, it is now presumed that the value of heritage can only be realized through continuous development.

Duanfang Lu explains the wider phenomenon of aggressive destruction and construction as being driven neither by some vague respect for the past nor mindless demolition but by a "perpetual search for an alternative future" that assumes an "inner drive for creative destruction." In attempting to build modernity on the basis of real and perceived scarcity, China's "Third World" development strategy abhorred waste and dictated that urban space be reconstructed, reproduced, and transformed in the interest of advancing social order.[2]

Liang Sicheng had sought to counter the degradation of the historical artifact as well as the wider built environment by introducing the concept of conservation and in situ preservation. The measure would have taken control from the hands of politicians (or later commercial developers) and given it to conservators. Those conservators might have made the same "irrational" decisions as traditional caretakers who were known to reject economic or political opportunities in order to sustain the creative energy of ritual. Liang failed in his wider mission, leaving the Chinese urban environment vulnerable to the process of aggressive demolition and rebuilding, whereby only select relics could be retained and maintained as heritage under the condition that they symbolically or directly support economic productivity or other doctrines construed as socially progressive. In the twentieth century, Kong Temple lost the sense of authenticity drawn from its ritualized past and became subject instead to a political discourse that was more concerned with claiming and controlling the temple's space than upholding an aesthetic appreciation for time and the continuity of virtue. Yet even in the modern era, Qufu's ancient relics have never fully succumbed to political or economic opportunism because politics and economics have failed to resolve the temple's problematic history. Even stripped down and remade as heritage, the old home of Kongzi presents a continual challenge to modernity, thus retaining the traces of the perpetually actual aura that have sustained the relic throughout its notable history.

The Tourist Discovery of Qufu

As shown in previous discussion, Kong Temple had a long experience with pilgrimage before the twentieth century. Given the temple's exclusivity, however, the experience of traveling to Qufu was quite removed from that of the mass pilgrimages that involved destinations like Mt. Tai. Unlike the deities of this sacred mountain to the north, Kongzi was never a popular cultic figure, and although the sage also had his monuments on Mt. Tai, the common pilgrim seems to have felt little compulsion to continue southward to pay respects at his primary temple. Had they done so, they would in any case have been dissuaded by the local elitism. Consequently, Qufu never developed as a popular tour destination and never obtained the reputation or infrastructure necessary to make an easy transition to tourism once that elitism started to fade in the early twentieth century.

Travel conditions further complicated Qufu's tourist development. Even for those who were well equipped, the task of reaching Qufu was quite arduous. Chinese travel writers typically did not belabor their readers with descriptions of these conditions—Wanggiyan Linqing, for instance, merely noted three days of travel from Tai'an and an uneventful stay at a guesthouse.[3] Foreigners, in contrast, were more forthcoming in their tales of individual suffering. When Reverend J. Edkins and traveling companion James Legge visited in 1873, they reported that it was necessary to travel from the north by the native variety of cart that, having no springs, jolted violently across the limestone ridges from which the foundations of Kong Temple had been hewn. A second challenge facing casual visitors to Qufu was that most of the local attractions simply were not open to the public. Edkins and Legge were able to facilitate their visit through a mutual acquaintance's letter of introduction to the Duke of Fulfilling the Sage, and on the strength of that letter they were assigned officers of the third and fourth rank to lead them through the temple.[4] W. A. P. Martin arrived at the temple without such credentials and had the door literally slammed in his face—an act that he correctly interpreted as a demand for payment.[5] In 1891 Alexander Armstrong was either less wealthy or more easily dissuaded. He successfully negotiated a tour of the Kong Forest for the cost of five hundred "cash" (i.e., copper coins, haggled down from an initial demand for ten thousand) yet failed to gain an audience with the duke and never gained entrance to the temple.[6] In 1900 Ernst Von Hesse-Wartegg was likewise refused entry upon arrival, but on pledging to remain in Qufu as long as it took to get official credentials from Beijing, the adventurer was able to force the issue and become, by his reckoning, the first "white man" ever to penetrate the temple's inner sanctum.[7]

When sinologists V. M. Alexeev and Edouard Chavannes arrived in 1907, the situation had not significantly changed—it was still necessary to travel the entire distance from Tai'an by cart and to present credentials to the magistrate before being admitted to the temple proper.[8] With the construction of the Tianjin-Pukou Railway in 1908–1913, such journeys were eased considerably, and they might have been eased further had Duke Kong Lingyi not taken exception to the arrival of a German surveying team intent on driving a railway through Qufu and uncomfortably near to the tomb of Kongzi. Rising to the occasion, the duke made what has come to be known as a definitive stand against modernity, addressing the throne and arguing that the railway would "shake the tomb of the Sage," "stop the Sage's very pulse," and prevent the ancestors from resting in peace.[9] The success of the duke's protest meant the line would take a wide detour around Qufu, passing instead through Yanzhou and depositing Qufu's passengers at a quaint Wilhelmine station house on a deserted stretch of track eleven kilometers from the city center. The connecting journey to Qufu could take up to two hours, and, as the Sishui River had no bridge, travelers were forced to either wade through the stream or pay to be carried.[10]

By 1915 Qufu was nonetheless securely on the tourist map. The itinerary advertised by the Imperial Japanese Railway Guide in that year suggested that the traveler leave Jinan on the 7:30 a.m. train, arriving at Qufu Station five hours later. The visitor could then complete the journey by cart and spend the afternoon visiting the main attractions of Qufu, including Kong Temple, which was open to visitors, and Kong Forest, which was not, except to those who had proper letters of introduction from the local authorities or other "persons of distinction." Alternatively, access could be gained by "tipping the guardian."[11] At the end of the tour, travelers were advised to make their way back to Qufu Station, where they would wait for the 1:45 a.m. train to Tai'an, ascend Mt. Tai at first light, and descend in time to catch the 3:29 p.m. train back to Jinan. This itinerary did not include time for sleeping, although this feature was not advertised as a drawback since it permitted the visitor to avoid the "indescribably filthy" local inns that were the only accommodations available to the general public.[12]

The escalation of conflict and banditry in North China during the 1920s pushed Qufu off the tourist itinerary until 1928, when the completion of the Guomindang Northern Expedition revived the possibility of casual visitation. Seeing the return of some modest demand after that time, the Kong family and the Shandong provincial government began to consider the merits of building Mengzi and Kongzi memorial halls in Zouxian and Qufu, respectively, along with a museum and a library facility to house the antiques and the literature collected by the Kong family.[13] The tour traffic was never sufficient to justify the realization of these projects, but the increasing numbers of visitors did make it necessary for the local managers to implement basic conservation measures to protect Kong Temple, especially the prized Han-Tang steles in the Gate of Unified Texts, from ardent seekers of stele rubbings. There was nothing new in this—the steles had long since been eroded by generations of antiquarians. The managers nonetheless moved to curtail rubbing by isolating the steles behind high picket fences and pasting them over with paper strips that warned off souvenir hunters. The Pictures of the Sage's Traces in the Hall of the Sage's Traces were also off-limits. In lieu of authentic rubbings, the temple gatekeepers offered books of reproduction rubbings for $1.50. Copies of other texts and images, such as Wu Daozi's famous *Picture of Kongzi as Itinerant Teacher* (*Kongzi xingjiao tu*), were also available at local shops for ten cents, as were facsimiles of the calligraphy of the late Kong Lingyi.[14]

The marginal recovery in tourism in the early 1930s was accompanied by marginal improvements in the tourist facilities. Qufu Station was served by an inn consisting of three doorless rooms furnished with straw mattresses and savage dogs, although the city was still without anything that qualified as a hotel.[15] The situation did improve somewhat by 1934, when a railway hotel was constructed at Yanzhou, and Qufu had gained at least one respectable guesthouse. The Datong Inn, located on Gulou Street near the temple and mansion, catered to both domestic and international tourists. However, its fifteen rooms were seldom filled to capacity, and the majority of the tenants were in fact antique dealers from Beijing.[16] Transportation continued to present a challenge. Those who did make the effort to reach Qufu had the option of disembarking at Qufu Station and continuing via mule cart, donkey, or rickshaw. A guidebook of the time warned that the road was rough, the dust thick, and the rickshaw drivers unscrupulous. Alternatively, one could travel a slightly longer distance after disembarking at Yanzhou Station. In 1933–1934 this became the favored route owing to the construction of the Kong Highway, but this golden age of transportation was short—by 1936 the road had so deteriorated that motorized passage from Yanzhou took a bone-shaking forty minutes.[17]

Just as Qufu was beginning to develop a rudimentary infrastructure, escalating tensions brought on by a growing Japanese military presence broke the promise of sustainable tourism. By May 1937 it was only possible to visit the local relics as part of a tour group—in one case organized by a nearby county-level "constructive citizenship training" (*jianmin shunji*) program.[18] The group's declared "anti-imperialist fervor" had little influence on the trajectory of events, and later that year Qufu and Kong Temple succumbed quietly to Japanese occupation. The temple remained open to Axis civilians throughout the occupation, although the relentless conflict that continued beyond the Anti-Japanese War and into the late-1940s thoroughly suppressed any possibility of developing a tourist industry during the remaining years of the mainland republic.[19]

Stagnation continued to grip Qufu into the first years of the Communist era, when parts of the temple were left more or less open to the pedestrians and loiterers who had access to the convenient shortcut through its side gates, as well as the park-like setting of the front courtyards. The core facilities beyond the Gate of the Great Ensemble were technically closed for repairs, but under the guidance of provincial authorities, the Chamber of Gold and Silk, the Hall of Fathering the Sage, and the Fathering the Sage Hall of Repose were reorganized to house local artifact exhibits that opened to the public on May 4, 1949.[20] As the political situation continued to stabilize, the temple began to receive occasional visits from the upper echelons of the Communist Party such as Mao Zedong and Liu Shaoqi and foreign delegates from India, Burma, Afghanistan, Mongolia, the Soviet Union, Romania, Yugoslavia, Indonesia, and Norway.[21] When British embassy staff arrived in 1956 they reported open hostility and were sharply discouraged from touring the temple. When the ambassador arrived a week later he commented that while Chinese tourists were nowhere to be found, his visit was "in every way delightful."[22]

While these records indicate, at worst, an ambiguous official attitude toward Kongzi's relics, the trickle of visitors arriving in the 1950s could not sustain the temple as a public artifact. With no ritual or tourist activity to speak of, the Qufu municipal government was compelled to find useful applications for Kong Temple and the Kong Family Mansion. These uses could be quite utilitarian—in 1954 it was observed that the Gate of the Lattice Star was closed and its courtyard put to the task of drying grain.[23] The Qufu County Ancient Cultural Artifact Management Association led a more formal occupation. In 1956 the association permitted exhibitions and classes on archaeology to be held in the Pavilion of the Literary Constellation and the Chamber of Odes and Rites and opened an exhibition of *Historical Artifacts, Calligraphy of Qing Dynasty Celebrities of Qufu,* and *Exhibit of Donated Artifacts* in the duke's former Abstinence Quarters after 1958.[24]

With China's turn toward economic liberalism in the early 1960s, the temple began to resume its role as a historical tourist center. Although growth was stunted by any measure, the temple's managers did take concrete steps toward building a tourist infrastructure. The Hall of Repose became the temple's primary display space, hosting the *Qufu Historical Artifact Exhibit* while the Hall of the Great Ensemble exhibited a complete set of ancient musical instruments alongside the statues of Kongzi and his disciples.[25] When the local government revived the traditional Linmen Festival as a three-day agricultural trade fair in 1962, the temple received some thirty thousand visitors daily.[26] The majority of those were presumably local residents eager for a glimpse of their problematic patrimony, although Qufu's leaders also sought a wider clientele by opening a branch of the National Travel Society and taking over management of the Kong Mansion Hotel in 1964.[27]

These initiatives would shortly come to a halt with the beginning of the Cultural Revolution, yet Qufu's experience with tourist development over its first fifteen years of public management demonstrates an ongoing contradiction between local and national authorities over how to use the temple. Conservation and political usage, as shown previously, had fluctuated as a state priority, and yet the state had no inclination to exploit the site for commercial purposes. Local authorities, on the other hand, eager to find a practical application for the temple, were concerned with developing an infrastructure, occupying the premises, and claiming ownership of the relic and its resource potential.

Once the Cultural Revolution passed, city managers faced the renewed problem of taking an object known for producing symbolic capital and making it generate income while satisfying both state ideological and local conservation interests. This delicate operation would involve a multipronged strategy. First, local and regional political authorities needed to secure state funding by promoting the idea of Kongzi as national and international heritage; second, they also needed to promote Qufu as a national and international tourist destination. State-funded "heritage conservation," therefore, had to be balanced against the needs of modern tourists and their vastly greater revenue potential.[28] Finally, Kongzi had to be made relevant beyond heritage and tourist interests by literally promoting his image as a brand that would anchor the regional investment strategy. Faced with the dual and contradictory motives of preserving "national" heritage and maximizing financial returns for the locality, the challenge—not always met—would be to keep heritage and commerce from negatively impacting one another.

Urban Planning and Confucian Modernity

In spite of Qufu's reputation for unyielding tradition, by the 1970s many of the city's notable historical properties had already fallen under pressure from development. In the 1930s Qufu was home to a Fire God Temple near the West Gate; a small Guandi Temple to the west of Kong Temple; a Yue Fei Temple in the east; the Wuma Shrine, for which Wumaci Street had been named; a Wenchang Shrine in the Gupan district; and Huatuo and City God Temples in the north.[29] Of these a portion of the City God Temple survived into modern times, owing to its initial occupation by the city police department and subsequent conversion to a hospital ward. Wenchang Shrine, which Kong Lingyi had built in the 1890s in order to block the construction of a Christian church on the same grounds, had been converted to a primary school.[30] The available literature does not describe the fate of the Wuma Shrine, although its appearance amid the recent demolition of its former neighborhood suggests that it survived into the present as a neighborhood committee office. Following its Republican-era occupation by county offices,

FIGURE 39. Former Qufu County Yamen, ca. 1530. After a period of abandonment, the structure was renovated in 2014 to serve as part of Qufu's network of historical architecture.

the former Yamen grounds were given over to a cadre school, and while one of the original buildings still stands (fig. 39), a jailhouse was demolished in 1999, in spite of having earned heritage designation in 1986.[31] A substantial amount of the urban space in Qufu had once been occupied by lesser Kong family mansions built in the Qianlong era. While some of these were incorporated into new schools or hospitals, most were demolished and their spaces reassigned to residential use, military barracks, or commercial space (fig. 40). Eastern sections of the Kong Family Mansion were pushed down to allow a thoroughfare to proceed directly between the North Gate and the Drum Tower, rather than along its traditionally oblique route through the famed Humble Alley of Yanzi's descendants. The Yan Family Mansion to the east of Yan Temple collapsed under its own weight in the 1950s, and until the recent erection of reproduction buildings to house a new Yan Research Center, the grounds were assigned to a printing enterprise.[32]

Still, by the 1970s Kong Temple, Yan Temple, and most of the Kong Family Mansion were intact. So was much of the city's vernacular architecture and

FIGURE 40. Former site of the twelfth Kong Family Mansion, ca. Qing dynasty. Modern tablet indicating city-level heritage protection status, overwritten by commercial agent telephone numbers. Compound occupied by Kongzi Tour Corporation.

overall spatial identity. That space had originally been defined in the Ming dynasty when key streets of the relocated city were developed in relation to the primary temples and mansions. Those streets were then populated by government buildings, secondary mansions, and smaller temples, with residential neighborhoods developing organically in the remaining space within the new city walls.[33] In the twentieth century, Qufu had not followed the national trend of demolishing city ramparts, and within the confines of its walls the emphasis had always been on spatial reassignment rather than reorganization. By the 1970s Qufu continued to follow the logic of discontinuous space that was bounded by the wall and centered on Kong Temple, the Kong Family Mansion, and Yan Temple. On the strength of these surviving artifacts and a substantial reorganization grant from the state, the city council prepared to reopen the city to tourism in 1978. In making those preparations, however, civic leaders demonstrated how badly they wanted to shed the city's conservative reputation and reclaim a role in the performance of national identity by following the prevailing trends of Chinese urban planning.

By the 1970s the Beijing example was well established as the standard for urban development in China. After the Communists moved the capital from Nanjing to Beijing in 1949, Liang Sicheng and Chen Zhanxiang had called upon the central government to protect not just prominent examples of ancient architecture but the entire historical environment by building a new administrative center in the western suburbs and retaining the old city of Beijing in situ. The official reaction to Liang's recommendations was to declare a "major danger" in showing an "extreme respect for old architecture, such that it constricts our perspective of development."[34] Instead, Beijing's planners set in motion the transformative machinery that would replace the city wall with a ring road; demolish blocks of imperial architecture to create Tiananmen Square; and raze temples and courtyard houses in order to accommodate wider roads, factories, and high-density apartment blocks. Although the process has been ongoing, by 1978 it was already apparent that Beijing intended to incorporate a select few symbolically important imperial relics into a grid of broad avenues, high-rise apartments, and modernist architecture.

Having no appreciable bureaucratic function, little industrial potential, and an old-city urban space of no more than four square kilometers, it seems less obvious why the Qufu City Council would ignore the protection measures implemented in 1957 and adopt the Beijing strategy for urban renewal. Nonetheless, in 1977 the city moved to enhance its new north–south thoroughfare by widening South Gulou Street from the original seven meters to twenty-two meters, which necessitated the demolition of existing structures along the route.[35] The city government was not entirely insensitive to architectural balance, on one occasion blocking construction of a new theater directly opposite the gates of Yan Temple, although the emptied site eventually became a parking lot. Other replacement buildings, especially the multistory Xinhua Bookstore directly opposite the Drum Tower, paid no respect to the former architectural environment.[36]

These developments paled in comparison to the city's grandest scheme. Pondering how best to impress "foreign tourists," the council decided that "the old gloomy wall should be taken away to give the city a modern image."[37] Whether local officials actually believed that anyone would be drawn to Qufu by its perceived modernity is difficult to say, but critics have noted the more cynical motive of capitalizing on the wall's masses of building material and the valuable real estate it occupied. Furthermore, because the city wall limited urban expansion, demolition was the first step toward claiming the surrounding countryside as part of Qufu city.[38] It is also worth considering that during the Ming dynasty the wall had helped to consolidate the feudal interests of the Kong family, so the relic was not without political symbolism for the civic officials who were trying to exert control over the site. In any case the city proceeded with demolition even before submitting the appropriate application to the province in 1978 and nearly completed the project before provincial authorities returned a preservation order a half year later. By then, just the Gate of the Esteemed Sage, the North Gate, and two corners on the northwest and the southeast of the city remained standing.[39]

If nothing else, the episode earned Qufu some attention, including a visit from Wu Liangyong. As a former assistant and colleague of Liang Sicheng and now one of China's leading architects and urban planners, Wu shared his mentor's views on the conservation of historic cities. Having witnessed the failure to preserve old Beijing, however, Wu had begun work on a theory of conservation that would accord with modernization. In conducting a somewhat belated survey of Qufu, the architect made three recommendations: (1) conserve antiquities as representations of "the wisdom and labors of historical people"; (2) facilitate tourism, recognizing that since Kongzi had an international reputation, his relics would attract an international tourist clientele; and (3) control construction and retain the character of Qufu as a historical relic attractive to tourists. The plan did not call for the arrest or reversal of development in Qufu. Instead, it explained the need to preserve the historical environment rather than displace it with hotels and theaters, since without the former there would be no use for the latter. Wu proposed that Qufu take pressure off the old city by developing a culture and education quarter in the vicinity of Qufu Normal College to the west and establishing a new administrative/commercial center to the east. The development of a scenic area to the south, which would connect to a green belt covering the grounds of the former city wall and continue northward to Kong Forest, would enhance the aesthetic value of the old city. Gupan Pond, the long-abandoned scenic spot in the southeast of the city, could be revitalized as part of a hotel district. The new inns, Wu suggested, could follow the example of the site's former Xinggong Palace (used as the Qianlong emperor's temporary residence on his frequent visits) by employing low profiles, whitewashed walls, and gray tile roofs.[40] Within the city Wu proposed the removal of the so-called rural population and the demolition of their residences to provide more green space. Vehicular traffic would be kept away from the historical architecture by replacing streets and parking lots with pedestrian malls. Where necessary, new architecture would avoid the "international style" and seek to maintain harmony with the classical Chinese surroundings.[41]

Although the city never fully adopted the proposal, it incorporated some of Wu's recommendations into the first city plan in 1982. The results can be seen in the construction of Qufu's first world-class hotel. It would occupy a block of property next to Kong Temple and the Kong Family Mansion rather than Wu's preferred location near Gupan Pond. Nonetheless, the Queli Guesthouse represented a bold step toward balancing concepts of architectural tradition and modernity. By this time China had already experienced two periods of architectural revivalism—the "adaptive architecture" of the Nanjing decade was known for wedding masonry structures with arching tile roofs and extended eaves.[42] In the early 1950s, Liang Sicheng promoted a similar style until his views were formally denounced during the so-called big roof controversy.[43] Both these movements bypassed the developmentally challenged Qufu, but in its third stage of development "national form" architects would find Qufu an ideal testing ground for these distinctively Chinese designs. Following the example of I. M. Pei's Fragrant Hills Hotel (Xiangshan Fandian) in Beijing (1982), the Queli Guesthouse (Queli Binshe) adopted demonstrably native design elements like whitewashed exterior walls, luxuriant gardens, water features, and heavy tiled roofs (fig. 41). In designing the Queli, architect Dai Nianci issued a challenge to the assumption that historic architecture had to be isolated from new, that modern functional requirements were contrary to traditional architecture forms, and that the traditional form of Chinese architecture was incompatible with modern technology.[44]

FIGURE 41. Queli Guesthouse, front entrance, 1986. Double gable-hip roof and reflecting pond. Design by Dai Nianci.

Having kept the balance of Wu Liangyong's recommendations in reserve since 1978, the second city plan issued in 1985 began to pay some respect to his vision, beginning with the development of a green belt on the former wall zone in 1987. That project faced a minor inconvenience in that some sixty families had been settled there after their homes were destroyed to make room for the Queli Guesthouse, and two dozen work units had been allowed to develop the remaining land and fill in the moat.[45] Nonetheless, the 780 residents were relocated, and in a show of mass mobilization, some seven thousand laborers restored the moat and completed the green zone by July 1989.[46] As a bonus the city rebuilt the Gate of the Esteemed Sage gatehouse, destroyed during the Central Plains War of 1930.

Wu Liangyong had also called for a scenic zone along the banks of the river to the south of the city, but in moving forward on this proposal, the city did not think in terms of public space and instead developed much of the prime riverside land as a series of commercial theme parks. The Analects Stele Garden/Gallery (1993), installed on the north bank of the river directly south of Kong Temple, emulated the local tradition of embedding fine calligraphy and classical Confucian references in its landscape and architecture. A more ambitious project was Wu's own design for the new Kongzi Research Institute, begun in 1996 and opened in 2000 as a combination scholarly institute and museum. Both provide pleasant environments that suit the vision of the original plan, although in commanding substantial entrance fees, they and the riverfront land they occupy are essentially off-limits to all but the occasional tour group.[47]

In contrast to the refined pretence of the Analects Stele Gallery and the monumentality of the Kongzi Research Institute, the Ancient City of Lu State (1992) foundered in its attempt to send the visitor back to the age of the Duke of Zhou through a combination of ersatz Zhou dynasty architecture and costumed mannequins within a miniature walled city. With the development of Olympic fever and the promise of an official torch visit in 2008, the complex was mercifully demolished to make way for a new stadium and public square. Nearby, the Six Arts City (1992) survives as a marginally more successful theme park based on the premise that Kongzi aspired to master six specific skills basic to the Zhou-era educational system and essential to the development of the superior man—rites, music, archery, mathematics, literature, and chariot driving. Seeking solidarity with its visitors, the park emphasizes the theme of Kongzi as a traveller, beginning with a larger-than-life bronze sculpture titled *Confucius Travelling the States* by Zhang Dedi of the Shanghai Art Academy (a replica appears at the city's freeway exit) (fig. 42). The theme is repeated in the Hall of Driving, which takes the visitor on a shabby subterranean amusement park tram ride that reenacts Kongzi's travels through the Warring States. A geodesic globe that is literally a tourist trap containing a maze of interlocking spiral staircases represents mathematics. A miniature Lu State, with a cast of thousands of three-inch figurines arrayed in the performance of grand sacrifice, represents rites. The Hall of Books focuses on a diorama of Kongzi lecturing his seventy-two students, with ample space left for the exhibition and sale of calligraphic scrolls. The Hall of Archery challenges the visitor to shoot targets from the back of a mechanical horse, and the Hall of Music is a dinner theater. A separate performance hall containing scale models of the Apricot Altar and the Hall of the Great Ensemble serves as a venue for performing "rites and music" in loose imitation of Kong Temple sacrifices. Those acts,

FIGURE 42. *Kongzi Travelling the States* by Zhang Dedi, 1992. Located inside Six Arts City, with the Hall of Mathematics in the background.

however, are likely to be executed by young women wearing diaphanous costumes more appropriate to the Tang dynasty exoticism of Xi'an than the stodgy patriarchy of Qufu, where women were not even permitted to enter the temple during rituals—much less dance there with bared midriffs.[48]

Wu Liangyong also called for the redevelopment of Wumaci Market Street. In carrying out those instructions, planners again turned to national form in search of traditional styles that could nonetheless withstand the rigors of modern shopping. Like Beijing's Liulichang, most of the existing brick and timber shop fronts dating to the Qing dynasty were razed and replaced with buildings that suggest the northern Chinese building tradition. In fact, these interpretations bear a stronger resemblance to what Jeffrey Cody refers to as the "adaptive architecture" of the mid-twentieth century: gray brick (or brick veneer) walls capped by a "Chinese" tiled roof (fig. 43). Other buildings adopted the angular façade, black roof tiles, and whitewashed walls of southern *matouqiang* architecture, as seen in Nanjing's redeveloped Fuzimiao District.[49] This divergence was justified on the grounds that although Qufu had always adhered to the northern school of architecture, geograph-

FIGURE 43. China Agricultural Bank, Qufu, ca. 1990s.

ically, the city was situated "half-way between north and south," so a blend of regional architectures was deemed appropriate. Other designs pursued a more radical interpretation of national form that referenced Chinese design elements but was fundamentally modern in execution (fig. 44). Although Wumaci Street preserved a handful of vintage buildings, the re-development gave little consideration to scale. Where the narrow lanes of the city had once enhanced vernacular architecture, that architecture is now dwarfed by adjoining concrete edifices and marginalized by the expansive pedestrian mall. As it is, the vintage architecture only contributes to the temporal and stylistic discontinuity of the street.

Having committed to continuous space through the demolition of the city wall and the construction of urban thoroughfares, in 2000 the city made the remarkable decision to strand those developments behind a resurrected city wall. There is nothing unusual about rebuilding historical relics in China. After the Golden Week holiday initiative in 1999, localities across the country scrambled to construct sites of historical interest in the hope of cashing

FIGURE 44. Wumaci Street, 2011, showing commercial building designed in the shape of an ancient Chinese knife coin, ca. 1990s.

in on the tourist boom. Few such projects can compare to the scale of Qufu's ¥100,000,000 experiment in refeudalization. Fused to the Ming dynasty Gate of the Esteemed Sage, the wall was intended as a replica of the original. When rebuilding the ramparts, however, the designers realized that the purely decorative structures could be left hollow. This measure not only saved the trouble of bringing back tons of fill hauled away during the original demolition and moat restoration but also created useable space within the wall. And because the wall was not an actual relic, there were few limits on how it could be exploited. Although it is now mostly vacant, the wall has periodically housed museums of ancient Chinese wine vessels, a *Yellow River Culture* exhibit, and a Kongzi portrait gallery, as well as a Qufu product and planning showcase. An exhibit opening near the Gate of the Esteemed Sage in 2006 displayed one of the world's largest collections of Cultural Revolution-era Mao badges and claimed to be recognized nationally as a "site of patriotic education" and as a "site of red tourism." Organized by a former vice-mayor of Qufu, the interpretation of the collection offered no recognition of the damage inflicted on Kong Temple in Mao's name.[50]

Although Qufu aggressively pursued urban development through the 1980s and the 1990s, the line between commercial exploitation of the environment and the historic preservation of the Three Kongs had generally been respected. Technically subordinate to the regional, provincial, and national cultural heritage management offices, the City of Qufu's Cultural Relics and Tourist Services Office, in fact, controlled the local architectural relics. Recognizing, perhaps, the inherent contradiction between conservation and tourist promotion, in 1999 the municipal government decided to separate the Qufu Cultural Relics Administration Committee (QCRAC) from the Cultural Relics and Tourist Service Division (CRTSD). Administrative responsibility for the Three Kongs and other ancient relics in the region, however, was given not to QCRAC but to the CRTSD.[51] The tourism agency then led a local consortium in partnering with Shenzhen OCT Tourism Development—an organization best known for creating the Splendid China and the Folk Culture Village theme parks in the southern metropolis of Shenzhen—to form the China Confucius International Tourism Company. This might have been an important step toward professionalizing Qufu's awkward arrangement of theme parks and exhibition halls and synchronizing them with the actual historical relics, except that the CRTSD's business acumen was not matched by its questionable skill in maintaining or conserving the antiquities. The problem first emerged in November 2000 when the management initiated a cleanup of Kong Temple grounds using a truck, which happened to collide with and smash a 1.75 meter stele dating to the Yuan dynasty. One month later the management took it upon itself to clean a series of steles, wooden plaques, and painted wooden beams in the temple and the mansion. The State Bureau of Cultural Relics later accused the company of using water and scrub brushes to accomplish the task and causing extensive damage to the delicate artifacts.[52]

The case raised a host of questions about the appropriate uses of material heritage and brought instant celebrity to the Qufu municipal government. In its own defense, the government insisted on the correctness of what it called "reform" to attract higher earnings. Although the relics were technically state owned, the CRTSD was little different from any of the thousands of state-owned enterprises across the country that underwent massive restructuring to improve economic performance. Indeed, in a strictly legal interpretation, there was nothing in the 1982 Law of the PRC on Protection of Cultural Relics that prohibited management from "reforming" heritage artifacts. Article 15 of the law stated only that

> units in charge of these sites as well as specially established organs, such as museums, must strictly abide by the principle of keeping the cultural relics in their original state, and must be responsible for the safety of the buildings and of the affiliated cultural relics, and may not damage, rebuild, extend or dismantle them. Units which use memorial buildings or ancient architectural structures shall be responsible for the maintenance and repair of these buildings or structures.[53]

A formal investigation of the incident ruled that the City of Qufu was responsible for the damage, although not until 2002 was this law revised to state that "no immovable cultural relics owned by the state may be transferred or mortgaged. No state-owned sites protected for their historical and cultural value, which are established as museums or cultural relics preservation institutes or used as tourist sites, may be made enterprise assets for business operation."[54] By then, control over maintenance of the historical relics had already reverted to QCRAC, although general administration of the relics remains under the control of the CRTSD.[55]

Legal and commercial conflicts may define the tensions emerging at Kong Temple and Qufu in general. However, my argument has been that the problem facing Kong Temple and other historical artifacts more essentially concerns aesthetics and politics. The ritualized past had once been the dominant aesthetic in Qufu, and the management principle, as Kong Lingyi had once implied when standing up to the German railroad, had been to "permit the ancestors to rest in peace." Kong Lingyi evidently understood that the best way to preserve that aesthetic was to reject all but the best-heeled visitors and to entertain them in the context of ritual. With the advent of modern tourism, the municipal government entered into a tortuous and convoluted process of trying to reinvent Qufu in the image of the modern tourist. In its view the city had to become open, bright, clean, and direct. Respecting tourists, or "welcoming friends from afar," as the *Analects*-derived slogan reads, meant eliminating anything that might interfere with tourist comfort and packaging the remaining antiquities into a modern infrastructure. That only compounded the problem because, as Michael Meyer argues in his study of the decline of old Beijing, the "truly old artefacts . . . evince the decrepitude of the past, instead of its glory."[56] Like the vintage structures on Wumaci Street, Kong Temple in relation to the Queli Hotel, or the new wall in relation to the Gate of the Esteemed Sage, it is not the new structure that looks out of place but rather the old one. And thus develops the compelling need to synchronize the antique with the modern, not through in situ conservation, but by giving the relic a polished façade that reflects on its sponsors as well as the patina of age once reflected on the dukes of Fulfilling the Sage.

"Isn't It a Pleasure . . .": Creating the Kongzi Brand

Ever since the beginning of the reform era in 1978, Qufu had identified tourism as its target industry. But while tour groups arrived at the Three Kongs with extraordinary frequency, the city struggled to attract the long-term visitors and investments essential to developing a full-fledged tourist industry. Qufu had never been able to retain its tourists, especially in the early twentieth century when visitors' explicit priority was to avoid spending the night. Although the transport and accommodation situation had improved dramatically since then, by the beginning of the 1980s it was apparent that Qufu could not hold visitors' attention for more than a few hours. Of the 1.4 million tourists reportedly arriving in 1984, just 20 percent stayed beyond their first day, resulting in a hotel occupancy rate of less than 35 percent.[57]

Seeing tourists rush through the Three Kongs and leave the city in as little as an hour, the relevant authorities sought to diversify the tourist experience. By developing a wider range of cultural activities, they hoped to encourage the tourist to look beyond the veneer of the cultural relics and to identify with the temple and its environment on a more personal level. The key to accomplishing this goal was to augment the narrative and create an identity for Kongzi, reclaiming a reputation for the city as the home of China's greatest sage. This was not a new phenomenon—earlier chapters of this book demonstrate a long history of attaching material substance to Kongzi by re-creating him in effigy or, more abstractly, through temple architecture and historic sites. Descendants and devotees also sought to make the sage more concrete by telling his story through serial engravings in the Hall of the Sage's Traces or by preserving or fabricating relics such as the Kongzi juniper; Kongzi's well; Kongzi's tomb; and in earlier generations, even his putative carriage, shoe, and inkstone. This materiality provided some balance to the ritual performances, although as Abigail Lamberton argues, it also strengthened the connection to the Kong family, growing their stock in the temple and securing their special status under the state.[58] With the loss of that connection in the modern era, the relics gradually became products over which Qufu could claim ownership and bring to market. In literally developing the "Kongzi brand," Qufu, its parent entities (Jining Prefecture/ Shandong Province), and its partners (Kongzi Foundation, Shandong Travel Bureau) were able to transform the "old Kong shop" into a dynamic (if conflicted) force in the developing market economy.[59]

The first step in creating the Kongzi brand was the most straightforward: to return Kongzi to his place of honor. Acting on the advice of no less than CCP chairman Hu Yaobang, in 1982 the relics administration began work on a new statue of Kongzi to replace the effigy the Red Guards had crushed sixteen years earlier.[60] This was not simply a matter of creating a sculpture and dressing it in a facsimile of a historical costume. Julia Murray has demonstrated that sculpting Kongzi statues had always been a serious business involving the most highly skilled imperial craftsmen.[61] Yet for all their care and detail, those craftsmen left no instructions regarding their sculptural techniques. Since no prototype survived the Cultural Revolution, the modern craftsmen were compelled to undertake a detailed and symbolically rich investigation of the effigy's true form. The result, naturally trumpeted as a masterpiece, was said to exhibit a broad lower body and shoulders narrowing to the head, giving the statue a pyramidal shape and a "grand and forceful appearance." As to the face, the sculptors relied mainly on photographic models and, at the same time, claimed to follow the spirit of ancient texts such as *The Analects,* which described Kongzi both as a patient teacher and a ruler at the peak of his power.[62] When the work was unveiled in 1984, those familiar with the Yongzheng-era statue agreed that while the original had been somewhat frightening the new version seemed pleasantly benevolent. Liu Haisu, a modern artist who had seen the original at the Republican state sacrifice in 1935, commented that the statue was "very good, very peaceful, and all-embracing with nice countenance, expression and temperament. The costume design and color is full of traditional oriental style. Although we have not laid eyes on Kongzi himself we can see him in his statue."[63] The photographic evidence shows that except for a more finely combed beard, a slightly more pronounced smile, and relative cleanliness, the reproduction is very close to the Yongzheng-era original.[64] The real difference lay not in its appearance but in how it was publicly represented as dignified yet humble and welcoming, or as tour guides proclaim, like a "great man of Shandong" (Shandong *dahan*).

Having thus symbolically rehabilitated Kongzi, the Qufu and Shandong tourism bureaus began to take tentative steps toward restoring his commemoration by developing a program initially advertised as the Kongzi Birthday and Hometown Tour Activity (Kongzi Danchen Guli You Huodong). At its inception in 1984, the organizers ignored the later Republican precedent of recognizing September 28 as Teachers' Day and scheduled the tour activity according to the Qing and early Republican precedent of marking "The First Teacher's" lunar calendar birthday (*xianshi dan*) on the twenty-seventh day of the eighth lunar month (September 22, 1984; October 11, 1985).[65] In 1986 a chance convergence in calendars, a nine-day extension, and daily performances of the sacrifice dance allowed organizers to commemorate both solar and lunar birth dates by opening the festival on September 26.[66] When the calendars diverged again, the opening date returned to the lunar *xianshi dan* until 1989, when the event was rebranded as the Kongzi Culture Festival (Kongzi Wenhua Jie, or Confucius Culture Festival in English language advertising) and extended to a full two weeks. The Zijinshan Astronomical Observatory in Nanjing confirmed that Kongzi had indeed been born on September 28, 551 BCE, and accordingly, September 26 was fixed as the permanent opening date for the festive commemoration of Kongzi.[67]

The new schedule implied the abandonment of the historically symbolic but commercially impractical *xianshi dan*. More importantly, it allowed the festival to span the holiday and eventual holiday week mandated for observing the October 1 National Day. And although the festival was launched with countless platitudes for Kongzi, virtually every form by which Kongzi could be honored had to be reviewed and adjusted to meet the demands of practicality. In developing the opportunity, the Shandong Tourism Bureau was careful to avoid controversy, calling on tour operators and developers to "respect history" and to adopt a "scientific" attitude toward Kongzi that accorded with contemporary political attitudes. That is, Confucianism was to be a doctrine, not a religious faction, and Kongzi was to be a man and not a god. On the other hand, in the interest of capitalizing on holiday revenue, the bureau also said there was little point in striving for historical accuracy in public displays or performances because strict interpretations of the past were neither technically possible nor of interest to the ordinary observer. Instead, operators were advised to develop an "exuberant" interpretation of the sage.[68]

In keeping with that position, the Kongzi Culture Festival embarked upon a continuing cycle of innovation designed both to satisfy the contemporary standards for "respecting the past" and to whet the appetite of the modern tourist. In 1989 festival goers could progress from an exhibition on Kongzi and the history of Confucianism in the temple's former Abstinence Quarters to a permanent exhibit of modern Pictures of the Sage's Traces, in the style of Han dynasty tomb engravings, installed at the Chamber of Odes and Rites. Outside the temple, the festival offered displays on local history; exhibitions of fine arts and handicrafts; and a parade with floats depicting themes of *Kongzi Travelling the States, Kongzi Lecturing at Apricot Altar,* and each of the six arts advocated by Kongzi (archery, mathematics, rites, etc.).[69] In 1990 the festival opening ceremony was augmented with music and dance performances, beginning (after a two-thousand-year hiatus) with the *shao* music that famously caused Kongzi to forget the taste of meat. In 1992 the opening ceremony delved even further into the past to re-create the mythical rites of the Yellow Emperor (Yunmen Dajuan), although performed in the present by energetic dancers in grass skirts and faux-fur loincloths. Later opening ceremonies were comparatively subdued in using established forms of Chinese classical and folk dance, but neither did they eschew more sensuous forms of dance featuring Tang courtesans and Buddhist flying *asparas*.[70]

Auxiliary performances outside the temple also continued to develop through the 1990s, when visitors were encouraged to attend dance performances, musicals, and spoken word plays with titles like *Kongzi Rhapsody* (*Kongzi changxiang qu*); *Dream of Datong* (*Datong meng*); *Kongzi the Commoner* (*Buyi Kongzi*); and a biographical costume drama, *Kongzi*.[71] By 1998 the festival had added the Fuji Cup photography competition, a national race-walking championship, and a Three Kong Beer Night sponsored by a local brewery. Another evening event, sponsored by a local cement manufacturer in 1998, featured nationally prominent performers such as the PLA chanteuse Fan Linlin and celebrity couple Fu Disheng and Ren Jing.[72] In 2001 the opening ceremony likewise adopted the gala format, moving its proceedings from morning to evening and from Kong Temple to the newly constructed Apricot Altar Theatre, where it became a full-scale sound-and-light show.[73]

Amid the host of invented traditions, one of the few with actual roots in Qufu's past was the state sacrifice. Aside from a single performance as a "research exercise" in 1957, the sacrifice music and dance known as the *jiKong yuewu* had been obsolete since the end of the Qing dynasty and extirpated on the Chinese mainland since 1948. From practically the moment that it became politically viable do so, however, local researchers began the work of reviving the long-abandoned ensemble. In 1984 a team of students and teachers from Qufu Normal University began to piece together the music and dance. In 1986 the Qufu Department of Culture and the Qufu Theatrical Association developed a full-scale production of the thirty-six-dancer version of the *jiKong yuewu*, and in 1987 the performance was finally upgraded to the sixty-four-dancer performance last used in Qufu at the end of the Qing dynasty.[74]

By 1989 the performance was relatively complete, although with significant omissions and alterations that distinguished it from historical practice and obvious additions that marked it as a tourist product. No purification rituals were held in advance of the sacrifice, and Kong Decheng, although still presiding over traditional ceremonies in Taiwan, was not on hand to legitimize the performance through his role as chief sacrificial officer. The music and dance formerly controlled by the Kong clan and performed by Confucian acolytes was executed by actors in cheap costumes and makeup who performed their routine with theatrical flourishes that would have been sacrilege in an earlier age. The dancers also departed from imperial protocol by facing the audience rather than the altar of Kongzi, which was, in any case, kept behind closed doors, thereby dispelling any suggestion of actual sacrifice.[75] The mock sacrifice, meanwhile, included only one offering of wine, and because the "three animal sacrifices" (also facing the audience rather than Kongzi) were made of plaster, there was no burning or burying of blood and fur.[76]

It is not clear who, if anyone, actually bothered to complain about the execution and manipulation of the sacrifice dance, but producers and directors nonetheless defended their choreography against any charge that it lacked authenticity. The dance, it was argued, had never been intended as a replica of past practice. Instead, it was labeled as *fanggu*—a term that refers to the classical artistic tradition of honoring the old masters by recapturing their artistic spirit, if not form. Considering the long recess in its performance, this was not an unreasonable argument, and Joseph Lam makes the point that given the historical ambiguity of the musical and dance notation, directors had always relied on their own frame of mind to complete the score handed down from the past.[77] Indeed, accepting that the modern director felt the need to bend the performance to meet practical constraints and tourist sensibilities, the entertaining quality of the tour activity/cultural festival suited the community's needs perfectly well.

The inherent problem with that strategy was that as long as Kongzi was treated as a tourist novelty, Qufu and its parent district of Jining stood little chance of propelling their brand to national and international prominence. From the first time the tour activity/cultural festival was held, Qufu had sought to balance its more frivolous entertainments with the serious study of Kongzi and Confucianism. The local inauguration of the China Kongzi Foundation and a six-day academic conference on the subject of "Kongzi's Thought Regarding Education" immediately followed the first celebration of 1984.[78] In 1985 the Preparatory Meeting of the China Kongzi Research Association was set to coincide exactly with the tour activity.[79] The local Kongzi studies establishment began to pursue internationalization by

linking the festival to the first International Confucian Studies Conference in 1987.[80] Two years later the Kongzi Foundation won the support of
the UNESCO in using Qufu to stage part of the International Kongzi/
Confucius 2540th Birthday Memorial and Academic Conference. When
Shandong's head of propaganda established the Kongzi Academic Assembly in 1990, the group was granted the use of a chamber in the Kong Family
Mansion and the continuing privilege of incorporating their annual symposium into the festival. During the 1990s and early 2000s, the Confucian
Thought Academic Reporting Conference established itself as the festival's principal scholarly meeting, bringing in high-profile speakers such as
"Master of National Learning" Ji Xianlin; diplomat Yuan Xiaoyuan; jour-
nalist Chen Xiangmei (Anna Chan Chennault); historians Yang Xiangkui, Li Xueqin, and Zhang Qizhi; philosopher Luo Guojie; and Harvard
professor Tu Weiming.[81] The Academic Reporting Conference became
the World Confucian Conference in 2007, and since 2010 the International Kongzi Festival has been linked to the Nishan Forum of World
Civilizations, held at the acknowledged birthplace of Kongzi twenty kilometers to the southwest of Qufu. Hosting academics and spiritual leaders
from China and the West, the conference is now billed as a dialogue between
the world's "two predominant civilizations, Confucianism and Christian-
ity," with the goal of drawing upon the comparative wisdom of Kongzi and
Jesus.[82]

Anna Sun's study of contemporary Confucianism shows that rituals performed in Confucian temples throughout China have, in recent years, begun to recover elements of worship and spirituality.[83] In Qufu the Nishan
Forum flirts with religion, and there are currently few obstacles to the
private worship of Kongzi in Kong Temple and elsewhere in Qufu. However, the official interpretation of Confucian ceremony remains strictly
secular. Sponsorship of the festival has always rotated between a shifting
coalition of the Qufu City Standing Committee and government, the Jining Prefecture Standing Committee and government, the provincial and
national tourism bureaus, and the Shandong provincial government. The
representatives of those offices, however, are careful to distinguish their
roles at the opening ceremony from the sacrifices performed in their aftermath. In the early years the distinction between the opening ceremony and

the sacrifice, both staged in front of the Hall of the Great Ensemble, had been blurred by their coincidence on the *xianshi dan*. With the extension of the festival and the adoption of the solar calendar, the official ceremony was effectively detached from the "popular" sacrifice. One—probably unintended—consequence was that so long as it could be identified as an elaborate folk dance performed exclusively for tourists and select members of the Kong family, the sacrifice was allowed to recover some of its ritual elements. From the early 1990s, the door to the Hall of the Great Ensemble was opened during the sacrifice to Kongzi, and after 1996 this sacrifice was allowed to include flesh-and-blood animal sacrifices (although still facing the audience); the recitation (although not full performance) of the sacrifice program; and the option for devotees to bow, kneel, or even kowtow (ideally without touching the head to the ground) before the altar of Kongzi.[84]

When the ceremony was televised to a national audience in 2004, the protocol was revised again to include the formal participation of public officials, and when Qufu's mayor stood to read the eulogy the event was recategorized as an "official sacrifice" (*guanji*). This was a critical development for the temple. The temple had recovered its role as an object of state patronage, although as a consequence, it became necessary for the temple's management to secularize the sacrifice to save these public officials from a potentially embarrassing association with former "feudal officials." Although the three animal sacrifices were on display and costumed proxies continued to perform the kowtow on the sidelines, the dignitaries substituted an offering of flowers and performed a bow from the waist. Only after the dignitaries had left the platform did the traditional performance commence, with a master of ceremonies dressed in Qing formal attire calling out the order of sacrifice amid a performance of the *jiKong yuewu*. Acts such as the burning and burying of hair and blood and welcoming the spirits again received lip service, but no rituals were actually performed.[85]

The revisions to the ceremony in 2004 effectively separated ritual from state and configured the space and performance to provide for official participation and recognition. Yet there was evident discomfiture with the close proximity between modern officials and their imagined premodern counterparts, as well as with the unclear distinction between the official ceremony and the sacrifice that followed. In 2005 the directors finally elected to "stop simply copying the ancient practice" and began to pursue a "modern interpretation of Kongzi thought and traditional culture." This meant that the family sacrifice was to be clearly distinguished from the official, not commencing until after the televised official proceedings had drawn to a close. This expedient satisfied the Kong family's interests, and it gave the directors a free hand to selectively use the more aesthetically interesting elements of tradition and to choreograph the performance as a public spectacle. The modern sacrifice now consisted of a temple opening ceremony followed by a procession of costumed actors and dignitaries from the Gate of the Esteemed Sage to the Hall of the Great Ensemble, where the eulogy and offering procedure established in 2004 was repeated, though now without the three animal sacrifices. The *jiKong yuewu* that followed was likewise purged of any residual ritual elements, yet by introducing certain performance elements and costumes noted in the Ming dynasty texts *Shengmen li zhi* and *Queli zhi*, directors were able to claim that their performance of *jiKong yuewu* was actually *more* traditional than any since the 1980s (plate 10).[86]

In one sense the directors might be credited with making the ceremony culturally relevant. However, the stylistic choices were driven by the need to coordinate the optics of the ceremony with the expectations of a modern television audience. Visually, amid an ongoing national discourse over appropriate Chinese clothing styles, the Manchu garments formerly worn by ceremonial officers were abandoned in favor of "Han clothing" (*Hanfu*). Sonically, the piercing tones of Chinese woodwinds were silenced in favor of a prerecorded and amplified arrangement dominated by bells and an overbearing chorus singing phrases from the Confucian classics.

Although it was primarily a Shandong showcase, the International Kongzi/Confucius Culture Festival had gradually begun to act as an agent of the state, first, by serving as a photo opportunity for the Shandong political elite, and second, by implicitly supporting the initiatives of the CCP. Anthony DeBlasi argues that the dominant themes in modern state-led Confucianism are cultural nationalism, China's contribution to a global culture, and self-improvement and self-actualization.[87] Those same themes regularly appear at the state-sponsored sacrifices in Qufu. When President Hu Jintao rolled out his policies of "peaceful rise" and "build a harmonious society" in 2005, the festival adopted the theme "Raise Outstanding

Traditional Culture, Build a Civilized and Harmonious Culture, Promote Openness and Innovate Development." The ceremony that year was coordinated with affiliated temples and organizations around the world, and the proceedings were televised as a "global unified sacrifice to Kongzi."[88] When China moved to ease tensions with Taiwan in 2006, the festival chose the theme "Raise Outstanding Traditional Culture, Strengthen Cross Straits Communication, Promote Openness and Cooperate in Development." The sacrifice that year, synchronized with similar events in Taipei and Tainan, included the spectacle of children emptying urns of soil and water from Taiwan's Sun Moon Lake and Ali Mountain into the incense burner in front of Dacheng Hall.[89] Sebastian Billioud and Joël Thorvald provide a detailed account of the 2007 event, noting that the theme for the year was Confucian "Chineseness" (Zhongghua Qing); that the opening ceremonies were headlined by Korean pop star Mina; and that the "state sacrifice" featured Yu Dan, the author of a highly popular series of self-help books advocating the incorporation of Confucianism into daily life.[90]

The list of themes and the nature of "Confucian values" continues to develop into the present, and the investment in commemoration has paid dividends in many forms. The most tangible return, however, has been economic. In contrast to their economically conservative "Confucian" predecessors, late twentieth-century entrepreneurs and city managers are unencumbered by reservations about associating the sage with their business transactions. Once relieved of their ritual duties in the 1950s, the representatives of the Kong family who remained in Qufu moved decisively toward commercial pursuits. Kong Family Mansion Limited, which had originated as the private distillery of the Kong family, was incorporated as the Qufu Distillery in 1958 and became the provider of the "official liquor of the Kongzi Festival" in 1984. In 1985 the distiller began to distribute Kong Mansion Family Liquor, and after it reincorporated as the Kong Mansion Family Distillery in 1986 the enterprise emerged as one of the major sponsors of the commemoration of Kongzi. In exchange, the distillery assumed the right to use the image and the reputation of the sage and his temple in marketing its products; printing their respective images on its packaging; and in one advertising campaign, distributing porcelain Kongzi figurines together with its premium wine.[91]

Beyond the involvement of the Kong Mansion Family Distillery (later the Kong Mansion Family Industrial Group), the organizers of the tour activity/cultural festival actively promoted the commemorative day/weeks as an opportunity to hold "economic technology consultations."[92] When festival authorities organized the commemoration around the solar calendar in 1989, they implicitly moved to optimize the event's economic potential by accommodating tourist as well as business interests invited to participate in the festival's associated trade fair. Between 1991 and 1993, the conveners were able to boast that hundreds of foreign and thousands of domestic businesses had signed letters of intent worth over ¥5 billion and that commercial organizations had approved more than a thousand science and technology development projects.[93] In the early years, many of these business promotions concerned products that were vaguely cultural or involved bringing together business-minded members of the Kong, Meng, and Yan clans. By the early twenty-first century, that sodality included a host of unrelated business and professional meetings, ranging from a career fair for Chinese doctoral students educated in the United States to a symposium for Chinese engineers to trade seminars for Fortune 500 enterprises. The keynote event was undoubtedly the *Chinese Patent and New High-Tech Products Exhibition,* which boasted more than ¥13 billion in trade and contracts in 2004 alone.[94]

Rather than attempting to pay respect to Kongzi by staking out a niche in a narrow cultural product industry, the entrepreneurs conceived the idea of a Confucian Business Association, united not by a shared interest in writing brushes and inkstones but by a shared system of values. As John Makeham observes, delegates to the 1999 International Conference Commemorating the 2550th Anniversary of Kongzi's Birth and Rushang in the Twenty-First Century spent much of their time debating the meaning of the term *rushang* (Confucian business).[95] Various definitions were arrived at, but the one that surfaced as the association's web-based manifesto prior to 2011 declared that the new Confucian business follows both "traditional virtue" and the "new moral concept bred by the market economy." The ideal Confucian entrepreneur, it was noted, should have "modern thinking, regional and global consciousness, should know a foreign language (preferably English), and should be able to use a computer."[96] As to the Confucian business spirit, adherents might combine profit with justice and the fulfillment

FIGURE 45. Profit in the Precious Land, ca. 2005. Monument featuring enlarged coins, commissioned by the Confucian Business Association and installed to the northeast of the Gate of the Esteemed Sage.

of other Confucian values; alternatively, they might use an "oriental style of management" to "oppose Western cultural hegemony" and to "address the deficiencies of instrumental rationality and analytical thinking" inherent in the Western business spirit. To its credit, the Confucian business strategy also addressed the question of limits, even stating that "some things should be left undone." Yet this maxim seems an afterthought in an environment where the actual business philosophy is to leave no opportunity unexploited (fig. 45).[97] We might, however, consider this statement as a structural theme of the sort that Kong Temple has inspired since its early days in the Han dynasty. In bringing that which should be left undone together with that which is actually done within the same monumental complex, the temple continues to perform its traditional mandate. It contrasts the ideal with the actual and gives cause to reflect upon the meaning of both.

7 | Epilogue

The Transformative Power of Heritage

I N 1907 EDOUARD CHAVANNES aimed his camera and snapped a photograph of the Hall of the Great Ensemble in the heart of Kong Temple (fig. 46). The resulting distorted composition owes as much to accident as it does to timing, yet from that chance alignment of light and celluloid the image is all the more striking: the backlit temple hall is dimly outlined but the sweeping eaves stand out in powerful contrast to a hazy sky and seem, as Eliade proposed of sacred places in general, to effect a "break in the plane" that "makes possible ontological passage from one mode to another."[1] In capturing the scene in the denouement of the Qing dynasty, the traveler archived that aura for future reference, but at the same time, it must be asked: Did Chavannes' photograph merely capture the "heat death" of a degrading memorial?

This study has focused on the particular history of Kong Temple. The broader goal, however, has been to understand how monuments achieve iconic status, how architecture engages its inhabitants through contingency, and how space and time intersect in the formation of place. In reference to the premodern regime, it was argued that although the built environment was subject to constant change, change was seen less as innovation than as an ongoing contribution toward an ageless architecture that honored the ancient home of Kongzi and embodied his ideals. The permanence of space, the poetics of building, and the continual performance of ritual encouraged patrons or clients to believe they were participating in the ways of the ancients. This is how the illusion of antiquity was created—by never distinguishing ancient from contemporary, the new was ultimately absorbed into the old. With the debasement of ritual and the rise of legalistic and politicized interpretations of heritage in the twentieth century, however, the artifact and its management/restoration aesthetic became subject to forms of

FIGURE 46. Hall of the Great Ensemble, northeast corner. Photograph by Edouard Chavannes, 1907.

political and commercial exploitation that thrived on the constructed division of new from old. The effect of the heritage regime has been to create a legal distinction between present and past; a technical definition of what constitutes heritage; and at least in theory, a mandatory set of practices deemed suitable for heritage maintenance, including the principles of "rational use," "historic authenticity," and "maintaining the historical condition."[2] The past was made static while the present was set in motion, and once that distinction was made, it was inevitable that the past would be made to serve the present (*gu wei jin yong*). That arrangement resulted in the deterioration of the historical environment, the adoption of unbalanced criteria regarding the definition of historical relics, and weak regulation concerning even the most highly regarded and uncontested examples of heritage. The 1978 demolition of the Qufu city wall and the reassignment of its former space to a local work unit, for example, were seen as necessary to the city's progress. A decade later, progress meant the removal of that work unit and the completion of the green zone. A decade after that Qufu finally moved to reconstruct the city wall on its original foundations, thus completing a perfectly rationalized cycle of destruction and construction.

Nor is there any sign of an end to this cycle. In 2008 the Jining District, which now has administrative authority over Qufu, announced its plan to build a ¥30 billion "Cultural City" to the south of the modern-day city. When first introduced the project did not go unopposed, even facing an unusual challenge from a significant faction within the usually docile Chinese People's Political Consultative Conference. In defending the project's motives, its spokesman explained: "Our primary aim is not to build houses or ritual architecture for worshipping. We want to arouse our nation's consciousness, *through a materialized way,* in treasuring and protecting our national spirits."[3] Although still under development, it is now apparent that the architects of the Cultural City aim to create an infrastructure that will bind the region's scenic spots, archaeological dig sites, and historical relics into a comprehensive tourist network fed by high-speed rail and supported by convention centers, art galleries, and luxury hotels.

By 2014 Qufu had seen the completion of a major Kongzi Culture Exhibition Center, its first international chain hotel, and a seventy thousand-square-meter Grand Masters of the Century (Bainian Jujiang) commercial art gallery district. The ground was also being prepared for a new Kongzi museum and an ancient Lu City archaeological park.[4] Many of the recent architectural contributions show respect to the designs that Wu Liangyong and Dai Nianci first introduced. Others simply place a Chinese-style roof, or in case of the Shangri-La Hotel, an entire Chinese-style hall atop a high-rise tower (fig. 47). At the same time, the city has taken a bold step toward the postmodern through constructing a giant tourism service center that preserves the prescribed color scheme while eschewing the ubiquitous roof tiles that defined national form and its less inspired antecedents (fig. 48). In this new articulation of cultural heritage, the ritual overtones are all but gone, and sagely connections are secondary to economic opportunities. Relics once claimed by family interests and linked by classical literary notations are now claimed by cultural relics bureaus and tied by strands of commerce masquerading as Confucian revivalism. Yet even in the twenty-first century, it is apparent that heritage plays a key role in determining and sustaining regional, social, cultural, and political identity.

The recent treatment of the Gupan District in the southeastern corner of Qufu provides a case in point. Since the late 1980s, and until recently, there

FIGURE 47. Shangri-La Hotel, Qufu, 2013. Includes two towers and one low-rise building with gable-hip roofs and vermillion column supports, suggesting the post and beam structure of traditional architecture. Other buildings under construction emulate the Shangri-La style but are not associated with the hotel.

FIGURE 48. Tourist Service Center, Qufu, 2008.

had been an effective freeze on the development of property within the walls of the old city. It seemed for a while that Liang Sicheng's concerns for preserving the historical environment, as well as the historical relic, were at last being taken seriously. That impression, however, was dispelled in 2013 when heavy equipment entered Gupan and proceeded with a wholesale demolition of the five-hundred-year-old neighborhood. The conservation principle was summed up—unintentionally, one presumes—by President Xi Jinping, who was at the same time using Kong Temple to showcase his campaign to revive traditional culture. While paying his respects to the relics of Kongzi in November 2013, Xi asked his constituents to "use the past to serve the present" and to "keep the essential while discarding the dross."[5] City planners had already begun to apply the principle by selecting the great majority of the Gupan District as expendable dross. By the summer of 2014, only two or three ramshackle houses remained standing, in addition to the modern compound that claims the site of the Qianlong emperor's former Temporary Palace; the remains of the Wenchang Shrine (Wenchangci); and the Wuma Shrine (fig. 49). These institutional relics appear to have been selected as the "essential" remains of a neighborhood that will be filled in with hotels, modern courtyard houses, parks, and traditional shopping streets.

FIGURE 49. Wuma Shrine (Wumaci), Gupan District, ca. Ming dynasty. The building is among the few former residents to remain in the district after demolition in 2013.

Assuming the relics do survive as heritage, they will only earn that designation once they have been defiled and stripped down to their bricks and rafters. Paradoxically, the city may claim that in rehabilitating these few relics the neighborhood will be even more traditional than in the past. Gupan Pond will presumably be converted to a public park, the Wuma and Wenchang Shrines seem set to resume service as working temples, and the vicinity of the Temporary Palace will be converted to luxury accommodation based on the *siheyuan* style of courtyard housing that once defined the upscale neighborhoods of urban Qufu. These conversions will not actually recover the residential past, of which there is little left to recycle, but they are a product of the heritage system, and they will contribute nonetheless toward the evolving sense of heritage.

Indeed, it could be said that no architectural relic in Qufu has ever attained heritage status without having undergone a similar form of sacrifice, release, and redevelopment at the hands of militarists, radical activists, or developers—most on multiple occasions. Although Kong Temple has technically been spared such extreme interventions, the relic's heritage development has been no less a response to the demands of the moment, and the resulting product is inevitably relieved of any sense of the sacred, heroic, or

FIGURE 50. Security entrance to Kong Temple.

mythical that once inspired its pilgrims. This sensitivity to the present was demonstrated in an especially blunt form in 2014, when the cultural relics bureau installed a new entrance to the southern extreme of the temple's fore-court (fig. 50). These gates were inspired not by classical architecture or ritual propriety but by the pragmatic demands of a modern security regime. Modestly constructed, filled with electronic scanning equipment, and oc-cupied by paramilitary staff, the new entrance was evidently designed to screen out terrorists. Yet the new gates are not entirely dissimilar from the Tones of Bronze and the Resonances of Jade or the Original Qi of Supreme Harmony archways. By their symbolic presence, their appearance, and their control of access to the site, they materialize an external reality, expose the frailty of the temple, and compensate for the erosion of a unitary ideal through the application of creative excess.

Like contemporary sacrifices, both the realities and the ideals of Kong Temple have changed fundamentally from a time when abstract aes-thetic principles like *siwen* stood as sufficient reason to follow supposedly ancient precedents. Yet it is still necessary to ask what is behind the regimes of analysis, criticism, commercial exploitation, and security that produce the modern heritage relic. What do markets, laws, and controls actually describe? Modern Qufu is arguably a model of what Walter Benjamin elsewhere observed to be a generational shift in social values from cultural production to cultural consumption.[6] However, tourism, commercial development, and modern conservation regulations and practices still encompass a managerial regime that is not entirely divorced from the past.[7] Even when conservation ethics are breached, as during the abortive consignment of Kong Temple to commercial management, the transgressions serve, over time, to strengthen the commitment to maintaining the core artifact as something that can uphold a claim to antiquity and authenticity. Heritage architecture is not reduced to the role of signpost on a constantly changing urban map, and because of Qufu's preponderance of "ancient relics," every act of worship, tourism, building, or destruction becomes an engagement with heritage.[8] Even when relieved of the universal values that once defined them, historical relics like Kong Temple still complicate matters for those who would use them to fulfill personal, political, corporate, or even cultural goals. Heritage is continually implicated in the changing environment, so in spite of itself, Kong Temple continues to influence the way in which the community makes sense of its past—and its present.

Appendix

Chronology of Construction, State Patronage, and Assets and Entitlements of Kong Temple and the Kong Family

Year	Recorded construction/ destruction	State patronage	Assets and entitlements of Kong family
478 BCE	Home of Kongzi established as a memorial.		
195 BCE		Han Gaozu offers Sacrifice of the Large Beast.	Kongzi descendant named as Lord Heir.
48 BCE			Descendant named as Lord Baocheng, with fief of eight hundred households.
8 BCE			Descendant named as Marquis Who Continues and Honors the Yin.
1 CE		Kongzi as Duke XuanNi of Baocheng.	Descendant as Baocheng Marquis.
153		Temple placed under state management.	Descendant conferred title of Hundredweight of Grain (*Baishi zushi*).
156	Restored.		
168	Restored.		
169–170		Beginning of regular spring and autumn sacrifices.	
178	Kongzi's portrait added to temple.		
189–220	Observed in ruins.		
220	Restored.		Descendant as Zongsheng Marquis.

Appendix (*continued*)

Year	Recorded construction/ destruction	State patronage	Assets and entitlements of Kong family
389	Observed in ruins and restored.		
442	Restored.		
495			Various entitlements.
541	Kongzi effigy installed in temple.		
550	Restored.		
580		Kongzi as Duke of Zou.	
585	Restored.		
611	Restored.		
626			Descendant named as Baosheng Marquis with endowment of land and servants.
628		Kongzi as First Sage.	
647		Enshrinement of twenty-two commentators and exegetes.	
666	Restored.	Imperial tour of Emperor Gaozong.	
719	Restored.		
720		Enshrinement of disciples.	
739		Kongzi as King of Exalted Culture.	Descendant named as Duke of Exalted Culture.
773	Restored.		
869	Observed in ruins.		
952	Restored.		
983	Restored.		
997	Addition of the Pavilion of the Literary Constellation.		

Appendix (*continued*)

Year	Recorded construction/ destruction	State patronage	Assets and entitlements of Kong family
1008		Kongzi as Profound (or Dark) Sage and King of Exalted Culture. Emperor Zhenzong offers Sacrifice of the Large Beast.	Ten households appointed to manage tomb and temple.
1013		Kongzi's title altered to Ultimate Sage and King of Exalted Culture.	
1018–1022	Expanded, Apricot Altar constructed.		
1038	Five Sages Hall constructed.		
1048	Hall of Matron of Lu constructed.		
1084		Mengzi as correlate.	
1093			Endowment of one hundred *qing* in land, one hundred *qing* as endowment for temple.
1104	Main hall titled Hall of the Great Ensemble.	Wang Anshi enshrined as correlate.	
1126		Wang Anshi demoted to scholar.	
1129	Damaged or destroyed.		
1140			Descendant named as Duke of Fulfilling the Sage, endowment of one hundred households.
1142	Restored.		
1179	Restored, addition of Hall of Matron of Zou, etc.		
1190–1194	Rebuilt.		Endowment of 123 *qing* of land, 65 *qing* of sacrifice land, and four hundred *jian* of houses.
1214	Damaged or destroyed.		
1237–1238	Partially restored.		One hundred households appointed to serve temple.

Appendix (*continued*)

Year	Recorded construction/ destruction	State patronage	Assets and entitlements of Kong family
1267	Repairs to pavilions, Apricot Altar, etc.		
1282	Temple wall repaired.		
1297–1302	Restored.		Endowment of one hundred thousand *qian*/month, fifty *qing* in land, twenty-eight sweeping households.
1307		Kongzi as Great Completer, Ultimate Sage, and King of Exalted Culture.	
1316		Zengzi and Zisi offered correlate sacrifices.	
1329	Restored.		
1330		Shuliang He named as King Who Fathered the Sage.	
1331–1336	Upgrades to reflect kingly title.		
1369		Sacrifices confirmed for Queli only.	Endowment of large estate.
1374	Restored.	Dancers and musicians trained in Nanjing.	
1387	Restored.		
1407			Endowment of seventy-three *qing* in land.
1411–1412	Restored.		
1439			Endowment of five hundred households to cultivate sacrifice grain.
1465	Restored.		
1477		Sacrifice vessels and dancers appointed and increased in number.	

Appendix (*continued*)

Year	Recorded construction/ destruction	State patronage	Assets and entitlements of Kong family
1483–1487	Reconstructed and expanded.		
1496		Sacrifice dancers increased in number.	
1499–1505	Destroyed and reconstructed.		Appointments to Hanlin Academy and Court of Imperial Sacrifice.
1511	Damaged and repaired.		
1530–1567		Great Rites Controversy. Ritual downgraded, Kongzi's title downgraded to First Teacher, Master Kong.	
1538	Addition of Tones of Bronze, Resonances of Jade archway.		
1544	Addition of Taihe Yuanqi archway.		
1553	Restored.		
1569	Restored, Apricot Altar upgraded.		
1577	Restored.		
1592	Addition of Hall of the Sage's Traces.		
1594	Restored.		
1601	Restored.		
1608	Western Cloister restored.		
1619	Damaged.		
1626	Gate of the Great Mean restored.		
1656	Pavilion of Literary Constellation restored.		
1663	Partially restored.		

Appendix (*continued*)

Year	Recorded construction/ destruction	State patronage	Assets and entitlements of Kong family
1677	Partially restored.		
1684	Restored.	Kangxi emperor offers sacrifice.	Kong Shangren appointed to Imperial Academy.
1690	Partially restored.		
1723		Kingly status for five generations of ancestors.	
1724–1730	Destroyed and recon-structed.		Forty men appointed as temple managers.
1748			Kong Jifen promoted to Grand Secretariat.
1754	Reconstruction of Gate of the Lattice Star.		
1756	Restoration of stele pavilions.		
1801	Partial restoration of Hall of the Great Ensemble.		
1816–1819	Partially restored.		
1869	Restored.		
1896–1897	Restored.		
1906	Temple materially upgraded.	Kongzi promoted to rank of emperor, ritual upgraded.	
1915	Hall of Repose, Jinshui Creek restored.		
1925	Hall of Repose restored.		
1927	Ming stele pavilions and Gate of Unified Texts reconstructed.		
1930	Damaged by shelling.		
1934		First Republican sacrifice.	
1936			Kong Decheng as chief sacrifice officer.

Appendix (*continued*)

Year	Recorded construction/ destruction	State patronage	Assets and entitlements of Kong family
1948			Kong Decheng evacuates to Taiwan.
1949		Temple placed under Cultural Relics Management Committee.	
1959	Restored.		
1961		Temple recognized as national heritage site.	
1966	Damaged, effigies destroyed.	Kongzi branded "#1 Hooligan."	
1978–1980	Restored.		
1983	Effigies restored.		
1984		Commencement of Kongzi's birthday festival.	
1985	Restored.		
1994		Temple as UNESCO World Heritage Site.	
2004		Sacrifices resume under state sponsorship.	

Notes

Abbreviations

SSZ = Shandong Sheng Difang Shizhi Bianzuan Weiyuanhui, ed. *Shandong shengzhi. Kongzi gulizhi* (Shandong provincial annals: The native place of Confucius) (Beijing: Zhonghua shu ju, 1994).

QLZ (1575) = Kong Zhengcong, *Queli zhi* (Annals of Queli), 1575.

QLZ (1505) = Chen Hao, *Queli zhi* (Annals of Queli), 1505.

QFXZ = Pan Xiang, *Qufu xianzhi* (Qufu county annals), 1774 (Jinan: Shandong Youyi chubanshe, 1998).

Preface

1. Brian Dott, *Identity Reflections: Pilgrimages to Mount Tai in Late Imperial China* (Cambridge, MA: Harvard University Asia Center, 2004); Susan Naquin, *Peking: Temples and City Life, 1400–1900* (Berkeley: University of California Press, 2000); Tobie S. Meyer-Fong, *Building Culture in Early Qing Yangzhou* (Stanford, CA: Stanford University Press, 2003).

Terms and Dates

1. Lionel Jensen, *Manufacturing Confucianism: Chinese Traditions and Universal Civilization* (Durham, NC: Duke University Press, 1997), 143.

2. Thomas Wilson, introduction to *On Sacred Grounds: Culture, Society, Politics, and the Formation of the Cult of Confucius,* Harvard East Asian Monographs 217 (Cambridge, MA: Harvard University Asia Center, 2002. Distributed by Harvard University Press), 24–25.

Chapter 1

1. Arjun Appadurai, *The Social Life of Things* (Cambridge: Cambridge University Press, 2011), 5 (emphasis in original). See also Craig Clunas, *Superfluous Things: Material Culture and Social Status in Early Modern China* (Honolulu: University of Hawai'i Press, 1991), 2.

2. Emile Durkheim, *The Division of Labor in Society* (1893; repr., New York: Free Press, 1997); Maurice Halbwachs, *The Collective Memory* (1950; repr., New York: Harper and Row

Colophon Books, 1980); Frances Yates, *The Art of Memory* (London: Routledge and Kegan Paul, 1966).

3. Jun Jing, *The Temple of Memories: History, Power, and Morality in a Chinese Village* (Stanford, CA: Stanford University Press, 1996).

4. Jun Jing, "Knowledge, Organization, and Symbolic Capital: Two Temples to Confucius in Gansu," in *On Sacred Grounds: Culture, Society, Politics, and the Formation of the Cult of Confucius,* ed. Thomas Wilson (Cambridge, MA: Harvard University Asia Center, 2002), 339.

5. Yves Alain Bois and Rosalind Krauss, *Formless: A User's Guide* (New York: Zone Books, 1997), 36.

6. Christopher Agnew, "Culture and Power in the Making of the Descendants of Confucius, 1300–1800" (PhD diss., University of Washington, 2006), 171–182.

7. Angela Zito, *Of Body and Brush: Grand Sacrifice as Text/Performance in Eighteenth-Century China* (Chicago: University of Chicago Press, 1997), 122.

8. Walter Benjamin, "The Work of Art in the Age of Mechanical Production," in *Illuminations,* ed. Walter Benjamin and Hannah Arendt (New York: Schocken Books, 1986), 223–224.

9. On the Opium War era marking the distinction between modern and premodern in Chinese architecture, see Sun Dazhang, *Zhongguo gudai jianzhu shi* (Beijing: CABP, 2002).

10. Pierre Nora, "Between Memory and History: Les Lieux de Mémoire," Special issue, Memory and Counter-Memory, *Representations,* no. 26 (1989): 7–9.

11. The use of *lieux de memoire* in Chinese history has been tested through a number of case studies in Marc Matten, ed., *Places of Memory in Modern China: History, Politics, Identity* (Leiden, Netherlands: E. J. Brill, 2012).

12. Madeleine Yue Dong, *Republican Beijing: The City and Its Histories* (Berkeley: University of California Press, 2003), 11.

13. On the debasement of religious cults in the Republican era, see Rebecca Nedostup, *Superstitious Regimes: Religion and the Politics of Chinese Modernity* (Cambridge, MA: Harvard University Asia Center, 2010).

14. Dong Wang, "Internationalizing Heritage: UNESCO and China's Longmen Grottoes," *China Information* 24, no. 2 (2010).

15. Xiaobo Su and Peggy Teo, *The Politics of Heritage Tourism in China: A View from Lijiang* (New York: Routledge, 2009).

16. Robert J. Shepherd, *Faith in Heritage: Displacement, Development and Religious Tourism in Contemporary China* (Walnut Creek, CA: Left Coast Books, 2013).

17. Anna Sun, *Confucianism as a World Religion: Contested Histories and Contemporary Realities* (Princeton, NJ: Princeton University Press, 2013), 1–2.

Chapter 2

1. Victor Segalen, "For Ten Thousand Years," in *Steles,* trans. and ed. Timothy Billings and Christopher Bush (Middletown, CT: Wesleyan University Press, 2007), 99–101; Simon

Leys, "The Chinese Attitude toward the Past," *China Heritage Quarterly,* no. 14 (2008), http://www.chinaheritagequarterly.org/.

2. F. W. Mote, "A Millenium of Chinese Urban History: Form, Time and Space Concepts in Soochow," *Rice University Studies* 59, no. 4 (1973): 51.

3. See, for example, Cary Y. Liu, "Chinese Architectural Aesthetics: Patterns of Living and Being between Past and Present," in *House, Home, Family: Living and Being Chinese,* ed. Ron Knapp and Kai-yin Lo (Honolulu: University of Hawai'i Press, 2005), 142; Anita Chung, *Drawing Boundaries: Architectural Images in Qing China* (Honolulu: University of Hawai'i Press, 2004), 157–158; Yinong Xu, *The Chinese City in Space and Time: The Development of Urban Form in Suzhou* (Honolulu: University of Hawai'i Press, 2000), 178–179. Tobie S. Meyer-Fong expresses more of an interest in the role of construction and renovation in the making of Yangzhou but, finding little evidence of buildings being treated as physical relics, turns instead to the "performance of place, or the creation of a site through culturally informed actions." Meyer-Fong, *Building Culture in Early Qing Yangzhou,* 3. Peter Carroll problematizes the Mote thesis by questioning whether "building materials and the survival of structures reveal a conscious philosophical preference for impermanence" and by calling attention to the "anachronistic historical intentionality" ascribed to European builders who are implicitly understood to be the epistemological opposites of Chinese builders. *Between Heaven and Modernity: Reconstructing Suzhou, 1895–1937* (Stanford, CA: Stanford University Press, 2006), 177.

4. Wu Jingzi, *The Scholars,* trans. Yang Xianyl and Gladys Yang (Peking: Foreign Languages Press, 1964), 455–456, 714.

5. Ibid., 496–503.

6. Ibid., 713.

7. The different forms of "trace" that observers historically identified with Chinese ruins are identified by Wu Hung as the divine trace (*shenji*), the historical trace (*guji*), the timeless or renowned trace (*shengji*), and the remnant trace (*yiji*). Wu Hung, *A Story of Ruins: Presence and Absence in Chinese Art and Visual Culture* (London: Reaktion Books, 2012), 62–91.

8. Wei Shang discusses the problem of the dissolution of literati culture and the deterioration of Taibo Temple in Shang, "The Collapse of the Taibo Temple: A Study of the Unofficial History of the Scholars" (PhD diss., Harvard University, 1995), 249–265.

9. Peter Kees Bol, *"This Culture of Ours": Intellectual Transitions in T'ang and Sung China* (Stanford, CA: Stanford University Press, 1992), 2.

10. On the grand shrines of Ise and Izumo, see William Coaldrake, *Architecture and Authority in Japan* (New York: Nissan Institute/Routledge, 1996), chap. 2.

11. Segalen, "For Ten Thousand Years," 99–101.

12. Tracy Miller, *The Divine Nature of Power: Chinese Ritual Architecture at the Sacred Site of Jinci* (Cambridge, MA: Harvard University Asia Center, 2007), 18.

13. Michael Nylan and Thomas Wilson, *Lives of Confucius: Civilization's Greatest Sage through the Ages* (New York: Doubleday, 2010), 150.

14. This anatomy has been thoroughly dissected in both Liang Sicheng, *Qufu Kongmiao jianzhu jiqi xiuqi jihua* (Beiping, China: Zhongguo yingzao xueshe, 1935); and Pan Guxi, *Qufu Kongmiao jianzhu* (Beijing: Zhongguo jianzhu gongye chubanshe, 1987). Ernst Boerschmann's brief study of 1911 was also interested in the architectural detail but did not achieve the technical

proficiency of later scholars. See Boerschmann, *Die baukunst und religiöse Kultur der Chinesen,* vol. 2, *Gedachtnistempel* (Berlin: Druck und Verlag Von Georg Reimer, 1914), 199–229.

15. Christopher Agnew in particular demonstrates how the Kong family manipulated local histories to perpetuate their regional power. Agnew, "Culture and Power."

16. Qufu was formally declared a sacred precinct by the Kangxi emperor in the Qing dynasty. Richard Strassberg, *The World of K'ung Shang-jen: A Man of Letters in Early Ch'ing China* (New York: Columbia University Press, 1983), 78.

17. There are, of course, a range of opinions concerning the relationship between Neolithic cultures and early states, some of which see the relationship as highly problematic. For a summary of the literature, see Liu Li, *The Chinese Neolithic: Trajectories to Early States* (Cambridge: Cambridge University Press, 2004), 223–225.

18. For an archaeological account of the ancient Lu City, see Zhang Xuehai et al., "Discussion of the Periodization and Basic Groundplan of the Lu City at Qufu" and "Conclusions from the Ancient City of the Lu State," *Chinese Sociology and Anthropology* 19, no. 1 (1986).

19. An alternate history argues that the state of Lu was founded elsewhere and relocated to Qufu by Duke Yang, a descendant of Bo Qin. See Zhang Xuehai et al., "Conclusions from the Ancient City," 49.

20. The cave known as Fuzidong (The master's cave) is still well known as a tourist attraction. For further discussion of the narrative qualities of the many Kongzi legends, of which this is only the most prominent, see Lionel M. Jensen, "Legends of Confucius," in *Hawai'i Reader in Traditional Chinese Culture,* ed. Victor H. Mair, Nancy Steinhardt, and Paul R. Goldin (Honolulu: University of Hawai'i Press, 2004).

21. Lionel Jensen has demonstrated that Sima Qian's Kongzi story should be read less as a biography than as the amalgamation of several narratives. The appearance of concrete artifacts such as Kongzi's books, carriage, clothes, and ritual vessels were essential to supporting the otherwise ambiguous claims of Kongzi's putative descendants. Jensen, "The Genesis of Confucius in Ancient Narrative: The Figurative as Historical," in *On Sacred Grounds: Culture, Society, Politics, and the Formation of the Cult of Confucius,* ed. Thomas Wilson (Cambridge, MA: Harvard University Asia Center, 2002), 177–178.

22. Sima Qian, in John Knight Shryock, *The Origin and Development of the State Cult of Confucius* (New York: Century, 1932), 95, passage translated by Edouard Chavannes. Original romanization altered to pinyin.

23. Ai, 16:3, in Yang Bojun and Ming Zuoqiu, *Chunqiu Zuozhuan zhu: Xiuding ben,* rev. ed., Zhongguo gudian mingzhu yiz hu congshu (Beijing: Zhonghua shu ju, 1990), 1697–1699; *Mencius,* 3:1, chap. 4, verse 13, in *The Four Books: Confucian Analects, the Great Learning, the Doctrine of the Mean, and the Works of Mencius,* trans. James Legge (Shanghai: Commercial Press, 1945), 634–635.

24. These legends are recorded in Shryock, *Origin and Development of the State Cult of Confucius,* 96; Henri Doré and M. Kennelly, *Researches into Chinese Superstitions,* vol. 13 (Taipei, Taiwan: Ch'eng-wen, 1966), 92; Reginald Fleming Johnston, *Confucianism and Modern China* (London: V. Gollancz, 1934), 129–131; *Queli guangzhi* (1673; repr. 1870), 6.5b–6a. The *Shengjitu* (Pictures of the Sage's Traces) also recorded such tales and enshrined them

in the temple itself. See Julia K. Murray, "Illustrations of the Life of Confucius: Their Evolution, Functions, and Significance in Late Ming China," *Artibus Asiae* 57, no. 1/2 (1997).

25. Sima Qian, *Shiji* (92 BCE), 47.23a.

26. Rafe de Crespigny, *A Biographical Dictionary of the Later Han to the Three Kingdoms* (Leiden, Netherlands: E. J. Brill, 2006), 1100.

27. "Yi Ying zhishou miao baishi zushi bei" (Stele of Yi Ying serving as temple *baishi zushi*) (153), in Luo Chenglie, *Shitou shang de Rujia wenxian: Qufu bei wen lu*. Zhongguo Kongzi jijinhui wenku (Jinan, China: Qi Lu shushe, 2001), 11–12.

28. "Han Chi zao liqi bei" (Stele of Han Chi commissioning ritual vessels) (156), in ibid., 19–24.

29. Li Daoyuan, *Shui jing zhu* (Taibei: Taiwan shangwu yinshuguan, 1965), 25.6b.

30. The Wei building code was identified, but not detailed, by Emperor Yuan of the Liang dynasty in the text *Jinlou zi* (ca. 550). Joseph Needham, *Science and Civilization in China*, vol. 4, part 3 (Cambridge: Cambridge University Press, 1971), 81.

31. "Kong Xian bei" (Stele of Kong Xian), a.k.a. "Lu Kongzimiao bei" (Stele of the Kongzi Temple of Lu) (220), in Kong Fanyin, *Qufu de lishi mingren yu wenwu*, 349–350.

32. Shen Yue, *Song shu* (Reprint, Taibei: Taiwan shangwu yinshuguan, 1965), 492–493, 5.21b.

33. Li Daoyuan, *Shui jing zhu* 25.7a–b.

34. "Li Zhongxuan bei" (Stele of Li Zhongxuan) (541), in Kong Fanyin, *Qufu de lishi mingren yu wenwu*, 355–356.

35. "Chen Shuyi xiu Kongzimiao bei" (Stele of Chen Shuyi restoring the Temple of Kongzi) (611), in Luo Chenglie, *Shitou shang de Rujia wenxian*, 90–92.

36. "Zeng Taishi Luguo Kong XuanNi bei" (Stele honoring Kongzi as a great teacher) (edict of 666, inscribed 668, postscript 677), in Kong Fanyin, *Qufu de lishi mingren yu wenwu*, 361–368. The text also refers to the restoration of Lingguang Hall (Lingguangdian). Although it is not directly associated with Kongzi or Kong Temple, in the Han dynasty it was regarded as one of the most exemplary buildings of the age. It was said that Prince Gong was motivated to create the magnificent building in ca. 150 BCE by the many auspicious signs that appeared in the state of Lu. In the chaotic years of the later Han, most such structures were destroyed, but Lingguang Hall famously survived "possibly because it had the protection of the gods who wished to preserve it as a symbol of the continuity of the dynasty, and also because it was built in accordance with the celestial system (i.e., 'lunar lodges' *xingxiu*)." *QFXZ* 50.1a. It is not clear when Lingguang Hall finally disappeared, although it still appears in texts dating to as late as 1190. See Fei Kun, *Liangchi manzhi*, in Needham, *Science and Civilization in China*, 132. For Wang Yanshou's description of the hall's murals, see Wu Hung, *The Wu Liang Shrine: The Ideology of Early Chinese Pictorial Art* (Stanford, CA: Stanford University Press, 1989), 73. Julia Murray suggests that the murals may well have included the figure of Kongzi. Murray, "Varied Views of the Sage," in *On Sacred Grounds: Culture, Society, Politics, and the Formation of the Cult of Confucius*, ed. Thomas Wilson (Cambridge, MA: Harvard University Asia Center, 2002), 222n2.

37. "Kongfuzimiao bei" (Stele of the Temple of Kongzi) (719), in Kong Fanyin, *Qufu de lishi mingren yu wenwu*, 369–370.

38. Ouyang Xiu, *Xin Tang shu,* in Fu Chonglan, *Qufu miaocheng yu Zhongguo Ruxue* (Beijing: Zhongguo shehui kexue chubanshe, 2002), 104–105.

39. Luo Chenglie, "Wenxuanwangmiao xinmen ji" (Record of the new gate of Wenxuanwang Temple) (773), in *Shitou shang de Rujia wenxian,* 115–117.

40. "Xinxiu Wenxuanwangmiao bei" (Stele of the newly restored Wenxuanwang Temple) (870), in Luo Chenglie, *Shitou shang de Rujia wenxian,* 372–374.

41. "Chongxiu Wenxuanwangmiao bei" (Stele of restoring the Wenxuanwang Temple) (983), in Kong Fanyin, *Qufu de lishi mingren yu wenwu,* 377–378. For an example of how the structures may have appeared at the time, see the Guanyin Pavilion of Dule Monastery in Ji County, Hebei, completed in 984.

42. These temples, the Jinglinggong and the Taijigong, rivaled or even exceeded Kong Temple and the Kong Family Mansion in scale through most of the Song and Yuan before falling into ruin in the late Yuan or early Ming. Currently, only a few foundation stones remain as physical evidence of their existence. See *QFXZ* 26.11b, and the diagram of "The Hometown of Kongzi" (1037–1121) showing the combined temples to be substantially larger than Kong Temple, in Valerie Hansen, *The Open Empire: The History of China to 1600* (New York: Norton, 2000), 69.

43. *QFXZ* 4.7a; Tuotuo (Toghto), *Song shi* (1345), 105.1a–2a.

44. *QFXZ* 24.17a. This may refer to materials left over from the construction of the building that would be turned over to the Kong family as Yanbinzhai. *QFXZ* 49.8a.

45. Fu Chonglan, *Qufu miaocheng yu Zhongguo Ruxue,* 122–123; *SSZ,* 294.

46. Kong Yuancuo, *Kongshi zuting guangji* (Reprint, Taibei: Taiwan shangwu yinshuguan, 1966), 3.13a.

47. Dang Huaiying, "Chongjian Yunguofurendian" (Reconstruction of the Hall of the Matron of Yun) (1181), in Kong Fanyin, *Qufu de lishi mingren yu wenwu,* 387–388; *QFXZ* 26.4a. Mote writes that Shizong, although strongly identifying with his steppe heritage, showed an appreciation for the idealized version of the Chinese past, which could be contrasted to the less than ideal circumstances of the present. The "barbarians" in this passage are presumably the Khitan, who had rebelled against Shizong at the outset of his regime F. W. Mote, *Imperial China, 900–1800* (Cambridge, MA: Harvard University Press, 1999), 237–238.

48. Dang Huaiying, "Chongjian Yunguofurendian," in Kong Fanyin, *Qufu de lishi mingren yu wenwu,* 387–388; *QFXZ* 26.4a.

49. Dang Huaiying, "Zhuan chongxiu Zhisheng Wenxuanwangmiao bei" (Stele of rebuilding the Zhisheng Wenxuanwang Temple) (1197), in Luo Chenglie, *Shitou shang de Rujia wenxian,* 196–204. See also *QFXZ* 26.5a.

50. On the difficulties faced by the Jin at this time, see Herbert Franke, "The Chin Dynasty," in *The Cambridge History of China: Alien Regimes and Border States, 907–1368,* vol. 6, ed. Frederick W. Mote and Denis Twitchett (Cambridge: Cambridge University Press, 1994), 246.

51. "Dang Huaiying zhuan chongxiu Zhisheng Wenxuanwangmiao bei" (Stele of repairing the Zhisheng Wenxuanwang Temple, composed by Dang Huaiying) (1197), in Luo Chenglie, *Shitou shang de Rujia wenxian,* 196–204. *QFXZ* 26.5a.

52. "Chongjian Zhisheng Wenxuanwangmiao bei" (Stele of rebuilding the Zhisheng Wenxuanwang Temple) (1301), in Luo Chenglie, *Shitou shang de Rujia wenxian,* 247–249; *QLZ* (1575), 8.3a; *QFXZ* 26.9b.

53. *QFXZ* 26.11a–b; "Chongjian Zhisheng Wenxuanwangmiao bei" (Stele of rebuilding the Zhisheng Wenxuanwang Temple) (1301), in Luo Chenglie, *Shitou shang de Rujia wenxian,* 247–249.

54. "Yang Yuan zhuan chongxiu Queli miao yuan ji bei" (Stele recording the restoration of Queli temple walls, composed by Yang Yuan) (1282), in Luo Chenglie, *Shitou shang de Rujia wenxian,* 222; *QFXZ* 26.14a–b.

55. "Chongjian Zhisheng Wenxuanwangmiao bei" (Stele of rebuilding the Zhisheng Wenxuanwang Temple) (1301), in Luo Chenglie, *Shitou shang de Rujia wenxian,* 247–249. Construction of the Confucian temple in Beijing would begin the next year.

56. The "model of the royal palace" presumably refers to the Mongol capital at Dadu, although as Cary Liu points out, Dadu was itself modelled on the ideal of the building manual *Kaogongji* and so referred to the "model of the ancients," which held strong Dao School implications. Cary Y. Liu, "The Yuan Dynasty Capital, Ta-Tu: Imperial Building Program and Bureaucracy," *T'oung Pao,* no. 78 (1992): 267. The same upgrades were approved for the Confucian temple in Beijing in 1331. Zhang Dainian, ed., *Kongzi da cidian* (Shanghai: Shanghai cishu chuban she, 1993), 54.

57. "Chongxiu Xuanshengmiao timing bei" (Stele praising the restoration of Xuansheng Temple) (1332), in Luo Chenglie, *Shitou shang de Rujia wenxian,* 280–281; "Chi xiu Qufu Xuanshengmiao bei" (Stele of the official order to restore the Xuansheng Temple) (1339), in ibid., 291–294; Kong Jifen, *Queli wenxian kao* 12.7a. In 1111 the Northern Song had effectively recognized the temple's "royal" status by granting it the right to display twenty-four halberds, although this concession was not reflected in the architecture. Kong Yuancuo, *Kongshi zuting guangji* 3.28b.

58. Christopher Agnew in particular questions the scale of the land grants that were allegedly provided to the Kong family by the first Ming emperor. Agnew, "Culture and Power," 22.

59. *SSZ,* 298; Zhang Tingyu, *Ming shi* 2.11a.

60. "Yuzhi chongxiu Kongzi miao bei" (Imperial stele of restoring the Kongzi Temple) (1417, re-erected in 1503), in Luo Chenglie, *Shitou shang de Rujia wenxian,* 442–443; Zhang Tingyu, *Ming shi* 284.1a–10a.

61. *QFXZ* 28.9b–28.10a.

62. Luo Chenglie, "Chongjian Jinsitang ji" (Record of rebuilding Jinsitang) (1435) in *Shitou shang de Rujia wenxian,* 389–390.

63. *QLZ* (1575), 10.58a.

64. "Chongxiu Shengmiao beiji" (Stele record of repairing the Saint's Temple) (1468), in ibid., 10.59b; "Chongxiu Queli Xianshengmiao bing yuzhi miao beiji" (Record of restoring the Saint's Temple and preparing the stele) (1468), in Luo Chenglie, *Shitou shang de Rujia wenxian,* 404–406.

65. Luo Chenglie, "Chongxiu Xuanshengmiao ji" (Record of restoring the Xuansheng Temple) (1488), in *Shitou shang de Rujia wenxian,* 416–417; *SSZ,* 299.

66. *QFXZ* 29.5b.

67. *QLZ* (1575), 12.10b.

68. "Yuzhi chongjian Kongzimiao bei" (Imperial Stele of rebuilding the Temple of Kongzi) (1504), in Luo Chenglie, *Shitou shang de Rujia wenxian,* 444; *QFXZ* 29.6a.

69. Christine Moll-Murata notes that this was the principle later in the Qing dynasty. See "Maintenance and Renovation of the Metropolitan City God Temple and the Peking Wall during the Qing Dynasty," in *Chinese Handicraft Regulations of the Qing Dynasty: Theory and Application,* ed. Christine Moll-Murata, Song Jianze, and Hans Ulrich Vogel (Munich: IUDICIUM Verlag, 2005), 242.

70. "Chongxiu Queli miao tuxu bei" (Stele of the preface to a drawing showing the restored Queli temple) (1504), in Luo Chenglie, *Shitou shang de Rujia wenxian,* 447–449; *QFXZ* 29.7b–10a. On the quality of the stones from Guan'goushan, see *QFXZ* 37.4a. For Huizhou artisans, see Wang Ziyun, *Zhongguo diaosu yishu shi,* vol. 1 (Beijing: Renmin meishu chubanshe, 1988), 435.

71. *QLZ* (1505), 4.6a; see also Liang Sicheng, *Qufu Kongmiao jianzhu jiqi xiuqi jihua,* 46.

72. *QFXZ* 29.7a.

73. *QFXZ* 29.12b; "Cheng Queli jibei" (Stele record of the Queli wall) (1525), in Luo Chenglie, *Shitou shang de Rujia wenxian,* 506–507.

74. *QFXZ* 29.13b.

75. Christopher Agnew points out that the relocation of the county seat also allowed the ducal mansion to assert greater control over the region. Having already gained the authority to appoint the magistrate, the magistrate's office was now effectively adjunct to the mansion. Agnew, "Culture and Power," 107–108.

76. "Cheng Queli jibei" (Stele record of the Queli wall) (1525), in Luo Chenglie, *Shitou shang de Rujia wenxian,* 506–507; Strassberg, *World of K'ung Shang-jen,* 3.

77. On the development and idealization of the concept of the "kingly city," see Nancy Shatzman Steinhardt, *Chinese Imperial City Planning* (Honolulu: University of Hawai'i Press, 1990).

78. "Chongxiu Queli linmiao jibei" (Stele record of restoring the forest and temple) (1555), in Luo Chenglie, *Shitou shang de Rujia wenxian,* 557–559.

79. "Queli chongxiu Kongzimiao bei" (Stele of restoring the Temple of Kongzi) (1580), in Luo Chenglie, *Shitou shang de Rujia wenxian,* 590–593.

80. *QFXZ* 30.7a; Murray, "Varied Views of the Sage," 243–244.

81. "Queli chongxiu linmiao jibei" (Stele of restoring the forests and temples of Queli) (1594), in Luo Chenglie, *Shitou shang de Rujia wenxian,* 658–662.

82. "Chongxiu Queli Kongzi miao bei" (Stele of restoring the Kongzi Temple in Queli) (1603), in Luo Chenglie, *Shitou shang de Rujia wenxian,* 666–668. The figure of two thousand *liang* of gold (*jin erqian liang*) is provided in *QFXZ* 30.10b. On Vice-Military Commissioner Wang Guozhen, see *QFXZ* 30.11b.

83. "Lu Weiqi Kongmiao shu jie" (Stele of Lu Weiqi repairing Kong Temple) (1619), in Luo Chenglie, *Shitou shang de Rujia wenxian,* 680–697.

84. Kong Jifen, *Queli wenxian kao* 12.8; Kong Fanyin, *Qufu de lishi mingren yu wenwu,* 205.

85. "Yuzhi chongxiu Queli Kongzi miao bei" (Imperial stele of restoring the Kongzi Temple in Queli) (1683), in Luo Chenglie, *Shitou shang de Rujia wenxian,* 795–796.

86. Kong Jifen, *Queli wenxian kao* (1762), 12.9a.

87. Klaas Ruitenbeek, "Building Regulations (*Zeli*) and Their Context," in *Chinese Hand-icraft Regulations of the Qing Dynasty: Theory and Application,* ed. Christine Moll-Murata, Song Jianze, and Hans Ulrich Vogel (IUDICIUM Verlag, Munich 2005), 175.

88. *QFXZ* 33.6a; Kong Fanyin, ed., *Qufu Kongfu Dang'an shiliao xuanbian,* 3.3, 4985/307–309, 4990/310–311, 4985/312–314. See also Abigail Lamberton, "The Kongs of Qufu: Power and Privilege in Late Imperial China," in *On Sacred Grounds: Culture, Society, Politics, and the Formation of the Cult of Confucius,* ed. Thomas Wilson (Cambridge, MA: Harvard University Asia Center, 2002), 297–332.

89. Before the high Qing era, project administration and construction methods were based on Ming precedents. Only during the Yongzheng reign period did the Qing begin to compile and consolidate texts detailing building costs and regulations in 1731 and 1736. See Christine Moll-Murata and Song Jianze, "Notes on Qing Dynasty 'Handicraft Regulations and Precedents' (*jiangzuo zeli*), with Special Focus on Regulations on Materials, Working time, Prices, and Wages," *Late Imperial China* 23, no. 2 (2002): 89. The detailed financial calculations evident in the Kong Temple reconstruction budget at the beginning of the Yong-zheng reign indicate that codes were already in place, although the administrative scandals that emerged during the project show that they were not authoritative.

90. "Shu dong fu deng wei xiuli Kongmiao gongshi gujia zouwen shi," in *Qufu Kongfu Dang'an shiliao xuanbian,* ed. Kong Fanyin, 3.3, 4985/312–314. As the subtotals do not equal the total, this is presumably a partial list. Otherwise, the extraordinarily precise figures re-flect the character of the *Gongbu gongcheng zuofa,* which prescribed exact measurements and exact man hours. Together with price lists for materials issued by the Board of Works, it was possible to determine the budget down to the last copper. It should not be presumed that these budgets were actually met, but without final tallies they must be accepted as the best estimates for what building works actually cost. For comparative discussion, see Klaas Ruitenbeek, *Carpentry and Building in Late Imperial China: A Study of the Fifteenth-Century Carpenter's Manual* Lu Ban Jing (Leiden, Netherlands: E. J. Brill, 1993), 3, 27–29; Lian-sheng Yang, "Economic Aspects of Public Works in Imperial China," in *Excursions in Sinol-ogy,* ed. Liansheng Yang (Cambridge, MA: Harvard University Press, 1969), 191–248. For a less detailed memorial from Duke Kong Zhuanze, see Lamberton, "Kongs of Qufu," 303.

91. Compare the more candid (although still fictional) estimate proposed by Wu Jingzi for the repairs to Yuanwu Pavilion. Including the hiring of masons to rebuild the outer walls and stairway and a "great many" carpenters to replace beams and pillars and rafters, the to-tal cost was estimated at three hundred to five hundred *liang.* Wu Jingzi, *The Scholars,* 618.

92. *QFXZ* 33.8b–9a.

93. While there is no detailed information about the numbers of craftsmen or common laborers involved in the project, it is possible to get a sense of the activities on a mid-Qing dynasty imperial building site from documents concerning construction of the "Three Rear Palaces" in the Forbidden City. When that complex was rebuilt after a fire of 1797, the list of expenses included wages for two different grades of carpenters, masons, tile and bricklay-ers, scaffolders, earthwork laborers, varnishers and painters, window paperers, glazed ridge tile layers, and tinsmiths. Ruitenbeek, "Building Regulations (*Zeli*) and Their Context," 182. See also Ruitenbeek, "The Rebuilding of the Three Rear Palaces in 1596–1598," in *Study on*

Ancient Chinese Books and Records of Science and Technology, ed. Hua Jueming (Zhengzhou, China: Elephant Press, 1998).

94. "Chongxiu xianshi Kongzimiao bei" (Stele of restoring the Temple of First Teacher Kongzi) (1730), in Luo Chenglie, *Shitou shang de Rujia wenxian,* 863–866; Kong Fanyin, ed., *Qufu Kongfu Dang'an shiliao xuanbian,* 3.3, 4990/310–311.

95. "Washang Li Longzhang bingwei qiangba shantu fanxing diaowu qiyi xian yanshen zhengfa shi" (Tile merchant Li Longzhang reports that he was collecting materials for tiles but was extorted by a thug), in *Qufu Kongfu Dang'an shiliao xuanbian,* ed. Kong Fanyin, 3.3, 4985/305.

96. *QFXZ* 33.8b–9a. Kent Guy notes that both Chen Shiguan (son of Governor Chen Shen) and Yue Jun (son of General Yue Zhongqi) were chosen to serve in Shandong because of their political reliability. Guy, *Qing Governors and Their Provinces: The Evolution of Territorial Administration in China, 1644–1796* (Seattle: University of Washington Press, 2010), 191. Chen Shiguan, however, had also developed a close kinship with the Duke of Fulfilling the Sage, which may have interfered with his ability to run a graft-free building site. See Agnew, "Culture and Power," 126.

97. "Shu dong fu deng wei xiuli Kongmiao gongshi gujia zouwen shi" (Shandong governor and others report the cost estimate for rebuilding Kong Temple), in *Qufu Kongfu Dang'an shiliao xuanbian,* ed. Kong Fanyin, 3.3, 4985/312.

98. *QFXZ* 33.8a–10a, 13b; "Yuzhi chongjian Queli Shengmiao bei" (Imperial stele of restoring the Saint's Temple in Queli) (1730), in Luo Chenglie, *Shitou shang de Rujia wenxian,* 861–863.

99. *SSZ,* 312.

100. A general description of ridge beasts is provided in Rose Kerr and Nigel Wood, *Chemistry and Chemical Technology in Science and Civilization in China,* vol. 5, part 12, "Ceramic Technology" (Cambridge: Cambridge University Press, 2004), 496. It is apparent that the nature, if not the number, of these beasts at Kong Temple has changed over the course of the twentieth century. Chavannes' photograph of the Hall of the Great Ensemble, taken after the Qing court had advanced the local sacrifices to the highest rank but before the work was formally completed (fig. 46), shows nine beasts but no immortal at the head of the procession. Currently, the same roof-ridge includes eight beasts and one "fish" arranged behind the hen-riding immortal.

101. On the development of building manuals, see Ruitenbeek, "Building Regulations (*Zeli*) and Their Context."

102. Liang Sicheng and Wilma Fairbank, *A Pictorial History of Chinese Architecture: A Study of the Development of Its Structural System and the Evolution of Its Types* (Cambridge, MA: MIT Press, 1984), 103.

Chapter 3

1. Joseph Lam, *State Sacrifices and Music in Ming China: Orthodoxy, Creativity, and Expressiveness* (Albany: State University of New York Press, 1998), 15–16.

2. Kai-wing Chow, *The Rise of Confucian Ritualism in Late Imperial China: Ethics, Classics, and Lineage Discourse* (Stanford, CA: Stanford University Press, 1994), 13. See also Thomas Wilson, "The Ritual Formation of Confucian Orthodoxy and the Descendants of the Sage," *Journal of Asian Studies* 55, no. 3 (1996): 564.

3. *QLZ* (1575), 12.18b.

4. Sima Qian, *Shiji* 17(47), 29b, trans. Shryock, *Origin and Development of the State Cult of Confucius,* 95.

5. Ban Gu, *Hanshu* 1(2), 12b; Sima Qian, *Shiji* 17(47), 29b; *QLZ* 2.19a. On the travels of Gaozu and motives for visiting Qufu, see Howard Wechsler, *Offerings of Jade and Silk: Ritual and Symbol in the Legitimation of the Tang Dynasty* (New Haven, CT: Yale University Press, 1985), 162.

6. Sima Qian, in Nylan and Wilson, *Lives of Confucius,* 26–27.

7. Wu Hung, *Monumentality in Early Chinese Art and Architecture* (Stanford, CA: Stanford University Press, 1995), 111.

8. For details on these appointees, see Michael Loewe, *A Biographical Dictionary of the Qin, Former Han and Xin Periods (221 BC–AD 24)* (Leiden, Netherlands: E. J. Brill, 2000); de Crespigny, *Biographical Dictionary of the Later Han to the Three Kingdoms.*

9. Ban Gu, *Hanshu* 81(51), 17a; Kong Yuancuo suggests that in the seventeenth year of Lu Aigong there were already "one hundred households protecting the temple and tombs" and that the land was used to support sacrifice to Kongzi. See Kong Yuancuo, *Kongshi zuting guangji* (1227), 3.1a. The claim appears to be apocryphal.

10. On Kongzi's genealogy, see Robert Eno, "The Background of the Kong Family of Lu," *Early China,* no. 28 (2003); Thomas Wilson, "Ritualizing Confucius/Kongzi: The Family and State Cults of the Sage of Culture in Imperial China," in *On Sacred Grounds: Culture, Society, Politics, and the Formation of the Cult of Confucius,* ed. Thomas Wilson (Cambridge, MA: Harvard University Asia Center, 2002), 58–61.

11. Ban Gu, *Hanshu* 18(6), 9a. Ban Gu indicates the recipient of this title as Kong Ji, *Hanshu* 10(10), 15b. See also Wilson, "Ritualizing Confucius/Kongzi," 61.

12. Ban Gu, *Hanshu* 12(12), 4a.

13. Fan Ye, *Hou Han shu* 445/1(1), 25a.

14. Kong Zhencong, *QLZ* 2.20a; Fan Ye, *Hou Han shu* 1(2), 9a–11a.

15. Fan Ye, *Hou Han shu* 2.16b, 3.16a–b, 5.21b. The term "uncrowned king" had been coined by the new text (or modern text) school of Confucians in the Han dynasty to refer to Kongzi as an institutional reformer and author of the six classics. See Thomas Wilson, *Genealogy of the Way: The Construction and Uses of the Confucian Tradition in Late Imperial China* (Stanford, CA: Stanford University Press, 1995), 30–31.

16. "Yi Ying zhishou miao baishi zushi bei" (Yi Ying requests the establishment of Baishi Zushi) (153), in Luo Chenglie, *Shitou shang de Rujia wenxian,* 11–12; de Crespigny, *Biographical Dictionary of the Later Han to Three Kingdoms,* 11.

17. "Kong Zhou bei" (Stele of Kong Zhou) (164), in Wu Hung, *Monumentality in Early Chinese Art and Architecture,* 221–222.

18. "Han Chi zao liqi bei" (Stele of Han Chi commissioning ritual vessels) (156), in Luo Chenglie, *Shitou shang de Rujia wenxian,* 19–24.

19. de Crespigny, *Biographical Dictionary of the Later Han to Three Kingdoms,* 1140–1141.

20. Wu Hung, *Monumentality in Early Chinese Art and Architecture,* 217–218.

21. Michael Loewe, "The Conduct of Government and the Issues at Stake, A.D. 57–167," in *The Cambridge History of China,* vol. 1, *The Ch'in and Han Empires, 221 BC–AD 220,* ed. Denis Twitchett and John K. Fairbank (Cambridge: Cambridge University Press, 1986), chap. 4, 315.

22. B. J. Mansvelt Beck, "The Fall of Han," in *The Cambridge History of China,* vol. 1, *The Ch'in and Han Empires, 221 BC–AD 220,* ed. Denis Twitchett and John K. Fairbank (Cambridge: Cambridge University Press, 1986), chap. 5, 319–322.

23. "Shi Chen qianhou bei" (Shi Chen Stele) (169 CE), in Kong Fanyin, *Qufu de lishi mingren yu wenwu,* 333–336. The elaborate pictorial inscriptions recorded in the Wuliang Shrine of nearby Jiaxiang a few years earlier do not refer directly to Kong Temple, but they openly express the sentiment that the scholar is obliged to censure the despot. See Wu Hung, *Monumentality in Early Chinese Art and Architecture,* 193, 218.

24. de Crespigny, *Biographical Dictionary of the Later Han to Three Kingdoms,* 394–395. The descendant Kong Yu is listed as one of the cosponsors of the Shi Chen Stele, although by the time it was inscribed in 169 Kong had resigned his office and returned to private life.

25. "Kong Xian bei" (Stele of Kong Xian), a.k.a. "Lu Kongzi miao bei" (Stele of the Kongzi Temple in Lu) (220), in Kong Fanyin, *Qufu de lishi mingren yu wenwu,* 348–350.

26. Titles during this time included Marquis of Sagely Ancestry (Zongshenghou), Master of Revering the Sage (Chongshengdafu), and Chongsheng Marquis (Chongshenghou) for the descendants of Kongzi and Duke of Zou (Zouguogong), First Teacher Master Ni (Xianshi Ni Fu) and Sage of Culture and Venerable Ni (Wensheng Ni Fu) for Kongzi. See Kong Jifen, *Queli wenxian kao,* 6.1.

27. Liu Xu, *Jiu Tang shu* (945), 24.7b. See also Thomas Wilson, "Sacrifice and the Imperial Cult of Confucius," *History of Religions* 41, no. 3 (2002): 263; Wilson, "Ritualizing Confucius/Kongzi," 63.

28. "Xinxiu Qufu xian Wenxuanwangmiao ji" (Record of the new restoration of Wenxuanwang Temple in Qufu), a.k.a. "Tang Luguogong xiu miao ji ji xinxiu Wenxuan Wang miao bei" (Record of Duke of Tang Luguo restoring the temple and stele of the new restoration of the Wenxuanwang Temple) (869), in Luo Chenglie, *Shitou shang de Rujia wenxian,* 118–120.

29. *QFXZ* 23.11a–b, 60.4.b–5a; see also Wilson, "Ritualizing Confucius/Kongzi," 64. Lamberton suggests that the Later Tang were motivated more by Kong Mo's failure to pay taxes than any sincere interest in preserving the bloodline of the sage. Lamberton, "Kongs of Qufu," 312–313.

30. On the Later Tang, see Ouyang Xiu and Richard L. Davis, *Historical Records of the Five Dynasties* (New York: Columbia University Press, 2004), 105; Agnew, "Culture and Power," 143–144. On the patronage of Song Taizu, see Tuotuo (Toghto), *Song shi* (1345), 105.1a–b.

31. Tuotuo (Toghto), *Song shi* 105.1a–2a, trans. after Chavannes in Shryock, *Origin and Development of the State Cult of Confucius* (Wade-Giles romanization altered to pinyin). The

passage continues with details on further titles, privileges, and gifts to the Kong family and the form of sacrifices to be used at regional temples.

32. Douglas Skonicki, "Employing the Right Kind of Men: The Role of Cosmological Argumentation in the Qingli Reforms," *Journal of Song-Yuan Studies*, no. 38 (2008): 57–58.

33. "Wuxiantang jibei" (Stele of the Chamber of the Five Sages) (1038) in Luo Chenglie, *Shitou shang de Rujia wenxian*, 157–159. On the status of these sages, see Wilson, *Genealogy of the Way*, 41. The Jin dynasty temple diagram in Kong Yuancuo, *Kongshi zuting guangji*, shows that the Chamber of the Five Sages had been moved away from the courtyard's south–north axis to a position on the western side of the compound. However, it had effectively become obsolete by the late eleventh century when Mengzi was promoted to the main hall in position of correlate, and Xunzi, Yang Xiong, and Han Yu were ennobled with the lower rank of earls and enshrined with the exegetes in the cloisters. Because his historical existence could not be verified, this privilege was not immediately extended to Wang Tong, and the famed emulator of Kongzi was sidelined until 1530 when the Jiajing emperor returned him to the temple. He would finally be raised to the title of *xianxian* (former worthy) in 1641. See Howard Wechsler, "The Confucian Teacher Wang T'ung (584?—617): One Thousand Years of Controversy," *T'oung Pao* 63, no. 4–5 (1977).

34. "Wuxiantang jibei" (Stele of the Chamber of the Five Sages) (1038), in Luo Chenglie, *Shitou shang de Rujia wenxian*, 157–159.

35. On Fan Zhongyan's construction of the temple in Suzhou, see Carroll, *Between Heaven and Modernity*, 105.

36. The substantive issues in eleventh-century Chinese reformist thought and the influence of Mengzi are covered in James T. C. Liu, *Reform in Sung China: Wang An-shih (1021–1086) and His New Policies* (Cambridge, MA: Harvard University Press, 1959).

37. *QFXZ* 25.9a–b. See also Wilson, *Genealogy of the Way*, 41; Nylan and Wilson, *Lives of Confucius*, 156.

38. Julia K. Murray, "Heirloom and Exemplar: Family and School Portraits of Confucius in the Song and Yuan Periods," *Journal of Song-Yuan Studies*, no. 41 (2011): 231.

39. Of this one hundred *qing*, twenty were to support the costs of the annual sacrifice, twenty were to support students of the temple school, ten were to buy ritual wares for the temple, and the remaining fifty were to generate funds for temple repairs and maintenance. *QFXZ* 25.10b–11a; see also Strassberg, *World of K'ung Shang-jen*, 18.

40. Nylan and Wilson, *Lives of Confucius*, 156.

41. Peter K. Bol, "Government, Society and State: On the Political Visions of Ssu-ma Kuang and Wang An-Shi," in *Ordering the World: Approaches to State and Society in Sung Dynasty China*, ed. Robert P. Hymes and Conrad Schirokauer (Berkeley: University of California Press, 1993), 152.

42. Ibid., 186.

43. The title changed from Duke of Exalted Culture in 1055 because it was deemed inappropriate for descendants to inherit the posthumous title of the sage. *QFXZ* 25.4b.

44. Kai-wing Chow, *Rise of Confucian Ritualism in Late Imperial China*, 100–101.

45. Tuotuo (Tohgto), *Jinshi* (1343), 105.5b. For more on the tortured family politics of this period, see Agnew, "Culture and Power," 88–89.

46. *QFXZ* 26.5a–b, 26.6b.

47. *QFXZ* 26.11a; Lamberton, "Kongs of Qufu," 314.

48. On the family feud that precipitated these events, see Agnew, "Culture and Power," 90–91. This state of affairs would continue until the early Ming, when descendants of Kong Sihui finally gained control of the magistracy, which they retained until the Qianlong emperor revoked the office amid yet another scandal. Agnew, "Culture and Power," 107–108.

49. "Haimei Shiyong ye miao timing jie" (Stele of Haimei Shiyong visiting the Temple) (1269), in Luo Chenglie, *Shitou shang de Rujia wenxian,* 217.

50. For discussion of the intricate intellectual and political issues connected with the development of the Dao School and the notion of the "true sages of antiquity," see Wilson, *Genealogy of the Way,* 35–51.

51. The head of the northern line would later be recognized as the only legitimate claimant on the title of Duke of Fulfilling the Sage and provided with an official salary of the fourth rank, fifty *qing* (five thousand *mu*) in land, and twenty-eight households to serve as *sasao hu.* "Chongjian Zhisheng Wenxuanwangmiao bei" (Stele of rebuilding the Wenxuanwang Temple) (1301), in Luo Chenglie, *Shitou shang de Rujia wenxian,* 247–250. The text as recorded by Luo claims "2008 households (*erqianba hu*)," although this is presumably a transcription error for "twenty eight households (*ershiba hu*)."

52. *QFXZ* 26.15b; "Queli jiqi bei" (Stele of Queli ritual vessels) (1294), in Luo Chenglie, *Shitou shang de Rujia wenxian,* 226–227.

53. "Jigao Xuanshengmiao bei" (Stele of making offerings to Xuansheng Temple) (1311), in Luo Chenglie, *Shitou shang de Rujia wenxian,* 257–258; *QFXZ* 27.5b; Wilson, *Genealogy of the Way,* 45–47.

54. *QFXZ* 27.8.a; Gong Yanxing and Wang Zhengyu, *Kongmiao zhushen kao: Kongmiao suxiang ziliao bian* (Jinan, China: Shandong youyi chubanshe, 1994), 162–163.

55. *QFXZ* 27.5b–27.8.a–b; Huang Chin-shing, "Cultural Politics of Autocracy," 276n40; Wilson, "Ritual Formation of Confucian Orthodoxy," 559. Yanzi was enfeoffed as Duke of Yan, Mengzi as Duke of Zou, Zengzi as Duke of Cheng, and Zisi as Duke of Yi. The mothers of Kongzi and Mengzi, who raised the sages in the absence of their fathers, also received special recognition, although still as adjuncts to their husbands.

56. "Chongxiu Xuanshengmiao timing bei" (Stele praising the restoration of Xuansheng Temple) (1332), in Luo Chenglie, *Shitou shang de Rujia wenxian,* 280–281; "Chi xiu Qufu Xuanshengmiao bei" (Stele of the official order to restore the Xuansheng Temple) (1339), in ibid., 291–294; Kong Jifen, *Queli wenxian kao* 12.7a. In 1111 the Northern Song had effectively recognized the temple's "royal" status by granting it the right to display twenty-four halberds, although this concession was not reflected in the architecture. Kong Yuancuo, *Kongshi zuting guangji* 3.28b.

57. Wilson, "Ritualizing Confucius/Kongzi," 55.

58. "Zhongshu pingzhang si Xuanshengmiao ji bei" (Administrator of the Secretariat performs sacrifice at Xuansheng Temple) (1361) in Luo Chenglie, *Shitou shang de Rujia wenxian,* 335. See also Agnew, "Culture and Power," 94–96.

59. *QFXZ* 28.1a; see also Huang Chin-shing, "The Cultural Politics of Autocracy: The Confucius Temple and Ming Despotism, 1368–1530," in *On Sacred Grounds: Culture, Society,*

Politics, and the Formation of the Cult of Confucius, ed. Thomas Wilson (Cambridge, MA: Harvard University Asia Center, 2002), 283.

60. Zhang Tingyu, *Ming shi* (1739), 284.1a; Zhongguo shehui kexueyuan, jindai shi yanjiu suo, ed., *Kongfu dang'an xuan bian,* 2 vols. (Beijing: Zhonghua shuju, 1982), 1:17.

61. Agnew, "Culture and Power," 99.

62. Zhang Tingyu, *Ming shi,* 139.1a–b; Lam, *State Sacrifices and Music in Ming China,* 19–22; Romeyn Taylor, "Official Religion in the Ming," in *The Cambridge History of China,* vol. 8, *The Ming Dynasty, Part 2: 1368–1644,* ed. Denis Twitchett and Frederick W. Mote (Cambridge: Cambridge University Press, 1998), 849–850. Mengzi was briefly removed from the temple between 1372 and 1373. Huang Chin-shing, "Cultural Politics of Autocracy," 286.

63. *QFXZ* 28.3a.

64. Nicholas Standaert, "Ritual Dances and their Visual Representations in the Ming and the Qing," *East Asia Library Journal* 12, no. 1 (2006): 87.

65. Christopher Agnew casts some reasonable doubt on these figures, noting that they first appear in local records dating to the Qing dynasty and do not appear in official Ming records. Agnew, "Culture and Power," 22.

66. *QFXZ* 28.2a.

67. *QFXZ* 28.9a, 28.13b.

68. L. Carrington Goodrich, *Dictionary of Ming Biography, 1368–1644* (New York: Columbia University Press, 1976), 879; Agnew, "Culture and Power," 104.

69. *QFXZ* 29.3a

70. *QFXZ* 29.5a.

71. *QFXZ* 29.6a.

72. *QFXZ* 29.6b; Lamberton, "Kongs of Qufu," 321–322; Strassberg, *World of K'ung Shang-jen,* 21.

73. Lamberton, "Kongs of Qufu," 321–323.

74. "Yuzhi chongjian Kongzi miao bei" (Imperial stele of building the Kongzi Temple) (1504), in Luo Chenglie, *Shitou shang de Rujia wenxian,* 444–445.

75. Sommer, "'Destroying Confucius': Iconoclasm in the Confucian Temple," in *On Sacred Grounds: Culture, Society, Politics, and the Formation of the Cult of Confucius,* ed. Thomas Wilson (Cambridge, MA: Harvard University Asia Center, 2002); Huang Chin-shing, "Cultural Politics of Autocracy."

76. Sommer, "'Destroying Confucius,'" 125.

77. Huang Chin-shing, "Cultural Politics of Autocracy," 267, 292. On the Jiajing controversy, see also Carney Fisher, *The Chosen One: Succession and Adoption in the Court of Ming Shizong* (Boston: Allen and Unwin, 1990); on the politics of music in the Jiajing court, see Lam, *State Sacrifices and Music in Ming China,* chap. 4.

78. Imperial Censor Li Guan did once point out that because Kongzi's title of king had been revoked it would be appropriate to reduce the scale of Kong Temple and eliminate the double eaves of its central halls. Knowing the position of the scholars, however, Li probably intended this as a rhetorical point and not a serious proposition. See Huang Chin-shing, "The Cultural Politics of Autocracy," 274.

79. Goodrich, *Dictionary of Ming Biography,* 76.

80. Agnew, "Culture and Power," 106, 108.

81. Alexander Woodside, "The Ch'ien-lung Reign," in *The Cambridge History of China,* vol. 9, *The Ch'ing Empire to 1800, Part 1,* ed. Willard J. Peterson (Cambridge: Cambridge University Press, 2002), 247.

82. Lamberton, "Kongs of Qufu," 320; Agnew, "Culture and Power," 51–53.

83. Wilson, "Ritualizing Confucius/Kongzi," 57.

84. Kong Jifen, *Queli wenxian kao* 12.8.b, 14.42a; Strassberg, *World of K'ung Shang-Jen,* 79.

85. Ibid., 91–93.

86. *Qingshilu,* "Yongzheng," in Woodside, "Ch'ien-lung Reign," 247; *QFXZ* 33.3a.

87. Huang Chin-shing, *Philosophy, Philology and Politics in Eighteenth Century China: Li Fu and the Lu-Wang School under the Ch'ing* (Cambridge: Cambridge University Press, 1995), 155–156.

88. *QFXZ* 33.12b. Regarding salary, Wu Jingzi's contemporary novel *The Scholars* sees Yu Yude, a private tutor, provided with twenty *liang* as a base annual salary. Wu Jingzi, *The Scholars,* 485.

89. The rumor, still popular today, suggests that that the emperor was drawn to Qufu by the presence of a favored princess married to the ducal heir-apparent. It is said that the princess had first been adopted by Grand Secretary Yu Minzhong to avoid official sanctions against Manchu-Han marriages. Lamberton, however, notes that there is no compelling evidence, other than the imperial overtones of the marriage ceremony, to suggest that the bride was anyone other than the actual daughter of Yu Minzhong. Lamberton, "Kongs of Qufu," 325.

90. "Qin she zhishiguan timing bei (Imperial Stele of Appointing the Zhishi Minister)" (1749), in Luo Chenglie, *Shitou shang de Rujia wenxian,* 894–895; Kong Fanyin, *Qufu de lishi mingren yu wenwu,* 77.

91. The extensive background on the problem of the duke's control over the Qufu magistracy is provided in Agnew, "Culture and Power," chap. 2.

92. Ibid., 205. Kong Jifen's position that his reforms were to bring the music and dance into proper alignment with standards set by certain ritual texts is also discussed in Standaert, "Ritual Dances and Their Visual Representations," 139.

93. Huang Chin-shing, "Cultural Politics of Autocracy," 268. Huang's reference is in regard to the general institution of Confucius temples, not specifically Kong Temple in Qufu.

94. Zito, *Of Body and Brush,* 9.

95. Carroll, *Between Heaven and Modernity,* 110–111.

96. Lam, *State Sacrifices and Music in Ming China,* 15–16; Kai-wing Chow, *Rise of Confucian Ritualism,* 13.

97. The Kong family estates and the many complications that attended their management between the Yuan and Qing dynasties are detailed in Agnew, "Culture and Power," chap. 1. For eighteenth-century statistics, see also Christopher Agnew, "Bureaucrats, Sectarians, and the Descendants of Confucius," *Late Imperial China* 31, no. 1 (2010): 8.

98. *SSZ,* 382.

99. This quarterly sacrifice schedule was unique to the Queli temple. Elsewhere, the state sacrifices to Kongzi were performed only in the spring and the autumn.

100. Visitors had once been provided with a similar facility to the west of the Gate of Unified Texts, although this eventually fell out of use, and dignitaries were directed instead to the wings of the Pavilion of the Literary Constellation.

101. On the *jiKong yuewu,* see Joseph Lam, "Musical Confucianism: The Case of Jikong Yuewu," in *On Sacred Grounds: Culture, Society, Politics, and the Formation of the Cult of Confucius,* ed. Thomas Wilson (Cambridge, MA: Harvard University Asia Center, 2002). See also Standaert, "Ritual Dances and Their Visual Representations."

102. The text of these eulogies varied. See Rodney Taylor, *The Way of Heaven: Introduction to the Confucian Religious Life* (Leiden, Netherlands: E. J. Brill, 1986), 14–18. For comparative versions of the eulogies, see J. Edkins, "A Visit to the City of Confucius," *Journal of the North China Branch of the Royal Asiatic Society,* no. 8 (1874); G. E. Moule, "Notes on the Ting-chi or Half-Yearly Sacrifice to Confucius," *Journal of the North China Branch of the Royal Asiatic Society,* no. 33 (1900–1901): 49–52.

103. *SSZ,* 380–382. Variations of this performance are discussed in Wilson, "Sacrifice and the Imperial Cult of Confucius"; Lam, "Musical Confucianism"; Carroll, *Between Heaven and Modernity,* 110–111. A semifictional ceremony held for Tai Bo is described in Wu Jingzi, *The Scholars,* 496–503. Interested readers are well advised to review Michael Nylan and Thomas Wilson's account of how the young Duke Kong Zhaohuan may have experienced a similar ceremony held at a shrine in the Kong Family Mansion in the spring of 1749. Nylan and Wilson, *Lives of Confucius,* chap. 6.

104. Mote, "Millenium of Chinese Urban History," 52.

105. Kong Fanyin et al., "Yanjin rendeng shanzi churu Yucui Guande liang men gao shi" (Notice forbidding free entrance through Yucui Gate and Guande Gate), (n.d., ca. nineteenth century), in *Qufu Kongfu Dang'an shiliao xuanbian,* 3.3, 4930/277.

106. See, for example, Wanggiyan Linqing, "Observing the Rites at the Ancient Abode of Confucius," *Tracks in the Snow,* Episode 35 (1), trans. and annotated in *China Heritage Quarterly,* ed. John Minford and Rachel May, no. 17 (2009).

107. Goodrich, *Dictionary of Ming Biography*; Willard J. Peterson, "Confucian Learning in Late Ming Thought," in *The Cambridge History of China,* vol. 8, *The Ming Dynasty, 1398–1644, Part 2,* ed. Denis Twitchett and Frederick W. Mote (Cambridge: Cambridge University Press, 1998), 723.

108. The plaque seems to be related to the discovery of a tomb in Weishan County, to the south of Qufu, in 1516. Cui Wenkui (Board of Works) declared this to be the resting place of Liang Shanbo and Zhu Yingtai and had the tomb repaired as a means to "edify the people." See Fan Cunchang, *Liang Shanbo Zhu Yingtai jia zai Kong Meng guli* (Jinan: Shandong wenxian yinxiang chubanshe, 2003), 3–5.

109. Zhang Dai, *Tao'an mengyi,* in Richard E. Strassberg, *Inscribed Landscapes: Travel Writing from Imperial China* (Berkeley: University of California Press, 1994), 339.

110. For a discussion of trees as symbols of ruin and recovery in Chinese poetry and painting, see Wu Hung, *Story of Ruins,* 41–53. Wu notes that "their ruinous forms possess

at the same time an extraordinary energy and spirit. While displaying signs of death and winter, they also offer hope for rebirth and spring."

111. *QLZ* (1575), 12.7a–b.

112. *QLZ* (1575), 12.11b.

113. Nylan and Wilson, *Lives of Confucius,* 144–145.

114. *QLZ* (1575), 12.11a. It was said that the original shoe (*lü*) of Kongzi was destroyed in a fire, along with the sword of Han Gaozu, during the reign of Jin Huidi (r. 290–301). Liu Jingshu, *Yiyuan* (ca. fifth century CE), *juan* 2. http://www.guoxue123.com/zhibu/0401/01yy/001.htm.

115. *QLZ* (1575), 12.4b.

116. *QLZ* (1575), 12.17a, trans. Innes Herdan, *300 Tang Poems* (Taipei, Taiwan: Far East Book Company, 1973), 218.

117. *QLZ* (1575), 12.23a.

118. Wu Hung, *Story of Ruins,* 18. Wu follows Stephen Owen, who describes *huaigu* as a mode of knowing that recognizes "a gap of time, effacement, and memory. The master figure here is synecdoche, the part that leads to the whole, some enduring fragment from which we try to reconstruct the lost totality." Stephen Owen, *Remembrances: The Experience of the Past in Classical Chinese Literature* (Cambridge, MA: Harvard University Press, 1986), 2.

119. Jonathan S. Hay, "Ming Palace and Tomb in Early Qing Jiangning: Dynastic Memory and the Openness of History," *Late Imperial China* 20, no. 1 (1999): 20.

120. *QLZ* (1575), 12.6a–b.

121. Confucius, *The Analects of Confucius,* trans. James Legge (Salt Lake City: Project Gutenberg), 7.14. (Electronic resource).

122. *QLZ* (1575), 12.15a.

123. Shao Yiren, in Julia K. Murray, "The Temple of Confucius and Pictorial Biographies of the Sage," *Journal of Asian Studies* 55, no. 2 (1996): 279. (Wade Giles altered to pinyin).

124. Kong Shangren, *Chushan yishu ji,* trans. Huang Chin-shing, *Philosophy, Philology and Politics in Eighteenth Century China,* 153.

125. *QLZ* (1575), 12.14a.

Chapter 4

1. Mircea Eliade, *The Sacred and the Profane: The Nature of Religion* (Orlando, FL: Harcourt, 1959), 26. Gottried Semper made an earlier but similar observation about memorial architecture: "An interesting phenomenon is the combination of two elements—the multiple series and the unified memorial—into a monumental overall effect by surrounding the unified element with rhythmically arranged circles of stone, a tangible illustration of pluralities merging into a unity. Such a combination presents the *memorial* as a unified idea opposing *plurality,* which becomes a unity itself through the peripheral rhythmic sequence, and at the same time contributes powerfully to strengthening the authority of the memo-

rial." Gottfried Semper, *Style in the Technical and Tectonic Arts, Or, Practical Aesthetics,* trans. H. F. Mallgrave and M. Robinson (1860; repr., Los Angeles: Getty Publications, 2004), 93 (emphasis in original).

2. Kenneth Frampton, "*Rappell à l'ordre:* The Case for the Tectonic," in Kenneth Frampton, *Labour, Work and Architecture: Collected Essays on Architecture and Design* (London: Phaidon Press, 2002), 82.

3. Li Zehou, *The Path of Beauty: A Study of Chinese Aesthetics* (Beijing: Morning Glory, 1989), 78.

4. *The Analects,* book 19, chap. 23, verse 2–3, trans. Legge, *Four Books,* 296–297.

5. The cultural dimensions of Chinese city walls are discussed in Yinong Xu, *Chinese City in Space and Time,* 90. See also Naquin, *Peking,* 4–8.

6. The phrase *Taihe yuanqi* was first written for Kong Temple by another provincial official for a stele erected in the same vicinity in 1514. Luo Chenglie, "Shen Jiao timing ji jie" (Stele report of praise for Shen Jiao), (1514), in *Shitou shang de Rujia wenxian,* 545.

7. *Mengzi* 5:2.5–7 (Wan Zhang: *xia*). Translation based on Mencius, P. J. Ivanhoe, and Irene Bloom, *Mencius, Translations from the Asian Classics* (New York: Columbia University Press, 2009), 111.

8. On *taihe* and *yuanqi* as separate concepts, see entries by Don J. Wyatt and and Deborah Sommer in *RoutledgeCurzon Encyclopedia of Confucianism,* ed. Xinzhong Yao (London, New York: Routledge, 2003), 588, 788.

9. The same "progeny of the dragon" are found atop the *huabiao* pillars in front of Tiananmen Square in Beijing and at the Ming tombs. See Ann Palundan, *The Imperial Ming Tombs* (New Haven, CT: Yale University Press, 1981), 21.

10. Liu, "Chinese Architectural Aesthetics," 141–142.

11. Hok-Lam Chan provides a relatively practical guide to the role of astrology in Chinese building in *Legends of the Building of Old Peking* (Seattle: University of Washington Press, 2008).

12. Based on an earlier diagram, Pan Guxi speculates that a version of the Gate of the Lattice Star may have been erected farther to the north during the Jin dynasty. Pan Guxi, *Qufu Kongmiao jianzhu,* 23.

13. *Shijing* "Praise Odes of Lu" (*Lu song*), in James Legge, *The Chinese Classics,* vol. 4, *The She King or The Book of Poetry* (London: Trübner, 1871), 616.

14. Li Daoyuan (d. 527) described the pond as indeterminate in shape in *Shui jing zhu* (Taibei: Taiwan shangwu yinshuguan, 1965). The pond seems only to have gained its current semicircular shape in the Ming dynasty. See Shen Yang, "Pan chi: Miaoxue lishui de yiyi ji biaoxian xingshi," *Zhongguo yuanlin,* no. 9 (2010): 62.

15. *QFXZ* 34.12b. I have not found any detailed descriptions of the original gate, although figure 1 includes a simplified drawing. It is speculated that when writing the gate's inscription in the Qing dynasty the Qianlong emperor formed the *ling* 欞 character as 櫺 without using the 巫 radical because it implies "sorcery" when written as an independent character. See Li Deming, *Dongfang shengcheng: Qufu* (Jinan, China: Shandong youyi chubanshe, 2001), 120.

16. The whole sordid affair has been documented by Agnew, "Culture and Power," 119–138.

17. Although a common feature of Confucius Temples, horse-dismounting steles date to as early as the Wei-Jin period and are also found outside a variety of imperial temples, palaces, and mortuaries, including the Forbidden City and the Ming tombs. By ordering passing officials to dismount when passing the residence or tomb, the steles defined the higher rank and status of the occupant.

18. "Shouwei baihu shen wei chuli Lin Zongwen niuche jingpao zhuangdao xiamabei yi'an qingjian heshi" (Security officer of the hundred households requests an investigation of the case of Lin Zongwen recklessly crashing his ox cart into the Horse Descending Stele), in Kong Fanyin et al., *Qufu Kongfu Dang'an shiliao xuanbian*, 3.3, 4930/274.

19. *QFXZ* 33.11a.

20. Jessica Rawson, *Chinese Jade from the Neolithic to the Qing* (London: British Museum, 1995), 247.

21. Ouyang Xiu, *Xin Tang shu*, 177–189.

22. Kong Zhencong, *QLZ* (1575), 11.20a. Liang Sicheng, *Qufu Kongmiao jianzhu jiqi xiuqi jihua* (Beiping, China: Zhongguo yingzao xueshe, 1935), 19.

23. The gates are formally known as Kuaidu, taken from the Tang scholar Han Yu: "What a pleasure to be among the first to lay eyes upon the sight (*zheng xian du zhe wei kuai*)," and Yanggao, taken from Yan Hui's praise for Kongzi's doctrines—"I looked up to them, and they seemed to become more high (*yang zhi mi gao*)." For Han Yu, see "Yu shao shi Li Shiyi shu" (Letter to Li Shiyi), in Ouyang Xiu, *Xin Tang shu*, 17.5. For Yan Hui, see *Analects* 9.10, trans. Legge, *Four Books*, 112.

24. Kong Fanyin et al., *Qufu Kongfu Dang'an shiliao xuanbian*, 3.3, 4930/278.

25. No catalogs survive for this library, although it is safe to say that no early modern Chinese library, least of all one associated with Kong Temple, could have been without a strong collection of dynastic histories, historiographies, and historical classics. The model for this type of library in late-imperial China would have been the Wenyuange in Beijing, the contents of which are well known. See Yang Shiqi, *Wenyuange cangshu shumu* (1441; repr., Taibei, Taiwan: Shangwu yinshuguan, 1967).

26. Kong Chuan, *Dongjia zaji* 16.b. The sources are inconclusive on whether the pavilion had been rebuilt, repaired, or merely renamed in the Jin dynasty. The stele of Dang Huaiying notes that one-third of this building work was repair, and two-thirds was reconstruction. In the Yuan dynasty, Yang Huan reported that the Pavilion of the Literary Constellation was "created," and Kaizhou prefect (*cishi*) supervised the construction. Yang Huan, *Dongyou ji, SSZ*, 694.

27. "Chongjian Zhisheng Wenxuanwangmiao bei" (Stele for rebuilding the Zhisheng Wenxuanwang Temple) (1301), in Lou Chenglie, *Shitou shang de Rujia wenxian*, 247–250; "Kuiwenge changshu jibei" (Stele recording the book collections at the Pavilion of the Literary Constellation) (1505), in Luo Chenglie, *Shitou shang de Rujia wenxian*, 438.

28. *QFXZ* 49.11a.; "Kuiwenge changshu jibei" (1505), in Luo Chenglie, *Shitou shang de Rujia wenxian*, 438. Considering that the building was substantially renewed and redesigned,

the architectural historian Liang Sicheng chose to date it not to 997 or 1191, but to 1504. Liang Sicheng, *Qufu Kongmiao jianzhu jiqi xiuqi jihua,* 26.

29. *QFXZ* 29.12b; "Kuiwenge zhongshu shuji jibei" (Stele record of sorting books in Kuiwenge) (1520), in Luo Chenglie, *Shitou shang de Rujia wenxian,* 483–485.

30. W. A. P. Martin, *A Cycle of Cathay, or, China, South and North with Personal Reminiscences* (New York: Fleming H. Revell, 1896), 284.

31. In 1192 Yang Huan noted the presence of six steles in the Eastern Cloister, including the Zhang Menglong Stele and five others "written in *lishu*" (i.e., of Han origin) and eight in the Western Cloister, four of which were written in *lishu* with the remainder being of Tang and Song origin. *Dongyou ji, SSZ,* 694.

32. In 1018 Kong Daofu noted that the pavilions had been repaired, indicating their earlier construction. Fu Chonglan, *Qufu miaocheng yu Zhongguo Ruxue,* 122–123. Those pavilions had disappeared by the Jin dynasty, although they were rebuilt between 1191 and 1196 and are pictured by Kong Yuancuo in 1227. See Kong Yuancuo, *Kongshi zuting guangji.* Their contents were listed later in the Yuan dynasty by Yang Huan: "In the east pavilion is a Song stele composed by Lü Mengzheng and written by Bai Chongju. It was erected in the tenth month of 983 (Taiping Xingguo 8). There is also one stele made in Jin times, composed and written by Dang Huaiying. All the steles located in the western pavilions are from Tang times. One of them was composed by Cui Xinggong and written by Sun Shifan. On the back of this stele is the imperial edict of the twelfth month of 626 (Wude 9) and a sacrifice document written in the second month of 666 (Qianfeng 1). Another stele was composed by Li Yong of Jiangxia, written by Zhang Tinggui of Fanyang, erected in the eleventh month of 719 (Kaiyuan 7). *Dongyou ji, SSZ,* 694.

33. "Zhu Yuanzhang yu Kong Kejian Kong Xixue duihua bei" (Stele of conversation of Zhu Yuanzhang and Kong Kejian, Kong Xixue) (1368), in Luo Chenglie, *Shitou shang de Ruxue wenhua,* 349–351.

34. The pavilions sheltering the earlier steles were destroyed in the fire of 1499 and subsequently rebuilt, along with pavilions for the Chenghua and Hongzhi steles. However, only the Hongwu stele pavilion endured into the Qing dynasty. After the fire of 1724, this sole survivor was joined by a reconstructed Yongle stele pavilion, and both endured into the twentieth century, although the extant pieces are attributed to Republican-era builders. *SSZ,* 305; Liang Sicheng, *Qufu Kongmiao jianzhu jiqi xiuqi jihua,* 13. The Manchus' treatment of other Ming relics is discussed in Hay, "Ming Palace and Tomb in Early Qing Jiangning."

35. Stele of Kongmiao in Queli, in Luo Chenglie, *Shitou shang de Ruxue wenhua,* 795–796.

36. Wu Hung, "On Rubbings: Their Materiality and Historicity," in *Writing and Materiality in China: Essays in Honor of Patrick Hanan,* ed. Judith Zeitlin and Lydia Liu (Cambridge, MA: Harvard University Asia Center, 2003). See also Lillian Lan-Ying Tseng, "Retrieving the Past, Inventing the Memorable: Huang Yi's Visit to the Song-Luo Monuments," in *Monuments and Memory, Made and Unmade,* ed. Robert S. Nelson and Margaret Olin (Chicago: University of Chicago Press, 2003). Tseng's analysis considers how rubbings, and the paintings and diary entries associated with them, may have taken on a monumental form through reproduction.

37. This process is described in more detail by Wu Hung, *Story of Ruins,* 51–54.

38. *QFXZ* 33.9b; Kong Fanyin et al., "Shu dong fu deng wei xiuli Kongmiao gongshi gujia zouwen shi," in *Qufu Kongfu Dang'an shiliao xuanbian,* 3.3, 4985/312–314; *Doctrine of the Mean,* chap. 28, verse 3; trans. James Legge, *The Chinese Classics* (Hong Kong: Hong Kong University Press, 1960), 411.

39. Strassberg, *World of K'ung Shang-jen,* 95–98.

40. Luo Chenglie, *Shitou shang de Rujia wenxian,* 46. A complete list of the steles housed in the Gate of Unified Texts by the 1930s is provided in Liang, *Qufu Kongmiao jianzhu jiqi xiuqi jihua,* 23–24.

41. Xiping Canbei (CE 172), in Luo Chenglie, *Shitou shang de Rujia wenxian,* 43–44. On Huang Yi, see Tseng, "Retrieving the Past, Inventing the Memorable."

42. Wu Hung, "On Rubbings," 39.

43. Ma Zhiyuan, cited in Wu Hung, "On Rubbings," 68n50. A good selection of rubbings from Kong Temple steles, including the Stele of Kong Zhou, are available online through the Harvard University Library. See, for example, the Stele of Kong Zhou at http://viacs.hul.harvard.edu/via/deliver/deepcontent?recordId=olvwork291767.

44. On the great, or "perfect ensemble," see Mencius, Ivanhoe, and Bloom, *Mencius, Translations from the Asian Classics,* 111. The term *cheng,* for which the central hall and gate is named, has elsewhere been translated as "completion," "accomplishment," "consummation," and "symphony." All these terms are valid, depending on the context in which they are used, although with respect to the temple I think that "ensemble" is most appropriate because it pays respect to the strong musical analogies embedded in the architecture.

45. Chongjian Zhisheng Wenxuanwangmiao bei (Stele of repairing the Zhisheng Wenxuanwang Temple) (1302), in Luo Chenglie, *Shitou shang de Rujia wenxian,* 248.

46. Liang Sicheng, *Qufu Kongmiao jianzhu jiqi xiuqi jihua,* 42.

47. Zhang Dai, trans. Strassberg, *Inscribed Landscapes,* 339.

48. *QLZ* (1575), 12.9b.

49. *QLZ* (1575), 12.18a.

50. Ibid., 12.15b.

51. Translated in Strassberg, *Inscribed Landscapes,* 339.

52. The stump of the earlier tree remained in place and was preserved in a glass case into the 1960s. See Shandong Provincial Artifact Management Office and the Jinan Branch of the Chinese International Travel Agency, *Qufu mingsheng guji* (Jinan: Shandong renmin chubanshe, 1958). For more discussion of temple trees, see also chapter 3 and Wu Hung, *Story of Ruins,* 41–53.

53. It was said that the apricots planted around Xing Altar blossomed in the second month, with double flowers having double pistils. This phenomenon was attributed to the fact that they grew in the place where Kongzi taught. Bi Jingyan, *Queli linmiao tongji shi* (Li dong tang bi shi, 1918), 23a.

54. Zhuangzi, *The Zhuangzi,* chap. 31, trans. James Legge, *The Sacred Books of China: The Texts of Taoism,* part 2 (New York: Dover, 1962).

55. "Dang Huaiying zhuan chongxiu zhisheng wenxuanwangmiao bei" (Stele written by Dang Huaiying for the reconstruction of Zhisheng Wenxuanwang Temple) (1197),

in Luo Chenglie, *Shitou shang de Rujia wenxian,* 196–203. Kong Yuancuo, *Kongshi zuting guangji.*

56. *QFXZ* 26.12b, 30.1b; *QLZ* (1575), 10.71a–73a.

57. Certain details of the organization of exegetes are given in chapter 4, although the complete history of canonization, which is standard for all Confucius temples, has been studied elsewhere in much greater detail. For an introduction to individual tablets, see Watters' *Guide to the Tablets in a Temple of Confucius* (Shanghai: American Presbyterian Mission Press, 1879). For a political analysis, see Huang Chin-shing, *Youru shengyu: Quanli xinyang yu zhengdangxing* (Taibei, Taiwan: Yun-chen, 1994). Thomas Wilson studies the formation of the Dao School of Confucianism in *Genealogy of the Way.*

58. Ouyang Xiu, *Xin Tang shu,* in Fu Chonglan, *Qufu miaocheng yu Zhongguo Ruxue,* 104–105.

59. Tuotuo (Toghto), *Song shi* 105.4a; Kong Yuancuo, *Kongshi zuting guangji* 3.28b.

60. Kong Fanyin, *Qufu de lishi mingren yu wenwu,* 230; Zhou Boqi in Kong Zhencong, *Queli zhi* 12.7a.

61. Chen Hao, *QLZ* (1505), 4.6a. See also Liang, *Qufu Kongmiao jianzhu jiqi xiuqi jihua,* 46.

62. Liang and Fairbank, *Pictorial History of Chinese Architecture,* 117. Liang, *Qufu Kongmiao jianzhu jiqi xiuqi jihua,* 47–53. Kongzi was promoted to the rank of emperor at the end of the dynasty, although his architecture was never altered to reflect that fact. See chapter 5.

63. "Shi Chen qianhou bei" (Shi Chen stele) (169 CE), in Kong Fanyin, *Qufu de lishi mingren yu wenwu,* 333–336.

64. Li Daoyuan, *Shui jing zhu* 25.7b; Julia K. Murray, "'Idols' in the Temple: Icons and the Cult of Confucius," *Journal of Asian Studies* 68, no. 02 (2009): 377.

65. "Li Zhongxuan bei" (541), in Kong Fanyin, *Qufu de lishi mingren yu wenwu,* 355–356. See also Kong Shangren's account in Strassberg, *World of K'ung Shang-jen,* 91.

66. Liu Xu, *Jiu Tang shu* (945), 24.7b. The text refers to the Imperial Academy (Guozijian), and since earlier descriptions of Kong Temple, including the Li Zhongxuan Stele, do not indicate the original position for the local Kongzi effigy, it can only be assumed that it had faced west until this time. See Wilson, "Sacrifice and the Imperial Cult of Confucius," 263. On regalia see Murray, "'Idols' in the Temple," 378.

67. Murray, "'Idols' in the Temple," 383; Sommer, "'Destroying Confucius,'" 106–107; Wilson, "Ritual Formation of Confucian Orthodoxy," 566.

68. Murray, "'Idols' in the Temple," 385; Sommer, "'Destroying Confucius,'" 123–124. Huang Chin-shing, "Cultural Politics of Autocracy." There are many cases in which effigies were hidden or displayed in defiance of this directive. See Sommer, "'Destroying Confucius,'" 126–127. The current effigies are reproductions dating to the early 1980s and are near-replicas of the version that was installed after the fire of 1724 (see chapter 6).

69. Li Daoyuan, *Shui jing zhu* 25.7b.

70. *QFXZ* 26.4a. Dang Huaiying, "Chongjian Yunguo furen dian" (Rebuilding the Hall of the Matron of Yunguo), http://www.infobase.gov.cn/bin/mse.exe?seachword=&K=a&A=71&rec=952&run=13.

71. *QLZ* (1505), 4.6a.

72. Kong Jifen, *Queli wenxian kao* 12.9; Liang, *Qufu Kongmiao jianzhu jiqi xiuqi jihua,* 55.

73. Liang Sicheng notes that the structural elements and tile decorations are all appropriate to the Wanli era of the Ming dynasty. Liang, *Qufu Kongmiao jianzhu jiqi xiuqi jihua,* 55.

74. Murray, "Varied Views of the Sage," 241–247.

75. See, especially, Shao Yiren, cited in Murray, "Temple of Confucius and Pictorial Biographies," 279.

76. For an early account affirming that the Family Temple is coterminous with the original residence of Kongzi, see Li, *Shui jing zhu* 25.6b.

77. Ban Gu, *Hanshu* 30(10), 3b; 88(58), 11a; *QLZ* (1575), 8.3a; Kong Fanyin, *Qufu de lishi mingren yu wenwu,* 42–43, 242. See also Strassberg, *World of K'ung Shang-jen,* 16–17. There is no firm evidence to indicate where this house was located, although according to a statement in the *Book of Rites,* the disciple Zengzi served Kongzi "between the Zhushui and Sishui [rivers]." See *Li Ji: Tan gong shang,* in James Legge, Confucius, Mencius, and Ming Zuoqiu, *The Chinese Classics,* 2nd ed. (Oxford: Clarendon Press, 1893), part 2, verse 12. This would logically place the sage's last residence, and the original memorial hall, to the north of the modern city. The residence retained by his descendants and occupied by Liu Yu would not, therefore, have played any particular role in keeping his memory. The "discovery" of the ancient texts would have greatly enhanced the memorial qualities of the Kong residence. While the hypothesis is speculative, such a development may in turn have facilitated the eventual consolidation of the memorial temple and family home within the existing compound some time during the Eastern Han. See Fu Chonglan, *Qufu miaocheng yu Zhongguo Ruxue,* 77.

78. On the charges of later forgery of the documents, see Bernhard Karlgren, *Philology and Ancient China* (1926; repr., Philadelphia: Porcupine Press, 1980), 97. On the exposure of the forgery in the Ming dynasty, see the biography of Mei Zu in Goodrich, *Dictionary of Ming Biography,* 1060–1061. On the continuing acceptance of the texts as legitimate, see Murray, "Varied Views of the Sage," 242–244. The reemergence of the controversy in the late Qing is detailed by Anne Cheng, "Nationalism, Citizenship, and the Old Text/New Text Controversy in Late Nineteenth Century China," in *Imagining the People: Chinese Intellectuals and the Concept of Citizenship, 1890–1920,* ed. Joshua Fogel and Peter Zarrow (Armonk, NY: M. E. Sharpe, 1997).

79. "Xinxiu Wenxuanwangmiao bei" (Stele for the reconstruction of Wenxuanwang Temple) (870), in Luo Chenglie, *Shitou shang de Rujia wenxian,* 372–374.

80. On the classical belief that the home of Kongzi was near Jinsitang, see "Li Dongyang Jinsitang ming" (Li Dongyang's inscription for the Hall of Gold and Silk) (1505), which notes the discovery on the site of a carved stone that allegedly proved the theory, in Luo Chenglie, *Shitou shang de Rujia wenxian,* 461.

81. Ibid.

82. *QFXZ* 49.8a–b.

83. *Dongyou ji, SSZ,* 692–698; Zhang Xuzhong, "Miaoxue ji" (Record of the temple school) (Yuan dynasty), in ibid., 698–699. "Li Dongyang Jinsitang ming" (Li Dongyang's

inscription for the Hall of Gold and Silk) (1505), in Luo Chenglie, *Shitou shang de Rujia wenxian*, 461.

84. Ibid. For an account of the lecture delivered in the presence of the Kangxi emperor, see Strassberg, *World of K'ung Shang-jen*, 80–89.

85. *Lunyu* (The analects) 16.13.

86. As noted, the connection to the first descendant was represented pictorially in the Hall of the Sage's Traces later in the Ming dynasty. Much later, in the 1990s, the same theme was incorporated into the Chamber of Odes and Rites, with the installation of a new set of stone-cut Pictures of the Sage's Traces.

87. Wilson, *Genealogy of the Way*.

88. Kong Chuan, *Dongjia zaji, shang*, 17b–18a; Tuotuo (Toghto) *Song shi* 105.1a–2a, trans. Shryock, *Origin and Development of the State Cult of Confucius*, 153–154. *QFXZ* 24.17a; Fu, *Qufu miaocheng yu Zhongguo Ruxue*, 123; *SSZ*, 294.

89. *QFXZ* 27.8.a; Huang Chin-shing, "Cultural Politics of Autocracy," 276n40; Wilson, "Ritual Formation of Confucian Orthodoxy and the Descendants of the Sage," 559. "Chongxiu Xuanshengmiao timing bei" (Stele of recognition for rebuilding the Xuansheng Temple) (1332), in Luo Chenglie, *Shitou shang de Rujia wenxian*, 280–281; "Hou Zhiyuan wu nian chi xiu Qufu Xuanshengmiao bei" (Official rebuilding of Xuansheng Temple in the fifth year of Zhiyuan) (1339), in ibid., 291–294; Pan Guxi, "The Yuan and Ming Dynasties," in *Chinese Architecture, The Culture and Civilization of China*, ed. Nancy Shatzman Steinhardt (New Haven, CT: Yale University Press, 2002), 228.

90. Huang Chin-shing, "Cultural Politics of Autocracy," 276. Zhang Tingyu, *Ming shi*, 50.

Chapter 5

1. Georges Bataille, in Bois and Krauss, *Formless*, 21.

2. "Chongxiu Zhisheng miao beiji" (Record of restoring the Temple of Kongzi) (1872), in Luo Chenglie, *Shitou shang de Rujia wenxian*, 987–988; *SSZ*, 304; Li Jingye and Gong Zhaozeng, *QFXZ* (1934), 8.28b.

3. See William Woolridge, "Building and State Building in Nanjing after the Taiping Rebellion," *Late Imperial China* 30, no. 2 (2009).

4. *Shenbao*, 04, 18, 1872 (*Shenbao* dates prior to 1912 are according to the lunar calendar). Ding was later transferred to Sichuan, where he gained considerable fame for his efforts in conserving the Dujiangyan irrigation works.

5. "Chongxiu Zhisheng miao bei" (Stele of restoring the Zhisheng Temple) (1898), in Luo Chenglie, *Shitou shang de Rujia wenxian*, 998; *SSZ*, 304.

6. Wilson, *Genealogy of the Way*, 28.

7. "Xiuqi Kongmiao" (Repairing Kong Temple), *Shenbao*, 04, 14, 1908; "Xiujian Qufu Shengmiao" (Repairing the Saint's Temple in Qufu), *Shenbao*, 03, 24, 1908; *SSZ*, 305; Pan Guxi, ed., *Qufu Kongmiao jianzhu*, 418–419.

8. On this and other related reforms to Confucian education at the end of the Qing, see Carroll, *Between Heaven and Modernity*, 124–130; and Yapei Kuo, "The Emperor and the

People in One Body": The Worship of Confucius and Ritual Planning in the Xinzheng Reforms, 1902–1911," *Modern China* 35, no. 2 (2009).

9. Uno Tetsuto, *Shina bunmei ki* (Account of Chinese culture) (1912), in Joshua A. Fogel, *The Literature of Travel in the Japanese Rediscovery of China, 1862–1945* (Stanford, CA: Stanford University Press, 1996), 110–112. See also Joshua A. Fogel, *The Cultural Dimension of Sino-Japanese Relations: Essays on the Nineteenth and Twentieth Centuries* (Armonk, NY: M. E. Sharpe, 1995), 107.

10. Ibid.; Carroll, *Between Heaven and Modernity,* 117–124, 130.

11. "Baohu Qufu Kongling" (Protecting the tomb of Kongzi in Qufu), *Shenbao,* July 26, 1912; "Jiaoyubu guanyu ding Kongzi danchen wei Shengjie zhi ge sheng bu du deng dian" (Telegram from the Department of Education to provincial governors etc., regarding the recognition of the birthday of Kongzi as a holy holiday) (1913), in *Zhonghua Minguo shi dang'an ziliao huibian,* vol. 3, no. 2 (Nanjing: Jiangsu guji chubanshe, 1991), 2–3.

12. "Da zongtong fabu gui xia jiKong ling" (Grand president decrees the restoration of sacrifices to Kongzi) (1914) in ibid., 2, 6.

13. "Shandong Kongjiao dahui jisheng" (On the Association for Confucian Religion in Shandong), *Shenbao,* October 6, 1913; *Analects,* 1, 12, 21, trans. James Legge, *The Four Books,* 170. For a more detailed account of another association meeting in 1931, see Kong Xiangke, "Kongzi shengdan Qufu dahui ji," *Kongjiaohui zazhi* 1, no. 9 (1931): 1–6.

14. "Da zongtong fabu Chongsheng dian liling" (Grand president issues decree regulating sacrifices to the revered saint) (1914), in ibid., 8–10. See also "Neiwubu diaocha Kongmiao yueqi" (Ministry of Interior investigates the musical instruments of Kong Temple), *Shenbao,* November 30, 1914. The ministry had also taken responsibility for the management of the newly established government museum (Guwu Chenliesuo; Neiwubu Guwu Chenliesuo after 1916; expanded as the Gugong Bowuyuan [Palace Museum] in 1925).

15. A detailed description of this ceremony is available in Paul Samuel Reinsch, *An American Diplomat in China* (Garden City, NY: Doubleday, Page, 1922), 26–27. Reinsch also reported on the ceremony of 1917 in Paul Carus, "Ceremony Celebrated under the Chinese Republic in Honor of Confucius," *Open Court, A Quarterly Magazine* 32, no. 3 (March 1918).

16. Chow Tse-tsung, "Anti-Confucianism in Early Republican China," in *The Confucian Persuasion,* ed. Arthur F. Cahill and James Wright (Stanford, CA: Stanford University Press, 1960), 293.

17. Kam Louie, *Critiques of Confucius in Contemporary China* (New York: St. Martin's Press, 1980), 6, 8.

18. Chow Tse-tsung, *The May Fourth Movement: Intellectual Revolution in Modern China* (Cambridge, MA: Harvard University Press, 1960), 303–307; "Wu Yu wenlu xu" (Selections from Wu Yu's writings), in *Hu Shi xuanwen xuanji,* ed. Lin Na (Tianjin, China: Baihua wenyi chubanshe, 2004), 91. By the time of the Cultural Revolution, the slogan had been conflated with another May 4 era slogan, "Down with Kong the second son" (*Dadao* Kong *lao'er*), to produce "Down with the Kong Family Shop" (*Dadao* Kongjiadian). During the Cultural Revolution, it was also popular to invoke the phrase "Burn the Kong Family Shop" (*Huoshao* Kongjiadian).

19. Li Jingming, *Jiazu shixi*, Kongzi jiazu quanshu, vol. 2 (Shenyang, China: Liaohai chubanshe, 1999), 340. Kong Lingyi was also preparing to erect a monument to Zhang Xun in Qufu, but this plan was abandoned after the failure of the restoration; see Kong Demao, Ke Lan, and Frances Wood, *The House of Confucius* (London: Hodder and Stoughton, 1988), 19.

20. "Zongtong siKong zhi lijie" (On the etiquette of the president's sacrifice to Kongzi), *Shenbao*, September 24, 1917.

21. "Da Zongtong fabu chongsheng dian xianru ling" (The grand president issues decree regulating sacrifices to the revered saint and the former scholars) (1919), in *Zhonghua Minguo shi dang'an ziliao huibian*, vol. 3, 15.

22. Sun Zhuyou, *Jiazu jingying*, Kongzi jiazu quanshu (Shenyang, China: Liaohai chubanshe, 1999), 323.

23. For a discussion of the drastic reduction in Kong-controlled lands to as little as one thousand *qing* by the early nineteenth century, see Agnew, "Culture and Power," 82.

24. "Neiwubu diaocha Kongmiao yueqi" (Ministry of the Interior investigates the musical instruments of Kong Temple), *Shenbao*, November 30, 1914. The investigation was also to include the Temple of Kongzi (Fuxue Wenmiao) attached to the prefectural school in the provincial capital of Jinan.

25. "Wei Zhenghong xiumiao junshui bei" (Stele of Wei Zhenghong repairing the temple and dredging the waterways) (1915), in Luo Chenglie, *Shitou shang de Rujia wenxian*, 1025.

26. "Neiwubu niding baocun guwu zanxing banfa zhi ge shengzhang dutong chishu zunxing zi" (Ministry of the Interior drafts provisional plan for the protection of cultural artifacts on behalf of the provincial governments) (1916), in *Zhonghua Minguo shi dang'an ziliao huibian*, vol. 3, 197–199. The 1909 *Regulations for the Self-Government of Cities, Towns, and Villages* is discussed in Carroll, *Between Heaven and Modernity*, 178–182.

27. Ministry of the Interior, ed., *Minguo Jing Lu Jin Xiang gu qiwu diaocha minglu* (Beijing: Beijing tushuguan chubanshe, 2004).

28. "Zhang Zongchang Qufu siKong ji" (Account of Zhang Zongchang's sacrifice to Kongzi), *Shenbao*, October 17, 1925.

29. Pan Guxi, ed., *Qufu Kongmiao jianzhu*, 419; SSZ, 305. "Zhang Zongchang Qufu siKong ji," *Shenbao*, October 17, 1925; F. Dransmann, *Taischan-Tchufu Fuhrer* (*T'aishan-Ku'fow Guide*) (Yenchowfu, Shantung: Yenchow Missionary Press, 1934), 310; Kong Demao, *House of Confucius*, 36, 214.

30. Sun, *Confucianism as a World Religion*, 43. One branch of the Kongjiaohui would continue to operate out of Hong Kong.

31. *Sin Wan Pao*, February 22, 1928, as cited in *Chinese Recorder,* April 1928; Li Jingming, *Jiashi benmo*, Kongzi jiazu quanshu, vol. 4 (Shenyang, China: Liaohai chubanshe, 1999), 212. See also Nedostup, *Superstitious Regimes,* 269.

32. "1928 nian Guomindang Neizhengbu chengqing quxiao Yanshenggong fengjue bing moshou sitian" (On the 1928 request from the Ministry of the Interior of the Guomindang to rescind the title of Duke of Fulfilling the Sage and confiscate his landed estates) (1928), in Zhongguo shehui kexueyuan, jindai shi yanjiu suo, ed., *Kongfu dang'an xuanbian*

(Beijing: Zhonghua shuju, 1982), 715–719; "Neizhengbu tongling baohu Kongmiao" (Ministry of the Interior orders the protection of Kong Temple), *Shenbao,* May 7, 1928; Nedostup, *Superstitious Regimes,* 263.

33. Chen Huanzhang, *Gaige Qufu lin miao banfa boyi* (Jiulong, China: Yi qiang yin shua chang yin, 1962), 22. See also Agnew, "Culture and Power," 221.

34. "Fujian sheng Yang Shuzhuang zhuan Shi Pingfan deng chengqing zhongyang tongling ge sheng jiKong dadian" (Telegram from Yang Shuzhuang of Fujian, through Shi Pingfan to the central government on each province performing sacrifice to Kongzi) *Shenbao,* August 8, 1927; "Lan Wenbin, Rao Guohua deng yaoqiu Guomin zhengfu tongdian quanguo quxiao Daxueyuan feizhi siKong ling de kuaiyou daidian" (Telegram from Lan Wenbin, Rao Guohua, and others requesting that the Nationalist government rescind the Great Academy's nationwide order to cancel sacrifices to Kongzi), *Shenbao,* May 7, 1927; "Zhonghua Zong Shanghui fandui feizhi siKong dian" (Telegram from the Chinese Chamber of Commerce opposing the abolition of sacrifices to Kongzi), *Shenbao,* April 13, 1928; "Dianqing baohu Kongzi yichan" (Telegram calling for protection of Kongzi heritage), *Shenbao,* December 22, 1929.

35. "1928 nian Kong Xiangxi fandui moshou sitian, nichu sitian shouru fenji banfa" (In 1928, Kong Xiangxi opposed the confiscation of sacrifice lands and drafted plans for the distribution of tenancy) (1928), in Zhongguo shehui kexueyuan, jindai shi yanjiu suo, ed., *Kongfu dang'an xuanbian,* 719–720; "Han Rujia qingshe Guoxueyuan yi weihu gu you daode bing gong Zhongwai renshi yanjiu Zhongguo wenhua zhi Tan Yankai" (Han Rujia to Tan Yankai on building the Academy of Chinese Learning in order to maintain morality and encourage foreigners and Chinese alike to research Chinese culture) (1929), in *Zhonghua Minguo shi dang'an ziliao huibian,* vol. 1.1, no. 2, 523–524; Li Jingming, *Jiazu shixi,* 212–216.

36. Yutang Lin, *Confucius Saw Nancy and Essays about Nothing* (Shanghai: Commercial Press, 1936). Translation of Lin Yutang, *Zi jian Nanzi* (1928), 44–46.

37. Kong Demao, *House of Confucius,* 133–134.

38. Ni Jingyin and his fellow travelers happened to pass through Qufu on the same day as the visiting dignitaries that sparked the scandal but found the town in a state of unremitting lethargy. Ni Jingyin, *Qufu Taishan youji* (Shanghai: Zhonghua shuju, 1931).

39. Li Jingming, *Jiazu shixi,* 218–225; see also Diran John Sohigian, "Confucius and the Lady in Question: Power Politics, Cultural Production and the Performance of *Confucius Saw Nanzi* in China in 1929," *Twentieth-Century China* 36, no. 1 (2011).

40. *Yusi* (Threads of talk), August 11, 1929, 5, 24. Reprinted in Lu Xun, *Jiwai jishi yi bu bian* (Supplement to the addenda to the collected works) (Beijing: Renmin wenxue chubanshe, 1993). Lu Xun, writing as Qi Ming, had also criticized Japanese propagandists for accusing the Shandong provincial government under Feng Yuxiang of being "immoral" for attempting to cancel the sacrifices and "Break the Kongzi and Mengzi temples in Shandong." *Yusi* (1928), 4, 33. Reprinted in Zhang Liang, ed., *Yusi Zuopin xuan* (Selections from *Threads of Talk*) (Beijing: Renmin wenxue chubanshe, 1988), 64–66.

41. Johnston, *Confucianism and Modern China,* 133; Li Jingye and Gong Zhaozeng, *Qufu xianzhi* 5.12–14.

42. Jiang Jieshi telegram to Kong Decheng, in Ke Lan, ed., *Qiannian Kongfu de zuihou yi dai*, (Tianjin Shi, China: Tianjin jiao yu chu ban she, 1998), 131; Johnston, *Confucianism and Modern China*, 133.

43. A *Shenbao* editorial, for example, suggested that "this place, where culture originated several thousand years ago, a world famous architectural site, has never before suffered this manner of damage." "Qufu Shengji bei duan ji" (Account of smashing the relics of the Saint in Qufu), *Shenbao*, July 31, 1930.

44. Pak Yŏn-jo and An Sŭng-gwi, ed., *Kokpu Sŏngmyo Wian Sasilgi* (Sihŭng County, Korea: Noktong Sŏwŏn, 1931), 27.

45. Carroll, *Between Heaven and Modernity*, 207–208.

46. "Kongmiao caichan baoguan banfa" (On methods of protecting the property of Confucian temples) (1929), in *Zhonghua Minguo shi dang'an ziliao huibian*, vol. 5.1, no. 2, 549. This followed a precedent of 1928. See "Neiwubu tongling baohu Kongmiao" (Ministry of the Interior orders the protection of Kong Temple), *Shenbao*, May 27, 1928. In 1917 Shandong governor Zhang Jian had called upon his magistrates to protect and renovate their local temples "as a sign that our noble morality is not declining," but this appeal was never given legal authority. "Lu shi lingshi" (Shandong affairs), *Shenbao*, April 20, 1917.

47. "Shandong sheng mingsheng guji guwu baocun weiyuanhui guice" (Establishing a committee for the protection of scenic and historical sites and antiquities in Shandong), *Zhonghua Minguo shi dang'an ziliao huibian*, vol. 5.1, no. 2, 583–584.

48. "Guwu baocun fa" (Antiquities Protection Law), in ibid., 609, 622–625.

49. "Shandong shengli er shi xuesheng fan Kong zhuan dan" (Anti-Confucian leaflet from Shandong Second Normal College) (n.d.), in *Kongfu Dang'an xuan*, ed. Luo Chenglie, Zhu Fuping, and Luo Ming (Beijing: Zhongguo wenshi chubanshe, 2002), 219–220.

50. Nedostup, *Superstitious Regimes*, 264–265.

51. "Mujuan chongxiu Konglin Kongmiao" (Raising funds for the restoration of Kong Forest and Kong Temple), *Shenbao*, April 3, 1931.

52. "Dai Liu dui muxiu Konglin yijian" (Dai Liu's opinion concerning the restoration of Kong Forest), *Shenbao*, April 17, 1931.

53. The Nanjing government appointed a Central Committee for Rectifying the Distribution of Sacrificial Fields, but by the eve of the Japanese invasion the committee had failed to disentangle the complicated tenurial system. Ke, *Qianian Kongfu de zuihou yi dai*, 125; Kong Demao, *House of Confucius*, 125; "Ye Chucang deng fandi Jing" (On Ye Chucang and others returning to the capital), *Shenbao*, August 29, 1934, "Qufu Kongmiao shou xiupu" (Kong Temple in Qufu repaired), *Shenbao*, September 26, 1934.

54. "Zushe xiufu Kongmiao choubeihui" (Establishing preparatory committee for the restoration of Kong Temple), *Shenbao*, April 21, 1931.

55. "Kongmiao choubeihui chengli" (Kong Temple preparatory committee established) *Shenbao*, May 15, 1931; *Shandong sheng zhengfu gongbao* (Bulletin of the Shandong provincial government), no. 198, September 7, 1932, 63–64; Li Guannan, "Culture, Revolution and Modernity: The Guomindang's Ideology and Enterprise of Reviving China, 1927–1937" (PhD diss., University of Oregon, 2009), 447–449.

56. Translated in ibid., 449–450. A draft of the telegram is included in the report "Kongmiao choubeihui chengli," *Shenbao,* May 15, 1931.

57. *Shandong sheng zhengfu gongbao,* no. 198, September 7, 1932, 63–64; "Xiufu Kongmiao hui juankuan zongshu" (Total funds collected by the Committee for the Restoration of Kong Temple), *Shenbao,* January 28, 1934.

58. "Xiufu Kong Zhou Yan Si Meng ge miao" (Restoring each of the temples of Kong, Zhou, Yan, Si, and Meng), *Shenbao,* June 15, 1934; "Xiuli Kongmiao choubeihui zhang" (Chair of the preparatory committee for restoring Kong Temple), *Shenbao,* July 14, 1934; "Xiuli Kongmiao deng an" (Plans for restoring Kong Temple and others), *Shenbao,* September 8, 1934; "Qufu jian bowuguan tushuguan" (Qufu to build museum and library), *Shenbao,* September 13, 1934.

59. Qing Bi, Guang Hua, and Jing Yu, "Kongdao, Kongdao ting yu Kongdao xuexiao," *Qufu wenshi* (Qufu culture and history), no. 6 (1986): 5–8.

60. "Guomindang zhongyang zhixing weiyuanhui zhuanqing guomin zhengfu mingling gongbu siKong banfa" (Central Executive Committee of the Guomindang requests that Nationalist government order rites for Kongzi) (1934), in *Zhonghua Minguo shi dang'an ziliao huibian,* vol. 5.1, no. 2, 530–531. The simultaneous celebration of Kongzi's birthday in the Confucian temple in Suzhou is discussed in Carroll, *Between Heaven and Modernity,* 153–158.

61. "Guomin zhengfu ge bu yuan hui daibiao Qufu ji Kong jishi" (Factual record of each government department sending representatives to attend sacrifice in Qufu) (1934), in *Zhonghua Minguo shi dang'an ziliao huibian,* vol. 5.1, no. 2, 534–535.

62. Kong Demao, *House of Confucius,* 116.

63. "Guomin zhengfu ge bu yuan hui daibiao Qufu jiKong jishi" (1934), in *Zhonghua Minguo shi dang'an ziliao huibian,* vol. 5.1, no. 2, 534–535.

64. Ibid. An abbreviated account of this ceremony appears in Kong Demao, *House of Confucius,* 116.

65. Li Guannan, *Culture, Revolution and Modernity,* 452.

66. "Guomindang zhongyang guanyu xiuli weichi Qufu Kongzi ling miao banfa ji xianshi fengsiguan teyu deng wenti zhi Guomin zhengfu" (Guomindang central government to Nationalist government concerning regulations for repairing and maintaining the tomb and temple of Kongzi in Qufu and remuneration of the sacrifice officer to the first teacher) (1934), in *Zhonghua Minguo shi dang'an ziliao huibian,* vol. 5.1, no 2, 547–548; "Xiufu Qufu Kongmiao" (Restoring Kong Temple in Qufu), *Shenbao,* October 13, 1934; *The Chinese Recorder,* November 1934, 699. Yunnan Governor Long Yun also promised to send ¥4,000, and additional funds were raised by auctioning off a quantity of dry timber. "Kong Yan miao gongcheng jiji jinxing" (Work on the Kong and Yan temples proceeding), *Shenbao,* October 29, 1934.

67. Liang Sicheng and Fairbank, *Pictorial History of Chinese Architecture,* 320. On Liang Sicheng's preference for Tang and Song architecture, see Nancy Shatzman Steinhardt, "The Tang Architectural Icon and the Politics of Chinese Architectural History," *Art Bulletin* 86, no. 2 (2004).

68. Carroll, *Between Heaven and Modernity,* 158–168.

69. Liang Sicheng, as cited in Guolong Lai, "Valuing the Past in China: The Seminal Influence of Liang Sicheng on Heritage Conservation," *Orientations* 35, no. 2 (2004): 85.

70. Liang Sicheng, *Qufu Kongmiao jianzhu jiqi xiuqi jihua*. Passage translated in ibid.

71. Ibid., 160.

72. Hu Shi, "Xie zai Kongzi danchen jinian zhihou" (Written after the birthday of Kongzi), *Duli pinglun* (Independent commentary), no. 111 (September 1934): 2–6, in Jerome Grieder, *Hu Shih and the Chinese Renaissance: Liberalism in the Chinese Revolution, 1917–1937* (Cambridge, MA: Harvard University Press, 1970), 284.

73. Quoted in Nedostup, *Superstitious Regimes*, 271.

74. "Guomindang zhongyang guanyu xiuli weichi Qufu Kongzi ling miao banfa ji xianshi fengsiguan teyu deng wenti zhi Guomin zhengfu," in *Zhonghua Minguo shi dang'an ziliao huibian* vol. 5.1, no. 2 (1934): 547–548.

75. "Kongzi danchen jinian hui" (Kongzi's birthday commemoration), *Shenbao*, August 28, 1935.

76. Cheng Zhizheng, "Wande Taishan Qufu Chuzhou jiyou," *Lüxing zazhi* 10, no. 10 (1936): 47; "Daibiao guofu zhiji Kongzi" (Sacrificing to Kongzi on behalf of the national government), *Shenbao*, August 28, 1936; "Qufu jiKong dianli longzhong" (Grand ceremony for Kongzi in Qufu), *Shenbao*, August 29, 1936.

77. "Qufu Kongmiao Fengsiguan Kong Decheng zai Hankou Diantai zuo Kongzi xueshuo yu kangdi jiuguo guanxi de boyin ci" (Broadcast from Hankow of the speech of Chief Sacrificial Officer Kong Decheng from Qufu on the relationship between Confucian teaching and the fight to save the nation), January 12, 1938 (transcript in *Zhonghua Minguo shi dang'an ziliao huibian*, vol. 5.2, no. 2, 577–581).

78. *SSZ*, 53–54. On proposed changes to the ceremony and alterations to the placement of honorees at Kong Temple, see "Wang wei xingzhengyuan huifu siKong dianli ling" (Executive committee of the Wang government ordered to restore sacrifice to Kongzi) (1942), in Zhongguo shehui kexueyuan, ed., *Kongfu dang'an xuan bian*, 41. On sacrifices in Qufu and Nanjing, see "Zuo Kong sheng danchen jinian zhongshu juxing juxing qiuji li" (Autumn ceremony held for yesterday's Kongzi birthday), *Shenbao*, September 29, 1943. For a detailed program of sacrifices held in Manchuria in 1933, see Manchoukuo Wenjiao Bu Lijiao Si, *Si Kong lu* (Record of sacrificing to Kongzi) (Changchun, China: Wenjiao Bu Lijiao Si, 1933). Rebecca Nedostup notes the Japanese project to support the Kong family and also points out that the New Life Movement may have been, in part, a response to Japanese appropriation of the sage. Nedostup, *Superstitious Regimes*, 270.

79. Kong Fanyin, *Yansheng gongfu jianwen* (Jinan: Qilu shushe, 1992), 178–179.

80. "Qufu chao sheng" (Pilgrimage to Qufu), *Shenbao*, December 27, 1947.

81. The historical background of the Qianlong bronzes is discussed in Hui-chun Yu, "The Intersection of Past and Present: The Qianlong Emperor and his Ancient Bronzes" (PhD diss., Princeton University, 2007), 126–129.

82. "Kongfu wei daoyun wenwu dian qing Jiang jun bafu cheliang" (Kong Family Mansion telegraphs Jiang requesting support vehicles) (1948), in Zhongguo shehui kexueyuan, ed., *Kongfu dang'an xuan bian*, 733–734. The artifacts remained in the church until 1952, whereupon they were returned to Qufu and put under the control of the Wenwu

Guanli Weiyuanhui (formerly Qufu Guwu Baoguansuo). During the Cultural Revolution, the bronzes were evidently buried to protect them from the Red Guards. See Liang Wang, "The Confucius Temple Tragedy of the Cultural Revolution," in *On Sacred Grounds: Culture, Society, Politics, and the Formation of the Cult of Confucius*, ed. Thomas Wilson (Cambridge, MA: Harvard University Asia Center, 2002), 384–385.

83. Mao Zedong, "Role of the Chinese Communist Party in the National War," *Selected Works*, 4 vols. (Peking: Foreign Languages Press, 1967), 155–156. Romanization altered to pin-yin.

84. Kong Fanyin, *Yansheng gongfu jianwen*, 178–179, 388.

85. *Dazhong ribao,* June 21, 1948 (reprinted in *SSZ*, 712).

86. Kong Fanyin, *Yansheng gongfu jianwen*, 388–389.

87. Ibid., 305–306; Kong Fanyin, *Qufu de lishi mingren yu wenwu*, 207–208.

88. Kong Derun, "Jianguo chu Qufu wenhua gongzuo yi shi liang ze," 80; for text of 1957 regulations governing management of historical sites and antiquities, see *SSZ*, 712–714.

89. Kong Fanyin, *Qufu de lishi mingren yu wenwu*, 207–208.

90. Joseph Needham, "Archeological Study Tour in China, 1958," *Antiquity* 33, no. 130 (1959): 116. That perspective is confirmed by a pictorial volume sponsored by the Shandong Provincial Artifact Management Office and the Jinan branch of the Chinese International Travel Agency published in that same year. The album shows temple and vicinity in situ, with Kong Xiangxi's pavilion standing prominently on the Saint's Road to the south of the temple and *pailou* commemorating virtuous women in the streets around the temple remaining intact. A pair of Han dynasty "stone giants" had been moved to the temple grounds from their prior location in Juexiangpo southwest of the temple, and the ancient steles of the Gate of Unified Texts and the stump of the original Kongzi juniper are untouched. Even the ritual apparatus remains in place—the Hall of the Great Ensemble is fitted with a full complement of musical and sacrifice wares, the Kangxi emperor's parasol is displayed in its ceremonial position, and most remarkably, a company of dancers is seen performing the *jiKong yuewu*, albeit as a "research exercise." See Shandong Provincial Artifact Management Office and Jinan Branch, Chinese International Travel Agency, *Qufu mingsheng guji*. The *jiKong yuewu* was performed by the Chinese Dance Research Association in 1957.

91. *SSZ*, 541.

92. Guo Moruo, "You Kongmiao" (Touring Kong Temple), "Guan Dachengdian" (Viewing Hall of the Great Ensemble), and "Song Qufu" (Sending off from Qufu), in *Dazhong ribao,* February 21, 1959.

93. "Qufu xian renmin weiyuanhui guanyu baohu gudai wenwu de tongzhi" (Qufu People's Committee notification concerning the protection of antiquities) (1957), in *SSZ*, 712–714. *Guangming ribao, Renmin ribao,* April 8, 1962; *Huaqiao ribao* (China daily news), April 16, 1962; *Shijie ribao,* April 24, 1962.

94. Louie, *Critiques of Confucius in Contemporary China,* 51

95. "Jinian danchen 100 zhou nian huigu Deng Xiaoping yu Shandong dashiji" (Commemorating the one-hundredth birthday of Deng Xiaoping, recounting his important affairs in Shandong), *Dazhong ribao,* August 13, 2004.

96. *Guangming ribao,* September 23, 1964.

97. From Mao's poem "Qinyuan chun—Changsha" (Spring in the Garden of Qin—Changsha) (1925).

98. *TaoKong xuanyan,* originally published in volume 3 of the Red Guard publication "TaoKong zanbao" (Report on the crusade against Kongzi), November 1966.

99. Liang Wang, "Confucius Temple Tragedy," 385–386.

100. Ibid., 389–395.

101. Sang Ye and Geremie Barmé, "The Fate of the Confucius Temple, The Kong Mansion, and the Kong Cemetery," *China Heritage Quarterly* 20 (2009), http://www.china heritagenewsletter.org/scholarship.php?searchterm=020_Kongzi.inc&issue=020.

102. Liang Wang, "Confucius Temple Tragedy," 395.

103. For fuller accounts of the wider destruction perpetrated outside of the temple, see ibid.; David Ho, "To Protect and Preserve: Resisting the Destroy the Four Olds Campaign, 1966–67," in *The Chinese Cultural Revolution as History,* ed. Joseph Esherick, Paul Pickowicz, and Andrew G. Walder (Stanford, CA: Stanford University Press, 2006), 84–92.

104. Liang Wang, "Confucius Temple Tragedy," 396.

105. Li Deming, *Dongfang shengcheng,* 305; *SSZ,* 542.

106. Louie, *Critiques of Confucius in Contemporary China,* 111–112; see also Qi Sihe, "Pingpan Kongzi de fandong weixin shiguan," *Beijing daxue xuebao: Zhexue shehui kexue xueban* 4 (1973): 90–94.

107. Louie, *Critiques of Confucius in Contemporary China,* 101.

108. "Qufu gong nong bing pi Lin pi Kong," *Wenwu,* no. 3 (1974): 1; Li Rongde, "Chongfeng zai qian: Shandong Qufu zhujun piLin piKong jishi," *Jiefang jun wenyi,* no. 3 (1974): 19–20. For photographs see Thomas H. Hahn Docu-images, http://hahn.zenfolio.com /p936730597/h1fa5a74a#h1fa5a74a.

109. *Piping Qufu "sanKong"* (Beijing: Wenwu chubanshe, 1974); see also Yu Shulie, "Yunyong lishi wenwu henjie mengpi Kong Meng zhi dao de zui e shizhi," *Wenwu,* no. 3 (1974): 6–7; "Pipan sanKong Cailiao," Shandong sheng pi Lin pi Kong zhanlanguan (1975). In the same vein, *Kaogu* employed material remains to critique Kongzi and the "feudal ruling class." See Gu Chun, "Cong Qufu Kongmiao kan fengjian tongzhi jieji zunKong de fandong shizhi he nongmin de fanKong douzheng," *Kaogu,* no. 1 (1974): 40–45; Pu Ren, "Xiri zunKong chongru de 'shengdi' jinri piLin piKong de zhanchang," *Kaogu,* no. 3 (1974): 143–152; Pu Hong, "Eba dizhu zhuangyuan—Qufu 'Kong Fu,'" *Kaogu,* no. 4 (1974): 226–233.

110. Liu Yuanyan and Yuan Shuchuan, "Commenting on 'More on That Man Confucius,'" *Renmin ribao,* December 12, 1976. Cited in Kam Louie, *Critiques of Confucius in Contemporary China,* 140.

111. "Qufu wenwu guanli weiyuanhui guanyu Kuiwenge xiushan yusuan de qingshi baogao" (Budgetary report for the restoration of the Pavilion of the Literary Constellation by the Qufu Bureau of Cultural Relics), October 14, 1977, Jining Municipal Archive 67/3/106.

112. Li Qinglun et al. "Xiannian tongzhi shi wenwu guji," *Qufu wenshi,* no. 9 (1989): 4–5, 3.

113. Pang Pu, "Ping 'sirenbang' de jiapi Kong," *Lishi yanjiu,* no. 6 (1974): 37–42.

114. Pang Pu, "Kongzi sixiang zai pingjia," *Lishi yanjiu*, no. 8 (1978); see also Chen Lifu, "Guanyu Kongzi sixiang pingjia de jige wenti- jianyu Pang Pu tongzhi shangque," *Nanchang daxue xuebao (Renmin shehui kexue ban)*, no. 4 (1978): 47–60.

115. Zhang Dainian, "Kongzi zhexue jiexi," in *Zhongguo zhexueshi yanjiu fangfa taolun ji*, ed. Zhongguo shehui kexueyuan zhexue yanjiusuo (Taiyuan, China: Zhongguo zhexueshi yanjiushi, 1979). Reissued by Zhongguo shehui kexue chubanshe, 1980; Li Zehou, "Re-evaluation of Kongzi," *Social Sciences in China*, no. 2 (1980): 99–127, in *Sources of Chinese Tradition*, vol. 2, trans. Wm. Theodore DeBary (New York: Columbia University Press, 2000), 574–580.

116. "Wo yuan juxing Kongzi xueshu taolun hui," *Qilu xuekan*, no. 6 (1980): 91; Yan Beiming, "Yao zhengque pingjian Kongzi" (Correctly evaluate Kongzi), *Qilu xuekan*, no. 6 (1980): 24–31; see also "Kongzi xueshu taolunhui taolun de yixie wenti" (A few issues with the Kongzi Academic Symposium), *Guangming ribao*, January 20, 1981.

117. Yan Beiming, "Kongzi yao pingfan, Kongjiadian yao dadao," *Shehui kexue jikan*, no. 1 (1981): 3–13; "Kongjiadian yao dadao: Kongzi yao pingfan," *Wenhui bao*, March 20, 1981; "Kongzi yao zhengque pingjia: Kongjiadian yao dadao" (Accurately evaluate Kongzi, Beat the Kong family shop), *Nanfang ribao*, March 18, 1981; "Kongjiadian yao dadao, Kongzi yao pingjian," *Zhongguo jianshe*, no. 4 (1982): 16.

118. *Dazhong ribao*, September 24, 1984; Zhongguo Kongzi Jijinhui, "Zhongguo Kongzi jijinhui gonggao," *Qilu xuekan*, no. 6 (1984): 38–39.

119. *Guoyue* (1987), 17, quoted in Li Jinpu, "Xuanli duocai de Zhongguo Qufu guoji wenhua jie," *Yuejin renjian*, no. 00 (1994): 9.

120. *SSZ*, 67.

121. Ibid., 69–70; Wang Runyan, "Fahui wenhua mingcheng youshi jiakuai fazhan Qufu jingji," *Yuejin renjian*, no. 00 (1994): 1. The China Kongzi Foundation, later the International Kongzi Foundation, moved its head office to Beijing in 1987, leaving a branch in Qufu before finally relocating to Jinan and leaving a liaison office in Beijing.

122. You Shaoping and Wang Qingcheng, eds., "A Regular Report on the Implementation of the Convention for the Protection of World Cultural and Natural Heritage," Qufu City Cultural Relics Administration Committee, 2003, 8, 20, http://whc.unesco.org/archive/periodicreporting/apa/cycle01/section2/704.pdf. On the nature of Confucianism's impact on the Enlightenment, see David Mungello, *The Great Encounter of China and the West, 1500–1800* (Lanham, MD: Rowman and Littlefield, 2005).

123. Michael Nylan, *The Five Confucian Classics* (New Haven, CT: Yale University Press, 2001), 344–345.

Chapter 6

1. David Lowenthal, *The Heritage Crusade and the Spoils of History* (London: Viking, 1997), 89.

2. Duanfang Lu, *Remaking Chinese Urban Form: Modernity, Scarcity, and Space, 1949–2005,* Planning, History, and Environment Series (London: Routledge, 2006), 7.

3. Wanggiyan Linqing, "Observing the Rites at the Ancient Abode of Confucius," *China Heritage Quarterly,* no. 17 (2009). Online.

4. Edkins, "Visit to the City of Confucius," 85.

5. Martin, *Cycle of Cathay,* 283.

6. Alexander Armstrong, *In a Mule Litter to the Tomb of Confucius* (London: J. Nisbet, 1896), 85–91; see also Alexander Armstrong, *Shantung (China): A General Outline of the Geography and History of a Province, a Sketch of Its Mission; and Notes of a Journey to the Tomb of Confucius* (Shanghai: Shanghai Mercury, 1891), 181–186.

7. Ernst von Hesse-Wartegg, "China's 'Holy Land': A Visit to the Tomb of Confucius," *The Century Magazine,* no. 60 (1900): 813. The traveller seems to have overlooked the account of Rev. A. Williamson, who evidently had unobstructed access to the hall in 1865. See "Recent Visit to the Classic Grounds in China," in *Confucius and the Chinese Classics, or, Readings in Chinese Literature,* ed. A. W. Loomis (San Francisco: A. Roman, 1867), 371–392.

8. V. M. Alekseev, *China im Jahr 1907* (Leipzig, Germany: Gustav Kiepenheuer Verlag, 1989), 149.

9. Kong Demao, Ke Lan, and Wood, *House of Confucius,* 122; Zhongguo shehui kexueyuan, ed., *Kongfu dang'an xuan bian* 3.3, 4919/300–304.

10. Jiang Weiqiao, "Qufu jiyou" (Journey to Qufu), *Xiaoshuo yuebao,* no. 6 (1915): 12.

11. In 1934 foreigners were advised to pay between forty cents and one dollar "Mex" (silver dollar) for entrance to the temple and approximately the same for access to the forest. Dransmann, *Taischan-Tchufu Fuhrer,* 274.

12. *An Official Guide to Eastern Asia: Transcontinental Connections between Europe and Asia,* vol. 4, *China* (Imperial Japanese Government Railways, 1915), 98, 114. Delegates to the Dacheng Festival in 1913 were housed in a hostel on Wumaci Street, although this does not seem to have been available to other visitors. "Shandong jiaoyu dahui jisheng" (On the Shandong Education Conference), *Shenbao,* October 10, 1913; "Qufu ye sheng ji" (Account of visiting the saint in Qufu), *Shenbao,* November 8, 1917.

13. "Qufu jian bowu tushuguan" (Qufu to build museum and library), *Shenbao,* September 13, 1934; "Xiuzhu Kong Meng jinniantang" (Building Kongzi and Mengzi memorial halls), *Shenbao,* December 23, 1934.

14. Dransmann, *Taischan-Tchufu Fuhrer,* 314.

15. Ni Jingyin, *Qufu Taishan youji,* 73, 26.

16. Cheng Zhizheng, "Wande Taishan Qufu Cizhou jiyou," 10; Meng Qiuju, "Qufu zuizao de yi jia lüshe—Datong Lüshe," *Qufu wenshi,* no. 8 (1988): 26–27.

17. Cheng Zhizheng, "Wande Taishan Qufu Cizhou jiyou."

18. Zhang Shaotang, *Ziyang Qufu Taishan youxing xinying lu* (1937), Introduction, 1.

19. Meng Qiuju, "Qufu zuizao de yi jia lüshe—Datong Lüshe," 26–27.

20. Kong Fanyin, *Yansheng gongfu jianwen,* 388–389.

21. Hua Min, "Waiguo pengyou zai Qufu," *Lüxing jia,* no. 7 (1956): 23–24.

22. "Tours within China by members of UK diplomatic service in Beijing, 1956," Foreign Office Files China (UK): I. FO 371/120985, FO 371/120878.

23. Peng Lin, "Qufu jianwen," *Lüxing zazhi,* no. 3 (1954): 70–71. In 2008 I observed that the forecourt of Zhougong Temple was still being used for drying agricultural and forestry products.

24. Shandong Sheng Difang Shizhi Bianzuan Weiyuanhui, ed., *Shandong shengzhi: Kongzi gulizhi* (Beijing: Zhonghua shuju, 1994), 555–556; Luo Chenglie, personal communication, May 2008.

25. Ibid., 556; Li Jianyu, "Qufu youji," *Shandong wenxue,* no. 10 (1961): 54.

26. Shandong Sheng Difang Shizhi Bianzuan Weiyuanhui, *Shandong shengzhi: Kongzi gulizhi,* 557. The other notable exhibit from the 1960s was the Qufu County Agricultural Accomplishments Exhibit, which city officials moved from the Kong Family Mansion to the Hall of the Great Ensemble in a desperate but futile attempt to protect the statues of Kongzi and his disciples. During the Anti-Kongzi Anti-Lin Biao campaign, exhibitions illustrating the "reactionary" nature of Kongzi and his descendants were held in the Kong Family Mansion, but there were no further exhibits in Kong Temple until 1984.

27. Li Deming, *Dongfang shengcheng,* 558.

28. The "needs" of these tourists, of course, are highly diverse. The remainder of this chapter will focus on production of heritage, rather than consumption, although for a discussion of Confucian tourism/ritualism, including the spiritual concerns of the many visitors to Kong Temple and other Confucian temples throughout China, see Sun, *Confucianism as a World Religion,* 153–172.

29. Dransmann, *Taischan-Tchufu Fuhrer,* 360. For a complete inventory of relics within the city and elsewhere within the county, see "Qufu xian wenwu pucha hou wenwu baohu danwei gongbu mingdan" (Public list of protected cultural relic units following the Qufu County cultural relics survey) (1957), in Shandong Sheng Difang Shizhi Bianzuan Weiyuanhui, *Shandong shengzhi: Kongzi gulizhi,* 714–731.

30. Kong Deping, ed., *Qufu guji tonglan* (Beijing: Wenwu chubanshe, 2010), 53.

31. In June 2014 the remaining Yamen building had been fully restored, although the purpose of the completed project was not yet apparent.

32. Dransmann, *Taischan-Tchufu Fuhrer,* 360; Zhang Jie, "City Building, Conservation and Architecture in China with Special Reference to Qufu" (PhD diss., University of York, 1991), 319; Kong Deping, *Qufu guji tonglan,* 49–51. For photographs, including an archway on Queli Street honoring an eighteenth-century duchess and an "honorable widow" archway outside the North Gate on the Spirit Road, see Dransmann, *Taischan-Tchufu Fuhrer.* These arches were pulled down during the Cultural Revolution. For a detailed discussion and map of palaces and the Five Terraces, see Kong Lingzhi, "Kongzi houyi fudi," *Qufu wenshi,* no. 5 (1985): 42–46.

33. Zhang Jie, *City Building, Conservation and Architecture in China,* 413.

34. "Draft on Reconstructing and Expanding Beijing Municipality" (1954), in Guolong Lai, *Valuing the Past in China,* 86. See also Thomas Campanella, *The Concrete Dragon: China's Urban Revolution and What It Means for the World* (New York: Princeton Architectural Press, 2008), 96–106.

35. For a comparative view of Gulou Street in the early twentieth century, see http://www.sd.xinhuanet.com/sdsq/2010–04/02/content_19412543.htm.

36. Zhang Jie, *City Building, Conservation and Architecture in China*, 320–321.

37. Ibid.

38. For aerial photos of Qufu showing the division of urban and rural along the lines of the city wall in 1976, see Li Min, "Archaeology of the Confucian Landscape: A Multidisciplinary Research Project at Qufu," http://dissertationreviews.org/archives/7034.

39. Zhang Jie, *City Building, Conservation and Architecture in China*, 320–321.

40. A drawing of the original Xinggong compound appears in *QFXZ* 3.2a–b.

41. Wu Liangyong, "Shilun lishi guji lüyou chengshi de guihua yu jianshi," *Guowai chengshi jihua*, no. 2 (1980): 9.

42. See Jeffrey W. Cody, *Building in China: Henry K. Murphy's "Adaptive Architecture," 1914–1935* (Seattle: University of Washington Press, 2001).

43. See Wilma Fairbank, *Liang and Lin: Partners in Exploring China's Architectural Past* (Philadelphia: University of Pennsylvania Press, 1994).

44. Dai Nianci, "Queli Binshe de sheji jieshao," *Jianzhu xuebao*, no. 1 (1986).

45. Zhang Jie, *City Building, Conservation and Architecture in China*, 320.

46. Ibid., 361.

47. In 2014 the Analects Stele Garden was opened to the public, free of charge, as the Kongzi Culture Garden (Kongzi Wenhuayuan).

48. These observations were made in the summer of 2008.

49. On Fuzimiao, see Campanella, *Concrete Dragon*, 269–271.

50. Chairman Mao Memorial Hall information pamphlet, 2006; *People's Daily*, December 21, 2003. Online. The collection was compiled by local notable Yang Chunbing, a retired army officer who, in addition to vice-mayor, had served as commune secretary, county vice-party secretary, and board member of the Kongzi Research Institute in Qufu. The institute hosted the original badge exhibit in 2003.

51. Sun Wanzhen and Wang Degang, "Systematic Contradiction between Heritage Conservation and Tourism Development: Cleaning the Temple and Cemetery of Confucius and the Kong Family Mansion in Qufu," *Chinese Journal of Population, Resources and Environment* 5, no. 1 (2007): 84. Another report is available through UNESCO: http://whc.unesco.org/archive/periodicreporting/apa/cycle01/section2/704.pdf.

52. Lu Xinning, " 'Shuixi wenwu' beihou (tebie baodao) Qufu sanKong wenwu shousun de baodao he sikao" (Behind the incident of using "water to wash cultural relics," special report, reporting and reflecting on the damage to the Three Kongs of Qufu), *Renmin wang*, February 09, 2001, http://www.people.com.cn/GB/paper40/2621/385450.html; also published in *Renmin ribao, Huadong xinwen*, September 2, 2001.

53. Law of the People's Republic of China on Protection of Cultural Relics, 1982, http://www.china.org.cn/english/environment/34304.htm.

54. Law of the People's Republic of China on Protection of Cultural Relics, rev. 2002, Article 24, http://www.gov.cn/english/laws/2005–10/09/content_75322.htm.

55. See consecutive reports in *China Daily*, overseas version, February 6, 9, 14, 19, 2001, http://www.chinadaily.cn.com; Sun Wanzhen and Wang Degang, "Systematic Contradiction," 84–87; Qufu City Cultural Relics Administration Committee, "A Regular Report on the Implementation of the Convention for the Protection of World Cultural and Natural

Heritage," 2003, http://whc.unesco.org/archive/periodicreporting/APA/cycle01/section2/704.pdf, 12. Other studies of the convoluted interaction of heritage conservation, commercial exploitation, and state management can be found in Wei Zhao, "Local versus National Interests in the Promotion and Management of a Heritage Site: A Case Study from Zhejiang Province, China," and Yujie Zhu and Na Li, "Groping for Stones to Cross the River: Governing Heritage in Emei," in *Cultural Heritage Politics in China,* ed. Tami Blumenfield and Helaine Silverman (New York: Springer, 2013).

56. Michael J. Meyer, *The Last Days of Old Beijing: Life in the Backstreets of a City Transformed* (New York: Walker, 2008), 110.

57. Zhang Jie, *City Building, Conservation and Architecture in China,* 297.

58. Lamberton, "Kongs of Qufu," 301–306.

59. For an overview of the Qufu tourism strategy in recent years, see Ma Aiping, Si Lina, and Zhang Hongfei, "The Evolution of Cultural Tourism: The Example of Qufu, the Birthplace of Confucius," in *Tourism in China: Destination, Cultures and Communities,* ed. Chris Ryan and Huimin Gu (New York: Routledge, 2009), 182–196.

60. Qufu Kongmiao Dachengdian huifu gongcheng bangongshe, "Kongmiao Dachengdian xiangkan huifu gaikuang," *Qufu wenshi,* no. 3 (1984): 40.

61. Murray, "'Idols' in the Temple," 386–388.

62. Gong Yanxing and Wang Zhengyu, *Kongmiao zhushen kao,* 56–58.

63. Ibid., 62; Chi Qingquan and Zhang Kunlun, "Qufu Kongmiao Dachengdian suxiang zaoxing fuyuan gongcheng jishi," *Qilu yiyuan,* no. 00 (1984): 19.

64. Often obscured by regalia, graffiti, or poor light, most photographs do not give a clear impression of the Yongzheng-era statue. One exception is Stéphane Passat's image taken in 1913, in Murray, "'Idols' in the Temple," fig. 3, 389. Ernst Boerschmann also captured superior images in *Die baukunst und religiöse Kultur der Chinesen,* 222–223.

65. "Cujin ge guo ge diqu jingji wenhua jiaoliu yu hezuo: Kongzi danchen guli you huodong juxing" (Encourage economic and cultural exchange and cooperation with each country and region visiting the Kongzi hometown birthday tour activity), *Dazhong ribao,* October 12, 1985; Fan Youde, "Qufu juxing di'erci Kongzi danchen guli you huodong" (Qufu holds the second annual Kongzi hometown birthday tour activity), *Guangming ribao,* October 16, 1985.

66. *Qufu nianjian* (Qufu, China: Qufu Bianzuan weiyuanhui, 1986), 128; "Kongzi danchen guli you huodong zai Qufu juxing" (Kongzi birthday and hometown tour activity held in Qufu), *Dazhong ribao,* September 27, 1986; Paula Swart and Barry Till, "A Revival of Confucian Ceremonies in China," in *The Turning of the Tide: Religion in China Today,* ed. Julian F. Pas (Hong Kong: Royal Asiatic Society; New York: Oxford University Press, 1989).

67. "Zhongguo Qufu guoji Kongzi wenhua jie jishi," *Dongfang wenhua shengdian: 1984 nian–2008 nian: Documentary on China Qufu International Kongzi Culture Festival, 1984–2008* (Jinan: Qilu chubanshe, 2009), 52.

68. Zi Mu, "Qiantan Kongzi jiaxiang lüyou de duiwai xuanchuan," *Shandong lüyou,* no. 5 (1989): 12.

69. Xiao Xi, "Shouce Kongzi wenhua jie huodong fengfu duocai," *Shandong lüyou* no. 5 (1989): 29–30.

70. "Zhongguo Qufu guoji Kongzi wenhua jie jishi," 78, 119, 131.

71. Li Kesheng, "Zhengque chuli wenhua yu jingji de guanxi nuli tigao liangge xiaoyi," *Yuejin renjian,* no. 1 (1994): 7; Zhao Yuanshan, "Rang 'jieqing' zhi hua gengjia xianyan," *Yuejin renjian,* no. 1 (1994): 17.

72. Zhang Dongwei, ed. *Qufu nianjian* (Qufu: Bianzuan weiyuanhui, 1999–2000), 124–125.

73. "Zhongguo Qufu guoji Kongzi wenhua jie jishi," 144.

74. Ma Dongfeng, "JiKong yuewu huodong gaishu," *Zhongguo yinyue nianjian* (1990): 488–489; Yang Anbang, "Wenyi fanggu jiKong yuewu biaoyan," in *Qufu nianjian* (Qufu, China: Qufu Bianzuan Weiyuanhui, 1986), 128; Che Yanfen, "Zai faming zhong yanxu chuantong yi jiKong yuewu de dangdai fuxing wei ge'an," *Journal of Wenzhou University* 23, no. 1 (2010): 22–27.

75. Bill Bramwell and Hongliang Yan, "Cultural Tourism, Ceremony and the State," *Annals of Tourism Research* 34, no. 4 (2008): 981.

76. Joseph Lam, "The Yin and Yang of Chinese Music Historiography: The Case of Confucian Ceremonial Music," *Yearbook for Traditional Music,* no. 27 (1995): 38. See also Swart and Till, "Revival of Confucian Ceremonies in China," 213.

77. Lam, "Yin and Yang of Chinese Music," 44.

78. "Kongzi jijinhui chengli" (The establishment of the China Kongzi fund), *Dazhong ribao,* September 24, 1984; "Qufu juxing Kongzi jiaoyu sixiang xueshu taolunhui: Zhongguo Kongzi jijinhui he Kongzi yanjiuhui choubei zu chengli" (Qufu holding conference on Kongzi's educational philosophy: The establishment of the preparatory group for the China Kongzi fund and the Kongzi Research Association), *Dazhong ribao,* September 28, 1984.

79. "Zhongguo Kongzi yanjiuhui yubei huiyi zhaokai" (Preparatory meeting of the China Kongzi Research Association held), *Guangming ribao,* October 15, 1985.

80. "1987 nian Kongzi danchen guli you Kongzi danchen 2538 zhou nian" (Visiting the Kongzi hometown birthday tour activity on the 2538th birthday of Kongzi in 1987), http://www.sdsqw.cn/bin/mse.exe?searchword=&K=d00&A=2&rec=143&run=13.

81. "Zhongguo Kongzi Jijinhui Qufu banshichu gongzuo" (The office of the China Kongzi Foundation begins work), in *Qufu nianjian* (1999–2002), http://www.infobase.gov.cn/bin/mse.exe?seachword=&K=c8a&A=3&run=12.

82. "Confucian-Christian Dialogue Points Way in Turbulent Times," *People's Daily,* September 27, 2010, http://en.people.cn/90001/90782/90873/7152317.html. The Nishan Forum of World Civilizations continues to be held annually.

83. Anna Sun, *Confucianism as a World Religion.* See, especially, chapter 8.

84. Yuan Baoyin and Zhang Xiaoyu, "Song xianshi fenggong houde, yang ruxue lishi zhendi: Zhongguo Qufu Kongzi wenhua jie fanggu jiKong jishi" (Praising the great achievements and virtues of the first teacher, relying on the true meaning of Confucianism, reporting on imitating the ancient sacrifice to Kongzi in Qufu China), *Zouxiang shijie,* no. 6 (1995–1996): 34–36; "Zhongguo Qufu guoji Kongzi wenhua jie jishi," 114; "Kongzi guli yu jiKong dadian" (The hometown of Kongzi and the JiKong ceremony), video, from *Zhongguo kexue wenhua chubanshe,* 2002. The sacrifice performance recorded in this video corresponds to 1999.

85. "Xin Zhongguo shouci juxing guanfang jisi Kongzi dadian" (New China holds its first official sacrifice ceremony for Kongzi)," http://www.china.com.cn/chinese/2004/Sep/670444.htm; *Qufu nianjian,* 658. CCTV video coverage of the 2004 event can be viewed at http://v.youku.com/v_playlist/f1005599o1p0.html, and http://www.chinanews.com.cn/news/2004/2004–09–29/26/489358.shtml. For differently edited video from a Japanese source, see http://www.youtube.com/watch?v=-oAfWBlWGMU&feature=related. The 2005 ceremony is available at http://v.youku.com/v_show/id_XNDg5MzE3MTI=.html.

86. "Quanqiu lianhe jiKong longzhong juxing" (Holding the grand global joint sacrifice to Kongzi), *Qufu nianjian,* 2005, http://sd.infobase.gov.cn/bin/mse.exe?seachword=&K=c8a&A=2&rec=309&run=13.

87. Anthony DeBlasi, "Selling Confucius: The Negotiated Return of Tradition in Post-Socialist China," in *The Sage Returns: Confucian Revival in Contemporary China,* ed. Kenneth Hammond and Jeffrey Richey (Albany: State University of New York Press, 2015), 70–71.

88. "Zhongguo Qufu guoji Kongzi wenhua jie jishi," 180.

89. Ibid., 187; "Tongji xianshi gongxiang hexie" (Joint sacrifice to the first teacher, enjoy harmony together), http://news.cctv.com/special/C19322/01/index.shtml.

90. Sebastian Billioud and Joël Thorvald, "*Lijiao:* The Return of Ceremonies Honoring Confucius in Mainland China," *China Perspectives,* no. 4 (2009): 94–96. Beyond the "official" ceremonies, Billioud and Thorvald note several grassroots Confucian organizations promoting their own brand of neoritualism and supporting President Hu Jintao's pseudo-Confucian "harmonious society" campaign. Although excluded from the main ceremony, these groups were able to validate their organizations by conducting rituals in the Mengzi Temple in Zoucheng and at Mt. Ni.

91. Qufu Kongfu jiajiu ye youxian gongsi (Kong Mansion Family Distillery Ltd. of Qufu), http://www.kfj.com.cn/.

92. "Kongzi danchen guli you huodong zai Qufu juxing" (Kongzi hometown birthday tour activity held in Qufu), *Dazhong ribao,* September 27, 1986; Niu Guodong, "Lüyou fuwuye—disan jie Kongzi danchen guli you" (Travel service—the third Kongzi hometown birthday tour), in *Shandong nianjian,* ed. Li Huacheng and Xi Xingjia (Jinan, China: Shandong renmin chubanshe, 1987), 409–410.

93. Li Kesheng, "Zhengque chuli wenhua yu jingji de guanxi nuli tigao liangge xiaoyi," 7.

94. Meng Fanliang and Zhu Taiming, "Rujia jieqing: 2004 Zhongguo guoji Kongzi wenhua jie," *Zhongguo ruxue nianjian,* 2005, 134–136; Meng Fanliang, "Da wenhua tai, chang jingmao xi, ban hao guoji Kongzi wenhua jie," *Qufu nianjian,* 2003–2005, http://sd.infobase.gov.cn/bin/mse.exe?seachword=&K=c8a&A=2&rec=91&run=13.

95. John Makeham, *Lost Soul: Confucianism in Contemporary Chinese Academic Discourse* (Cambridge, MA: Harvard University Asia Center, 2008).

96. Jining shi jingji maoyi weiyuanhui xieban, "Rushang wenhua" (Confucian merchant culture), http://www.chinakongzi.net/2550/rushang/rushang1.htm.

97. Ibid., http://www.chinakongzi.net/2550/rushang/rushang2.htm.

Chapter 7

1. Eliade, *Sacred and the Profane,* 63.

2. See article 4, article 23, and principle 3 of "Principles for the Conservation of Heritage Sites in China," trans. and ed. Neville Agnew and Martha Demas, The Getty Conservation Institute.

3. Wu Zhong, "Stumbling towards Confucius-ville," *Asia Times Online,* March 20, 2008, http://www.atimes.com/atimes/China/JC20Ad01.html.

4. Although it has been superseded, the elements of the initial plan are outlined in Ma Aiping et al., "Evolution of Cultural Tourism," 182–196. Current plans are outlined on the Qufu government website, http://www.qufu.gov.cn/xxgk/E_ReadNews.asp?NewsID =1566.

5. Dexter Roberts, "Xi Jinping Extols Confucian Values," *Bloomberg Business Week,* November 27, 2013, http://www.businessweek.com/articles/2013–11–27/xi-jinping-extols -confucian-values.

6. Benjamin, "Work of Art in the Age of Mechanical Production," in Benjamin and Arendt, *Illuminations,* 223–224.

7. On the importance of suppressing feelings of cynicism when approaching Chinese heritage, see Steven Harrell, "China's Tangled Web of Heritage," in *Cultural Heritage Politics in China,* ed. Tami Blumenfield and Helaine Silverman (New York: Springer, 2013).

8. Consider, for example, a 2010–2011 case wherein a Qufu Christian congregation made international headlines with its abortive plan to construct a church steeple that would have violated the long-standing principle of not permitting any structure in the vicinity of Kong Temple to exceed the height of the Hall of the Great Ensemble. Cara Anna, "Planned Church in Confucius' Native City Draws Protest," *China Post,* December 26, 2010, http:// www.chinapost.com.tw/china/national-news/2010/12/26/285130/Planned-church .htm; Wang Fanfan, "New Church to Tower over Home of Confucius," *Global Times,* January 19, 2011, http://special.globaltimes.cn/2011–04/613615.shtml. See also Anna Sun, *Confucianism as a World Religion,* 174.

Glossary

Aigong 哀公
ancha 按察
ancha fushi 按察副使
anchashi 按察使
Andi 安帝
ang 昂
baihu banshi ting 百戶辦事廳
baihu guan 百户官
Bainian Jujiang 百年巨匠
baishi zushi 百石卒史
banguan 伴官
banshiguan 辦事官
Baochenghou 褒成侯
Baochengjun 褒成君
Baochengxuan Nigong 褒成宣尼公
baoluo wanxiang 包羅萬象
Baoshenghou 褒聖侯
bi 璧
Bi Maokang 畢懋康
bian 籩
bingxun fushi 兵巡副使
Bishuiqiao 璧水橋
Bo Qin 伯禽
Boyu 伯魚
Buyi Kongzi 布衣孔子
Cangshulou 藏書樓
Cantongmen 參同門
Cao Pi 曹丕
Chai Zuyin 柴祖蔭
Changping 昌平
chaotianhou 朝天吼
Chen Duxiu 陳獨秀
Chen Fan 陳蕃

Chen Huanzhang 陳煥章
Chen Shuyi 陳叔毅
Chen Xiangmei 陳香梅
Chen Zhanxiang 陳占祥
Cheng Hao 程灝
Cheng Yi 程頤
Chengdi 成帝
Chengguanzhen 城關鎮
Chenghua 成化
Chengshengmen 承聖門
chengxiuguan 承修官
chezhuan 撤饌
chong xin zhi 崇新制
Chongshengci 崇聖祠
Chongshengdafu 崇聖大夫
Chongshenghou 崇聖侯
Chu 楚
Chu Minyi 褚民誼
Chunqiutai 春秋台
chuxian 初獻
ci 祠
Cui Wenkui 崔文魁
da Kongjiadian 打孔家店
dacheng 大成
Dacheng Zhisheng Wenxuan Xianshi 大成
    至聖文选先师
Dachengdian 大成殿
Dachengjie 大成節
Dachengmen 大成門
Dadao Kong *lao'er* 打倒孔老二
Dadao Kongjiadian 打倒孔家店
Dai Jitao 戴季陶
Dai Nianci 戴念慈

255

dai xianguan 代獻官
Damen 大門
Dang Huaiying 黨懷英
daotong 道統
Daoxue 道學
Datong meng 大同夢
Dawenkou 大汶口
Daxueyuan 大學院
Dazhongmen 大中門
Deng Xiaoping 鄧小平
Deng Yingchao 鄧穎超
dianji 典籍
ding 丁
Ding Baozhen 丁寶楨
ding ji 丁祭
Ding Wencheng 丁文誠
diwen 地文
Dong Zhongshu 董仲舒
Dongmeng 東蒙
Dongxi Liangwu 東西兩廡
Dou Wu 竇武
dougong 斗拱
Duan Qirui 段祺瑞
Fan Linlin 範琳琳
Fan Zhongyan 范仲淹
fen xianguan 分獻官
Feng Guozhang 馮國璋
Feng Yuxiang 馮玉祥
fengsiguan 奉祀官
fengsijun 奉嗣君
Fu Disheng 付笛聲
fushou 符守
Fuxue wenmiao 府學文廟
gaige kaifang 改革開放
Gaozong 高宗
Gaozu 高祖
Gongbu 工部
gouxin doujiao 勾心鬥角
Gu Menggui 顧夢圭
Gu Mu 谷牧
gu wei jin yong 古为今用
Guandemen 觀德門
guangchusi langzhong 廣儲司郎中

guan'gou 管勾
Guangwu 光武
Guangxu 光緒
guanji 官祭
guanku xianjin 莞庫羨金
Guanneihou 關內侯
Gugong Bowuyuan 故宮博物院
Guo Moruo 郭沫若
guojia siwen 國家斯文
Guozijian Boshi 國子監博士
Gupan 古泮
Gupanchi 古泮池
Guwu Baocun Fa 古物保存法
Guwu Chenliesuo 古物陳列所
Han (dynasty) 漢
Han Chi 韓勑
Han Fuju 韓復榘
Han Lu xiang Shichen 漢魯相史晨
Han Yu 韓愈
hanfu 漢服
Hanlin 翰林
Hanlinyuan Wujingboshi 翰林院五經博士
He Jian 何鑑
Hongdaomen 弘道門
Hongwu 洪武
Hongzhi 弘治
Houtuci 后土祠
Hu Qiaomu 胡喬木
Hu Shi 胡適
Hu Yaobang 胡耀邦
Hu Zuanzong 胡纘宗
huaigu 懷古
Huandi 桓帝
Huang Yi 黃易
Huangdi 黃帝
huanran yixin 煥然一新
Hubu 戶部
Huizong 徽宗
Huoshao Kongjiadian 火烧孔家店
ji dacheng 集大成
Ji Xianlin 季羨林
jiaji 家祭
Jiajing 嘉靖

Jiamiao 家廟
jian 間
jiancha yushi 監察御史
Jiang Jieshi 蔣介石
Jiang Zemin 江泽民
jiangshi 殭屍
Jiangzuo 將作
jianmin shunji 建民訓結
jianxin 薦新
Jiaqing 嘉慶
Jiaxiang 嘉祥
jigao 祭告
jiKong yuewu 祭孔樂舞
Jin 金
Jinglinggong 景靈宮
jinian hui 紀念會
Jinsheng Yuzhen 金聲玉振
jinshi 金石
Jinsitang 金絲堂
jizou 奮奏
Juexiangpo 矍相圃
jun 郡
juntian zhi gong 鈞天之宮
Kang Youwei 康有為
Kangxi 康熙
keji fuli 克己復禮
Kong Ba 孔霸
Kong Daofu 孔道輔
Kong Decheng 孔德成
Kong Duancao 孔端操
Kong Duanyou 孔端友
Kong Fu 孔鮒
Kong He 孔穌
Kong Hongxu 孔弘緒
Kong Jifen 孔繼汾
Kong Kejian 孔克堅
Kong lao'er 孔老二
Kong Li 孔鯉
Kong Lingyi 孔令貽
Kong Mo 孔末
Kong Qiu 孔丘
Kong Renyu 孔仁玉
Kong Shangli 孔尚立

Kong Shangren 孔尚任
Kong Shangxian 孔尚贤
Kong Sihui 孔思晦
Kong Wenyu 孔溫裕
Kong Xiangxi 孔祥熙
Kong Yuancuo 孔元措
Kong Yuqi 孔毓圻
Kong Zhaohuan 孔昭煥
Kong Zhen 孔滇
Kong Zhen'gan 孔貞幹
Kong Zong 孔摠
Kongdao 孔道
Kongfu 孔府
Kongjiaohui 孔教會
Konglin 孔林
Kongmiao 孔廟
Kongzi 孔子
Kongzi Danchen 孔子誕辰
Kongzi Danchen Guli You Huodong 孔子
    誕辰故里遊活動
Kongzi Danchen Jinian Ri 孔子誕辰紀念日
Kongzi guzhai 孔子故宅
Kongzi Wenhua Jie 孔子文化節
Kongzi xingjiao tu 孔子行教圖
Kuang Yaming 匡亞明
Kuiwenge 奎文閣
kun 坤
kuping wenyin 庫平紋銀
Lee Kuan Yu 李光耀
Li Daoyuan 酈道元
Li Dongyang 李東陽
Li Guan 黎貫
Li Hongzhang 李鴻章
Li Jiantang 李鑑堂
Li Jie 李傑
Li Peng 李鵬
Li Ruihuan 李瑞環
Li Xian 李賢
Li Xiannian 李先念
Li Xueqin 李學勤
Li Yong 李邕
Li Yuanhong 黎元洪
Li Zehou 李澤厚

Li Zhongxuan 李仲璇
Li Zicheng 李自成
Lian Biao 連標
Liang Shanbo 梁山伯
Liang Sicheng 梁思成
liangtai zhi shuhuan 兩台之贖鍰
Liaosuo 燎所
Libu 禮部
Lin Biao 林彪
Lin Sen 林森
ling 靈
Lingdi 靈帝
lingguang 靈光
linghua guibei 菱花龜背
Lingxingmen 欞星門
lingzhi 靈芝
Linmen hui 林門會
Linqingguan jiekuan 臨清關節款
Liqiku 禮器庫
Liu Bao 劉保
Liu Bin 劉斌
Liu Cang 劉滄
Liu Haisu 劉海粟
Liu Jiwen 劉紀文
Liu Shaoqi 劉少奇
Liu-Song (dynasty) 劉宋
lishu 隸書
Longmen 龍門
Longshan 龍山
Lu 魯
Lu Aigong 魯哀公
Lü Mengzheng 呂蒙正
Lu Tong 盧曈
Lubi 魯壁
Luguo taifuren 魯國太夫人
Luguogong 魯國公
Luo Guojie 羅國傑
Mei Fu 梅福
Meng Xiujian 孟休鑒
Mengzi 孟子
min 緡
Ming (dynasty) 明
Mingdi 明帝

nanmu 南木
neige zhongshu 內閣中書
neisheng waiwang 內聖外王
neitang 內帑
Neiwubu 內務部
Neiwubu Guwu Chenliesuo 內務部古物陳列所
Neiwufu 內務府
ning shen qi 寧神棲
Niqiu 尼丘
Ouyang Xiu 歐陽脩
Pan Zhen 潘珍
pangong 泮宮
Panshui 泮水
Panshuiqiao 泮水橋
pi-Lin, *pi*-Kong 批林批孔
Pingdi 平帝
Pu Ti 溥偊
Puyi 溥儀
puzuo 鋪作
Qi (state) 齊
qian 乾
qianguan jigao 遣官祭告
qianguan zhiji 遣官致祭
Qianlong 乾隆
Qiguan 亓官
Qiguogong 啟國公
Qiguogongdian 啟國公殿
Qin Shihuang 秦始皇
Qindian 寢殿
qing (area of land) 頃
Qing (dynasty) 清
Qishengci 啟聖祠
Qishengdian 啟聖殿
Qishengqindian 啟聖寢殿
Qishengwang 啟聖王
Qishengwangdian 啟聖王殿
Qiu Jun 邱濬
Queli 闕里
Queli Binshe 闕里賓舍
Qufu 曲阜
Quzhou 衢州
Ren Jing 任靜

Renzong 仁宗
ru 儒
Ruan Yuan 阮元
rushang 儒商
Saileng'e 塞楞額
sangui jiukou 三跪九叩
sanshixue jiaoshou 三氏學教授
sasaohu 灑掃戶
Shandong *dahan* 山東大漢
Shang (dynasty) 商
shanhou 善後
Shanhouju 善後局
shanzhang 山長
shao 韶
Shao Hao 少昊
Shaozheng Mao 少正卯
she xianguan 攝獻官
Shenchu 神廚
sheng zhi shizhe ye 聖之時者也
shengji 胜迹
Shengjidian 聖蹟殿
Shengshimen 聖時門
shengyu 聖諭
shenji 神迹
Shenpao 神庖
shenzuo 神坐
Shi Chen 史晨
shicai 釋菜
shilang 侍郎
Shilitang 詩禮堂
shixiang 時享
shiyi 食邑
Shizhe 十哲
Shizong 世宗
Shouqiu 壽丘
shouzhihui 手指檜
Shuliang He 叔梁紇
shuxie 書寫
shuxue 書學
Sima Guang 司馬光
Sima Qian 司馬遷
sipei 四配
Sishui 泗水

siwen 斯文
siyue 司樂
sizhu 絲竹
Song (dynasty) 宋
Song Feiqing 宋斐卿
Song guo 宋國
Song Na 宋訥
Song Zheyuan 宋哲元
Song Ziwen 宋子文
songshen 送神
Sui 随
Sun Zhongshan 孫中山
suwang 素王
Tai Bo 泰伯
Taichangsi 太常寺
Taichangsi Boshi 太常寺博士
Taihe Yuanqi 太和元氣
Taijigong 太極宮
tailao 太牢
Taishan 泰山
Taizong 太宗
Taizu 太祖
Tan Houlan 譚厚蘭
Tang (dynasty) 唐
Tang (King Tang) 湯
tianwen 天文
Tongwenmen 同文門
touhao da hundan 頭號大混蛋
Tu Weiming 杜維明
tunguan 屯官
Wan Li 萬里
wang 王
Wang Anshi 王安石
Wang Gen 王艮
wang gong zhizhi 王宮之制
Wang Jingwei 汪精衛
Wang Mang 王莽
Wang Tong 王通
Wang Yun 王惲
Wangcheng 王城
wangdao 王道
wanggong 王宮
Wanren Gongqiang 萬仞宮牆

wanshi shibiao 萬世師表
Wanyan Linqing 完顏麟慶
Wei (dynasty) 魏
wen 文
Wenchangci 文昌祠
Wendi 文帝
Wensheng Ni Fu 文聖尼父
Wenxuangong 文宣公
Wenxuanwang 文宣王
Wenxuanwangdian 文宣王殿
Wenxuanwangmiao 文宣王廟
Wenzong 文宗
Wu Jingzi 吳敬梓
Wu Liangyong 吳良鏞
Wu Yu 吳虞
Wudi 武帝
Wufuqu 五父衢
Wumaci 五馬祠
Wutai Shan 五台山
Wuxiantang 五賢堂
Wuyutai 舞雩台
Wuyutan 舞雩壇
Xi Jinping 习近平
Xia (dynasty) 夏
Xiandi 獻帝
xiang (image) 像
xiang (prime minister) 相
xiang yin da she 鄉飲大射
Xiangshan Fandian 香山飯店
xianguan 獻官
xianling 縣令
xianru 先儒
Xiansheng 先聖
xianshi 先師
xianshi dan 先師誕
Xianshi Ni Fu 先師尼父
xianxian 先賢
Xianyuan 仙源
xiaoliguan 効力官
Xiaowu 孝武
xiexiuguan 協修官
Xinggong 行宮
Xingtan 杏壇

xingwei 行慰
xingxiang 行香
xingxiu 星宿
xiujian rongxiang 修建容像
Xizong 熙宗
Xu Shichang 徐世昌
Xu Yuan 徐源
Xuansheng Wenxuanwang 玄聖文宣王
Xuanzong 玄宗
Xuelu 學錄
xunchayuan 巡查員
xunfu 巡撫
xunshiguan 巡視官
Xunzi 荀子
Yan Fu 閣復
Yan Hui 顏回
Yan Song 嚴嵩
Yan Xishan 閻錫山
Yan Zhengzai 顏徵在
Yanbinzhai 延賓齋
Yandi 炎帝
Yang Huan 楊奐
Yang Weicong 楊維聰
Yang Xiangkui 楊向奎
Yang Xiong 揚雄
Yangshengmen 仰聖門
Yangshengzhen 仰聖鎮
Yanshenggong 衍聖公
Yanzhou 兗州
Yanzi 顏子
yaxian 亞獻
Ye Chucang 葉楚傖
Yi Baisha 易白沙
Yi Ying 乙瑛
yifeng 遺風
yiji 遺迹
yimaoxue 瘞毛血
Yimen 儀門
Yin shaojiagong 殷紹嘉公
Yin shaojiahou 殷紹嘉侯
yinfu shouzuo 飲福受胙
yingshen 迎神
yixiang chaoque 以像朝闕

yizhuan 瘞饌
Yongle 永樂
Yongping 永平
Yongzheng 雍正
youguan 右官
Yu Dan 于丹
Yu Lian 餘廉
Yu Minzhong 於敏中
Yuan (dynasty) 元
Yuan Shikai 袁世凱
Yuan Xiaoyuan 袁曉園
Yuandi 元帝
yuanqi 元氣
Yucuimen 毓粹門
Yue Jun 岳濬
yuesi xiangshui 岳祀香稅
Yunguo 鄆國
Yunguo furen 鄆國夫人
Yunmen Dajuan 雲門大卷
Yuzandian 禦贊殿
Zao Bao 皂保
Zeng Guofan 曾國藩
Zeng Xian 曾銑
Zengzi 曾子
Zhaisu 齋宿
zhaiting 齋廳
Zhang Cheng 張程
Zhang Dai 張岱
Zhang Dedi 張得蒂
Zhang Ji 張繼
Zhang Jian 張兼
Zhang Qizhi 張豈之
Zhang Xun 張勛
Zhang Yanling 張延齡
Zhang Zai 張載
Zhang Zongchang 張宗昌
Zhangdi 章帝
zhangshu 掌書
Zhangzong 章宗

Zhao Huang 趙璜
Zhao Xian 趙賢
Zhao Ziyang 趙紫陽
Zheng Guangwan 鄭光琬
zheng xianguan 正獻官
Zheng Yun 鄭芸
Zhengde 正德
Zhenzong 真宗
Zhisheng 至聖
Zhishengmiao 至聖廟
zhishi 執事
zhitong 治統
zhiyin 知印
Zhong Liyi 锺离意
Zhongni 仲尼
zhongxian 終獻
zhongxian guan 終獻官
Zhongyong 中庸
Zhou Boqi 周伯琦
Zhou Chen 週忱
Zhou gong 周公
Zhou Yang 周揚
Zhougongmiao 周公庙
Zhu Gun 朱袞
Zhu Xi 朱熹
Zhu Yingkui 朱應奎
Zhu Yuanzhang 朱元璋
zhuanyunshi 轉運使
Zhushui 洙水
Zi jian Nanzi 子見南子
Zigong 子貢
Zisi 子思
zongguan fushi 總管府事
Zongshenghou 宗聖侯
Zou 鄒
Zoucheng 鄒城
Zouguogong 鄒國公
zuting zhifu 祖庭之複

Selected Bibliography

Agnew, Christopher. "Bureaucrats, Sectarians, and the Descendants of Confucius." *Late Imperial China* 31, no. 1 (2010): 1–27.

———. "Culture and Power in the Making of the Descendants of Confucius, 1300–1800." PhD diss., University of Washington, 2006.

———. "Memory and Power in Qufu: Inscribing the Past of Confucius' Descendants." *Journal of Family History* 34, no. 4 (2009): 327–343.

Alekseev, V. M. *China im Jahr 1907* (China in the year 1907). Leipzig, Germany: Gustav Kiepenheuer Verlag, 1989.

An Official Guide to Eastern Asia: Transcontinental Connections between Europe and Asia. Vol. 4. China: Imperial Japanese Government Railways, 1915.

Appadurai, Arjun. *The Social Life of Things.* Cambridge: Cambridge University Press, 2011.

Armstrong, Alexander. *In a Mule Litter to the Tomb of Confucius.* London: J. Nisbet, 1896.

———. *Shantung (China): A General Outline of the Geography and History of a Province, a Sketch of Its Mission; and Notes of a Journey to the Tomb of Confucius.* Shanghai: Shanghai Mercury, 1891.

Arnheim, Rudolf. *Entropy and Art: An Essay on Disorder and Order.* Berkeley: University of California Press, 1971.

Assmann, Jan. "Collective Memory and Cultural Identity." *New German Critique,* no. 65 (1995): 125–133.

Ban Gu. *Hanshu* (Book of Han). 92 CE. Reprint, Taibei: Taiwan shangwu yinshuguan, 1965.

Benjamin, Walter, and Hannah Arendt, eds. *Illuminations.* New York: Schocken Books, 1986.

Bi Jingyan. *Queli linmiao tongji shi* (General history of the forests and temples of Queli). Li dong tang bi shi, 1918.

Biallas, Franz. *Konfuzius und sein Kult* (Confucius and his cult). Peking: 1928.

Billioud, Sebastian, and Joël Thorvald. "*Lijiao:* The Return of Ceremonies Honoring Confucius in Mainland China." *China Perspectives,* no. 4 (2009): 82–100.

Bilsky, Lester James. *The State Religion of Ancient China.* 2 vols. Taipei, Taiwan: Chinese Association for Folklore, 1975.

Blanchon, Flora, and Rang-ri Park Barjot, eds. *Le nouvel âge de Confucius: Modern Confucianism in China and South Korea.* Paris: Presses de l'Université Paris Sorbonne, 2007.

Blumenfield, Tami, and Helaine Silverman, eds. *Cultural Heritage Politics in China.* New York: Springer, 2013.

Boerschmann, Ernst. *Die baukunst und religiöse Kultur der Chinesen* (Architecture and religious culture of the Chinese). Berlin: Druck und Verlag von Georg Reimer, 1914.

Bois, Yve Alain, and Rosalind Krauss. *Formless: A User's Guide*. New York: Zone Books, 1997.

Bol, Peter Kees. "Government, Society and State: On the Political Visions of Ssu-ma Kuang and Wang An-shi." In *Ordering the World: Approaches to State and Society in Sung Dynasty China*, edited by Robert P. Hymes and Conrad Schirokauer, 128–192. Berkeley: University of California Press, 1993.

———. *"This Culture of Ours": Intellectual Transitions in T'ang and Sung China*. Stanford, CA: Stanford University Press, 1992.

Bramwell, Bill, and Hongliang Yan. "Cultural Tourism, Ceremony and the State." *Annals of Tourism Research* 34, no. 4 (2008): 969–989.

Byatt, A. S. *The Biographers Tale*. London: Chatto and Windus, 2000.

Campanella, Thomas. *The Concrete Dragon: China's Urban Revolution and What It Means for the World*. New York: Princeton Architectural Press, 2008.

Carroll, Peter J. *Between Heaven and Modernity: Reconstructing Suzhou, 1895–1937*. Stanford, CA: Stanford University Press, 2006.

Carus, Paul. "Ceremony Celebrated under the Chinese Republic in Honor of Confucius." *Open Court, A Quarterly Magazine* 32, no. 3 (March 1918): 155–172.

Casey, Edward S. *Getting Back into Place: Toward a Renewed Understanding of the Place-World*. Bloomington: Indiana University Press, 1993.

Chan, Hok-Lam. *Legends of the Building of Old Peking*. Seattle: University of Washington Press, 2008.

Che Yanfen. "Zai faming zhong yanshu chuantong yi jiKong yuewu de dangdai fuxing wei ge'an" (Continuing tradition through invention: A case study of the contemporary recovery of the *JiKong yuewu*). *Journal of Wenzhou University* 23, no. 1 (2010): 22–27.

Chen Hao. *Queli zhi* (Annals of Queli). 1505.

Chen Huanzhang. *Gaige Qufu lin miao banfa boyi* (On the legal reforms to the forest and temple in Qufu). Kowloon, Hong Kong: Yi qiang yin shua chang yin, 1962.

Chen Lifu. "Guanyu Kongzi sixiang pingjia de jige wenti—jianyu Pang Pu tongzhi shangque" (Concerning several problems with the evaluation of Kongzi's thought—a discussion with Comrade Pang Pu). *Nanchang daxue xuebao (Renmin shehui kexue ban)*, no. 4 (1978): 47–60.

Cheng, Anne. "Nationalism, Citizenship, and the Old Text/New Text Controversy in Late Nineteenth Century China." In *Imagining the People: Chinese Intellectuals and the Concept of Citizenship, 1890–1920*, edited by Joshua Fogel and Peter Zarrow, 61–81. Armonk, NY: M. E. Sharpe, 1997.

Cheng Zhizheng. "Wande Taishan Qufu Chuzhou jiyou" (Journey to Wande, Mt. Tai, Qufu, and Chuzhou). *Lüxing zazhi* (Travel magazine) 10, no. 10 (1936): 39–50.

Chi Qingquan and Zhang Kunlun. "Qufu Kongmiao Dachengdian suxiang zaoxing fuyuan gongcheng jishi" (Report on the statue recovery project in the Hall of the Great Ensemble of Kong Temple). *Qilu yiyuan*, no. 00 (1984): 19.

Chow, Kai-wing. *The Rise of Confucian Ritualism in Late Imperial China: Ethics, Classics, and Lineage Discourse*. Stanford, CA: Stanford University Press, 1994.

Chow Tse-tsung. "Anti-Confucianism in Early Republican China." In *The Confucian Persuasion,* edited by Arthur F. Cahill and James Wright, 288–312. Stanford, CA: Stanford University Press, 1960.

———. *The May Fourth Movement: Intellectual Revolution in Modern China.* Harvard East Asian Studies. Cambridge, MA: Harvard University Press, 1960.

Chung, Anita. *Drawing Boundaries: Architectural Images in Qing China.* Honolulu: University of Hawai'i Press, 2004.

Clart, Philip. "The Concept of Ritual in the Thought of Sima Guang." In *Perceptions of Antiquity,* edited by Dieter Kuhn and Helga Stahl, 237–252. Heidelberg, Germany: Edition Forum, 2008.

Clunas, Craig. *Fruitful Sites: Garden Culture in Ming Dynasty China.* Durham, NC: Duke University Press, 1996.

Coaldrake, William. *Architecture and Authority in Japan.* Japanese Studies Series. New York: Nissan Institute/Routledge, 1996.

Cody, Jeffrey W. *Building in China: Henry K. Murphy's "Adaptive Architecture," 1914–1935.* Seattle: University of Washington Press, 2001.

Cody, Jeffrey W., Nancy Shatzman Steinhardt, and Tony Atkin, eds. *Chinese Architecture and the Beaux-Arts.* Spatial Habitus. Honolulu: University of Hawai'i Press, 2011.

Confucius (Kongzi). *The Analects of Confucius.* Translated by James Legge. Salt Lake City, UT: Project Gutenberg. Electronic resource.

Dai Nianci. "Queli Binshe de sheji jieshao" (Introduction to the design of the Queli Guesthouse). *Jianzhu xuebao,* no. 1 (1986): 2–3.

de Crespigny, Rafe. *A Biographical Dictionary of the Later Han to the Three Kingdoms.* Leiden, Netherlands: E. J. Brill, 2006.

DeBary, Wm. Theodore, ed. *Sources of Chinese Tradition.* 2 vols. New York: Columbia University Press, 2000.

DeBlasi, Anthony. "Selling Confucius: The Negotiated Return of Tradition in Post-Socialist China." In *The Sage Returns: Confucian Revival in Contemporary China,* edited by Kenneth Hammond and Jeffrey Richey, 67–92. Albany: State University of New York Press, 2015.

Dong, Madeleine Yue. *Republican Beijing: The City and Its Histories.* Berkeley: University of California Press, 2003.

Doré, Henri, and M. Kennelly, trans. *Researches into Chinese Superstitions.* Taipei, Taiwan: Cheng-wen, 1966.

Dott, Brian Russell. *Identity Reflections: Pilgrimages to Mount Tai in Late Imperial China.* Harvard East Asian Monographs 244. Cambridge: Harvard University Asia Center, 2004.

Dransmann, F. *Taischan-Tchufu Fuhrer* (T'aishan-Ku'fow guide). Yenchowfu (Yanzhou), Shantung, China: Yenchow Missionary Press, 1934.

Durkheim, Emile. *The Division of Labor in Society.* 1893. Reprint, New York: Free Press, 1997.

Ebrey, Patricia, and James L. Watson, eds. *Kinship Organization in Late Imperial China.* Berkeley: University of California Press, 1986.

Edkins, J. "A Visit to the City of Confucius." *Journal of the North China Branch of the Royal Asiatic Society,* no. 8 (1874): 79–92.

Eliade, Mircea. *The Sacred and the Profane: The Nature of Religion.* Orlando, FL: Harcourt, 1959.

Eno, Robert. "The Background of the Kong Family of Lu." *Early China,* no. 28 (2003): 1–41.

Esherick, Joseph, Paul Pickowicz, and Andrew G. Walder. *The Chinese Cultural Revolution as History.* Stanford, CA: Stanford University Press, 2006.

Fairbank, Wilma. *Liang and Lin: Partners in Exploring China's Architectural Past.* Philadelphia: University of Pennsylvania Press, 1994.

Fan Cunchang. *Liang Shanbo Zhu Yingtai jia zai Kong Meng guli* (The home of Liang Shanbo and Zhu Yingtai is in the native place of Kongzi and Mengzi). Jinan, China: Shandong wenxian yinxiang chubanshe, 2003.

Fan Ye. *Hou Han shu* (Book of the Later Han). 445. Reprint, Taibei: Taiwan shangwu yinshuguan, 1965.

Fang Xuanling. *Jin shu* (Book of Jin). 646. Reprint, Taibei: Taiwan shangwu yinshuguan, 1965.

Feuchtwang, Stephan. *The Imperial Metaphor: Popular Religion in China.* London: Routledge, 1992.

Fisher, Carney. *The Chosen One: Succession and Adoption in the Court of Ming Shizong.* Boston: Allen and Unwin, 1990.

Fogel, Joshua. *The Cultural Dimension of Sino-Japanese Relations: Essays on the Nineteenth and Twentieth Centuries.* Armonk, NY: M. E. Sharpe, 1995.

———. *The Literature of Travel in the Japanese Rediscovery of China, 1862–1945.* Stanford, CA: Stanford University Press, 1996.

Fogel, Joshua, and Peter Zarrow, eds. *Imagining the People: Chinese Intellectuals and the Concept of Citizenship, 1890–1920.* Armonk, NY: M. E. Sharpe, 1997.

Flam, Jack, ed. *Robert Smithson: The Collected Writings.* Berkeley: University of California Press, 1996.

Flath, James. "Managing Historical Capital in Shandong: Museum, Monument and Memory in Provincial China." *Public Historian* 24, no. 2 (2002): 41–59.

———. "Setting Moon and Rising Nationalism: Lugou Bridge as Monument and Memory." In *Beyond Suffering: Recounting War in Modern China,* edited by James Flath and Norman Smith, 244–261. Vancouver: University of British Columbia Press, 2011.

———. "'This Is How the Chinese People Began Their Struggle': Humen and the Origins of Modern China." In *Sites of Memory in China,* edited by Marc Matten, 167–192. Leiden, Netherlands: Leiden University Press, 2011.

Flath, James, and Norman Smith, eds. *Beyond Suffering: Recounting War in Modern China.* Vancouver: University of British Columbia Press, 2011.

Frampton, Kenneth, ed. "*Rappell à l'ordre:* The Case for the Tectonic." In *Labour, Work and Architecture: Collected Essays on Architecture and Design,* edited by Kenneth Frampton, 99–103. London: Phaidon Press, 2002.

Franke, Herbert. "The Chin Dynasty." In *The Cambridge History of China: Alien Regimes and Border States, 907–1368,* edited by Frederick W. Mote and Denis Twitchett, 215–320. Cambridge: Cambridge University Press, 1994.

Fu Chonglan. *Qufu miaocheng yu Zhongguo Ruxue* (Qufu, city of temples and Chinese Confucianism). Beijing: Zhongguo shehui kexue chubanshe, 2002.

Fu, Xinian. "Survey: Chinese Traditional Architecture." In *Chinese Traditional Architecture*, edited by Nancy Shatzman Steinhardt, 9–33. New York: China Institute in America, China House Gallery, 1984.

Gong Yanxing and Wang Zhengyu. *Kongmiao zhushen kao: Kongmiao suxiang ziliao bian* (Survey of the spirits in Kong Temple: Collected materials on the statuary of Kong Temple). Jinan, China: Shandong youyi chubanshe, 1994.

Goodrich, L. Carrington. *Dictionary of Ming Biography, 1368–1644.* New York: Columbia University Press, 1976.

Goossaert, Vincent, and David A. Palmer. *The Religious Question in Modern China.* Chicago: University of Chicago Press, 2011.

Grieder, Jerome. *Hu Shih and the Chinese Renaissance: Liberalism in the Chinese Revolution, 1917–1937.* Cambridge, MA: Harvard University Press, 1970.

Gu Chun. "Cong Qufu Kongmiao kan fengjian tongzhi jieji zunKong de fandong shizhi he nongmin de fanKong douzheng" (The reactionary nature of the worship of Kongzi by the feudal ruling class and the anti-Confucian struggles of the peasants as seen from the history of Kong Temple at Qufu). *Kaogu*, no. 1 (1974): 40–45.

Guy, R. Kent. *Qing Governors and Their Provinces: The Evolution of Territorial Administration in China, 1644–1796.* Seattle: University of Washington Press, 2010.

Halbwachs, Maurice. *The Collective Memory.* 1950. Reprint, New York: Harper and Row Colophon Books, 1980.

Hammond, Kenneth, and Jeffrey Richey, eds. *The Sage Returns: Confucian Revival in Contemporary China.* Albany: State University of New York Press, 2015.

Hansen, Valerie. *The Open Empire: The History of China to 1600.* New York: Norton, 2000.

Harrell, Steven. "China's Tangled Web of Heritage." In *Cultural Heritage Politics in China*, edited by Tami Blumenfield and Helaine Silverman, 285–294. New York: Springer, 2013.

Hay, Jonathan S. "Ming Palace and Tomb in Early Qing Jiangning: Dynastic Memory and the Openness of History." *Late Imperial China* 20, no. 1 (June 1999): 1–48.

Herdan, Innes, trans. *300 Tang Poems.* Taipei, Taiwan: Far East Book Company, 1973.

Hesse-Wartegg, Ernst von. "China's 'Holy Land': A Visit to the Tomb of Confucius." *The Century Magazine* 60 (1900): 803–819.

Ho, David. "To Protect and Preserve: Resisting the Destroy the Four Olds Campaign, 1966–67." In *The Chinese Cultural Revolution as History*, edited by Joseph Esherick, Paul Pickowicz, and Andrew G. Walder, 84–92. Stanford, CA: Stanford University Press, 2006.

Hobsbawm, Eric, and Terence O. Ranger. *The Invention of Tradition.* Cambridge: Cambridge University Press, 1992.

Hua Min. "Waiguo pengyou zai Qufu" (Foreign friends in Qufu). *Lüxing jia*, no. 7 (1956): 23–24.

Huang Chin-shing. "The Confucian Temple as Ritual System: Manifestations of Power, Legitimacy and Belief in Imperial China." *Qinghua Xuebao* (Tsing-hua journal of Chinese studies) 25, no. 2 (1995): 115–136.

———. "The Cultural Politics of Autocracy: The Confucius Temple and Ming Despotism, 1368–1530." In *On Sacred Grounds: Culture, Society, Politics, and the Formation of the*

Cult of Confucius, edited by Thomas Wilson, 267–296. Cambridge, MA: Harvard University Asia Center, 2002.

———. *Philosophy, Philology and Politics in Eighteenth Century China: Li Fu and the Lu-Wang School under the Ch'ing.* Cambridge: Cambridge University Press, 1995.

———. *Youru shengyu: Quanli xinyang yu zhengdangxing* (Entering the master's sanctuary: Power, belief and legitimacy in traditional China). Taipei, Taiwan: Yun-chen, 1994.

Hucker, Charles O. *A Dictionary of Official Titles in Imperial China.* Stanford, CA: Stanford University Press, 1985.

Hymes, Robert P., and Conrad Schirokauer, eds. *Ordering the World: Approaches to State and Society in Sung Dynasty China.* Berkeley: University of California Press, 1993.

Ingold, Tim. "Materials against Materiality." *Archaeological Dialogues* 14, no. 1 (2007): 1–16.

———. "Writing Texts, Reading Materials: A Response to My Critics." *Archaeological Dialogues* 14, no. 1 (2007): 31–38.

Jensen, Lionel. "The Genesis of Kongzi in Ancient Narrative: The Figurative as Historical." In *On Sacred Grounds: Culture, Society, Politics and the Formation of the Cult of Confucius,* edited by Thomas Wilson, 175–221. Cambridge, MA: Harvard University Asia Center, 2002.

———. "Legends of Confucius." In *Hawai'i Reader in Traditional Chinese Culture,* edited by Victor H. Mair, Nancy Shatzman Steinhardt, and Paul R. Goldin, 234–238. Honolulu: University of Hawai'i Press, 2004.

———. *Manufacturing Confucianism: Chinese Traditions and Universal Civilization.* Durham, NC: Duke University Press, 1997.

Jiang Weiqiao. "Qufu jiyou" (Journey to Qufu). *Xiaoshuo yuebao* 6, no. 12 (1915): n.p.

Jing, Jun. "Knowledge, Organization, and Symbolic Capital: Two Temples to Confucius in Gansu." In *On Sacred Grounds: Culture, Society, Politics, and the Formation of the Cult of Confucius,* edited by Thomas Wilson, 335–375. Cambridge, MA: Harvard University Asia Center, 2002.

———. *The Temple of Memories: History, Power, and Morality in a Chinese Village.* Stanford, CA: Stanford University Press, 1996.

Johnston, Reginald Fleming. *Confucianism and Modern China.* London: V. Gollancz, 1934.

Karlgren, Bernhard. *Philology and Ancient China.* 1926. Reprint, Philadelphia: Porcupine Press, 1980.

Ke Lan, ed. *Qiannian Kongfu de zuihou yi dai* (The last generation of the thousand-year-old Kong Mansion). Tianjin, China: Tianjin jiaoyu chubanshe, 1998.

Kerr, Rose, and Nigel Wood. "Chemistry and Chemical Technology." In *Science and Civilization in China.* Volume 5, part 12, Ceramic Technology. Cambridge: Cambridge University Press, 2004.

Knapp, Ron, and Kai-yin Lo, ed. *House, Home, Family: Living and Being Chinese.* Honolulu: University of Hawai'i Press, 2005.

Kong Chuan. *Dongjia zaji* (Miscellaneous records of the Eastern House). 1134. Kongzi wenhua daquan. Reprint, Jinan, China: Shandong youyi chubanshe, 1990.

Kong Demao, Ke Lan, and Frances Wood. *The House of Confucius.* London: Hodder and Stoughton, 1988.

Kong Deping, ed. *Qufu guji tonglan* (An overview of Qufu antiquities). Beijing: Wenwu chubanshe, 2010.

Kong Deping et al. *JiKong yuewu* (The music and dance of the sacrifice to Kongzi). Beijing: Zhongguo shehui chubanshe, 2010.

Kong Derun. "Jianguo chu Qufu wenhua gongzuo yi shi liang ze" (Two significant cultural works in early post-liberation Qufu). *Qufu wenshi*, no. 9 (1989): 74, 81–82.

Kong Fanyin. *Qufu de lishi mingren yu wenwu* (Noted historical figures, texts and relics of Qufu). Jinan, China: Qi Lu shushe, 2002.

———. *Yansheng gongfu jianwen* (The mansion of the Dukes of Fulfilling the Sage). Jinan, China: Qilu shushe, 1992.

Kong Fanyin, Shandong Sheng Qufu Wenwu Guanli Weiyuanhui, Zhongguo Shehui Kexueyuan Lishi Yanjiusuo, and Qufu Shifan Xueyuan Lishi Xi. *Qufu Kongfu Dang'an shiliao xuanbian* (Selection of historical materials from Kong Archive in Qufu). Jinan, China: Qi Lu shushe, 1980.

Kong Jifen. *Queli wenxian kao* (Investigation of documents in Queli). 1762. Reprint, Taipei, Taiwan: Zhongding wenhua gongsi, 1967.

Kong Lingzhi. "Kongzi houyi fudi" (Household of Kongzi's descendants). *Qufu wenshi*, no. 5 (1985): 42–46.

Kong Xiangke. "Kongzi shengdan Qufu dahui ji" (Record of the conference marking the birthday of Kongzi in Qufu). *Kongjiaohui zazhi* (Confucian association monthly) 1, no. 9 (November 1931): 1–6.

Kong Yuancuo. *Kongshi zuting guangji* (Extensive record of the Kong family ancestral precinct). 1127. Reprint, Taibei: Taiwan shangwu yinshuguan, 1966.

Kong Zhencong. *Queli zhi* (Annals of Queli). 1575.

"Kongjiadian yao dadao, Kongzi yao pingjian" (Beat the Kong family shop, evaluate Kongzi). *Zhongguo jianshe*, no. 4 (1982): 16.

Kuhn, Dieter, and Helga Stahl, eds. *Perceptions of Antiquity in Chinese Civilization*. Heidelberg, Germany: Edition Forum, 2008.

Kuo, Yapei. "'The Emperor and the People in One Body': The Worship of Confucius and Ritual Planning in the Xinzheng Reforms, 1902–1911." *Modern China* 35, no. 2 (2009): 123–154.

Lai, Guolong. "Valuing the Past in China: The Seminal Influence of Liang Sicheng on Heritage Conservation." *Orientations* 35, no. 2 (2004): 82–89.

Lam, Joseph S. C. "Musical Confucianism: The Case of Jikong Yuewu." In *On Sacred Grounds: Culture, Society, Politics, and the Formation of the Cult of Confucius*, edited by Thomas Wilson, 134–172. Cambridge, MA: Harvard University Asia Center, 2002.

———. *State Sacrifices and Music in Ming China: Orthodoxy, Creativity, and Expressiveness*. Albany: State University of New York Press, 1998.

———. "The Yin and Yang of Chinese Music Historiography: The Case of Confucian Ceremonial Music." *Yearbook for Traditional Music*, no. 27 (1995): 34–51.

Lamberton, Abigail. "The Kongs of Qufu: Power and Privilege in Late Imperial China." In *On Sacred Grounds: Culture, Society, Politics, and the Formation of the Cult of Confucius,* edited by Thomas Wilson, 297–332. Cambridge, MA: Harvard University Asia Center, 2002.

Le Shan. "Kongmiao jianxiu shuchang" (Renovatiing Kong Temple). *Qufu wenshi,* no. 1 (1982): 30–36.

Ledderose, Lothar. *Ten Thousand Things: Module and Mass Production in Chinese Art.* A. W. Mellon Lectures in the Fine Arts 1998. Princeton, NJ: Princeton University Press, 2000.

Lefebvre, Henri. *The Production of Space.* Translated by Donald Nicholson-Smith. Malden, MA: Blackwell, 1991.

Legge, James. *The Chinese Classics.* Vol. 4, *The She King or The Book of Poetry.* London: Trübner, 1871.

———. *The Four Books: Confucian Analects, the Great Learning, the Doctrine of the Mean, and the Works of Mencius.* Shanghai: Commercial Press, 1945.

———. *The Sacred Books of China: The Texts of Taoism.* New York: Dover, 1962.

Legge, James, Confucius, Mencius, and Ming Zuoqiu. *The Chinese Classics.* 2nd ed. Oxford: Clarendon Press, 1893.

Leys, Simon. "The Chinese Attitude toward the Past." *China Heritage Quarterly,* no. 14 (2008). Online.

Li Daoyuan. *Shui jing zhu* (Commentary on the Water Classic). Taibei: Taiwan shangwu yinshuguan, 1965.

Li Deming. *Dongfang shengcheng: Qufu* (Qufu: Eastern holy city). Jinan, China: Shandong youyi chubanshe, 2001.

Li Dongyang. *Da Ming huidian* (Collected statutes of the Ming dynasty). 1587.

Li, Guannan. "Culture, Revolution and Modernity: The Guomindang's Ideology and Enterprise of Reviving China, 1927–1937." PhD diss., University of Oregon, 2009.

Li Hongzhang, ed. *Da Qing huidian shili* (Collected statutes of the Qing dynasty). 1899.

Li Huacheng and Xi Xingjia, eds. *Shandong nianjian* (Shandong yearbook). Jinan, China: Shandong renmin chubanshe, 1987.

Li Jianyu. "Qufu youji" (Journey to Qufu). *Shandong wenxue,* no. 10 (1961): 54.

Li Jingming. *Jiashi benmo* (Family history). Kongzi jiazu quanshu. Shenyang, China: Liaohai chubanshe, 1999.

———. *Jiazu shixi* (Family lineage). Kongzi jiazu quanshu. Shenyang, China: Liaohai chubanshe, 1999.

Li Jingye and Gong Zhaozeng. *Qufu xianzhi* (Qufu county annals). Jinan, China: 1934.

Li Jinpu. "Xuanli duocai de Zhongguo Qufu guoji wenhua jie" (The brilliance and color of the international culture festival in Qufu, China). *Yuejin renjian,* no. 00 (1994): 8–11.

Li Kesheng. "Zhengque chuli wenhua yu jingji de guanxi nuli tigao liangge xiaoyi" (Correctly manage the relationship between culture and economics and aggressively promote two benefits). *Yuejin renjian,* no. 1 (1994): 6–7.

Li, Liu. *The Chinese Neolithic: Trajectories to Early States.* Cambridge: Cambridge University Press, 2004.

Li Qinglun et al. "Xiannian tongzhi shi wenwu guji" (Comrade Xiannian inspects cultural artifacts). *Qufu wenshi,* no. 9 (1989): 3, 4–5.

Li Rongde. "Chongfeng zai qian: Shandong Qufu zhujun piLin piKong jishi" (Charge forward: An account of criticizing Lin and Kong, by the Shandong, Qufu garrison). *Jiefang jun wenyi,* no. 3 (1974): 19–20.

Li, Zehou. *The Chinese Aesthetic Tradition.* Translated by Maija Bell Samei. Honolulu: University of Hawai'i Press, 2010.

———. *The Path of Beauty: A Study of Chinese Aesthetics.* Translated by Gong Lizeng. Beijing: Morning Glory, 1989.

———. "Re-evaluation of Kongzi." *Social Sciences in China,* no. 2 (1980): 99–127. In *Sources of Chinese Tradition,* Vol. 2, translated by Wm. Theodore DeBary, 574–580. New York: Columbia University Press, 2000.

Liang Sicheng. *Qufu Kongmiao jianzhu jiqi xiuqi jihua* (Plans for the construction and renovation of Kong Temple in Qufu). Beiping, China: Zhongguo yingzao xueshe, 1935.

Liang Sicheng, and Wilma Fairbank. *A Pictorial History of Chinese Architecture: A Study of the Development of Its Structural System and the Evolution of Its Types.* Cambridge, MA: MIT Press, 1984.

Liang Zhang, ed. *Yusi zuopin xuan* (Selection from *Threads of Talk*). Beijing: Renmin wenxue chubanshe, 1988.

Lin Na, ed. *Hu Shi xuanwen xuanji* (Collected essays of Hu Shi). Tianjin, China: Baihua wenyi chubanshe, 2004.

Lin, Yutang. *Confucius Saw Nancy and Essays about Nothing.* Shanghai: Commercial Press, 1936.

Liu, Cary Y. "Chinese Architectural Aesthetics: Patterns of Living and Being between Past and Present." In *House, Home, Family: Living and Being Chinese,* edited by Ron Knapp and Kai-yin Lo, 139–159. Honolulu: University of Hawai'i Press, 2005.

———. "The Yuan Dynasty Capital, Ta-Tu: Imperial Building Program and Bureaucracy." *T'oung Pao,* no. 78 (1992): 264–301.

Liu Houqin. *Jiazu chunqiu* (Family spring and autumn). Kongzi jiazu quanshu. Shenyang: Liaohai chubanshe, 1999.

Liu, James T. C. *Reform in Sung China: Wang An-shih (1021–1086) and His New Policies.* Cambridge, MA: Harvard University Press, 1959.

Liu Jun. *Kong Yan Meng sanshi zhi* (Annals of the three families of Kong, Yan, and Meng). 1482. Reprint, Beijing: Beijing tushuguan guji zhenben yekan 14, 1987.

Liu, Kwang-ching, ed. *Orthodoxy in Late-Imperial China.* Berkeley: University of California Press, 1990.

Liu Xu. *Jiu Tang shu* (Old book of Tang). 945. Reprint, Taibei: Taiwan shangwu yinshuguan, 1965.

Loewe, Michael. *A Biographical Dictionary of the Qin, Former Han and Xin Periods (221 BC–AD 24).* Leiden, Netherlands: E. J. Brill, 2000.

———. "The Conduct of Government and the Issues at Stake, A.D. 57–167." In *The Cambridge History of China.* Vol. 1, *The Ch'in and Han Empires, 221 BC–AD 220,* edited by Denis Twitchett and John K. Fairbank, 291–316. Cambridge: Cambridge University Press, 1986.

Loomis, A. W., ed. *Confucius and the Chinese Classics, or, Readings in Chinese Literature.* San Francisco: A. Roman, 1867.

Louie, Kam. *Critiques of Confucius in Contemporary China.* New York: St. Martin's Press, 1980.

Lowenthal, David. *The Heritage Crusade and the Spoils of History.* London: Viking, 1997.

Lu, Duanfang. *Remaking Chinese Urban Form: Modernity, Scarcity, and Space, 1949–2005.* Planning, History, and Environment Series. New York: Routledge, 2006.

Lu Xun. *Jiwai ji shiyi* (A supplement to the Addenda collection). Beijing: Renmin wenxue chubanshe, 1993.

Luo Chenglie. *Shitou shang de Rujia wenxian: Qufu bei wen lu* (Confucian writing in stone: A catalog of Qufu stele inscriptions). Zhongguo Kongzi jijinhui wenku. Jinan, China: Qi Lu shushe, 2001.

———. *Wenwu guji* (Ancient texts and relics). Kongzi jiazu quanshu. Shenyang, China: Liaohai chubanshe, 1999.

Luo Chenglie, Zhu Fuping, and Luo Ming, eds. *Kongfu Dang'an xuan* (Selections from the Kong family archives). Beijing: Zhongguo wenshi chubanshe, 2002.

Ma Aiping, Si Lina, and Zhang Hongfei. "The Evolution of Cultural Tourism: The Example of Qufu, the Birthplace of Confucius." In *Tourism in China: Destination, Cultures and Communities,* edited by Chris Ryan and Huimin Gu, 182–196. New York: Routledge, 2009.

Ma Dongfeng. "JiKong yuewu huodong gaishu Ma Dongfeng" (Brief introduction to the JiKong yuewu). *Zhongguo yinyue nianjian* (1990): 488–489.

Makeham, John. *Lost Soul: Confucianism in Contemporary Chinese Academic Discourse.* Cambridge, MA: Harvard University Asia Center, 2008.

Manchoukuo Wenjiao Bu Lijiao Si. *Si Kong lu* (Record of sacrificing to Kongzi). Changchun, China: Wenjiao bu lijiao si, 1933.

Mansvelt Beck, B. J. "The Fall of Han." In *The Cambridge History of China.* Vol. 1, *The Ch'in and Han Empires, 221 BC–AD 220,* edited by Denis Twitchett and John K. Fairbank, 317–376. Cambridge: Cambridge University Press, 1986.

Mao Zedong. *Selected Works.* 4 vols. Peking: Foreign Languages Press, 1967.

Martin, W. A. P. *A Cycle of Cathay, or, China, South and North with Personal Reminiscences.* New York: Fleming H. Revell, 1896.

Matten, Marc, ed. *Places of Memory in Modern China: History, Politics, and Identity.* Leiden, Netherlands: E. J. Brill, 2012.

McMullen, David. *State and Scholars in T'ang China.* Cambridge Studies in Chinese History, Literature, and Institutions. Cambridge: Cambridge University Press, 1988.

Mencius (Mengzi), P. J. Ivanhoe, and Irene Bloom. *Mencius, Translations from the Asian Classics.* New York: Columbia University Press, 2009.

Meng Fanliang. "Da wenhua tai, chang jingmao xi, ban hao guoji Kongzi wenhua jie" (Build the stage of culture, perform the play of economics and trade, properly manage the international Kongzi culture festival). *Qufu nianjian.* Qufu: Qufu Bianzuan weiyuanhui, 2003–2005. Online.

Meng Fanliang and Zhu Taiming. "Rujia jieqing: 2004 Zhonggyuo guoji Kongzi wenhua jie" (Confucian festival: The 2004 China international Kongzi cultural festival). *Zhongguo ruxue nianjian,* 2005, 134–136.

Meng Qiuju. "Qufu zuizao de yi jia lüshe—Datong Lüshe" (Qufu's earliest hotel—the Datong Hotel). *Qufu wenshi,* no. 8 (1988): 26–27.

Meyer, Michael J. *The Last Days of Old Beijing: Life in the Backstreets of a City Transformed.* New York: Walker, 2008.

Meyer-Fong, Tobie S. *Building Culture in Early Qing Yangzhou.* Stanford, CA: Stanford University Press, 2003.

Miller, Tracy. *The Divine Nature of Power: Chinese Ritual Architecture at the Sacred Site of Jinci.* Cambridge, MA: Harvard University Asia Center, 2007.

Minford, John, and Rachel May, eds. "Observing the Rites at the Ancient Abode of Confucius." *China Heritage Quarterly,* no. 17 (2009). Online.

Ministry of the Interior, ed. *Minguo Jing Lu Jin Xiang gu qiwu diaocha minglu* (Republican Beijing, Shandong, Shanxi, Hunan ancient relics investigation). Beijing: Beijing tushuguan chubanshe, 2004.

Moll-Murata, Christine, and Song Jianze. "Note on Qing Dynasty 'Handicraft Regulation and Precedent' (*jiangzuo zeli*), with Special Focus on Regulations on Materials, Working Time, Price, and Wage." *Late Imperial China* 23, no. 2 (2002): 87–126.

Moll-Murata, Christine, Song Jianze, and Hans Ulrich Vogel, eds. *Chinese Handicraft Regulations of the Qing Dynasty: Theory and Application.* Munich: IUDICIUM Verlag, 2005.

Mote, F. W. *Imperial China: 900–1800.* Cambridge, MA: Harvard University Press, 1999.

———. "A Millennium of Chinese Urban History: Form, Time and Space Concepts in Soochow." *Rice University Studies* 59, no. 4 (1973): 35–65.

Mote, Frederick W., and Denis Twitchett, eds. *The Cambridge History of China: Alien Regimes and Border States, 907–1368.* Vol. 6. Cambridge: Cambridge University Press, 1994.

Moule, G. E. "Notes on the Ting-chi or Half-Yearly Sacrifice to Confucius." *Journal of the North China Branch of the Royal Asiatic Society,* no. 33 (1900–1901): 49–52.

Mukerji, Chandra. *Territorial Ambitions and the Gardens of Versailles.* Cambridge Cultural Social Studies. Cambridge: Cambridge University Press, 1997.

Mungello, David. *The Great Encounter of China and the West, 1500–1800.* Lanham, MD: Rowman and Littlefield, 2005.

Murck, Christian F., ed. *Artists and Traditions: Uses of the Past in Chinese Culture.* Princeton, NJ: Art Museum, 1976.

Murray, Julia K. "Heirloom and Exemplar: Family and School Portraits of Confucius in the Song and Yuan Periods." *Journal of Song-Yuan Studies,* no. 41 (2011): 227–266.

———. "'Idols' in the Temple: Icons and the Cult of Confucius." *Journal of Asian Studies* 68, no. 2 (2009): 371–411.

———. "Illustrations of the Life of Confucius: Their Evolution, Functions, and Significance in Late Ming China." *Artibus Asiae* 57, no. 1/2 (1997): 73–134.

———. "The Temple of Confucius and Pictorial Biographies of the Sage." *Journal of Asian Studies* 55, no. 2 (May 1996): 269–300.

———. "Varied Views of the Sage: Illustrated Narratives of the Life of Confucius." In *On Sacred Grounds: Culture, Society, Politics, and the Formation of the Cult of Confucius,* edited by Thomas Wilson, 222–264. Cambridge, MA: Harvard East Asia Center, 2002.

Museé National des Arts Asiatiques Guimet. *Confucius: A l'aube de l'humanisme chinois.* Paris: Réunion des Musées Nationaux, 2004.

Naquin, Susan. *Peking: Temples and City Life, 1400–1900.* Berkeley: University of California Press, 2000.

Nedostup, Rebecca. *Superstitious Regimes: Religion and the Politics of Chinese Modernity.* Cambridge, MA: Harvard University Asia Center, 2010.

Needham, Joseph. "Archeological Study Tour in China, 1958." *Antiquity* 33, no. 130 (1959): 113–119.

———. *Science and Civilization in China.* Cambridge: Cambridge University Press, 1971.

Nelson, Robert S., and Margaret Olin, eds. *Monuments and Memory, Made and Unmade.* Chicago: University of Chicago Press, 2003.

Ni Jingyin. *Qufu Taishan youji* (Journey to Qufu and Mt. Tai). Shanghai: Zhonghua shuju, 1931.

Niu Guodong. "Lüyou fuwuye—Disan jie Kongzi danchen guli you" (Travel service—the third Kongzi hometown birthday tour). In *Shandong nianjian,* edited by Li Huacheng and Xi Xingjia, 409–410. Jinan, China: Shandong renmin chubanshe, 1987.

Nora, Pierre. "Between Memory and History: Les Lieux de Memoire." Special issue: Memory and Counter-Memory, *Representations,* no. 26 (Spring 1989): 7–24.

Nylan, Michael. *The Five Confucian Classics.* New Haven, CT: Yale University Press, 2001.

Nylan, Michael, and Thomas Wilson. *Lives of Confucius: Civilization's Greatest Sage through the Ages.* New York: Doubleday, 2010.

Ouyang Xiu. *Xin Tang shu* (New book of Tang). 1060. Reprint, Taibei: Taiwan shangwu yinshuguan, 1965.

Ouyang Xiu and Richard L. Davis. *Historical Records of the Five Dynasties.* New York: Columbia University Press, 2004.

Owen, Stephen. *Remembrances: The Experience of the Past in Classical Chinese Literature.* Cambridge, MA: Harvard University Press, 1986.

Pak Yŏn-jo and An Sŭng-gwi, eds. *Kokpu Sŏngmyo Wian Sasilgi* (True account of bringing comfort to the saint's temple in Qufu). Sihŭng County, Korea: Noktong Sŏwŏn, 1931.

Palundan, Ann. *The Imperial Ming Tombs.* New Haven, CT: Yale University Press, 1981.

Pan Guxi, ed. *Qufu Kongmiao jianzhu* (The architecture of Kong temple in Qufu). Beijing: Zhongguo jianzhu gongye chubanshe, 1987.

———. "The Yuan and Ming Dynasties." In *Chinese Architecture, the Culture and Civilization of China,* edited by Nancy Shatzman Steinhardt, 199–260. New Haven, CT: Yale University Press, 2002.

Pan Xiang. *Qufu xianzhi* (Qufu county annals). 1774. Reprint, Jinan, China: Shandong Youyi chubanshe, 1998.

Pang Pu. "Kongzi sixiang zai pingjia" (Reevaluating Kongzi's thought). *Lishi yanjiu,* no. 8 (1978): 48.

———. "Ping 'sirenbang' de jiapi Kong" (Critique the Gang of Four's False Criticism of Kongzi). *Lishi yanjiu,* no. 6 (1974): 37–42.

Pas, Julian. *The Turning of the Tide: Religion in China Today.* Hong Kong: Royal Asiatic Society, 1989. In association with Oxford University Press.

Peng Lin. "Qufu jianwen" (What I saw and heard in Qufu). *Lüxing zazhi,* no. 3 (1954): 70–71.

Peng Yanhua. "Zhongguo Kongzi Jijinhui Qufu banshichu gongzuo." In *Qufu nianjian* (Qufu yearbook), edited by Zhang Dongwei. Qufu, China: Qufu Bianzuan weiyuanhui, 1999–2000. Online.

Peterson, Willard J. "Confucian Learning in Late Ming Thought." In *The Cambridge History of China.* Vol. 8, *The Ming Dynasty, 1398–1644, Part 2,* edited by Denis Twitchett and Frederick W. Mote, 708–788. Cambridge: Cambridge University Press, 1998.

Peterson, Willard J., ed. *The Cambridge History of China.* Vol. 9, *The Ch'ing Empire to 1800, Part 1.* 1st ed. Cambridge: Cambridge University Press, 2002.

"Pipan sanKong Cailiao" (Materials criticizing the three Kongs). Shandong sheng pi Lin pi Kong zhanlanguan, 1975.

Piping Qufu "sanKong" (Criticize the three Kongs of Qufu). Beijing: Wenwu chubanshe, 1974.

Pu Hong. "Eba dizhu zhuangyuan—Qufu 'Kong Fu'" (The Kong Family Mansion at Qufu—a manor of landlord tyrants). *Kaogu,* no. 4 (1974): 226–233.

Pu Ren. "Xiri zunKong chongru de 'shengdi' jinri piLin piKong de zhanchang" (Qufu, once a shrine of Kongzi and his followers, becomes a battlefront for criticizing Lin Biao and Kongzi. *Kaogu,* no. 3 (1974): 143–152.

Qi Sihe. "Pingpan Kongzi de fandong weixin shiguan" (Criticizing Kongzi's idealistic reactionary historical view). *Beijing daxue xuebao; zhexue shehui kexue xueban.* Vol. 4. 1973, 90–94.

Qing Bi, Guang Hua, and Jing Yu. "Kongdao, Kongdao ting yu Kongdao xuexiao" (Kong highway, Kong highway pavilions, and Kong highway school). *Qufu wenshi* (Qufu culture and history), no. 6 (1986): 5–8.

Queli guangzhi. (Expanded annals of Queli). 1673. Reprinted 1870.

"Qufu gong nong bing pi Lin pi Kong" (Qufu workers, peasants and soldiers criticize Lin and Kong). *Wenwu,* no. 3 (1974): 1.

Qufu Kongmiao Dachengdian huifu gongcheng bangongshe. "Kongmiao Dachengdian xiangkan huifu gaikuang" (General situation with recovering the statues and shrines of Dacheng hall in Kong temple). *Qufu wenshi,* no. 3 (1984): 40–43.

Qufu nianjian (Qufu yearbook). Qufu, China: Qufu Bianzuan weiyuanhui, 1986.

Qufu nianjian (Qufu yearbook). Qufu, China: Qufu Bianzuan weiyuanhui, 2003–2005.

Rawson, Jessica. *Chinese Jade from the Neolithic to the Qing.* London: British Museum, 1995.

Reinsch, Paul Samuel. *An American Diplomat in China.* Garden City, NY: Doubleday, Page, 1922.

Robson, James. *The Power of Place: The Religious Landscape of the Southern Sacred Peak (Nanyue) in Medieval China.* Cambridge, MA: Harvard University Asia Center, 2009.

Ruitenbeek, Klaas. "Building Regulations (*Zeli*) and Their Context." In *Chinese Handicraft Regulations of the Qing Dynasty: Theory and Application,* edited by Christine

Moll-Murata, Song Jianze, and Hans Ulrich Vogel, 175–190. Munich: IUDICIUM Verlag, 2005.

———. *Carpentry and Building in Late Imperial China: A Study of the Fifteenth-Century Carpenter's Manual* Lu Ban Jing. Leiden, Netherlands: E. J. Brill, 1993.

———. "The Rebuilding of the Three Rear Palaces in 1596–1598." In *Study on Ancient Chinese Books and Records of Science and Technology,* edited by Hua Jueming, 201–209. Zhengzhou, China: Elephant Press, 1998.

Ryan, Chris, and Huimin Gu, eds. *Tourism in China: Destinations, Cultures and Communities.* New York: Routledge, 2009.

Sang, Ye, and Geremie Barmé. "Commemorating Confucius in 1966–67: The Fate of the Confucius Temple, the Kong Mansion and Kong Cemetery." *China Heritage Quarterly,* no. 20 (2009). Online.

Segalen, Victor. *Steles.* Translated by Andrew Harvey and Iain Watson. London: Cape, 1990.

Semper, Gottfried. *Style in the Technical and Tectonic Arts, Or, Practical Aesthetics.* 1860. Translated by H. F. Mallgrave and M. Robinson. Reprint, Los Angeles: Getty Publications, 2004.

Shandong Provincial Artifact Management Office (*Shandong sheng wenwu guanli chu*) et al. *Qufu mingsheng guji* (Famous sites and relics of Qufu). Jinan, China: Shandong renmin chubanshe, 1958.

Shandong Sheng Difang Shizhi Bianzuan Weiyuanhui, ed. *Shandong shengzhi: Kongzi gulizhi* (Shandong provincial annals: The native place of Kongzi). Beijing: Zhonghua shu ju, 1994.

Shandong Shifan Daxue, ed. *Qing shilu Shandong shiliao xuan* (Veritable records of the Qing, collection of Shandong historical records). Vol. 1. Jinan, China: Qi Lu shushe, 1984.

Shang, Wei. "The Collapse of the Taibo Temple: A Study of the Unofficial History of the Scholars." PhD diss., Harvard University, 1995.

Shen Yang. "Pan chi: Miaoxue lishui de yiyi ji biaoxian xingshi" (Ideas of the layout of waters and expression of Panchi). *Zhongguo yuanlin* (Chinese landscape architecture), no. 9 (2010): 59–63.

Shen Yue. *Song shu* (Book of Song). 492–493. Reprint, Taibei: Taiwan shangwu yinshuguan, 1965.

Shepherd, Robert J. *Faith in Heritage: Displacement, Development and Religious Tourism in Contemporary China.* Walnut Creek, CA: Left Coast Books, 2013.

Shryock, John Knight. *The Origin and Development of the State Cult of Confucius.* New York: Century, 1932.

Sima Qian. *Shiji* (Records of the grand historian). 91 BCE. Reprint, Taibei: Taiwan shangwu yinshuguan, 1965.

Skonicki, Douglas. "Employing the Right Kind of Men: The Role of Cosmological Argumentation in the Qingli Reforms." *Journal of Song-Yuan Studies,* no. 38 (2008): 39–98.

Smithson, Robert. "Entropy Made Visible (Interview with Alison Sky) 1973." In *Robert Smithson: The Collected Writings,* edited by Jack Flam, 301–309. Berkeley: University of California Press, 1996.

Sohigian, Diran John. "Confucius and the Lady in Question: Power Politics, Cultural Production and the Performance of *Confucius Saw Nanzi* in China in 1929." *Twentieth-Century China* 36, no. 1 (2011): 23–43.

Sommer, Deborah. "'Destroying Confucius': Iconoclasm in the Confucian Temple." In *On Sacred Grounds: Culture, Society, Politics, and the Formation of the Cult of Confucius,* edited by Thomas Wilson, 95–133. Cambridge: Cambridge University Press, 2002.

Standaert, Nicholas. "Ritual Dances and their Visual Representations in the Ming and the Qing." *East Asia Library Journal* 12, no. 1 (2006): 68–181.

Steinhardt, Nancy Shatzman, ed. *Chinese Architecture: The Culture and Civilization of China.* New Haven, CT: Yale University Press, 2002.

———. *Chinese Imperial City Planning.* Honolulu: University of Hawaiʻi Press, 1990.

———. "The Tang Architectural Icon and the Politics of Chinese Architectural History." *Art Bulletin* 86, no. 2 (2004): 228–254.

Stille, Alexander. *The Future of the Past.* New York: Picador, 2002.

Strassberg, Richard E. *Inscribed Landscapes: Travel Writing from Imperial China.* Berkeley: University of California Press, 1994.

———. *The World of K'ung Shang-jen: A Man of Letters in Early Ch'ing China.* New York: Columbia University Press, 1983.

Su, Xiaobo, and Peggy Teo. *The Politics of Heritage Tourism in China: A View from Lijiang.* New York: Routledge, 2009.

Sun, Anna. *Confucianism as a World Religion: Contested Histories* and *Contemporary Realities.* Princeton, NJ: Princeton University Press, 2013.

———. "The Revival of Confucian Rites in Contemporary China." In *Confucianism and Spiritual Traditions in Contemporary China and Beyond,* edited by Fenggang Yang and Joseph Tamney, 309–328. Leiden, Netherlands: E. J. Brill, 2012.

Sun Dazhang. *Zhongguo gudai jianzhu shi* (History of Chinese ancient architecture). Beijing: CABP, 2002.

Sun Wanzhen and Wang Degang. "Systematic Contradiction between Heritage Conservation and Tourism Development: Cleaning the Temple and Cemetery of Confucius and the Kong Family Mansion in Qufu." *Chinese Journal of Population, Resources and Environment* 5, no. 1 (2007): 84–90.

Sun Zhuyou. *Jiazu jingying* (Family talents). Kongzi jiazu quanshu. Shenyang, China: Liaohai chubanshe, 1999.

Swart, Paula, and Barry Till. "A Revival of Confucian Ceremonies in China." In *The Turning of the Tide: Religion in China Today,* edited by Julian F. Pas, 201–214. Hong Kong: Royal Asiatic Society, New York: Oxford University Press, 1989.

Taylor, Rodney. *The Way of Heaven: Introduction to the Confucian Religious Life.* Leiden, Netherlands: E. J. Brill, 1986.

Taylor, Romeyn. "Official Religion in the Ming." In *The Cambridge History of China.* Vol. 8, *The Ming Dynasty, Part 2: 1368–1644,* edited by Denis Twitchett and Frederick W. Mote, 840–892. Cambridge: Cambridge University Press, 1998.

Tilley, Charles. "Materials *in* Materiality." *Archaeological Dialogues* 14, no. 1 (2007): 16–20.

Tschepe, P. A. *Heligtümer des Kongfuzianismus in K'ü-fu und Tschou-hien* (Sacred sites of Confucianism in Qufu and Zouxian). Jentschoufu (Yanzhou), China: Druck und Verlag der Katholishchen Mission, 1906.

Tseng, Lillian Lan-Ying. "Retrieving the Past, Inventing the Memorable: Huang Yi's Visit to the Song-Luo Monuments." In *Monuments and Memory, Made and Unmade,* edited by Robert S. Nelson and Margaret Olin, 37–58. Chicago: University of Chicago Press, 2003.

Tuotuo (Tohgto). *Jinshi* (History of Jin). 1343. Reprint, Taibei: Taiwan shangwu yinshuguan, 1965.

———. *Song shi* (History of Song). 1345. Reprint, Taibei: Taiwan shangwu yinshuguan, 1965.

Twitchett, Denis, and John K. Fairbank, eds. *The Cambridge History of China.* Vol. 1, *The Ch'in and Han Empires, 221 BC–AD 220.* Cambridge: Cambridge University Press, 2008.

Twitchett, Denis C., and Frederick W. Mote, eds. *The Cambridge History of China.* Vol. 8, *The Ming Dynasty, 1368–1644.* Cambridge: Cambridge University Press, 1998.

Wang, Dong. "Internationalizing Heritage: UNESCO and China's Longmen Grottoes." *China Information* 24, no. 2 (2010): 123–147.

Wang, Liang. "The Confucius Temple Tragedy of the Cultural Revolution." In *On Sacred Grounds: Culture, Society, Politics, and the Formation of the Cult of Confucius,* edited by Thomas Wilson, 376–398. Cambridge, MA: Harvard University Asia Center, 2002.

Wang Runyan. "Fahui wenhua mingcheng youshi jiakai fazhan Qufu jingji" (Take advantage of the famed cultural city, speed up the excellent development of Qufu's economy). *Yuejin renjian,* no. 00 (1994): 1.

Wang Ziyun. *Zhongguo diaosu yishu shi* (History of Chinese sculptural art). Beijing: Renmin meishu chubanshe, 1988.

Wanggiyan Linqing. "Observing the Rites at the Ancient Abode of Confucius." *China Heritage Quarterly,* no. 17 (2009). Online.

Watters, Thomas. *A Guide to the Tablets in a Temple of Confucius.* Shanghai: America Presbyterian Mission Press, 1879.

Weschler, Howard. "The Confucian Teacher Wang T'ung (584?—617): One Thousand Years of Controversy." *T'oung Pao* 63, no. 4–5 (1977): 225–272.

———. *Offerings of Jade and Silk: Ritual and Symbol in the Legitimation of the Tang Dynasty.* New Haven, CT: Yale University Press, 1985.

Wei Shou. *Wei shu* (Book of Wei). 554. Reprint, Taibei: Taiwan shangwu yinshuguan, 1965.

Wei Zheng. *Sui shu* (Book of Sui). 621. Reprint, Taibei: Taiwan shangwu yinshuguan, 1965.

Wilson, Thomas. *Genealogy of the Way: The Construction and Uses of the Confucian Tradition in Late Imperial China.* Stanford, CA: Stanford University Press, 1995.

———. "The Ritual Formation of Confucian Orthodoxy and the Descendants of the Sage." *Journal of Asian Studies* 55, no. 3 (1996): 558–584.

———. "Ritualizing Confucius/Kongzi: The Family and State Cults of the Sage of Culture in Imperial China." In *On Sacred Grounds: Culture, Society, Politics, and the Formation of the Cult of Confucius,* edited by Thomas Wilson, 43–94. Cambridge, MA: Harvard University Asia Center, 2002.

———. "Sacrifice and the Imperial Cult of Confucius." *History of Religions* 41, no. 3 (2002): 251–287.

Wilson, Thomas, ed. *On Sacred Grounds: Culture, Society, Politics, and the Formation of the Cult of Confucius,* Harvard East Asian Monographs 217. Cambridge, MA: Harvard University Asia Center, 2002.

"Wo yuan juxing Kongzi xueshu taolun hui" (My institution holds an Kongzi academic symposium). *Qilu xuekan,* no. 6 (1980): 91.

Woodside, Alexander. "The Ch'ien-lung Reign." In *The Cambridge History of China.* Vol. 9, *The Ch'ing Empire to 1800, Part 1,* edited by Willard J. Peterson, 230–309. Cambridge: Cambridge University Press, 2002.

Woolridge, William. "Building and State Building in Nanjing after the Taiping Rebellion." *Late Imperial China* 30, no. 2 (2009): 84–126.

Wu Hung. *Monumentality in Early Chinese Art and Architecture.* Stanford, CA: Stanford University Press, 1995.

———. "Monumentality of Time: Great Clocks, the Drum Tower, the Clock Tower." In *Monuments and Memory, Made and Unmade,* edited by Robert S. Nelson and Margaret Olin, 107–132. Chicago: University of Chicago Press, 2003.

———. "On Rubbings—Their Materiality and Historicity." In *Writing and Materiality in China,* edited by Judith Zeitlin and Lydia Liu, 29–72. Cambridge, MA: Harvard University Asia Center, 2003.

———. *A Story of Ruins: Presence and Absence in Chinese Art and Visual Culture.* London: Reaktion Books, 2012.

———. *The Wu Liang Shrine: The Ideology of Early Chinese Pictorial Art.* Stanford, CA: Stanford University Press, 1989.

Wu Hung, ed. *Reinventing the Past: Archaism and Antiquarianism in Chinese Art and Visual Culture.* Chicago: University of Chicago Press, 2010.

Wu Jingzi. *The Scholars.* Translated by Yang Xianyi and Gladys Yang. Peking: Foreign Languages Press, 1964.

Wu Liangyong. "Shilun lishi guji lüyou chengshi de guihua yu jianshi" (Discussion of planning and construction in a tourist city of historical antiquities). *Guowai chengshi jihua,* no. 2 (1980): 1–12.

Wright, Arthur. *The Confucian Persuasion.* Stanford, CA: Stanford University Press, 1960.

Xiao Xi. "Shouce Kongzi wenhua jie huodong fengfu duocai" (The first Kongzi cultural festival activity was rich and colorful). *Shandong lüyou,* no. 5 (1989): 29–30.

Xinhua Tongxun She. *Juebu yunxu kai lishi daoche: Qufu renmin jiefa pipan Kong Fu zui e* (Do not reverse the wheel of history: Qufu people resolutely criticize the evils of Kong Mansion). Beijing, Renmin meishu chubanshe, 1974.

Xu, Yinong. *The Chinese City in Space and Time: The Development of Urban Form in Suzhou.* Honolulu: University of Hawai'i Press, 2000.

Yan Beiming. "Kongzi yao pingfan, Kongjiadian yao dadao" (Rehabilitate Kongzi, beat the Kong family shop). *Shehui kexue jikan,* no. 1 (1981): 3–13.

———. "Yao zhengque pingjian Kongzi" (Correctly evaluate Kongzi). *Qilu xuekan,* no. 6 (1980): 24–31.

Yang Anbang. "Wenyi fanggu jiKong yuewu biaoyan" (Imitating ancient art and culture in the performance of the *JiKong yuewu*). *Qufu nianjian.* Qufu, China: Qufu Bianzuan wei-yuanhui, 1986.

Yang Bojun and Ming Zuoqiu. *Chunqiu Zuozhuan zhu: Xiuding ben* (Annotation of Zuo's commentary to the *Spring and Autumn Annals,* revised edition). Zhongguo gudian ming-zhu yi zhu congshu. Beijing: Zhonghua shu ju, 1990.

Yang, Liansheng. *Excursions in Sinology.* Cambridge, MA: Harvard University Press, 1969.

Yang Shiqi. *Wenyuange cangshu shumu* (Catalog of the Wenyuan library). 1441. Reprint, Tai-bei: Shangwu yinshuguan, 1967.

Yao, Xinzhong, ed. *RoutledgeCurzon Encyclopedia of Confucianism.* London, New York: Rout-ledge, 2003.

Yates, Frances. *The Art of Memory.* London: Routledge and Kegan Paul, 1966.

Ye, Sang, and Geremie Barmé. "The Fate of the Confucius Temple, The Kong Mansion, and the Kong Cemetery." *China Heritage Quarterly,* no. 20 (2009). Online.

You Shaoping and Wang Qingcheng, eds. "A Regular Report on the Implementation of the Convention for the Protection of World Cultural and Natural Heritage." Qufu City Cul-tural Relics Administration Committee, 2003.

Yu, Hui-chun. "The Intersection of Past and Present: The Qianlong Emperor and His Ancient Bronzes." PhD diss., Princeton University, 2007.

Yu Shulie. "Yunyong lishi wenwu henjie mengpi Kong Meng zhi dao de zui e shizhi" (Use historical artifacts to expose and criticize the essence of the evil crimes of the way of Kongzi and Mengzi). *Wenwu,* no. 3 (1974): 6–7.

Yuan Baoyin and Zhang Xiaoyu. "Song xianshi fenggong houde yang ruxue lishi zhendi; Zhongguo Qufu Kongzi wenhua jie fanggu jiKong jishi" (Praising the great achieve-ments and virtues of the first teacher, relying on the true meaning of Confucianism, reporting on imitating the ancient sacrifice to Kongzi in Qufu China). *Zouxiang shijie* no. 6 (1995–1996): 34–36.

Zeitlin, Judith, and Lydia Liu, eds. *Writing and Materiality in China.* Cambridge, MA: Harvard University Asia Center, 2003.

Zhang Dainian. "Kongzi zhexue jiexi" (Analysis of Kongzi's philosophy). In *Zhongguo zhe-xueshi yanjiu fangfa taolun ji,* edited by Zhongguo shehui kexueyuan zhexue yanjiusuo. Taiyuan, China: Zhongguo zhexueshi yanjiushi, 1979. Reissue, Zhongguo shehui kexue chubanshe, 1980.

Zhang Dainian, ed. *Kongzi da cidian* (Dictionary of Kongzi). Shanghai: Shanghai cishu chu-ban she, 1993.

Zhang Dongwei, ed. *Qufu nianjian* (Qufu yearbook). Qufu, China: Qufu Bianzuan weiyuan-hui, 1999–2000. Online.

Zhang, Jie. "City Building, Conservation and Architecture in China with Special Refer-ence to Qufu." PhD diss., University of York, 1991.

Zhang Liang, ed. *Yusi Zuopin xuan* (Selection from *Threads of Talk*). Beijing: Renmin wenxue chubanshe, 1988.

Zhang Shaotang. *Ziyang Qufu Taishan youxing xinying lu* (Heartfelt record of travelling to Ziyang, Qufu, and Taishan). 1937.

Zhang Tingyu. *Ming shi* (History of the Ming). 1739. Reprint, Taibei: Taiwan shangwu yinshuguan, 1965.

Zhang Xuehai et al. "Discussion of the Periodization and Basic Groundplan of the Lu City at Qufu" and "Conclusions from the Ancient City of the Lu State." *Chinese Sociology and Anthropology* 19, no. 1 (1986): 35–48, 49–65.

Zhao Erxun. *Qingshi gao* (Draft of the history of the Qing). 1927. Reprint, Beijing: Zhonghua shuju, 1997.

Zhao, Wei. "Local versus National Interests in the Promotion and Management of a Heritage Site: A Case Study from Zhejiang Province, China." In *Cultural Heritage Politics in China*, edited by Tami Blumenfield and Helaine Silverman, 73–100. New York: Springer, 2013.

Zhao Yuanshan. "Rang 'jieqing' zhi hua gengjia xianyan" (Let the festive celebration bloom even more brightly). *Yuejin renjian*, no. 1 (1994): 17.

Zhongguo Kongzi Jijinhui. "Zhongguo Kongzi jijinhui gonggao" (An announcement from the China Kongzi Foundation). *Qilu xuekan*, no. 6 (1984): 38–39.

"Zhongguo Qufu guoji Kongzi wenhua jie jishi, Jining Shi Kongzi wenhua jie bangongshi." *Dongfang wenhua shengdian: 1984 nian—2008 nian* (A grand cultural ceremony of the Orient: Documentary on China Qufu International Confucius Culture Festival, 1984–2008). Jinan, China: Qilu chubanshe, 2009.

Zhongguo shehui kexueyuan, jindai shi yanjiu suo, ed. *Kongfu dang'an xuanbian* (Selections from the Kong Mansion Archives). Beijing: Zhonghua shuju, 1982.

Zhonghua Minguo shi dang'an ziliao huibian (Selected materials from the archives of the Republic of China). Nanjing, China: Jiangsu guji chubanshe, 1991.

Zhu Fuping. *Kongmiao shisan beiting* (Thirteen stele pavilions of Kong Temple). Beijing: Zhongguo dang'an chuban she, 2004.

Zhu Liangming. "Zhongguo Qufu guoji Kongzi wenhua jie" (International Kongzi Culture Festival in Qufu, China). In *Qufu nianjian*, edited by Zhang Dongwei. Qufu: Qufu Bianzuan weiyuanhui, 1999–2002. Online.

Zhu, Yujie, and Na Li. "Groping for Stones to Cross the River: Governing Heritage in Emei." In *Cultural Heritage Politics in China*, edited by Tami Blumenfield and Helaine Silverman, 51–72. New York: Springer, 2013.

Zhuangzi. *The Zhuangzi*. In *The Sacred Books of China: The Texts of Taoism*, Part 2, translated by James Legge. Oxford: Clarendon Press, 1891.

Zi Mu. "Qiantan Kongzi jiaxiang lüyou de duiwai xuanchuan" (A brief on external propaganda for tourism in the hometown of Kongzi). *Shandong lüyou*, no. 5 (1989): 11–13.

Zito, Angela. *Of Body and Brush: Grand Sacrifice as Text/Performance in Eighteenth-Century China*. Chicago: University of Chicago Press, 1997.

Index

About the Author

JAMES A. FLATH is associate professor in the Department of History at the University of Western Ontario, Canada.